HISTORY AND LEGEND

駱雪倫 著

歷史、講史與文化傳統

春樹 題

History and Legend

Ideas and Images in the Ming Historical Novels

Shelley Hsueh-lun Chang

Ann Arbor

THE UNIVERSITY OF MICHIGAN PRESS

Library of Congress Cataloging-in-Publication Data

Chang, Shelley Hsueh-lun, 1934–
  History and legend : ideas and images in the Ming historical
novels / Shelley Hsueh-lun Chang.
      p.   cm.
  Includes bibliographical references.
  ISBN 0–472–10117–X (alk. paper):
  1. Historical fiction, Chinese — Themes, motives. 2. Chinese
fiction — Ming dynasty, 1368–1644 — History and criticism.   I. Title.
PL2419.H57C46   1989
895.1'308109046 — dc20   89–39964
                                                                        CIP

This book is dedicated to
Chun-shu
with love and appreciation

Acknowledgments

The writing of this book started in 1974, and it was one of the projects under the broad subject of Chinese literature and society in early modern China I worked on in the 1970s. The first draft was completed in the summer of 1976, and a summary of the important issues and ideas in this draft was presented in a paper read at the Thirtieth International Congress of Human Science held in Mexico City, Mexico, in August, 1976. Then I temporarily put aside this project and devoted my time to complete other research projects. It was not until the spring of 1982, while I was teaching Ming history at Lanchou University in China, that I started thinking about revising the draft manuscript. One of the subjects in my lectures was the recurrent theme of violence in Ming historical novels, part of my primary sources for this book. I started the revisions in the fall of 1982, and the book was completed by the end of 1986, at which time I had already returned to the United States.

In the span of seven years of research work that resulted in this book, I have accumulated a heavy debt of gratitude to the many institutions and individuals who have helped me along the way. Space, however, can allow me to list here only a few of them. I owe much to our friends Wan Wei-ying and Ma Wei-yi and the staff of the Asia Library at the University of Michigan, who have put together one of the most complete collections of microfilms and primary and secondary materials on the Ming and Ch'ing periods. I wish to thank the senior staff members of Lanchou University Library, Nanking University Library, Shanghai Library, and Peking Library for their kindness in allowing Chun-shu and me to read in a short period all the materials we needed in their libraries. I am grateful to the Fu Ssu-nien Library of Academia Sinica and the National Central Library in Taipei for making rare materials available for my study.

In the long course of writing the present study, I have benefited from discussion and association with scholars of various institutions.

For example, twice in this continent I presented parts of my book in scholarly gatherings, at the 1976 International Congress of Human Science and at the 1987 Annual Meeting of the American Historical Association. At both meetings I benefited from questions and comments from fellow scholars when some of the main themes of my book were discussed.

To all scholars on the subjects of Chinese history and literature whose works are listed in the Bibliography, I feel an immense intellectual debt. Without their individual works, this first book-length study of Ming intellectual history through historical novels could never have been done. Several scholars have been more than generous with their advice and aid: They are Professors Chow Tse-tsung, Hao Yenp'ing, Ernest P. Young, and Paul Ropp. They all took time in their busy schedules to read the manuscript (at different stages of revision) with unusual attentiveness and took the trouble to write out comments for my use. Their thoughtful suggestions enabled me to explore more fully the dynamic of expression and interpretation. To them goes my profound gratitude.

My husband, Chun-shu, has been an inspiration to me throughout the years. With infectious enthusiasm, he has often performed the difficult job of being my constant critic. Without his guidance, none of my works could have been completed. I also want to thank our children, Jean Chien-ju, Debbie I-ju, and Victor Wei-chung, who have miraculously grown up with their parents' voluminous "big black books," which were packed and unpacked in the family car whenever the family traveled, and who were instructed repeatedly, "Whenever there is a fire, save the big black books first." I thank them for everything that they have contributed over the years to making my life richer and fuller. Victor also touched my heart when he, in the spring of 1987, read this manuscript in three days. His interest in my work moved me deeply.

Debbie Chang and Victor Chang skillfully and cheerfully helped with the preparation of the index, and I am pleased to acknowledge their contribution.

Finally I wish to express my appreciation to the editors of the University of Michigan Press, especially to Mary K. Erwin, who first encouraged me to submit my manuscript and has taken a special interest in its development.

Preface

This book is a study of ideas and images in fictionalized historical narratives in Ming China,* with a special focus on the interplay between history and legends in popularized chronicles and legendary tales written in either simplified *wen-yen* (Classical Chinese) or vernacular Chinese. These narratives, in spite of their pseudohistorical outlook, are fictional works in which historical events and characters blend thoroughly with legends and fictional elaborations. Collectively, they have been referred to as "historical novels" (*chiang-shih hsiao-shuo*) in modern times, covering various styles and qualities.

It should be pointed out that the historical novel per se is not the subject of this study. In this study, historical novels, as well as Official Histories, regular historical sources, classical and philosophical works, and traditional writings of various dimensions, are treated as primary sources. This is a study of the dominant motifs and formulae in historical novels, comparing them with those similar or related major ideas on the higher levels in historical and philosophical works. It explores how history — historical events and personages — were perceived, evaluated, and rewritten into colloquial novels for the ostensible purpose of popular consumption in Ming times, when such writings became a cultural and literary phenomenon for the first time in the history of China.

The Ming historical novels, as will be made clear in the Introduction, represent the collective efforts of both the oral and performing artists on the one hand, and the educated writers, editor-compilers, and editor-publishers on the other hand. The writers — without realizing it themselves — acted as mediators between the elite and the popular traditions by incorporating the various antecedent narrative materials, through a period of evolutionary developments, into the final recensions of these novels. Thus the ideas and images that emerged in the novels

---

* In this study, Ming China covers both the dynastic period from 1368 to 1644 and the Southern Ming reigns from 1645 to 1661.

reflect a long period of dynamic interaction between the elite and popular cultures.

The original Chinese terms for elite and popular traditions are *ta-tao* (the great Way) and *hsiao-tao* (the small Way). History, which was a "comprehensive mirror" for aid in government according to the Confucian tradition, was naturally part of the great Way. Fiction, in Chinese *hsiao-shuo*, which originally meant "the talk of the streets," belonged to the small Way. In this study the term *elite tradition* is adapted from Robert Redfield's definition of "great tradition"; it means a tradition "cultivated in schools or temples." The term *popular tradition* is adapted from Peter Burke's definition of "popular culture"; it refers to the "unofficial culture" of the nonelite that also includes elite participation—as a "second culture"—and the participation of the "mediators," the group who stood in between the elite and the nonelite.*

It should also be pointed out that the Ming historical novel, which was by design "popularized" historical narrative, was preoccupied with "historical" events and personages, especially the latter who were both makers and products of history. As "historical" personages command the full attention of the writers of the historical novels, they give rise to two overall impressions of these novels. The first is a profound faith in the ultimate justice of history—a belief that history will always have the last word on everyone—and the second is a great interest in the total complex of relations between people in the traditional Chinese society. These impressions also explain why, in spite of its seemingly outdated literary style and subject matter, the traditional historical novel has enjoyed enduring popularity among Chinese readers; to them as well as to those writers, history and politics are forever inextricably related to each other and that is why they are forever a fascinating subject.

The book is divided into seven chapters. Chapter 1, "Introduction," analyzes the main features and characteristics of the historical novel, describes its scope and contents, and examines the possible links between the vernacular fiction and the professional oral fiction. The

---

* For Redfield's discussion of two cultural traditions, see Robert Redfield, *The Little Community and Peasant Society and Culture* (Chicago: University of Chicago Press, 1960), pp. 40–43. Redfield's definition of the little tradition as "the tradition of the non-elite" was criticized by Peter Burke as "too narrow." For Burke's discussion, see his book *Popular Culture in Early Modern Europe* (New York: Harper Torchbooks, 1978), pp. 23–29, 58–64. See also the Prologue for his definition of popular culture.

discussion also touches the general setting and cultural milieu of the emerging vernacular novel, as well as related outstanding issues. The wide variety of source materials and the historical ties with both the traditional written historical literature and the professional oral literature suggest some degree of interaction between the elite and popular traditions.

Chapter 2, "The Pattern of History," examines the ideas and theories regarding the historical phenomena of the rise and fall of dynasties in the writings of both the historians and the vernacular writers. The transformation of infinite historical recurrence of dynastic wars in the Official Histories into infinite recurrence of "righteous revolts" of rustic heroes in historical novels is one manifestation of the observable samples of the interplay of the elite and popular traditions. Systematic analyses of the rebellious groups in the historical novels reveal the general patterns of these revolts, such as the plotting pattern, the organizing pattern, the pattern of the inner working of power transference, and so forth. Among these broad patterns, some familiar archetypes, which emerge to be the most noticeable characteristics of the "righteous revolts," can be traced back to either the Official Histories or the storytellers' oral traditions.

Chapter 3, "Man and History," puts forward some detailed analyses of different types of "men of distinction" in the historical novels, representing the variation and contrast in human motivation in traditional times. The assorted historical images, which are colorful, lively, and unforgettable, are the products of image makers from different traditions through a long period of development. Furthermore, among the assorted heroes the predominant feature of military supermen is significant. This militarism, which represents the rising force of popular heroism, is a sharp contrast to the disparagement of the military in the Confucian system of values.

Chapter 4, "Ethical Values and Sociopolitical Order," discusses dominant ethical values as the ideological framework of the Confucian state and society. Although the most celebrated virtues in the historical novels still include Confucian virtues, two noticeable traits of the rustic heroes—selfless friendship and martial valor—stand out as the all-time favorite themes among writers of historical novels. At the same time, the public spirit (*t'ien-hsia wei-kung*) of the legendary sage-kings, which represents the symbol of nobility and self-dedication in the Confucian scheme of values, was upheld in the writers' attempts to redefine the concepts of loyalty and righteousness regarding relationships between the individual and his sovereign, and between self and society.

Chapter 5, "Ideals and Reality," examines the ideals and reality of the imperial political institution in traditional China, emphasizing its tremendous impact on the mind-set of the Chinese, on their ideas and mental temperament, demonstrated by their actions and reactions described in the historical novels. The discussion centers on major areas of misgovernment: bureaucratic corruption, social and economic injustice, crime and violence, and the tyrannical rulers in history. In each of these areas, there are conflicting accounts and ill-reconciled emotions juxtaposed to indicate the existence of a society with multiple values.

Chapter 6, "The Cosmic and Religious Order," explores the general religious ideas and beliefs in popular pseudohistorical works, comparing them with those expressed in official histories. Historically speaking, the religions in the Ming period acquired a unique syncretic nature. The three religions — religious Taoism, Buddhism, and classical religion — that have diffused intimately into Confucian social and political institutions represented a generally accepted religious order in Ming times. However, the notion of the "Three Religions" (*san-chiao*) was often mixed up with another dominant notion about the combined practice of the "Three Teachings" (also *san-chiao*) — Confucianism, Taoism, and Buddhism — that became popular in the late Ming. This mix-up is most evident in the historical novels in which "Three Religions" and "Three Teachings" are used indiscriminately. Furthermore, in the novels the influence of both religious Taoism and Buddhism are overwhelming, as witnessed by their dominant themes of fatalism, predestination, retribution, incarnation, transmigration, and the inscrutable workings of Heaven.

Chapter 7, "Conclusion," sums up the dominant ideas and images in the historical novels that contributed to the general fund of ideas in Ming times. These ideas and images reveal the generally accepted popular assumptions and attitudes that have pervaded the novels. Since the traditional historical novels have enjoyed enduring popularity among the Chinese, these assumptions and attitudes provide a fundamental perspective for understanding the history and culture of the Chinese people.

Contents

Tables

Chronology: The Ming Reigns

Hung-wu	1368−98
Chien-wen	1399−1402
Yung-lo	1403−24
Hung-hsi	1425
Hsuan-te	1426−35
Cheng-t'ung	1436−49
Ching-t'ai	1450−56
T'ien-shun	1457−64
Ch'eng-hua	1465−87
Hung-chih	1488−1505
Cheng-te	1506−21
Chia-ching	1522−66
Lung-ch'ing	1567−72
Wan-li	1573−1619
T'ai-ch'ang	1620
T'ien-ch'i	1621−27
Ch'ung-chen	1628−44
Hung-kuang	1645
Lung-wu	1645−46
Yung-li	1647−61

Note about Romanization

I have followed the Wade-Giles system in my romanization of Chinese characters. But I have also made some necessary modifications, such as leaving out the umlauts for words like *yuan* (instead of *yüan*), *lueh* (instead of *lüeh*), *hsu* (instead of *hsü*), *hsueh* (instead of *hsüeh*), and so forth when pronunciation is clear. For place names, I have generally employed the "Postal System," thus Peking for Pei-ching, Nanking for Nan-ching, Chekiang for Che-chiang, and so on.

Chapter 1

Introduction

The Master said, "I have transmitted what was taught
to me without making up anything of my own. I have
been faithful to and loved the ancients. In these
respects, I make bold to think, not even our old P'eng
can have excelled me."

—*Lun-yü*

In ancient China, as in ancient Greece, history began with legend. In
ancient Greece, Clio was a muse for both epic poets and historians.
Legends were blended with historical facts in early Greek epic and
historical writing; Homer's epic and Herodotus's work are examples.
In ancient China, legends recorded in both lyric poetry and prose
narrative were admitted into the Confucian classics such as the *Shih-
ching* (Book of Poetry) and the *Shu-ching* (Book of History). Once
admitted into the venerable classics, legends were accepted as part of
the authentic history. The respect for ancient written records, the very
example set by Confucius (551–479? B.C.) himself, had exerted tremendous influence on the Chinese mind in traditional times. At the
same time Confucius also demonstrated great concern about compiling
history. In his *Ch'un-ch'iu* (the Spring and Autumn Annals), also one
of the Five Classics, he upholds the moral conviction that by "praise"
or "blame" of the historical personages in the Annals, history has the
last word on them. The profound moral significance that Confucius
assigned to history gave rise to the awareness of the need to distinguish
fact from fiction. Throughout the long history of imperial China,
although legends continued to be admitted into all sorts of orthodox
historical writings, the idea or ideal of separating fact from fiction
continued to grow among reflective scholars and thinkers. By the time
of the Ming dynasty (1368–1644), the emergence of a new genre of
narrative—the historical novel—added a new dimension to the issue
of "fact versus fiction," for the writers of historical novels not only
elaborated upon established historical records, they transformed them
into legends and myths.

In China, as in the West, the novel is a late development in the literary scene. When the full-length novels (most of the earliest ones are historical novels) eventually appeared in the Ming, China had already seen the golden ages of nearly all other major literary genres. The Chinese historical novel is very different from the historical novel in Western cultures. The Western concept of the novel as imaginary literature, for example, as in the novels of Sir Walter Scott, does not apply.[1] The Chinese historical novel is, by design, historical narrative rather than creative historical fiction.

The Chinese historical novels are believed to have evolved from professional storytelling during the Sung period (960−1279) and, as a genre of full-length novels, reached maturity by Ming times.[2] Since they developed from the storyteller's art, they inherited some of its traits, two of which stand out as the most influential. One is the tradition of narrating history based on popularized historical texts and developing the story within a fixed historical plot. The other is the tradition of glorifying historical or legendary figures and events that emphasize action and drama in the narration. The former is evident in the "popularized chronicle" style of the dynastic novels, and the latter in the prevailing "military romance" style of the heroic tales.[3]

As far as style is concerned, there is no comparison between the Western novel and the traditional Chinese novel; they are too different to compare. Regarding subject matter, the Chinese historical novel, which highlights the rise and fall of the past dynasties, may be compared with Western heroic literature (such as the Homeric epics), which deals with remarkable public deeds of historical or legendary heroes engaged in collective rather than individual enterprises.[4] Like the epic, in which warfare is essential rather than accessory, the Chinese historical novel, especially its branch of heroic tales, is preoccupied with warfare.[5] However, unlike the epic that is an oral and poetic genre, it is written mainly in prose but can include poems, songs, and set pieces of description.

In spite of its outdated traditional styles and subject matter, this old-fashioned genre of novels has enjoyed enduring popularity among its Chinese readers, both synchronically across space and diachronically through generations. Ever since their first appearance in the book markets of the early sixteenth century, these historical novels have been among the most popular books in China. The heroes and villains of these novels are household words for Chinese people all over the world. The heroic deeds and treacherous acts of the historical characters, together with legends and historical anecdotes of the past, have been so deeply entrenched in the consciousness of the Chinese that they have become part of China's cultural heritage. And it is one of the purposes of this study to demonstrate that the traditional Chinese historical novel, at least in its highest development, represents a living tradition that provides a fundamental perspective for understanding the life, culture, and history of the Chinese people.

With these general observations presented, I now turn to the more specific features of the Ming historical novel.

I

The first distinct feature of the Ming historical novel is its professed tie with authentic historical works. This is readily seen in the suggestive generic terms included in the titles. The most familiar generic titles are *t'ung-su yen-i* (to elucidate and popularize history; or popularized chronicle), *chih* (annal), *chuan* (chronicle), and *chih-chuan* (record). The generic title *t'ung-su yen-i* means to retell the profound and difficult Standard (or Official) History in plain language to make its meaning clearer, while the other generic titles, *chih*, *chuan*, and *chih-chuan* are actually purported to be authentic historical works. The pseudohistorical nature of these works is further evidenced by various phrases that were often added to the main titles, such as *an-chien yen-i* (to elucidate according to historical works, or to elucidate according to a chronological framework), *ts'an-ts'ai shih-chien* (to adapt materials with reference to standard historical works), or simply *an-chien* (according to historical works, or according to a chronological framework). The key word, *chien*, in these phrases probably originally stood for Ssu-ma Kuang's (1019–86) influential annals *Tzu-chih t'ung-chien* (The Comprehensive Mirror for Aid in Government; *T'ung-chien* hereafter).[6] Later, it referred to historical works in general, especially annalistic historical narratives.[7] This preoccupation with historical references reflects the tremendous prestige that traditional historiography held in the mind of the historical novelists. It also delineates, from the point of view of the novelists, the supposedly close relationship between the official historical works and the historical novel.

In principle, the relation between official historical works and

historical novels is like the one between the principal and the supplemental as signified by the declared guideline of historical novelists:
"to supply the omission for the Official Histories (*cheng-shih*)."[8]
This means that historical facts are the principal and the novelists'
stories the supplemental. In practice, however, this relation is flexible;
it fluctuates from novel to novel. In some cases, the novelists follow
the official historical works closely, in others the novelists rely heavily
on unofficial works and their own resources. Thus no matter what
approach the novelists chose in organizing their material, historical
novels are, by and large, a mixture of history and fiction in varying
proportions.

That historical novels are a mixture of history and fiction caused
concern among traditional scholars who recognized the unsurpassed
popularity of the novels but were afraid that they might confuse facts
and fiction for the readers.[9] Consequently scholars in Ming-Ch'ing
times took it upon themselves to distinguish fiction from the authentic
history. In so doing, they persistently asked one question: Does the
novel follow the Official History closely? The assumption underlying
the question was that the intrinsic authenticity of the official historical
texts was beyond doubt. Although most modern scholars question this
assumption,[10] nevertheless, it does represent the general acceptance of
a supposed close relation between the historical novel and the Official
Histories in traditional times.

To find out more information about this issue, we first examine the
general approaches of the novelists and the source material they used
for their novels. Take the famous *San-kuo-chih t'ung-su yen-i* (The
Romance of the Three Kingdoms; *San-kuo* hereafter), the most influential historical novel in the field. According to Yung-yü-tzu's (pseudo-
nym for Chiang Ta-ch'i) preface to the earliest extant edition of the
San-kuo, the novel was based on Ch'en Shou's (233–297) *San-kuo
chih* (The History of the Three Kingdoms), the Official History of the
period. This same preface also shows that the novelist's commitment to
an authentic and judicious account of history was most sincere and
genuine. In addition to the *San-kuo chih*, other standard historical
works relevant to the period were also consulted, such as P'ei Sung-
chih's (360–439) commentary on the *San-kuo chih*, Ssu-ma Kuang's
T'ung-chien, and Chu Hsi's (1130–1200) *Tzu-chih t'ung-chien kang-mu*
(Outlines and Details Based on the *T'ung-chien*; *Kang-mu* hereafter).[11]
In the same vein, Feng Meng-lung's (1574–1646) novel *Hsin lieh-kuo*

chih (New Records of the States; *Hsin lieh-kuo* hereafter) claims several historical classics as its sources, namely, the *Tso-chuan* (Tso's Commentary on the *Ch'un-ch'iu*), *Kuo-yü* (Discourses of the States), *Chankuo ts'e* (Stratagems of the Warring States), *Wu-Yueh ch'un-ch'iu* (The Spring and Autumn of the Wu and Yueh States), and the *Shih-chi* (Historical Records).[12] Some of the historical novels were copied verbatim from their respective Official Histories, such as the novel *Tung Hsi Chin yen-i* (Popular Elucidation of the History of the Western and the Eastern Chin Periods), which is based primarily on the Official History of the period, the *Chin-shu* (The History of the Chin), compiled under the direction of Fang Hsuan-ling (578–648).[13]

These examples demonstrate that some historical novels, especially those of the branch of popularized chronicles, rely heavily upon the established historical sources. On the other hand those that belong to the branch of legendary tales tend to pay less attention to standard historical sources. The most extreme case is the *Shui-hu chuan* (Outlaws of the Marsh; *Shui-hu* hereafter), which deals with legendary tales of the Liang-shan outlaws in the Northern Sung period.[14] Although we can recognize the general historical background of the period and can find the names of a few of the outlaw heroes in T'o T'o's *Sung-shih* (the Official History of the Sung Period), the novel finds no established historical texts to back up its stories. Nevertheless, the central plots of the *Shui-hu* evolve around the formation of an armed rebel force, the expansion of this armed force, the rise to power and glory of this rebel force, and its final disbandment. All these are essentially the same kind of scenarios of a dynastic struggle that are the dominant themes of the historical novels.

The second distinct feature concerns the established pattern of compiling a historical novel and the authors of the historical novels. This pattern was described in Chinese terms as *chui-chi*, literally to sew together or to mix together. It has been generally accepted that in compiling a historical novel (in the Ming times), the writer usually did not go ahead and create a new work; instead this individual edited, compiled, and modified various existent narratives on the same subject into something that can be accepted as a novel. Strictly speaking there was no single writer who could claim sole authorship, as today's novelist does, for any novel thus produced. The Ming writers, under the circumstance, were editor-compilers, editor-storytellers, editor-publishers, and so forth. In this study, I use the word *novelist* merely as a covenient piece of shorthand for the various writers, editors, and compilers of historical novels.

There are reasons for the existence of such a *chui-chi* compiling pattern; the Confucian tradition of "being faithful to and loving the ancients" is one, and the evolutionary nature of the traditional novel is another. All these will be discussed shortly. Complicating this already complex issue of composite authorship is the fact that we know very little about the individual novelists. We do not even know the names of some of them. For instance, scholars are now still debating on the identity of the author of the *San-kuo*, the most influential novel in the field. Not much information about the authors has been found, even for those novelists whose names we know. This lack of information about the novelists gives an impression of mystery and remoteness that hovers like a subtle aura around the historical novels as a whole.

The third distinct feature of the Ming historical novel concerns the concepts of unofficial history and fictitious history that reveal the novelists' self-image of the historical novel. To put them in proper historical perspective, a few key issues involved with the development of these concepts need to be further examined. They are the issue of fiction (*hsiao-shuo* or *pai-kuan hsiao-shuo*) versus history (*shih*); the issue of official history (*cheng-shih*) versus unofficial history (*yeh-shih*); the issue of the great Way (*ta-tao*) versus the small Way (*hsiao-tao*), which also includes the concepts of the refined (*ya*) versus the popular (*su*), the concepts of the polished (*wen*) versus the unpolished (*chih*). I will start with analyzing the meaning of the key terms.

The term *hsiao-shuo* originally meant "small talk of no great consequence" when it first appeared in the *Chuang-tzu* (by Chuang Chou, ca. 369–286 B.C.). In Pan Ku's (A.D. 32–92) authoritative *Han-shu* (History of the Former Han), *hsiao-shuo* means "the talk of the streets" when it appears together with the term *pai-kuan*, literally "petty official."[15] According to Pan Ku, in ancient times there were petty officials appointed to collect the gossip of the streets (for the purpose of letting the prince know people's sentiments), and he compared the *hsiao-shuo* to the *hsiao-tao*, the "small Way," contrasting it with the Confucian "great Way." From then on the term *pai-kuan hsiao-shuo* was established, sharing the same meaning as *hsiao-shuo*. There are altogether fifteen book titles listed as works of *hsiao-shuo* in the bibliographical section of the *Han-shu*. Judging from Pan Ku's comments, these *hsiao-shuo* were works attributed to ancient authors, anecdotes about ancient history, miscellaneous notes about the Chou period (ca. 1027–256 B.C.), and so forth.

Pan Ku's comments about *hsiao-shuo* make it clear that there has been a parallel development of two cultural traditions since the Chou period, the great Way and the small Way. The former represents the governing elite, the latter, the governed people. He also pointed out that from the very beginning there was two-way traffic between these two cultural traditions. Furthermore, this two-way traffic was institutionalized. It was an established institution to appoint petty officials to the job of collecting the talk of the streets.

Pan Ku referred the great Way to the Confucian tradition. The two parallel developments are abundantly clear in Confucius's teaching. In fact, it is one of the dominant themes throughout *Lun-yü* (The Analects of Confucius), in which the Master is seen constantly examining, exhorting, and expounding the importance of balancing two sets of values between the profound and the practical, the elegant and the simple, the refined and the popular, the polished and the unpolished. Take the issue of rites and music, the essence of the elite culture.

> The master said, "As far as the rites and music are concerned, the disciples who were the first to come to me were rustics [who resided in the countryside] while those who came to me afterwards were gentlemen [who resided in the city]. When it comes to putting the rites and music to use, I follow the former."[16]

We are told that it was Confucius's belief that those who first advance and take hold of rites and music are people residing in the countryside; those who reside in the city are slow in advancing and taking hold of the truth. Although Confucius appreciated the qualities of the gentleman, he constantly cautioned his disciples against the preponderance of acquired refinement over native substance. *Hsiao-shuo*, the talk of the streets, was the small Way, but it was as important as the great Way.

Next, we examine the term *shih*. The term *shih* (the writing of history, or historiography) was very loosely defined according to the conventional classification of books in imperial China, which divided books into four major categories: Confucian classics, historical writings, philosophical writings, and belles lettres. Under the broad umbrella of "historical writings" there is a wide range of works. For example, consider the bibliographical section of the Official History *Sui-shu* (History of the Sui Dynasty) by Ch'ang-sun Wu-chi, et al., there are altogether thirteen subheadings under the heading of "Historical Writings"![17] Of all kinds of historical works, the most important ones are the *cheng-shih*, the Official or Standard Histories, which start with *Shih-chi*, *Han-shu*, *Hou-Han shu*, *San-kuo chih*, and so forth.

The term *yeh-shih* (the unofficial history) is the opposite expression of the term *cheng-shih*, from the historian's point of view. It is also a very loosely defined term, referring to every sort of historical works that were not authorized by the government. In practice, however, *yeh-shih* chiefly referred to private records; these are miscellaneous works related to people and events of past. The fifteen *hsiao-shuo* listed by Pan Ku seemed to belong to this subclassification. In the following I will give two concrete examples of these *yeh-shih* and *hsiao-shuo*.

According to the classification of the above-mentioned book, the *Sui-shu*, there are thirteen subheadings under "Historical Writings," of which the sections "Chiu-shih pien" (The Old Records) and "Tsa-chuan pien" (The Miscellaneous Records) are in essence no different from *hsiao-shuo* and *yeh-shih* described above. The two examples are taken from these two sections: They are Kan Pao's (fl. fourth century) famous collection of strange tales, *Sou-shen chi* (The Records of Spirits), and Ko Hung's (283–363) *Hsi-ching tsa-chi* (Miscellaneous Notes of the Western Capital).[18] Kan Pao of the Eastern Chin Dynasty (317–420), who compiled the *Chin-chi* (History of the Chin), was a historian and writer of strange tales. In his own preface to *Sou-shen chi*, he points out the importance of bequeathing all kinds of records to posterity. The official records and histories, in spite of their completeness and thoroughness, still might omit something, Kan Pao reflected.[19] Therefore, it would be useful to preserve as many materials as possible, even those that seem strange and unbelievable.

Thinking along similar lines Ko Hung, Kan Pao's contemporary, actually claimed to "supply the omission" for the *Han-shu* by his work *Hsi-ching tsa-chi*.[20] Obviously, to Kan Pao and Ko Hung, compiling private records represented an earnest effort to collect miscellaneous materials, and this viewpoint prevailed for a long time. In the bibliographical section of the *Chiu T'ang-shu* (The Old History of the T'ang Dynasty), both Kan Pao's and Ko Hung's works were classified under the broad heading of "Historical Writings."[21] By the time of the Yuan dynasty, when the *Sung-shih* (The History of the Sung Dynasty) was compiled, Ko Hung's work *Hsi-ching tsa-chi* was still classified in the category of "Historical Writings," while Kan Pao's work *Sou-shen chi* finally emerged under the subheading of *hsiao-shuo* in the category of "Philosophic Treatises and Others."[22] It is clear that by the time of the Yuan dynasty, although overlapping between the boundaries of *hsiao-shuo* and historical writings was finally narrowed down, the process was still very slow.[23]

This blurring of the boundaries between historical writings and *hsiao-shuo* was most evident to the historical novelists who found plenty of *hsiao-shuo* materials in their standard historical sources. Again take the novel *San-kuo* as an example. Besides the official historical sources mentioned before, the novelist also consulted P'ei Sung-chih's commentary, which quotes more than two hundred old records and unofficial historical works as references.[24] Of these unofficial historical works, at least twenty-two provide important materials for the *San-kuo* stories: they are, among others, such works as Liu I-ch'ing's (403–444) *Shih-shuo hsin-yü* (New Specimens of Contemporary Talk) and the *Ts'ao Man chuan* (Biography of Ts'ao Man) by an anonymous author. The former falls into the group of *hsiao-shuo*, the latter that of *yeh-shih*. These unofficial and fictitious materials, which include all kinds of personal reminiscences, miscellaneous anecdotes, and legendary tales, are by nature far more entertaining than sober history. This explains why writers and compilers of historical novels, who were not subject to the restraints of responsibility common to historians, found these materials stimulating and incorporated them into their works.

I have just demonstrated how the historical novelists, under the influence of traditional historiography, might have conceived their novels along the line of unofficial histories and fictionalized histories. But the term *hsiao-shuo* also means story, legend, and fiction. There was a wide range of literary works (both in vernacular and Classical Chinese) that were regarded as modes of *hsiao-shuo* in Ming time, such as the *chih-kuai* (strange tales), the *ch'uan-ch'i* (romances), the *hua-pen* (short stories), the *p'ing-hua* (popular tales), the *pi-chi* (random notes), and so forth. While most historical novelists adapted all kinds of historical materials into their works, they also tended to freely admit the above-mentioned literary works. To understand how the novelists themselves arranged their source materials and how they defined their works, we will take a close look at some of their own prefaces. Note how little they said about their literary sources, compared with how much they were obsessed with a desire to justify their use of unofficial historical materials in their novels.

Hsiung Ta-mu (fl. 1552), a productive editor-publisher of historical novels, describes how he compiled his novel about a Sung general Yueh Fei (1103–41) in the preface of the *Ta-Sung chung-hsing t'ung-su yen-i* (Popular Elucidation of the Restoration of the Sung Dynasty; *Ta-Sung* hereafter).[25] He explained that he relied on Chu Hsi's *Kang-mu* for a chronological framework, and that he enlarged it with materials from Yueh Fei's official biography, from private family records, and from an early work of *hsiao-shuo* (story, legend), which he did not mention by title. In another of Hsiung's novels, the *Pei-Sung chih-chuan t'ung-su yen-i t'i-p'ing* (The Chronicle of the Northern Sung Dynasty; *Pei-Sung* hereafter), he wrote a short prefatory note explaining that he based the novel on "the *Records of the Yang Family* and the like (Yang-chia fu teng chuan)."[26]

It is evident that Hsiung Ta-mu used three kinds of source material for his novels: official historical writings, private records and unofficial historical writings, and some sort of fictional narratives or literary works. In the novel *Ta-Sung*, the "early *hsiao-shuo*" that Hsiung mentioned but did not identify by title, has been identified, according to a modern study, as a short story entitled "Hsu *Tung-ch'uang shih-fan*" (Sequel to the *Tung-ch'uang shih-fan*). This story, which deals with the retribution theme based on Yueh Fei's tragic death, appears in a fifteenth-century collection of *wen-yen* (Classical Chinese) stories entitled *Hsiao-p'in chi* (An Imitative Collection of Stories).[27] In the novel *Pei-Sung*, the novel was based on "*Yang-chia fu* teng chuan," according to Hsiung. Although the original texts of these antecedent narratives have not yet been found, Hsiung's own prefatory note makes it clear that they belong to either the category of unofficial historical writings or the category of fictional works.

Hsiung Ta-mu not only laid out his source material for his readers, he also attempted to define the function of historical novel. Again we take his novel *Ta-Sung* as example. In his preface to the novel, Hsiung admits that Official Histories and *pai-kuan yeh-shih* (private records and unofficial histories) are not of equal quality, but counters with the argument that the *yeh-shih* often retain materials omitted by Official Histories. He takes the story of the historically famous beauty Hsi Shih as an example, citing four references to her in historical and literary sources and pointing to their differing implications. His discovery that even established sources contradicted one another probably was his justification for including fictitious materials in his works, even those conflicting with the Official History. Thus, as far as source material was concerned, Hsiung did not prefer official historical sources to unofficial historical writings and fictitious materials. Nevertheless, he held firm to his view that the function of the historical novel is to retain materials omitted by Official Histories.

This line of argument was also taken by another novelist, Chen Wei (fl. 1573), who prefaced his own novel *Hsi-Han yen-i* (The Founding of the Western Han Dynasty; *Hsi-Han* hereafter) after the fashion of Hsiung Ta-mu.[28] In fact Hsiung's approach represents the general attitude among early historical novelists who consulted with official historical works but were not strictly guided by them. This openly defending the usefulness of unofficial histories and fictitious materials marks the beginning of a departure from history to imaginary historical romance. By the time of Yuan Yü-ling (1599–1674), who was to live through the Ming-Ch'ing dynastic transition period, the open admission of fictitious materials was advanced by a new and bold spirit exhibited in the preface (dated 1633) to his novel *Sui-shih i-wen* (Supplementary Records of the History of the Sui Dynasty; *Sui-shih* hereafter).[29] In this preface Yuan openly declares that history and fiction are not of the same nature, the former drawing on authenticity and the latter on imagination. This emphasis on imagination pointed to a new direction for the later vernacular novels, that is for the Ch'ing novels, in that it moved a step further in the direction of creative writing.

Yuan Yü-ling's emphasis on imagination also reflected his attitude toward source material; unlike Hsiung Ta-mu who relied more on historical sources (both official and unofficial), Yuan relied heavily on antecedent literary works as his source. This reliance on antecedent literary materials apparently was shared by other editor-compilers, as testified by Feng Meng-lung, the most productive and well-known writer and editor-compiler of vernacular fiction in the Ming time. Feng's novel the *Hsin lieh-kuo* is a rewrite of Yü Shao-yü's (fl. 1550s and 1560s) "old" work, the *Lieh-kuo chih-chuan* (Records of the States; *Lieh-kuo* hereafter).[30] The readily available examples of adapting antecedent literary materials among historical novelists are self-evident in the existence of a group of prose narratives known as the *p'ing-hua* (here referring to the popular tales written in vernacular Chinese on historical themes). These popular tales are generally regarded as the possible forerunner of the Chinese novel, according to modern studies.[31] There are at least seven extant *p'ing-hua* that were mostly published in the Yuan period, of which four are identifiable as possible sources for some Ming historical novels. The popular tales of the *Hsuan-ho i-shih* (Supplementary Records of the Hsuan-ho Period) provide the earliest extant written version of the *Shui-hu* legend; they also provide some background materials for the novel *Ta-Sung*.[32] The *San-kuo-chih p'ing-hua* (Popular Tales of the Period of the Three Kingdoms) contains the nucleus of the novel *San-kuo*.[33] The *Wu-tai shih p'ing-hua* (Popular Tales of the Five Dynasties) provides materials for *Nan-Sung chih-chuan* (The Founding of the Sung; *Nan-Sung* hereafter).[34] The *Wu-wang fa Chou p'ing-hua* (Popular Tales of King Wu's Expedition against the Tyrant Chou) provides materials for both the *Feng-shen yen-i* (The Investiture of Gods; *Feng-shen* hereafter) and the *Lieh-kuo* mentioned above.[35]

With *p'ing-hua* as the possible forerunner of traditional novels, the debate among literary scholars over the issue of whether these *p'ing-hua* are the original prompt-books of storytellers also comes into sight. For us the possible links between the historical novel and the oral fiction of professional storytellers is also one of the major areas of our concern. We now turn our attention to the fourth distinct feature of the historical novel, its possible relation with the professional oral fiction.

II

Two types of popular entertainment were most common in Ming-Ch'ing times: storytelling and opera (referring to the musical plays or popular drama of all kinds), which were performed regularly in the entertainment quarters in all urban centers as well as in the temples or marketplaces of every village and town. The popularity of these two performing arts was observed by one seventeenth-century writer, Liu Hsien-t'ing (1648–95) as follows:

> In my observation [of the ways of the world], there are very few common people who are not fond of going to the theatre and singing

the opera; this means that man by nature is receptive to [the *Book of*] *Poetry* and [the *Book of*] *Music*. There are very few common people who are not fond of reading fiction and listening to storytellers' tales; this means that man by nature is receptive to [the *Book of*] *History* and the *Spring and Autumn Annals*. There are very few common people who do not believe in divination and make sacrifice to gods and spirits; this means that man by nature is receptive to [the *Book of*] *Changes* and [the *Book of*] *Rites*. Thus it is self-evident that the Six Classics — the teaching of the sages — are based on the understanding of human nature.[36]

Liu's observation reveals two important points at issue. First, it suggests an assumption on his part that both fiction and professional storytelling centered on the subject of history, or stories of history. When he talked about reading fiction and listening to storytellers' tales, he assumed they were all about the stories of history. Second, there was no question in Liu's mind about the popularity of fiction and drama in his days. According to our studies, historical themes are also among the dominant themes in Ming fiction and drama.[37]

Liu Hsien-t'ing's observations about the common interest shared by both writers of fiction and professional storytellers, plus the fact that both the entertaining business of storytelling and the publishing business of fiction-writing were flourishing, suggest the possibility of interaction at some point between these two different areas of cultural activities. In order to put this interaction issue in proper historical perspective, the origin and development of both the vernacular fiction and the professional storytellers' art need to be further explored. Discussions of the possible influence of oral literature on the origin and development of the vernacular fiction generally center on two issues: first, the idea of the original model that traces the vernacular fiction back to the professional storytellers' art in Sung times; and second, the consensus among the literary scholars that all the early novels went through a series of evolutionary stages. We will start with the idea of the original model.

According to Sung works that contain descriptions of storytellers' art in the marketplaces in the capital,[38] for example Nai Te-weng's *Tu-ch'eng chi-sheng* (The Wonder of the Capital) written in 1235, there were four classes of narrators, of which two are particularly relevant to our study: those of *chiang-shih* (historical narration) and those of *hsiao-shuo* (stories).[39] The former specialized in reciting historical happenings and the latter specialized in telling stories—various types of stories including historical ones. The narrators of history were very popular, and they often specialized in a specific period of history such as the period of Three Kingdoms or the period of Five Dynasties, using popularized historical texts as their sources. The narrators of stories, on the other hand, covered a wide variety of subjects, such as love stories; supernatural stories; stories of the marvels; stories of crime, detection, and chivalry; and stories of soldiers, horses, weapons, and drums. Note that some of the stories classified under the Sung subjects of "chivalry" and "soldiers, horses, weapons, and drums" are in essence no different from the subject matter of legendary heroic tales in Ming historical novels.

Furthermore, the difference between the narrators of history and narrators of stories was observed by a Sung writer as follows: The narrators of history "recited the histories, records, and biographies of previous dynasties, the rise and fall of states and wars; [they] feared most the narrators of stories, for the latter can resolve the events of a whole dynasty or a generation in an instant."[40] Evidently, the fast-moving narrators of stories not only also dealt with historical subjects, but dealt with them more effectively than narrators of history.

The Sung descriptions about the differences between the two genres of storytellers' art remind us of the differences between the two genres of historical novels. First, the observation that the narrator of history was less efficient in exciting the audience than the narrator of stories also holds true for the two genres of historical novels: On the whole, the legendary heroic tales are more exciting and interesting than the popularized chronicles. Second, the difference between the two oral genres also lies in the nature of their source materials, on which their narrations were based. The narrators of history, we are told, dealt with the standard historical texts, while the narrators of stories dealt with miscellaneous court anecdotes and country anecdotes. The same kind of difference in source materials also holds true for the two genres of historical novels: The popularized chronicles rely more on standard historical sources and the legendary tales rely more on unofficial historical sources and fictitious materials. Is this a mere coincidence that the two classes of storytellers, the narrators of history and the narrators of stories, fit in rather nicely with the two genres of the historical novel, the popularized chronicles and the legendary tales?

We have just identified two genres of Sung professional oral fiction that shared the same types of source materials with Ming historical novels. Later, when some of these oral stories were written down, or when the original prompt-books were rewritten or reorganized, would they be the forerunners of the vernacular fiction? To answer the question we now examine the idea of the evolutionary nature of the early novels. Take the novel *San-kuo*, one of the earliest novels that appeared in the book market in Ming times. The legendary stories about the historical personages and events of the Three Kingdoms period had flourished for a long time among the various public recitalists' circles before the stories were gathered together and written down. These legendary stories, which we shall refer to as "Three Kingdoms stories," can be traced back as early as the T'ang dynasty, as evidenced by two Three Kingdoms stories cited in a popular Buddhist text in the T'ang dynasty.[41] One of these stories tells about the close rapport described as "like the fish enjoying the water" between Liu Pei, the ruler of the Shu kingdom, and his chief advisor Chu-ko Liang, and the other tells how "the dead Chu-ko scared away the living Chung-ta." Both stories were adopted and elaborated on by the novel *San-kuo*.[42]

By the time of the Sung dynasty, the Three Kingdoms stories were flourishing in the repertoires of the professional storytellers in the marketplaces. There is a Sung writer who testifies to the existence of a school of storytellers specializing in Three Kingdoms stories in the Northern Sung (960–1126) capital of Pien-liang (modern Kaifeng).[43] Although we have no extant Northern Sung storytellers' prompt-books about Three Kingdoms stories, we learn from Su Tung-po (1036–1101), the famous Northern Sung poet, that during his time the storytellers telling Three Kingdoms stories were already sympathetic toward Liu Pei and were hostile to Ts'ao Ts'ao,[44] a sentiment shared by the *San-kuo*.[45] By the time of the Southern Sung (1127–1279), storytellers who specialized in historical subject matter were flourishing: twenty-three of them were named in a Sung work describing the sights and professional entertainments of the Southern Sung capital of Lin-an (modern Hang-chow).[46] Naturally, Three Kingdoms stories would be in these story-tellers' repertoires. From the Sung dynasties through the Yuan dynasty (1260–1368), the Three Kingdoms stories were gradually revised as they were transmitted from place to place and disseminated through the medium of public entertainers such as storytellers and theatrical performers. At least by Yuan times, the widely propagated and circulated Three Kingdoms stories had been written down in the extant

Yuan edition of the *San-kuo-chih p'ing-hua* and numerous Yuan plays dealing with the Three Kingdoms themes.[47] This *San-kuo-chih p'ing-hua* marks an important stage in the evolution of the Three Kingdoms stories. It provides the rough sketch for the full-length novel that would not come into existence until Ming times. Many of the major stories in the Ming novel *San-kuo* are in embryonic form in the *San-kuo-chih p'ing-hua*.[48]

The evolution of the Three Kingdoms stories suggests the existence of a possible tie between oral tradition and vernacular literature, especially the novel. It was through the influence of oral artists that heroic sagas and folk legends left their imprints on historical novels. In this aspect oral tradition represents the influence of the common people in literature. We can also see the influence of the various media of popular entertainment; through the media of drama and public recital, the heroic sagas of historical personages were spreading and consolidating, and finally these heroic figures were transformed from history to myth. Judging from the wide-ranging locations of these media of popular entertainment (some of these forms were unique to their own provinces or districts), it is clear that many heroic sagas and folk legends enjoyed a national reputation. By the time these sagas and legends were compiled into written literature, all of the myths that were well entrenched in the writers' minds were incorporated into written forms, together with the added acquisitions of classic traditions and Confucian values contributed by Confucian-educated writers, poets, and playwrights. In a broad sense, the vernacular novels thus represent both the collective efforts of oral and performing artists on the one hand, and the individual contributions of educated writers, novelists, and playwrights on the other.[49] Legends and tales were treated again and again in different ages, by different authors, and in different literary media, so that it became an established convention to revise or rewrite an extant plot instead of creating a completely new one. This is especially true in the case of full-length novels; almost all of the major Ming works had gone through a series of rewriting.[50]

The convention of revising and/or expanding an extant plot instead of creating a completely new one is most revealing. It reveals a unique mentality of the Chinese writers of traditional vernacular novels in terms of comparing them with their counterparts in the West. Here, the conservative spirit of the ancient civilization, like the setting sun, lingers before our eyes. And we hear the teachings of Confucius echoed persistently through history:

> The Master said, "I have transmitted what was taught to me without making up anything of my own. I have been faithful to and loved the ancients. In these aspects, I make bold to think, not even our old P'eng can have excelled me."[51]

The Master's words, memorized by every educated Chinese in traditional times, represented parts of the Confucian influence that shaped the conservative intellectual character of traditional writers. In the field of historical novels, the writers' obsession with source materials reflects this character. Almost everything they wrote, they claimed, was based on some kind of old records.

It was through this repeated reworking of various antecedent narratives that many of the earlier oral formulae (verbal formulae as well as character archetypes) and recurrent motifs are adapted in the Ming historical novels. As adaptation always implies a modification according to changing circumstances, how Ming novelists adapted their source materials also reflects the signs of their time. In their ways of choosing their source materials and presenting their versions of history, the historical novelists tell us something about their sentiments and viewpoints. In fact, in many cases, the novelists offer their direct comments on some particular historical incidents or personages that reveal the shift in attitudes of the time or the unconscious acquisition of certain assumptions on the part of the novelists themselves. As shown by the following chapters, identifying and analyzing these attitudes and assumptions is both a challenging and rewarding experience.

III

We have examined the main features and characteristics of the Ming historical novels. Let us now turn our attention to their scope and contents. A few words need to be said first about the status of historical novels within the broader classification of all Ming novels. Generally speaking, Ming novels have been loosely classified by subject matter into three broad groups: historical novels (popularized chronicles and legendary tales), novels about gods and devils (supernatural tales and tales of marvels), and social and domestic novels (novels of manners).[52] Among all categories of Ming novels, the historical novel was the prevailing form in Ming times. Either in the genre of popularized chronicle or in the genre of legendary tale, the subject of history fascinated the Ming writers, as manifested by the output of the historical novels, which surpassed the combined total of all other kinds of Ming novels.[53] The fact that there are more historical novels than other kinds is not surprising. In a country where history and tradition were reverenced, it was only natural that writers were engrossed in the subject of history. An added factor was the long tradition of professional oral fiction just mentioned, of which history was one of its popular subjects.

With plenty of oral traditions, literary materials, and historical sources, the historical novels are able to cover all of the legendary periods and major dynasties in history, including the contemporary Ming era. In table 1 a representative list of titles is given, illustrating the scope and contents of the historical novels.[54] Both the Chinese titles and their English translations are given in the abbreviated form, with dating information from the earliest extant editions. If no dating information about a novel has been found, the dating information about the novelist or the dated preface is given. If the author or the specific dates of a publication are not known, but it was published during the Ming period, it is listed simply as "Ming edition."

Table 1 not only shows the general scope of the Ming historical novel, it also shows what is missing. The two missing historical periods include the Southern and Northern Dynasties (420—589), which covers a period of about one hundred and seventy years over a fragmentated China, and the Yuan Dynasty (1260—1368), which covers a period of about one hundred years under the Mongol empire. A survey of the field shows that there is only one historical novel that deals with the Yuan; it is the *Ta-Yuan lung-hsing chi* (The Glories of the Yuan; *Ta-Yuan* hereafter), of which we know very little.[55] The book *Ta-Yuan* could be a Ming work; it also could be a Ch'ing work. Most likely it was a Ch'ing work, based on our observation that "nationalism," which was represented by the tremendous popularity of Yueh Fei as a national hero against foreign invasion in Ming times, was a dominant theme in Ming fiction and drama. There is also one novel that deals with the period of the Southern and Northern Dynasties; it is Tu

TABLE 1. Historical Dynasties and Historical Novels of the Ming

Legendary Periods and Historical Dynasties	Historical Novels
The legendary periods (from the Creations to the Hsia)	*P'an-ku* (From P'an-ku to Kings T'ang and Yü) (preface attributed to Chung Hsing, 1574–1624)
	* *K'ai-p'i* (Legends of the Creation) (preface 1635)
	Yu-Hsia (Records of the Hsia) (preface attributed to Chung Hsing)
The Shang Kingdom (ca. 1600–ca. 1027 B.C.)	* *Yu Shang* (Records of the Shang) (Ming edition)
The Western Chou Kingdom (ca. 1027–771 B.C.)	*Shang-Chou* or *Feng-shen* (Records of the Shang and the Chou) (Shu Tsai-yang edition, ca. 1616–21)
The Eastern Chou Kingdom (770–256 B.C.)	*Lieh-kuo* (Records of the States) (1615 edition)
	Hsin lieh-kuo (New Records of the States) (by Feng Meng-lung, 1574–1646)
	Sun P'ang (Sun Pin and P'ang Chüan) (preface 1636)
The Ch'in Dynasty (221–207 B.C.)	*Hsi-Han* (The Founding of the Western Han) (1612 edition)
The Western Han Dynasty (202 B.C.–A.D. 8)	* *Ch'üan-Han* (Chronicle of the Han) (1588 edition)
The Eastern Han Dynasty (25–220)	*Tung-Han* (The Restoration of the Eastern Han) (1612 edition)
The Three Kingdoms (220–265)	*San-kuo* (Romance of the Three Kingdoms) (1522 edition; preface 1494)
The Western Chin Dynasty (265–317)	*Tung Hsi Chin* (Popularized Chronicles of the Western and Eastern Chin) (1612 edition)
The Sui Dynasty (589–618)	*Sui Yang-ti* (The Gay Life of Emperor Yang) (preface 1631)
	Sui-shih (Supplementary Records of the Sui) (preface 1633)
The T'ang Dynasty (618–906)	* *Sui-T'ang* (The Sui and T'ang Dynasties) (1619 edition)
	T'ang-shu (The Chronicle of the T'ang) (1553 edition)

(Continued)

Note: The novels listed are for the purpose of illustration, with no intention of being exhaustive. The full titles and bibliographic details of these novels are given in text whenever they are discussed. The four titles marked by an asterisk are the novels unavailable for examination (full titles are given in the glossary). For more information about them, see Sun K'ai-ti's bibliography of popular Chinese fiction, *Chung-kuo t'ung-su hsiao-shuo shu-mu* (1982 edition), pp. 27, 28, 32, 48.

TABLE 1— *Continued*

Legendary Periods and Historical Dynasties	Historical Novels
The Five Dynasties (907–960)	*Ts'an-T'ang* (The Late T'ang and Five Dynasties) (Ming edition)
The Northern Sung Dynasty (960–1126)	*Nan Sung* (The Founding of the Sung) (Ming edition) *Shui-hu* (Outlaws of the Marsh) (preface by T'ien-tu wai-ch'en [Wang Tao-kun] ca. 1589) *Pei-Sung* (The Generals of the Yang Family) (preface 1618)
The Southern Sung Dynasty (1127–1279)	*Ta-Sung* (The Sung Restoration Hero Yueh Fei) (1552 edition)
The Ming Dynasty (1368–1644)	*Ying-lieh chuan* (The Founding of the Ming) (1591 edition) *San-pao* (The Western Voyages) (preface 1597) *Yü Shao-pao* (The Life and Career of Yü Chien) (preface 1581) *Wang Yang-ming* (The Life and Career of Wang Yang-ming) (by Feng Meng-lung, 1574–1646)
The Southern Ming reigns (1645–61)	*Chiao Ch'uang* (The Ch'uang Rebellion) (1645 edition)

Kang's *Nan pei shih yen-i* (Popular Chronicle of the Southern and Northern Dynasties; 1793 original edition). Apparently Tu Kang, a Ch'ing writer, noticed this missing period in historical novels and decided to make amends for it.

The two "missing" periods tell something about the nature of the "collective memory" of historical novels. These periods represented a sort of "Dark Age" in Chinese history when the structural and ideological breakdown of Chinese society took place. The period of the Southern and Northern Dynasties was a period of disunity and great turmoil, while the Yuan Dynasty witnessed the disintegration of the Confucian orders under the alien Mongol empire. Without realizing it themselves, the storytellers, the writers of fiction and drama, the performing artists of all kinds — all seemed to try to block these national "nightmares" from their collective memories. This tradition seemed to be carried into Ch'ing times. As pointed out before, there is no historical novel or drama that glorified the founding of the Ch'ing Dynasty in Ch'ing times, compared with the many Ming novels and dramas glorifying the founding of every major dynasty in history with the only possible exception of the Yuan dynasty.

Besides the purpose of illustration of the scope and contents of the Ming historical novel, table 1 also serves as a checklist for representative works chosen for this study. In making up this checklist I have followed three criteria: to cover as completely as possible all legendary and historical periods; to cover a wide variety of the subjects; and to represent more novelists. These same criteria are also followed in choosing individual novels for a wide variety of thematic analyses throughout the book. Keep in mind here one major premise: that the historical novel per se is not the subject of this study; in this study, historical novels are treated as primary sources.

As primary sources, the literary merits of the individual novel are not the concern of this study. Take the novel *Chiao Ch'uang t'ung-su hsiao-shuo* (The Suppression of the Ch'uang Rebellion; by Hsi-wu lan-tao-jen [pseud.], *Chiao Ch'uang* hereafter). Published in 1645 right after the Ch'ing took over north China, it was a sort of eyewitness account of the fall of the Ming. To students of history, this is valuable source material in spite of the fact that the novel was so poorly written and poorly organized that it can hardly be called a novel by today's standards. In other words, as primary sources, historical novels are "measured" according to the information they provide; the more information they provide, the more attention they will receive in this study.

Generally speaking, there are two groups of novels that receive more attention: the novels that deal with the founding of a major imperial dynasty and the novels that deal with legendary heroes in history. Two examples: In our discussion of the pattern of history, we will study several novels to examine the pattern of dynastic cycle (which reflects dynastic wars in history), the nature and organization of the rebel groups, the pattern of attaining power, the pattern of establishing personal relationships among rebel heroes, and so forth. The novels (see tables 3, 4, 5, and 6) that provide source materials for these discussions will naturally be mentioned more often than others. In our discussion of heroes in history, we will analyze different archetypes in the novels. These novels (see table 8), when checked against the repertoires of professional oral fiction and popular dramas of all kinds, show that they share with these popular entertainments similar story plots and historical or fictional personages. It becomes clear that novels that provide a body of commonly accepted stories and legends will receive more attention.

IV

We have defined the scope and contents of the historical novels. We now turn to the outstanding issues surrounding these novels as a whole. The first important issue is the size of readership of these historical novels, a subject of tremendous interest to both historians and literary scholars. Different views and theories are advanced, but no matter how fascinating, they remain views and theories. The size of readership cannot be known unless we know the rate of literacy, the number of copies of a novel issued, and any reliable indications of how many copies actually sold. Unfortunately for all of these we have either only modern estimates based on general and imprecise statistics or statements, or no figures at all.

Theoretically speaking, estimates of China's literate population can logically be based on figures derived from civil service examination records. The central government established quotas for the maximum number of degree-holders, by administrative units, who would be allowed to pass each level of the civil service examinations on any occasion. Normally these examinations took place according to fixed schedules. Thus, based on the fixed quotas of the *sheng-yuan* (the first-degree holder) and the ratio between the successful and unsuccessful candidates for degrees, one can, theoretically, proceed to make a general estimate of the literate population during a given period of time. But there are complicated problems involved with this kind of estimation, for instance, how to consider the unsuccessful candidates for degrees who participated in the same examinations again and again. If half the candidates at any one examination were repeating the test, this would alter the estimate significantly. Yet it was a well-known fact that in Imperial China the unsuccessful degree candidates tended to persevere; men took the same examination again and again in the hope of ultimately passing it.

To estimate the size of readership, we need to know the economic aspects of the novel trade, especially the size of the final production for each novel. Although there are excellent studies containing useful information about the publishing business, including geographical distribution of publishing firms, the state of the art of the printers' craft, and the general conditions of the publishing industry such as detailed production costs for materials and services of all sorts, there is no information on the number of copies of any one edition, to say nothing of the size of novel sales.[56] Without these vital statistics, estimates of the size of readership will be too general to delineate the complexity of the reading audience. Therefore, instead of making more estimates and speculations, we will leave this matter open and wait for new evidence that may be discovered in the future.

Another need for more information concerns the writers of these historical novels. This involves two issues: the authorship of the early novels and biographical information on the writers of the later novels. Identifying the writers of the early novels is a major problem. Scholars are still debating the authorship of the novel *San-kuo* and the novel *Shui-hu*, as the two most notable examples. For the writers of the later novels, the authorship is not the problem; we generally know the names of the writers, although there are still a few anonymous or pseudonymous novels. The problem is that we know very little about these authors except for their names.

We do know some information about four writers of the later novels. The first is Feng Meng-lung (1574–1646). A native of Ch'ang-chou District, Soochow Prefecture, Feng wrote and edited three vernacular novels.[57] He was better known as a short-story writer and editor whose greatest contribution as a writer and scholar lay in the preservation, promotion, and creation of popular literature. Feng fared poorly in civil service examinations. It was only in 1631, at the age of fifty-seven, that he was sent to the National University by his local school, and then qualified for a minor appointment. From 1634 to 1638 Feng was the magistrate of Shou-ning, Fukien. Besides these facts, not much about his life is known.

Another better-known writer is Feng Meng-lung's close friend Yuan Yü-ling (1592–1674), from a distinguished family of Soochow literati. His grandfather Yuan Nien (1539–1617) was a *chin-shih* graduate of 1577 who served in a number of important provincial posts over a ten-year span late in the sixteenth century, but the name of Yuan's father is not known. Yuan Yü-ling is better known as a dramatist and poet than as a novelist, although he compiled three historical novels.[58] Yuan was renowned for his bohemian behavior that was described as morally repulsive by his contemporary detractors. The fact that he was among the first wave of Chinese literati to offer their services to the Manchus after the conquest also might have affected the popularity of his writings during the early Ch'ing. His enemies were legion, to judge from the number of uncomplimentary references to him in contemporary writings. One story said that he wrote a play to slander his rival for the favors of a local courtesan. This indiscretion cost him his academic degree. Like Feng Meng-lung, Yuan also fared poorly in civil service examinations, passing only the first academic degree. Another story identified Yuan as the man who pesonally sur-rendered the city of Soochow to Manchu invaders. The allegation is false because Yuan was in Peking during the conquest. However, he did offer his services to the Manchus even though he only served with them a very short period of time. All in all, it is clear that Yuan was a very unconventional man by any standards.

The next better-known writer of historical novels was Hsiung Ta-mu (fl. 1552), a native of Chien-yang District, Chien-ning Prefecture, who was the most productive historical novelist in late Ming times. Whether or not Hsiung received any academic degree is still a mystery. Recent studies suggest that Hsiung Ta-mu and Feng Meng-lung either owned or were closely connected with some printing concern.[59] Although solid evidence is yet to be found, this connection with a publishing firm would be significant because it demonstrates the close relation between the writers and the publishing firms of the time. The fourth writer, Yü Shao-yü (fl. 1566), also from Chien-yang, prefecture of Chien-ning, is known as a relative of Yü Hsiang-tou, an established publisher in Fukien Province.[60]

The connection with a publishing firm is interesting because publish-ing was a logical choice of occupation among the unsuccessful degree candidates. For example we know for certain that a well-known Ch'ing fiction writer and dramatist, Li Yü (1611−80), had been a government student (*sheng-yuan*) before he engaged in writing and publishing popular works of all sorts for a living after the collapse of the Ming empire.[61] As publishers knew the contemporary book market well, the suggestion that some of them or their relatives had actually written and published these long historical novels indicates the confidence the publishers had in their efforts to promote this particular genre of literature. It should be pointed out here that the Ming imperial government also played a role in promoting the book publishing business. Earlier in 1368 when the dynasty was just established, the founding emperor, Ming T'ai-tsu, decreed that the book tax be abolished.[62] This abolition of the book tax could be viewed as an incentive given to the publishing business by the imperial government. Throughout the Ming period, publishing firms took advantage of the exemption from taxation and were prosperous everywhere, especially in major urban centers such as Nanking, Peking, Chien-yang, Soochow, Ch'ang-chou, Yangchou, and Hui-chou. The apogee of Ming printing occurred around 1600; also about that time many historical novels were published. This brings us to the question of readership, a subject of tremendous interest to both historians and literary scholars. For whose benefit were these historical novels written?

The writers of historical novels wanted to reach a larger reading audience that included the less educated. For example, when Chiang Ta-ch'i wrote his preface to the novel *San-kuo* in 1494, he mentioned that the purpose of the historical novel was to explain the difficult Official History to *chung-jen* (the masses), which included both the educated and the uneducated. In 1552 when Hsiung Ta-mu wrote his preface to one of his own historical novels, *Ta-Sung*, he indicated that he was asked to write the novel for the benefit of *yü-fu yü-fu* (the common people) so that they (the people) could learn a few things about history. In a preface to the novel *Tung Hsi Han t'ung-su yen-i* (1612 edition) attributed to Yuan Hung-tao, the novel is said to be written for the benefit of all, the educated and the uneducated, the old and the young.[63] The sense of mission expressed in these prefaces echoed the spirit of the time represented by the T'ai-chou group of the left-wing Wang Yang-ming school of Confucianism in their efforts to popularize learning for all men.[64]

This goal of education for all was an aspiration of the Ming thinkers and writers, and has remained an ideal for the Chinese. By the end of the Ming period, this objective had been attained only to a certain extent, with a long way still to go for its complete realization. The writers of historical novels did try to elucidate and popularize history for all people, keeping in mind future generations and all posterity. They tried to retell the profound and difficult standard historical texts in plain spoken language, a language that when read aloud could be understood, at least partly, by most people. But the fact remained that the majority of the people, who were illiterate, were unable to read these novels themselves. Nor could they afford the novels, as most of them lived at or near the subsistence level.

Thus the most obvious social class who could afford the novels, read them, and take the leisure to enjoy them was the "educated elite," especially the wealthy and leisured stratum of that class. For students of history, the question is not who read the novels, but who else read the novels besides the "scholar-gentry." Did the "scholar-commoners" read the novels, since the majority of the educated consisted of unsuccessful degree candidates? Did the merchants read the novels, since there were so many degree candidates turned merchants? What about the women, since there were more educated women in the late Ming times? The question is a complex one, because it involves several unresolved but related issues, such as the rate of literacy, the economics of the novel trade, the size of novel sales, and the size of readership. Until further findings clear up these unresolved issues, we will leave this question open.

A few words more must be said here about the role played by writers of historical novels in the broad process of construction and transmission of tradition. They, together with the playwrights and short story writers of their own time, could be compared to what modern intellectual historians call "secondary" or "minor" intellectuals in terms of the quality of their intellectual works — from the vantage point of cultural originality rather than cultural borrowing — or in terms of their occupational roles as teachers, writers of vernacular fiction or drama, or popular entertainers. According to a modern study, it has become more and more apparent that these "secondary intellectuals" may indeed play a central role in the broad process of construction and transmission of tradition.[65] In other words, it is these secondary intellectuals, through their activities in teaching, writing popular works of all kinds, and entertainment, who served as channels of institutionalization, and even as possible creators of new types of symbols of cultural orientation, of tradition, and of collective and cultural identity. With Ming writers of historical novels this seems to be the case. They were "secondary intellectuals" whose works were not recognized as bona fide literature by the governing elite during Ming times. Nevertheless, as writers of fiction, their works reached a much wider audience than any other genre of literature in Ming and Ch'ing times. In the last analysis, the vernacular writers and playwrights had their works promoted not only by prosperous publishing firms but also by the mass media of the theater and professional storytelling; these writers and playwrights have played an important role in the process of shaping popular culture ever since Ming times.[66]

With this note we now turn to the general setting of an emerging vernacular and semivernacular literature on the Ming horizon.

V

The historical novels that first made their appearance in the book market in the late fifteenth and early sixteenth centuries ushered in a new era of vernacular literature in Ming China. The burgeoning of such a literature serves to indicate the presence of an opportune cultural and economic environment. Many factors contributed to the cultural growth in the late Ming: the spread of silver currency followed by general commercial prosperity, the economic affluence resulting from great progress in agriculture and handicrafts, the prosperous printing business that saw the emergence of an expanded reading public, and the blossoming of private and semiprivate academies and educational institutions that reflected a climate of optimism nourished and promoted by the Wang Yang-ming (1472–1529) school of Confucianism in the effort to popularize learning for all men. This climate of optimism was most significant, for it witnessed vigorous and conscientious efforts among concerned scholars who truly believed in transmitting education to the masses. Among them was Wang Ken (1483–1547) of the T'ai-chou school of thought, the famous left or radical wing of the Wang Yang-ming school; Wang Ken was the leader of this "mass" movement. Believing that all men had the capability for enlightenment, Wang Ken inspired many followers who viewed it as their mission to awaken the masses. As a result, popular lecturers of this radical school flourished and spread throughout the land, carrying with them their zealous effort to promote education among the masses.[67]

The impact of this cultural movement on Ming society cannot be overemphasized, for it was not just a matter of Wang Yang-ming's Confucianism being disseminated downward, but of popular thought penetrating upward. In other words, the popularization movement stimulated and accelerated the process of interaction between the elite culture of the great Way and the popular culture of the small Way. The fact that quite a few leading figures of the T'ai-chou group were commoners bore testimony to the extent of the movement. The significance of popular thought penetrating upward lay not only in the addition of fresh and vigorous blood to an old culture, but also in the opening up of new and boundless frontiers. Through this interaction between cultures, new thoughts made their appearance. The most important development was the rise of new romantic and spontaneous literature.[68]

Historically speaking, the pioneer, the one person whose ideas inspired the new romantic literary movement in the late Ming, was Li Chih (1527–1602), one of the most brilliant and complex figures in Chinese thought and literature. An admirer of Wang Yang-ming and Wang Ken, Li Chih drew upon and carried forward some of the main ideas and tendencies generated within the Wang Yang-ming school. But Li Chih himself did not belong to any school of thought. Being an individualist with a sharp, critical mind, he always did things with the ideas of others that they had not done. Take, for example, his theory of the "childlike mind." Influenced by Yang-ming's doctrine of the individual mind (as the ultimate source of morality), Li Chih propounds a theory of the childlike mind (*t'ung-hsin*) that inspired a whole generation of literati in their pursuit of a more spontaneous and less moralistic literature.[69] According to Li Chih, the childlike mind is, like man's nature, originally pure, and one should follow wherever it spontaneously leads. The same is true with literature; the best literature always follows where the emotions lead spontaneously. That is why the best in literature always springs from the childlike mind. It follows that if writing follows wherever the childlike mind leads, then the writing of any age, any form, any style, and any language should all be accepted as literature. In such a simple and forceful way, Li Chih upheld his belief that popular works of fiction and drama, written in either Classical Chinese or in the vernacular, should be accepted as literature as poetry and literary prose do.

Besides his attempt to theorize a more spontaneous and less moralistic literature, Li Chih actually worked on individual fictional works to promote their popularity, as in the case of the novel *Shui-hu*, for which he not only wrote the preface, but also commentaries on the text. In fact, it was from Li Chih's commentaries, the so-called *p'ing-tien* (marginal commentaries on the text) of the novel *Shui-hu*, that a unique form of fiction criticism developed. Together with the forms of preface (*hsu*) and colophon (*pa*), the *p'ing-tien* style of commentaries constitutes the essence of the late Ming and early Ch'ing fiction criticism. The late Ming reader-critics Yeh Chou, Feng Meng-lung, and the famous Chin Sheng-tan of the early Ch'ing were all influenced by Li Chih. As this fiction criticism was the guiding force behind the new literary movement, Li Chih's contribution to the vernacular literature is self-evident.[70]

Through his conscious effort and concrete examples, Li Chih popularized the concept that drama and fiction should be viewed as great literature. His ideas that literature changes with time and that each age has its particular literature found their echoes in the writings of many of his contemporary and later literati. Among Li Chih's contemporaries, the famous Yuan brothers—Yuan Tsung-tao (1560–1600), Yuan Hung-tao (1568–1610), and Yuan Chung-tao (1570–1624)—and the great Ming playwright, T'ang Hsien-tsu (1550–1616), were his admirers. Take Yuan Hung-tao, for example. Inspired by Li Chih's idea that literature changes with time, Yuan Hung-tao, the most articulate and influential of the three Yuan brothers, arrived at an evolutionary theory of literature. According to Yuan Hung-tao, after having reached its zenith each literary form naturally gives way to another new form, and in the same fashion, the worn-out literary practices of a certain period are superseded by more appropriate conventions.[71] Like Li Chih, the Yuan brothers also believed that literature must express one's own feelings and emotions naturally and spontaneously. The most important thing in writing, according to them, is to express what Hung-tao called one's "native sensibility" (*hsing-ling*), which sounds very much like Li Chih's concept of pure nature. Consequently, Hung-tao placed higher value on folksongs than literary poetry and prose — the belles lettres in orthodox literature — because folksongs were composed by unlettered but unaffected people (what he called *chen-jen*) and were invested with a genuine tone (*chen-sheng*). For the same reason he also compared the literary value of the novel *Shui-hu* with that of the Six Classics or even with that of Ssu-ma Ch'ien's *Shih-chi*.[72]

These emphases on "the unlettered but unaffected" common people and their "genuine tone" reveal, on the one hand, the emancipated spirit of the new literature movement. Here the word *emancipated* is used in the sense that the movement represented a defiant attitude toward the moralistic orthodox neo-Confucianism of the time—the Ch'eng-Chu school of Confucianism. The fact that common people became the dominant group of protagonists in Ming fiction and drama bore testimony to the strength of this spirit. On the other hand, this endorsement of the "unlettered and unaffected" could be also traced back to the ancient tradition of the two-way traffic between the governing elite and the governed people of the streets. In a broad sense, the endowment of the "childlike" purity was not much different from the Master's original ideas of "unpolished" and "unrefined" discussed in the *Analects of Confucius*. They complement each other in their basic optimistic views of human nature. These two seemingly conflicting elements, the defiant and the compliant, are the central threads of our discussions throughout the book; they are essential to our understanding of the cultural and intellectual development of the late Ming.

Almost simultaneous with the rise of vernacular literature was the development of printing. The expanding reading public and the rising interest in cultural activities among the lower classes of society were closely related to the great expansion of printing in late Ming China, which was marked with flourishing commercial book production including not only fiction and drama, but also popular works of Confucian culture and simplified means of preparing for civil service examinations. This sign of the times indicated the fact that the sixteenth and seventeenth centuries saw a general trend of transmitting education and popularizing learning to the lower classes of the society. As a result, the social base from which candidates (for civil service examinations) were drawn was widened, and this was made possible not only because of increasing affluence, but also because the means whereby the lower classes might educate themselves were available through the various types of new publications that were printed and sold in larger numbers.[73]

It becomes clear that the driving force behind the cultural and intellectual development of the late Ming was the belief in transmitting education and popularizing learning to the masses. Composing, writing, and publishing historical novels was only a very small part of this great enterprise. The ideal, the goal, that "in education there shall be no class distinction" was definitely nothing new, but the energy, the vigor, and the dynamics the Ming writers displayed in their attempts to popularize history for the masses are memorable. They happened to produce some of the most loved pieces of literature in traditional times.

VI

In summation, the Ming historical novels represent the influence of the lower folk stream in literature as well as the influence on the Chinese mind of the classical traditions and Confucian ideology. The vast quantity of historical novels attests to the tremendous interest in the historical past during Ming times, while the extensive historical scope of these novels — from the legendary Sage Kings through the pre-Ch'in classical period, and the long succession of dynasties of Imperial China down to the Ming dynasty — provides a supplementary folk history to the Official Histories. Through examination of the Ming historical novels we hope to obtain a general picture of the historical world of the Ming people, and by analyzing the ideological structure of that world we hope to obtain a penetrating look at ideas, beliefs, and feelings of every sort in Ming times, especially those unconventional ones. We can also investigate how these unconventional and unorthodox beliefs and feelings interacted with high societal and state ideologies.

As the historical novels represent the collective efforts of both plebeian artists and educated writers, they provide two groups of materials for the study of ideas: first, the popular ideas and beliefs in the realm of folklore and community sentiment; second, the attitudes, assumptions, and aspirations of the governing elite in the realm of popularized historical writing and imaginary literature.[74] While ideas on the level of popular acceptance are often in the nature of random remarks, those entertained by the educated vernacular writers also represented a lower level of thought that had seeped down from the high level, taking a vulgarized or distorted form. In order to put these ideas in their proper historical perspective, it is necessary to compare them with the higher level of thought available in Ming times and bring in background information that helps to access the dominant ideas of the times. The background information in the present study is drawn largely from the Standard Histories and various comprehensive histories, as well as the Confucian classics and other pre-Ch'in philosophical works that were an invariable part of the education of cultured Chinese in traditional times. Since education and a political career — usually via the universal civil service examination system—were closely interconnected in traditional China, the stock of convictions held by individuals within the governing elite varies only slightly from one person to another. This unusual ideological integration among the governing elite makes it possible to access the dominant ideas of the times.

In the present study, we concentrate on examining the ideas and images of Ming historical novels, approaching them through a thematic analysis of their dominant motifs, formulae, and archetypes. In such a descriptive analysis, thoughts and deeds are inextricably entangled, and intellectual history provides a way of treating this common material from the standpoint of the thought rather than the deed.[75] Furthermore, all materials in the present study have been integrated in a general structure of explanation covering all the interlocking cultural traditions from ancient times to the Ming period. Thus, in a broad sense, they become a constituent part of general cultural history. Finally, a study of this sort cannot avoid advancing hypotheses or "structuring" (as the social scientists say) its material. The best that can be hoped for by one who undertakes a new departure is that he or she may stimulate others to follow with new studies to better effect.

Chapter 2

The Pattern of History: Dynastic Cycle and Political Legitimacy

> They say the momentum of history was ever thus: the empire, long divided, must unite; long united, must divide.
>
> —*San-kuo yen-i*

In the classic *Meng-tzu* (The Works of Mencius), Mencius (371–289 B.C.) is said to have observed the pattern of history as follows: "A long time has elapsed since this world of men received its being, and there has been along its history now a period of good order, and now a period of confusion."[1] In his *Shih-chi* (Historical Records), the first comprehensive history in ancient China, Ssu-ma Ch'ien (145–86 B.C.) describes the pattern of history simply as "a cycle which, when it ends, must begin over again."[2] In the historical novel, the opening statement of the popular *San-kuo* sums up the following observations: "They say the momentum of history was ever thus: the empire, long divided, must unite; long united, must divide."[3] This opening statement of *San-kuo* speaks well for the popular diffusion of the concept of dynastic cycle. Accepting the cyclic alternation between order and disorder as a self-evident truth, the novel further asserts its author's belief that since periodic disorders and anarchies are inevitable, the heroes in history must bring back peace and order to the world. Thus heroes become the dynamic force in history as attested by the two most quoted phrases in historical novels: "Circumstances produce heroes" and "Heroes create circumstances." History is viewed as a record of the careers of these "heroes" who in their perpetual struggles for fame and power take advantage of the opportunities offered by periodic disorders and anarchies.

The theory of dynastic cycle is, of course, not the only theory interpreting the pattern of Chinese history in imperial times. Historians who view the past from different perspectives reach conclusions differently.[4] In historical novels, however, the theory of dynastic cycle is a dominant thought, because it blends well with ideas and beliefs related to the very being of a state, such as the cyclical theory of the Five Virtues (*wu-te chung-shih shuo*), the concept of dynastic legitimacy (*cheng-t'ung*), and the doctrine of the Mandate of Heaven (*t'ien-ming*).

The concept of dynastic cycles stemmed from an ancient observation over the mysterious cyclical process of nature. As nature shows its way by the established rhythm of the four seasons, so does life, through the cycle of birth, growth, maturity, senescence, and death. In the same vein of cyclical process, the rise and fall of dynasties is viewed as following an established rhythm of genesis, expansion, prosperity, and decline. On the surface, the dynastic cycle is a life-cycle analogy: politics, like men, follow an established rhythm prescribed by the mysterious natural forces of the universe. But at closer view the Chinese never interpreted the dynastic cycle as merely following the laws of nature; for them the dynamics behind the dynastic changes were moral, and the lessons to be drawn from them were moral lessons.[5] The historical novels in Ming times testified to the popular acceptance of this idea of dynastic cycle. Most novels, at least the majority, center on the changing of dynasties. The most critical issue arising from dynastic changes is a moral one: the concept of dynastic legitimacy that was derived from two ancient theories, the theory of grand unification of the *Ch'un-ch'iu* and the cyclical theory of the Five Virtues.[6] To understand this concept of dynastic legitimacy and its related issues, we first must examine the doctrine of the Mandate of Heaven, which explains the very existence of the ancient state.

The belief in an all-ruling Heaven and the notion that laws were derived from Heaven were basic elements in the theory of the Mandate of Heaven formulated during the Shang and Chou times.[7] According to this theory, China was a state created by and maintained under the direct supervision of the highest deity, Heaven (*T'ien*); its ruler had the status of the Son of Heaven (*T'ien-tzu*) who was chosen by Heaven to rule the country and to take care of the people. As the welfare of the people was Heaven's chief concern, the people were viewed as the most important element in the country. This sentiment was expressed in the words of "T'ai-shih" (The Great Declaration) in the *Shu-ching* (Book of History) as quoted in the *Meng-tzu*: "Heaven sees according as my people see; Heaven hears according as my people hear."[8] Thus, the key to the Mandate of Heaven (in theory, at least) was the people, whose approval and support spoke volumes for the justice and promise of the new regime in the eyes of Heaven. It follows that since the ruler was chosen by the people (in the name of Heaven), he could be deposed by the people if he betrayed the people's trust. Accordingly, a moral principle of political legitimacy was established to justify the changes of dynasties: In its genesis a dynasty received the mandate to rule from Heaven, which recognized the virtues and benevolence of its founder; at its end, a dynasty lost the mandate when its rulers failed to attend earnestly to government business and failed to protect or to benefit the people. The classic examples are stories about the founding of the Shang and the Chou dynasties that repeatedly appeared in standard histories and historical novels. In both cases, the doctrine of the Mandate of Heaven is applied. The last kings of the Hsia (ca. 2000−ca. 1600 B.C.), and the Shang (ca. 1600−ca. 1027 B.C.)−King Chieh and King Chou, respectively−were so tyrannous that they lost the mandate to rule, and their former vassals, the virtuous founders of the Shang and the Chou (ca. 1027−256 B.C.)−King T'ang and King Wu, respectively−were well justified in taking the throne from them, with Heaven's blessing. Implied in these stories is a unique belief that the Mandate of Heaven could and did pass repeatedly from one ruling house to another, but never, even for a moment, could it be interrupted. Nor at any one time could it be simultaneously held by more than one house or ruler.[9] This is the essence of the doctrine of the Mandate of Heaven; it means that there was only one line of legitimate succession to the throne.

The idea of establishing dynastic legitimacy based on moral principle represents the ancient concept of an ideal state that upholds the virtues and benevolence of the ruler of the state as the foundation of an acceptable government. But in reality, the established rule to justify dynastic legitimacy was the de facto recognition given to whoever unified China or occupied the largest part of the country. This political expediency to rationalize a de facto recognition was generally observed by traditional historiographers in all Official Histories. The unbroken line of dynastic succession, one after another in the long history of imperial China, witnessed the practice of this expediency. Nevertheless, the ideal of a benevolent state established to uphold virtue and humanity was so entrenched in the Chinese mind that it surfaced again and again in scholars' writings and in popular literature. The best example is the historical novel *San-kuo*, which reflects both the utopian tradition of that ideal and its popular support among the people. In this aspect the focus of the novel is the anti-Wei and pro-Shu sentiment that ignores the dynastic legitimacy of the Wei dynasty (220–265) long established in the Official History (the *San-kuo chih* by Ch'en Shou) and followed by Ssu-ma Kuang in his celebrated *T'ung-chien*.[10] In the novel *San-kuo*, the Shu (221–263), not the Wei, is regarded as the legitimate regime to succeed the Han dynasty. The different treatments of this subject by historians and novelists lie in their different attitudes toward the moral issue of usurpation; the pragmatic historians ignored it and the novelists denounced it.

The historical novel *San-kuo* covers a period of about one hundred years, from the last decades of the Later Han Dynasty (25–220) to the establishment of the Chin Dynasty in 265. During this period there were political and military struggles among rival groups contending for control of the Chinese empire. Three kingdoms emerged: Wei in the north, ruled by Ts'ao Ts'ao (155–220) and his son Ts'ao P'i (188–227); Shu in the southwest, ruled by Liu Pei (162–223), a kin of the royal house of the Han, and his son Liu Ch'an (207–267); and Wu in the southeast, ruled by Sun Ch'uan (181–252). When Ch'en Shou, the historian, wrote his *San-kuo chih*, he treated the three regimes differently by referring to the biographies of Wei rulers as *chi* (from *pen-chi*, which means imperial annal). These include "Wu-ti chi" (The Imperial Annals of Emperor Wu), "Wen-ti chi" (The Imperial Annals of Emperor Wen), and "Ming-ti chi" (The Imperial Annals of Emperor Ming). But he referred to the biographies of the Shu and Wu rulers merely as *chuan* (biography). These include "Hsien-chu chuan" (The Biography of the Former Ruler of Shu) and "Wu-chu-chuan" (The Biography of the Ruler of the Wu).[11] According to traditional historiographical convention since Ssu-ma Ch'ien's *Shih-chi*, the *pen-chi* is an exclusive designation in Official Histories for the biographies of emperors, while *chuan* is used to denote the biographies of any other person. Note also the contrast when Ch'en Shou used the word *ti* (emperor) to refer to the Wei rulers, and the word *chu* (ruler) to the Shu and Wu rulers. Thus it is clear that Ch'en Shou regarded the Wei as the legitimate regime.

Although as early as the fourth century there was already some doubt about the legitimacy of the Wei,[12] the historical position of the Wei was reinforced when Ssu-ma Kuang wrote his *T'ung-chien*, in which he recognized the Wei as the dynasty that succeeded the Han, not the Shu, whose ruler was a kin of the royal house of the Han. However, the fact that Ts'ao P'i of the Wei usurped the throne of the Han must have troubled Ssu-ma Kuang because he wrote a lengthy note to explain why he chose the Wei instead of the Shu as the legitimate succeeding dynasty of the Han.[13]

Throughout the Northern Sung period scholars generally followed Ssu-ma Kuang's example, until the legitimacy of the Wei was openly denounced by the great Neo-Confucianist Chu Hsi, who specifically took issue with Ssu-ma Kuang in his work *Kang-mu*. According to Chu Hsi the Shu should be the legitimate regime succeeding the Han since it was founded by a kin of the royal house of the Han, while the Wei should be classified as *ch'ien-kuo* (the usurped state) since its founder usurped the throne of the Han.[14] Chu Hsi's judgment, which was based entirely on moral conviction, represented the triumph of the *pao-pien* (praise and blame) tradition of Confucius's *Ch'un-ch'iu*. It also represented a strong pro-Han and pro-Shu sentiment in his time. Historically, this pro-Han sentiment also represented a trend of growing "national" sentiment in the Southern Sung period (1127–1279) as a result of the long struggle between the Chinese and their belligerent northern neighbors, particularly the Chin (Jurcheds), who not only demolished the Northern Sung regime, but also threatened the very existence of the Southern Sung. Having lost the North to the barbarians, the Chinese were wistfully longing for the glorious military accomplishment of the great Han dynasty. They now identified themselves as the Han people in order to distinguish themselves from those non-Han "barbarians." The ancient concept of "Chinese versus barbarians" (*Hua-Hsia* versus *I*) changed from a cultural and social distinction to politically oriented hostility toward foreign invaders. As the Chinese rallied around the "nationalistic" flag of the Han, they naturally developed an attachment for the Han empire, and this attachment for the Han was easily turned into resentment against the Wei, whose founder usurped the throne from the Han. This explains why Ts'ao Ts'ao of the Wei was forever branded as a villain in the world of popular drama and fiction.

Chu Hsi's pro-Shu and anti-Wei stand was completely in accord with popular sympathy for the Shu aroused by earlier storytellers and other public entertainers. Earlier, in the days of Su Tung-po, people sympathized with the Shu cause. Su once recalled that while listening to storytellers telling stories about the Three Kingdoms, people clapped their hands when they heard that the Shu were winning, and they sobbed when they were told about its defeat.[15]

By the time the novel was written down, the pro-Shu and anti-Wei sentiment had developed into a strong persuasion. The novelist makes it quite clear that his sympathy and affection are on the side of the Shu whom he regards as the legitimate successor to the Han dynasty.[16] In order to establish the Shu's legitimacy there are two possible approaches: one is to assert the Shu as being the legitimate successor to the Han dynasty; the other is to denounce the Wei as an illegitimate regime. The novelist adopted both approaches. He followed Chu Hsi's argument that Liu Pei, the founder of the Shu, was a scion of the imperial house of the Han, and at the same time, he denounced Ts'ao Ts'ao of the Wei as a traitor to the Han. For example, in chapter 20 of the novel, there is an episode about how the Han emperor Hsien-ti (190−220) recognized Liu Pei as his uncle by descent.[17] From this time on Liu Pei has been generally styled as "Liu, Uncle of the Emperor" (Liu Huang-shu). In this same chapter Ts'ao Ts'ao is denounced for humiliating his emperor and ruining the empire in the secret imperial edict, the famous "girdle decree" (*i-tai chao*), written in blood by the Emperor himself:

> Recently the wicked Ts'ao Ts'ao has exercised his rights abusively, treating even his sovereign ruler with indignities. With the support of his faction and his army he has destroyed the principles of government. By conferring rewards and inflicting punishments he has reduced me, the Emperor, to a nonentity. I have grieved over this day and night, and have feared the Empire would be ruined.[18]

Ts'ao Ts'ao's tyrannous and unscrupulous treacheries are further described in chapter 24, in his murder of Tung Kuei-fei (Lady Tung), one of the Emperor's consorts who was in her fifth month of pregnancy carrying the Emperor's offspring.[19] Again, in chapter 66, the Empress Fu was also murdered.[20] While Ts'ao Ts'ao is described as tyrannous and treacherous, Liu Pei is praised as being kind, modest, considerate, and righteous. Contrary to Ts'ao Ts'ao's hunger for power and ruthlessness in grabbing it, Liu Pei is described as a man of integrity. He never takes anything that does not belong to him. For example, three times he declined to take over Hsu-chou (in modern Kiangsu) even when it was offered to him by its governor, T'ao Ch'ien (fl. late second century to early third century). Only after T'ao died did Liu Pei reluctantly succeed as governor of Hsu-chou.[21] Again in chapter 40, Liu Pei declined to take over Ching-chou (in modern Hupeh) from its dying governor, Liu Piao (d. 218) who offered him the territory. When his chief advisor, Chu-ko Liang (181–234), warned him, "If you do not take this opportunity [to accept Ching-chou as part of your territory], you will regret it ever after," Liu Pei said, "I would rather perish than do what is wrong."[22] Thus Liu Pei's "rather perish than do what is wrong" conviction represents the sage-king image among the people, and this is the reason why there were always so many people eager to follow him.

Liu Pei never abandoned the people who had followed him, even when he was retreating. In chapter 41, when Liu Pei, pressured by Ts'ao Ts'ao's force, decided to abandon Fan Ch'eng (in modern Hupeh), his first concern was the people, as he anxiously said to Chu-ko Liang: "But what of the people who have followed us? They cannot be abandoned." After Chu-ko suggested, "You can tell them to do as they wish; they may come if they like, or remain here," boats were ordered to be prepared and the people were told that Ts'ao Ts'ao was coming, that the city could not be defended, and that those who wished to do so might cross the river with the army. And all the people cried, "We will follow the prince even if it be to death."[23] It is precisely such faith in their prince that justified Liu Pei's claim of legitimacy in the eyes of the people. At the same time, his supporters were also quick to point out that he carried the great heritage from his illustrious ancestor of the imperial Han house. In chapter 54, when the Wu envoy, Lu Su (fl. late second century to early third century), went to see Liu Pei, asking him to return Ching-chou to the Wu, Chu-ko Liang refused. One of his reasons is as follows:

Ever since our illustrious Emperor Kao-tsu raised a righteous revolt and founded the empire, the great heritage has descended in due course till today when, unhappily, evil doers have risen among the powerful and they have sledged upon such portions as they could. But, most likely with Heaven's favor and help, the legitimate (Han) regime will be restored. My lord is the direct descendant of Prince Chung-shan, a great great grandson of the Emperor Hsiao-ching [r. 156–141 B.C.]. Now, as the Emperor's Uncle, should he not have a share of the Empire?[24]

As a scion of the Imperial house, and with an image of sage-king, Liu Pei was thus firmly established in the people's eyes as the legitimate successor to the Han dynasty, according to *San-kuo*.

That the Shu should be regarded as the legitimate successor to the Han, even though it was defeated by the Wei in A.D. 263, presents a problem: Did Shu receive the Mandate of Heaven as the Han's successor? If so, why could the Shu not unify China and defeat the Wei? According to the novel, Liu Pei was the only leader who won over the people's hearts and established a sage-king image in the people's eyes. Yet Liu Pei failed to unify the country. Thus he could not claim that he did receive the Mandate of Heaven. This probably explains why, unlike other historical novels which usually include divine birth myths of respective dynastic founders, we cannot find that of Liu Pei in the *San-kuo*. Instead, we are told that it was the fates that forbade Liu Pei to restore the Han. Liu Pei was a sage-king who had the most brave, loyal, and competent advisors and warriors at his service. In people's minds there was no reason except the fates to explain why he could not succeed in unifying China. In fact, this belief in foreordination is one of the dominant themes in the later parts of the *San-kuo*. We will discuss in great details the aspect of predestination later in chapter 6 ("The Cosmic and Religious Order") of this book. In the meantime, we shall examine the general treatment of dynastic founders in historical novels.

The concept of divine sovereignty, an ideology that is related to dynastic legitimacy, also dominated the Chinese mind throughout the long imperial period. Among the dynastic founders many were members of the ruling class, including generals and prime ministers of a former dynasty. There are some exceptions, however. The most notable are Emperor Kao-tsu of the Han (Liu Pang, 247−195 B.C.; r. 202−195 B.C.), the founder of the Han dynasty, and Emperor T'ai-tsu of the Ming (Chu Yuan-chang, 1328−98; r. 1368−98), the founder of the Ming dynasty, both being from poor and obscure families. In order to assert their Mandate of Heaven, myths of their divine birth were created by their contemporaries and accepted by later generations. Even in Official Histories, these myths were accepted as facts, to say nothing of historical novels. We have stories of these great men being born with unusual signs and omens and growing up with an extraordinary endowment of talents.

In Chen Wei's novel *Hsi-Han* we have the myth of the divine birth of Liu Pang.[25] According to the story, Liu Pang was born after his mother dreamed that she had encountered a god. While his mother was dreaming she was resting on the bank of a pond. Suddenly the sky grew dark and was filled with thunder and lightning. When his father went to look for his mother, he saw a dragon over the place where she was lying. After this she became pregnant and gave birth to Liu Pang. This story of the dragon-origin of Liu Pang was obviously adopted from the historical classic, the *Shih-chi* by Ssu-ma Ch'ien, who, after telling the birth myth, went further to describe that Liu Pang had a dragon-like face:

> Kao-tsu [Liu Pang] had a prominent nose and dragonlike face, with beautiful whiskers on his chin and cheeks; on his left thigh he had seventy-two black moles.... He was fond of wine and women and often used to go to Dame Wang or old lady Wu's and drink on credit. When he got drunk and lay down to sleep, the old women, to their great wonder, would always see something like a dragon over the place where he was sleeping.[26]

There are also stories about the divine birth of Chu Yuan-chang, the founder of the Ming dynasty, Emperor T'ai-tsu. For example, among the several versions of the novel *Huang-Ming k'ai-yün Ying-lieh chuan* (*Ying-lieh chuan* hereafter), written in the sixteenth century, one birth myth is told this way.[27] Just before Chu Yuan-chang was born, people heard music coming from the heavens and a white sun ray was seen descending from the heavens carrying a holy child, held by many goddesses and fairies, to the Chu house. When people went to the Chu house, they saw at the front door two yellow dragons hovering overhead and a blazing fire coming from the house that made people bow their heads and close their eyes. Then they heard that a boy was born and he was the later Emperor T'ai-tsu. In the Official History, *Ming-shih* (The History of the Ming Dynasty), compiled by Chang T'ing-yü (1670–1756) and others, there is also a birth myth about Chu Yuan-chang.[28] According to the *Ming-shih*, when Chu Yuan-chang's mother was pregnant, she dreamed one night that God gave her a pill, which was luminous in her palm, and she swallowed it. Then she awakened, but she still smelled the wonderful scent of the pill. When she gave birth to Chu Yuan-chang, there were red rays all over the room. During the night of her labor, blazing fire appeared several times in her house. When neighbors who saw the fire rushed to put it out, they found that there was no fire at all. This official version of Chu Yuan-chang's birth myth seemed to borrow part of the story from the novel *Ying-lieh chuan*, since the Official History was compiled in the Ch'ing period and the novel was written in the Ming period.[29]

Liu Pang's and Chu Yuan-chang's stories tell the superstitious nature of these birth myths that existed for most of the major dynastic founders, such as Emperor Wen-ti of the Sui (Yang Chien, 541–604; r. 581–604) in the novel *Sui-shih*;[30] Emperor T'ai-tsung of the T'ang (Li Shih-min, 597–649; r. 627–649) in the *T'ang-chuan yen-i* (*T'ang-chuan* hereafter);[31] and Emperor T'ai-tsu of the Sung (Chao K'uang-yin, 927–976; r. 960–976) in the *Nan-Sung*.[32] Since these birth myths are very much like those of Liu Pang's and Chu Yuan-chang's, I will not repeat them here.

With these divine birth myths instilling the idea of divine origin into people's minds, they also strengthened the new dynasty's claim of legitimacy in the eyes of the people. This emphasis on supernatural, divine choice of a dynastic founder reflects the trend of increasing imperial despotism that reached its peak in Ming times. Historically speaking, by the Ming times the imperial institution, which had already existed for more than sixteen hundred years, was developing into a system of absolute monarchy.[33] The classic theory of the Mandate of Heaven, which originally emphasized the proven virtues and abilities of a ruler, was now used to assert the absolute right of the monarch who required no proven qualities defined by the job. In historical novels, the many divine birth myths indicate the general acceptance of the concept of divine origin of the monarch, which further popularized or propagated the existing imperial system.

Another aspect concerning the pattern and structure of history is the cyclic alternation of *unification* and *fragmentation*. In the long history of imperial China up to the Ming, the rise and fall of dynasties had been progressing spirally between two poles: the unified dynastic empire and the divided warring states, as shown by the diagram on table 2.

For the Ming Chinese who were looking back, the pattern of history was clear: the rise and fall of dynasties ran zigzag on the path of the past. There was no enduring disunity in the long history of imperial China to challenge the observation of the *San-kuo*. The world, when long divided, is sure to be reunited; when long united it is sure to be divided. The drama of history, for the novelists, thus naturally focused on the process of the fragmentation of an old empire and the emergence of a new one. And at the center of the drama were the dynastic contenders including both the successful and unsuccessful ones.

Generally speaking, there was an unwritten rule about the dynastic contenders in the world of realistic politics. The proverb "Those who succeed become emperors and those who fail are bandits" reveals the expedient nature of the dynastic game. The double-edged doctrine of the Mandate of Heaven, which served both the dynastic founders and their contestants (in the case of the former, the emphasis was on the unification as Heaven's blessing; in the latter, the emphasis was on the people's right to revolt against a tyrant), is another example of this expediency. In historical novels, in which writing in general is less

TABLE 2.   The Cyclic Alternation of Unification and Fragmentation

Unification of Dynastic Empires	Warring States among Dynastic Contenders
The Hsia Dynasty	Dynastic war between the Hsia and the Shang
The Shang Dynasty	Dynastic war between the Shang and the Chou
The Chou Dynasty	The Period of Warring States
The Ch'in Dynasty	"Righteous revolts of the heroes" during the Ch'in-Han transition
The Han Dynasty	The Period of Three Kingdoms
The Chin Dynasty	The Southern and Northern Dynasties
The Sui Dynasty	"Righteous revolts of the heroes" during the Sui-T'ang transition
The T'ang Dynasty	The Five Dynasties
The Sung Dynasty	Foreign invasions
The Yuan Dynasty	"Righteous revolts of the heroes" during the Yuan-Ming transition
The Ming Dynasty	Local upheavals and foreign invasions
The Ch'ing Dynasty	

refined when compared with Standard Histories, this expediency is expressed in a most simple and direct manner. For example, in the novel *Ts'an-T'ang Wu-tai shih yen-i chuan* (*Ts'an-T'ang* hereafter), the following statement is revealing: "Only those who have vigorous troops and stout horses could be the Son of Heaven [emperor]."[34] This simplistic statement sums up the outstanding characteristic of the "warring states" in which force of arms was the decisive factor in the making of an emperor.

Most historical novelists in Ming times did accept popular revolt by force of arms as the inevitable course of dynastic changes.[35] Almost all the major historical novels deal with armed rebellions that are generally referred to as "the righteous revolts of the heroes" (*ch'ün-hsiung ch'i-i*). Moreover, the majority of the heroes in these novels are men who excel either at martial arts or military strategy and commandership. Clearly, the popular conception of a hero, in Ming times, was a super-military man.

In addition to military interests, the heroes in historical novels share another common trait: most of them are men of humble origin. For example, in the novel *San-kuo*, the major heroes were all commoners before they involved themselves in a military struggle for control of the country: Liu Pei was a seller of straw sandals and grass mats in spite of his claim that he was a scion of the Imperial Han house; Chang Fei was a wine seller and a butcher; Kuan Yu was a fugitive; and Chu-ko Liang was a scholar-farmer. In the novel *Ts'an-T'ang*, the protagonists are also mostly men of humble origin: the major hero, Li Ts'un-hsiao, was a shepherd before being "discovered" by his lord, Li K'e-Yung; Wang Yen-chang was an illiterate soldier before he distinguished himself on the battlefield; Huang Ch'ao, the rebel, was the son of a salt merchant; and Li K'e-Yung was an "alien" soldier who was promoted to Prince Chin after he suppressed the rebellion of Huang Ch'ao. Here the most significant case is Huang Ch'ao, who is condemned by the Standard History as a chief villain, but is treated sympathetically in *Ts'an-T'ang*.[36] According to the novel, Huang Ch'ao is a gifted warrior who originally ranked first in the military service examination. But he was rejected by the T'ang court because the T'ang emperor Hsi-tsung (r. 874–888) did not like his looks. (He is said to have had a most strange and ugly face.) The novelist strongly deplores the fact that the talented warrior Huang Ch'ao was discarded because his face was ugly. Obviously the writer considers Emperor Hsi-tsung's injustice the cause of Huang Ch'ao's rebellion.

The historical novelists' admiration for military talents is furthered by the belief that the country needs military might. The writers seem to believe that periodic disorders in history are inevitable and that it is up to the heroes to bring back peace and order to the world. In other words, to them, heroes are the dynamic force in the historical world. The most significant characteristic of the heroes in historical novels is their superman quality. Almost all of them have the image of a superman who either has tremendous physical power and excels at martial arts or has an unusual endowment of wisdom and magic power and excels at military strategy and commandership. Those who are famous for their physical prowess are Kuan Yü, Chang Fei, Ch'in Ch'iung, Ch'eng Yao-chin, Shan Hsiung-hsin, Chao Yun, Li Ts'un-hsiao, Li K'uei, Wu Sung, Lu Chih-shen, and others. Those who are famous for their magic power and military strategy are Chiang Shang, Sun Pin, Chu-kuo Liang, Chiang Wei, Wu Yung, Hsu Shih-chi, and so forth.

Li Ts'un-hsiao, the leading hero of the novel *Ts'an-T'ang*, is an example of the superman. In the story, Li enters the stage in grand style. As a young shepherd, he single-handedly kills a ferocious tiger. Impressed by this display of sheer physical strength, Li K'e-yung, the founder of the Later T'ang dynasty (923–935) who happens to witness the whole breathtaking tiger-killing scene, enlists the young shepherd in his camp. From then on, Li Ts'un-hsiao, whose original name was An Ching-ssu but was changed to the present name by his new lord, dominates the story throughout. The outstanding characteristic of Li Ts'un-hsiao is his prowess, especially his physical strength. A typical treatment of Li's prowess is demonstrated in the section "Li Ts'un-hsiao li-sha ssu-chiang" (Li Ts'un-hsiao single-handedly kills four generals) in which the novelist makes it a point to emphasize Li Ts'un-hsiao's physical strength.[37] According to the novel, Li Ts'un-hsiao single-handedly kills four reputed generals of the adversary in one battle. He then plunges through the enemy's Long Snake Battle Formation (*Ch'ang-she Chen*), kills fifty or more warriors, and destroys the formation formed by over forty thousand hand-picked troops. Still not physically exhausted, he chases after the defeated enemies to their capital. All these battles happen continuously! In like fashion, he achieves numerous stupendous feats on the battlefield that represent the unique achievements of a "superman."

Significantly, the superman image of Li Ts'un-hsiao is only the novelist's creation. In the Official Histories of the period *Chiu Wu-tai-shih* (The Old History of the Five Dynasties, by Hsueh Chü-cheng) and *Wu-tai shih-chi* (The History of the Five Dynasties, by Ou-yang Hsiu), Li Ts'un-hsiao was only one of numerous warriors, and none of the stupendous feats described in the novel are reported.[38] Moreover, the tragic death of Li Ts'un-hsiao in the novel is completely different from the description in his official biographies. In the novel, Li Ts'un-hsiao is said to be loyal to his lord, Prince Chin, Li K'e-yung, to the end. He is executed by two jealous fellow warriors on a false pretense. But in the Official Histories, he is described as disloyal to Li K'e-yung at the end, and that he was executed by Li K'e-yung's direct order. Both Standard Histories, however, agree that Li Ts'un-hsiao's betrayal of Li K'e-yung was caused by Ts'un-hsiao's feeling of insecurity toward his lord because Li Ts'un-hsin, one of his fellow warriors, constantly slandered him before Li K'e-yung. Obviously the novelist made a hero out of Li Ts'un-hsiao by changing him from a traitor to a loyal and courageous hero who suffered injustice at the hands of evil men. Although it is possible that the novelist did not make up Li Ts'un-hsiao's stories all by himself (he could have adopted some of them from folk legends or storytellers' tales), the fact that he preferred fictional accounts to historical accounts testifies to his passion for the military superman.

Glorification of the military heroes is common among the writers of historical novels. As a matter of fact, the prominent position of the heroic tales in the field attests this passion for military heroes and miracles. They all give detailed descriptions of weapons, martial arts, military mazes, military strategies, and, above all, actual physical combat in the battlefield. The novelists' passion for military heroes is a sharp contrast to the disparagement of the military in the Confucian system of values. The proverb that "good iron is not used to make a nail nor a good man to make a soldier" well expresses this antimilitary sentiment. In the historical novels, however, this antimilitarism is notably absent. Accepting that periodic disorders in history are inevitable, the novelists regard as heroes those who used "armed forces" to bring peace and order back to the world. They believe that anyone with special military skills and physical strength can be a hero, but one hero alone cannot achieve the ultimate goal. He has to look for his kind and try to organize an armed force. The movement to organize an armed force is the beginning of a *righteous revolt*, which is, in many cases, also the beginning of a historical novel.

A systematic study of these righteous revolts described in the novels reveals certain significant patterns. The following four tables (tables 3–6) sum up the general outline of these patterns. In table 3, five novels are listed as examples, juxtaposed and compared to the major rival groups in each novel. The pattern of simultaneous revolts is self-evident. Numerous rebel groups were always competing with one another for the unification of the empire.

Since most so-called *righteous revolts* start with a small group of men, special bonds of union are formed among these rebels. Examples are the bonds of affection shared by sworn brothers and by adoptive father and adopted son. These special bonds and relationships are the most noticeable characteristics of the *righteous revolts* in the oral tradition of folk history. In table 4, some examples of this special bond are given. Moreover, the forming or shaping of these organized forces also follows a common pattern of development that reveals the basic

TABLE 3. Simultaneous Revolts

	Rival Power Groups	
	---	---
Novel	Leader	Dynasty
Hsi-Han	Hsiang Yü	Ch'u
	Liu Pang	Han
San-kuo	Ts'ao Ts'ao	Wei
	Liu Pei	Shu
	Sun Ch'üan	Wu
Sui-shih	Li Mi	Wei
	Wang Shih-ch'ung	Cheng
	Tou Chien-te	Hsia
	Li Yuan	T'ang
Nan-Sung	Chao K'uang-yin	Sung
	Li Yü	Southern T'ang
	Liu Ch'ung	Pei-Han
Ying-lieh chuan	Chang Shih-ch'eng	Chou
	Liu Fu-t'ung (with Han Lin-erh as figurehead)	Sung
	Hsü Shou-Hui (later was usurped by Ch'en Yu-liang)	Han
	Kuo Kuang-ch'ing Chu Yuan-chang	Ming

TABLE 4.   Special Relationship among Leading Heroes in Historical Novels

Novel	Special Relationship among Leading Heroes
Shui-hu	The 108 bandit-heroes swear allegiance to each other.
San-kuo	Liu Pei, Kuan Yü, and Chang Fei become sworn brothers.
Ts'an-T'ang	Li Ts'un-hsiao is adopted by Li K'e-yung as one of his many adopted sons.
Nan-Sung	Chao K'uang-yin has many sworn brothers, such as Ch'ai Jung and Cheng An.
Sui-shih	Ch'in Shu-pao has many sworn brothers, notably Ch'eng Yao-chin, Shan Hsiung-hsin, and Hsü Shih-chi.

nature of these righteous revolts. In the novels *Shui-hu* and *Sui-shih*, both the Liang-shan-po band and the Wa-kang-chai band are good examples. While Sung Chiang of the Liang-shan-po band does not aspire to build an empire (although the thought of his being an emperor does exist in some of his followers' minds),[39] Li Mi of the Wa-kang-chai band does proclaim himself king. In spite of this ostensible difference, these two bands share many things in common. Table 5 shows three stages of development that are shared by both the Liang-shan-po and the Wa-kang-chai bands. The three stages, "from among the rustics," "rapid expansion and reorganization," and "disbandment," represent the pattern of development among the rebel groups. During the first stage, leadership emerges and the nature of group relationship is defined. Although at this stage new members join the band, the pace is slow and gradual compared to the rapid expansion of the second stage. The second stage is generally a period when most bloodshed occurs. This is the time when rapid expansion occurs and reorganization takes place. The last stage, that of disbandment, does not represent the fate of all armed revolts; it only represents the fate of those who fail. As for those who succeed, they become the empire builders and dynastic founders, and the last stage becomes a series of military campaigns aimed at unifying the empire.

Table 6 shows two examples of successful revolts that tell the inner workings of power transference. The example of Chao K'uang-yin (in the novel *Nan-Sung*) follows the pattern of usurpation of the throne, which was the most frequent occurrence of power transference in imperial China. One the other hand, the example of Chu Yuan-chang (in the novel *Ying-lieh chuan*) demonstrates the natural process of

TABLE 5.   Pattern and Structure of Rebellious Groups

Group	*Shui-hu*		*Sui-shih*	
	Liang-shan-po Band		Wa-kung-chai Band	
First Stage: From among the Rustics				
1. Original members	1. Wang Lun Tu Chien Sung Wan	the leader 2d chair 3d chair	1. Ti Jang the leader	
2. Gradual expansion	2. Lin Ch'ung Chu Kuei	4th chair 5th chair	2. Shan Hsiung-hsin Hsü Shih-chi Wang Po-tung Li Mi	
Second Stage: Rapid Expansion and Reorganization				
1. New members join the band and reorganize it	1. Wang Lun killed by Lin Ch'ung when Ch'ao Kai and his group joined the band		1. Reorganization of the band Ti Jang Li Mi Shan Hsiung-hsin Ch'in Shu-pao Wang Po-tung Chia Yun-fu Ch'eng Yao-chin Hsu Shih-chi Lo Shih-hsin	1st chair 2d chair 3d 4th 5th 6th 7th 8th 9th
2. Bloodshed occurs, sometimes before reorganizing the band and sometimes after	2. Ch'ao Kai Wu Yung Kung-sun Sheng Lin Ch'ung Liu T'ang Yuan the Second Yuan the Fifth Yuan the Seventh Tu Ch'ien Sung Wan Chu Kuei	1st chair 2d 3d 4th 5th 6th 7th 8th 9th 10th 11th	2. Li Mi Proclaimed King, styled Wei	
3. New leadership emerges	3. Sung Chiang succeeded Ch'ao Kai when the latter was killed in one of the band's adventures. The number of the band reaches the peak of 108 members		3. Li Mi murdered Ti Jang	
Third Stage: Disbandment	Sung Chiang and his band surrender to the Sung court		Li Mi surrenders to Li Yuan	

TABLE 6.   Patterns of Attaining to Power

The Usurpation of the Throne (*Nan-Sung*)	Affiliation and Severance (*Ying-lieh chuan*)
Shih Ching-t'ang, the founder of the later Chin dynasty (936–49), usurped the throne of the later T'ang;	Kuo Kuang-ch'ing first joined the Red Turban Army of Liu Fu-t'ung, then severed the relation with the Red Turban Army and proclaimed himself King of Hsü-Yang.
Liu Chih-yuan, the founder of the later Han (947–50), usurped the throne of the later Chin;	
Kuo Wei, the founder of the later Chou (951–60), usurped the throne of the later Han;	Chu Yuan-chang first served under Kuo Kuang-ch'ing and married Kuo's adopted daughter. After Kuo died, Kuo's son was proclaimed King of Ho-yang, but at this time all power was already in the hands of Chu Yuan-chang. When the King of Ho-yang died, Chu Yuan-chang proclaimed himself King of the Wu.
Chao K'uang-yin, the founder of the Sung dynasty (960–1279), usurped the throne of the later Chou.	

affiliation and severance among the rebellious groups. However, these two examples only emphasize different circumstances in attaining power. The former emphasizes the vertical relationship in power transfer, the latter, the horizontal relationship. In most historical novels, the power struggles among rival groups involve both processes. For example, in the novel *San-kuo*, the usurpation of the throne occurs in the dynastic change between the Han and the Wei, while the process of affiliation and severance is most apparent in the formative stage of development among the rival groups, such as Liu Pei's first serving under Ts'ao Ts'ao, but later severing his relation with Ts'ao.

After discussing the four aspects of *righteous revolts* in historical novels, it becomes clear that the terms *righteous revolt* and *dynasty-building contest* describe different stages of the same historical drama. Although *righteous revolt* is a popular expression used mostly by story-tellers and historical novelists, the idea (the inspiration) itself may well be traced back to the Official History in the *Shih-chi*, in which Ch'en She's historical revolt is given a most vivid and detailed description.[40] The grand historian Ssu-ma Ch'ien announced to the world (through the mouth of Ch'en She, a commoner) that "Kings and nobles, generals and ministers—such men are made, not born,"[41] and the ambitious men in the long history of imperial China did just that—they made numerous emperors, nobles, generals, and ministers! In order to understand the historical precedent of the *righteous revolt*, a brief discussion of Ch'en She's revolt is necessary.

According to *Shih-chi*, the rebel Ch'en She was a man of humble origin. When he was young, he was working in the fields as a hired hand. One day he said to his fellow farmhands, "If I become rich and famous, I will not forget the rest of you!" The other farmhands laughed and answered, "You are nothing but a hired laborer. How could you ever become rich and famous?" Ch'en She then gave a great sigh and said: "Oh, well, how could you little sparrows be expected to understand the ambitions of a swan?"[42]

According to *Shih-chi*, during the first year of the Second Emperor of Ch'in (209 B.C.), in the seventh month, an order came for a force of nine hundred men to be sent to the garrison at Yü-yang (southwest of the modern Mi-yun District of Hopei). Ch'en She and Wu Kuang were among those whose turn it was to go and they were appointed heads of the levy of men. When the group had gone as far as Ta-tse County (southeast of modern Su-hsien of Anhui), they encountered such heavy rain that the road became impassable. It was apparent that the men would be unable to reach the appointed place on time, an offense punishable by death. Ch'en She and Wu Kuang accordingly began to plot together. They first planned to overawe the men in their group by enlisting supernatural aid in the following scheme. They wrote with cinnabar on a piece of silk: "Ch'en She shall be a King." Then they stuffed the silk into the belly of a fish someone had caught in a net. When one of the soldiers bought the fish and boiled it for his dinner, he discovered the message in the fish's belly and was greatly astonished. Also Ch'en She secretly sent Wu Kuang to a grove of trees surrounding a shrine that was close to the place where the men were making camp. When night fell, Wu Kuang lit a torch and, partly concealing it under a basket, began to wail like a fox and cry, "Great Ch'u shall rise again! Ch'en She shall be a king!" As a result, the soldiers were filled with alarm and overwhelmed by the idea that Ch'en She would be a king.

Meanwhile the two conspirators were waiting for the right moment to strike the first blow against the commanding officers. The movement came when the officer in command of the group became drunk. Wu Kuang made a point to openly announce several times that he was going to run away. In this way Wu Kuang hoped to arouse the commander's anger, get him to punish him, and so stir up the soldiers' ire and resentment (for Wu Kuang had always been kind to others and many of the soldiers would do anything for him). As Wu Kuang had expected, the commander began to beat him. In a dramatic act of self-defense, Wu Kuang killed the commander. Ch'en She rushed to Wu Kuang's assistance and they proceeded to kill the other two command-ing officers as well. Then they called together all the men of the group and announced:

> Because of the rain we encountered, we cannot reach our rendezvous on time. And anyone who misses a rendezvous has his head cut off! Even if you should somehow escape with your heads, six or seven out of every ten of you are bound to die in the course of garrison duty. Now, my brave fellows, if you are unwilling to die, we have nothing more to say. But if you would risk death, then let us risk it for the sake of fame and glory! Kings and nobles, generals and ministers — such men are made, not born![43]

With this inflammatory speech, they won the support of the group and together started the revolt against Ch'in.

Historically speaking, Ch'en She was a king for only six months. He was murdered by his carriage driver, Chuang Chia, who surrendered to Ch'in. Although Ch'en She died very early and did not see the downfall of the Ch'in, he has been remembered in history as the man who began the uprising that eventually succeeded in overthrowing the Ch'in.[44] However, in historical novels — for example, the *Hsi-Han* dealing with the overthrow of the Ch'in regime — the significance of Ch'en She's revolt has been ignored. There is only one sentence about Ch'en She; it simply says that Ch'en She and Wu Kuang "raised troops at Chi."[45] Since the central theme of *Hsi-Han* is the founding of the Han dynasty, it is understandable that the focus of attention is on the two leading rival power groups, the Ch'u and the Han. However, the historical precedent of Ch'en She's revolt must have had a tremen-dous impact on people's minds. The two basic tactics of Ch'en She's revolt — enlisting supernatural aid and skillfully maneuvering mass psychology by a scheming few — became familiar features in many later righteous revolts. Moreover the image of Ch'en She as a com-moner who "stepped from the ranks of the common soldiers, rose up from the paths of the field, and led a band of some hundred poor, weary soldiers in revolt against Ch'in,"[46] becomes the archetype of rebel-heroes in history, as evidenced by the humble origin of many rebel-heroes in historical times. In historical novels this image of the commoner as a rebel-hero is most noticeable because it captivates the imagination of both the writers and their readers.

To conclude our observation on the pattern of history, the dominant keynote is the motif of dynastic cycle that views the rise and fall of dynasties as part of historical inevitability. On the surface, patterns emerging from historical novels reflect the influence of traditional historiography. But at closer view, there are different emphases between the Official Histories and the historical novels. In the world of historical writings, in which the Confucian tradition of studying the past as a repository of relevant experience dominated, historians reflected long and hard on the causes of dynastic prosperity and failure.[47] In the world of historical novels, in which the weighty matters of the state were not the center of attention, novelists tended to simplify their subject matters and make them interesting and understandable to their readers. As a result, the merits and demerits of former ages do not concern them much. To the novelists, the drama of history lies in its periodic anarchy and disorder—the so-called righteous revolt of rustic heroes in the oral tradition of historical narration—which is regarded as a necessary process of rejuvenating or replacing a degenerating regime.

In both history and fiction, the rebellious heroes are mostly men of humble origins. Although in both cases the imperial institution is used as an automatic machine that instantly transforms heroes of humble origin into divine royalties and nobilities, there are, again, different emphases on their handlings of these heroes, especially the defeated ones. As mentioned before, the proverb "those who succeeded became emperors and those who failed became bandits" describes well the conventional pattern of handling dynastic contenders. Since those who succeeded were founding heroes of a new dynasty, they were the ones who subsequently ruled the country; consequently their places in history were secured. In Official Histories, which safeguard the established traditions for later generations, the achievements of the dynastic founders are always asserted. In order to glorify these winners, stereotyped divine myths were invented to cover up their humble origins, and their early lives and careers were generally ignored. As to the defeated dynastic contenders, with the exception of a few, they were either lightly brushed aside or treated as outlaws. While Official Histories cannot help being burdened with precedents and traditions, historical novels can escape such influence. Regarded as merely an item for entertainment, the historical novels were very much products of their authors' scruples and imaginations. Although historical novels, following the pattern established by Official Histories, glorify the founding emperors and their advisers and warriors, emphasis is more often on colorful and imaginative stories about the early lives and careers of these winning heroes. Some of these stories were created by the novelists and others were adopted from popular legends circulated among folk artists and storytellers. In a class-conscious society, people are forever fascinated by the idea that a man of humble origin could rise in the world. In historical novels this fascination with rugged heroes goes deeper than just applauding the winners; it also reflects the novelists' sympathy toward those who fail to fulfill their dreams. At times this sympathy toward defeated heroes extends to the extreme of contradicting established records.

In both history and fiction, the imperial institution is omnipresent. In both cases, the doctrine of the Mandate of Heaven and the theory of dynastic cycle worked hand in hand to justify dynastic changes and to give divine sanction to new regimes throughout the long history of imperial China. The ambition to build an empire and to found a dynasty was so deeply imprinted on the Chinese consciousness that it became a common dream for all "heroes" in time of war and disorder. In historical novels in which armed rebellions are glorified, it is natural for people to identify the dynastic ambitions of their heroes with their own hopes of better times. This might explain why the righteous revolts captured the fascination of the people and made the dynasty-founding theme the dominant keynote in historical novels.

Finally, we examine, through the motif of righteous revolt, the interplay of the elite and popular traditions in historical novels. As pointed out earlier, the historical novelists focused their attention on the disintegration of the dynasty, and the first signs of this disintegration were local upheavals that provided the opportunity to start a righteous revolt. Systematic analyses of the rebellious groups in the novels reveal the general patterns of these revolts, such as the plotting pattern, the organizing pattern, and the pattern of the inner working of power transference. Among these broad patterns, some of the basic tactics of a rebel group and some archetypes of the rebel-heroes and their special relationships, which emerge as the most noticeable characteristics of the righteous revolts, can be traced back to either the Official Histories or to the oral tradition of folk history, a manifestation of the gnarled roots and twisted knots of the elite and popular traditions.

Chapter 3

Man and History: Historical Figures and Legendary Heroes

A man has only one death. That death may be as
weighty as Mount T'ai, or it may be as light as a goose
feather. It all depends upon the way he uses it.... I
am shamed to think that after I am gone my writings
will not be known to posterity.... Before I had
finished my rough manuscript [of the *Shih-chi*, the
Historical Records], I met with this calamity. It is
because I regretted that it had not been completed
that I submitted to the extreme penalty without
rancor.... If it [the *Historical Records*] may be
handed down to men who will appreciate it, and
penetrate to the villages and great cities, then I should
suffer a thousand mutilations, what regret would I
have?

—*Ssu-ma Ch'ien's letter to his friend Jen An*

It is generally agreed that a culture's heroes form a system, and that
these heroes reveal the values and standards of that culture. In traditional China the nature of human ambition was characterized by the
so-called three immortalities (*san pu-hsiu*), which denoted three areas
in which man could achieve lasting fame. These were, in order of
importance: moral virtues, meritorious public service, and words. The
three immortalities, first referred to in the *Tso-chuan* under the entry
of the twenty-fourth year (549 B.C.) of Duke Hsiang of Lu (r. 572–542
B.C.),[1] define the general scope of recognized achievements in traditional times. A closer look at the headings of *Biographies* and *Men
of Distinction* in standard historical works reveals a more detailed
description of distinguishable deeds. Take both the Official History
Ming-shih and a local history, the *Ku-su chih* (The Gazette of Su-chou)
for examples.[2] Comparing the classifications of the Biographies of the
Official History with that of Men of Distinction of the local history, we
have the following common categories: *Ming-ch'en* (Famous Officials),
Chung-i (The Loyal and Righteous), *Hsiao-yu* (The Filial and

Brotherly), *Ju-lin* (Confucian Scholars), *Wen-hsueh* (Men of Letters), *Cho-hsing* (Men of Outstanding Behavior), *I-shu* (Artists), *Tsa-chi* (Men of Miscellaneous Techniques), *Yin-i* (Recluses), *Lieh-nü* (Virtuous Women), and *Shih Lao* (Buddhists and Taoists). Under each category, the achievements and/or notable deeds of these distinguished men and women are related, and they generally reflect the predominant criteria of real success in life. Since this coverage of Men of Distinction is typical of all local histories and Official Histories, general patterns dealing with model values and virtues are representative. In historical novels in which dynasty building is the dominant motif, the protagonists are the dynasty contenders, their advisers, and their warriors — who have priority over other types of Men of Distinction.

The general motivation for notable deeds and outstanding behavior is worth examining. Two driving forces can be seen behind all distinguishable deeds in traditional China. The first was the desire to achieve fame and immortality, as summed up by popular expressions such as *li-ming* (to make a name for oneself) or, more specifically, *ch'ing-shih liu-ming* (to earn a place in history). These popular terms are, in essence, a resonance of Confucius's saying, "The Superior Man hates the thought of his name not being mentioned after his death."[3] In this same spirit, Ssu-ma Ch'ien, the most revered literatus and historian in traditional China, completed his masterpiece, *Shih-chi*, after he suffered castration in 98 B.C. for his defense of General Li Ling (d. 74 B.C.), who surrendered to the Hsiung-nu after a disastrous defeat in 99 B.C. In a letter quoted below, Ssu-ma Ch'ien explained the driving force behind his writing to a friend:

> I am shamed to think that after I am gone my writings will not be known to posterity.... Before I had finished my rough manuscript [the *Shih-chi*], I met with this calamity. It is because I regretted that it had not been completed that I submitted to the extreme penalty without rancor.... If it [the *Shih-chi*] may be handed down to men who will appreciate it, and penetrate to the villages and great cities, then though I should suffer a thousand mutilations, what regret would I have?[4]

Ssu-ma Ch'ien suffered an extremely unjust penalty of mutilation when he spoke his mind to defend his friend Li Ling against Emperor Wu's wishes. His first instinct was to commit suicide to express his protest against unjust treatment from his lord, as most men of honor would do in his day. Then he thought of his unfinished work, the *Shih-chi*. It was far more important for him to finish his work than to take his life. He decided to continue to live, or to use his words, "to dwell in vileness and disgrace," in order to finish his writings, so that his work would not be unknown to posterity.

This idea of being known to posterity not only characterizes the ambition of Chinese intellectuals but also had a tremendous effect on the attitude of the common people in their pursuit of moral virtue under the influence of Confucian political and social ideology. There is plenty of evidence of this in both orthodox writings and popular literature. In historical writings, the various biographic sections of Men of Distinction are typical examples; in fiction and dramas, the numerous stories of righteous men and virtuous women are self-evident. The general model values will be discussed in the next chapter, "Ethical Values and Sociopolitical Order."

The second driving force among traditional Chinese intellectuals was devotion to governmental service. The inseparable relationship between "study" and "governmental service" is best described in the *Lun-yü* (Analects of Confucius) as follows: "The energy that a man has left over after doing his duty to the State, he should devote to study; the energy that he has left over after studying, he should devote to service of the State."[5] This belief in the importance of governmental service is the foundation of the philosophy of public service. This philosophy of public service, in which a man's greatest satisfaction is to serve his country in the best way he could and to achieve the kind of moral supremacy that would make him always be remembered in history, manifested the highest model values in traditional times.

There were many ways to enter the government. In ordinary times the most common ones were through the regular channels of the civil and military services. Through these services all ambitious men channeled their energies. In times of disorder, however, the story was completely different. In a turbulent period, ambitious men gave in to their hidden desires and rose to become rebel leaders, war-lords, emperor-aspirants, and empire-builders; they turned the whole country into a battlefield. Thus, in the long history of imperial China, the wax and wane of the dynasties went together with the cycles of order and disorder. Since historical novels usually highlight the vicissitudes of the dynasties, they are generally set in the turbulent period between two dynasties and their dominant theme is of dynasty building.

One might wonder: Who would want to build a new dynasty? And why? There are no special requirements for being a dynastic contender. Anyone could make such an attempt, provided that he had the ambition to be an emperor and was willing to risk execution. The classical observations on the nature of the ambition of these dynastic contenders can be found in Ssu-ma Ch'ien's *Shih-chi*, in which the ambitions of the two chief contenders for the first empire in history, Liu Pang (247– 195 B.C.) and Hsiang Yü (233–202 B.C.), were described vividly:

> Once the First Emperor of Ch'in came on a visit to K'uai-chi. When he was crossing the Che River, Hsiang Liang and Hsiang Yü went to watch the procession. "This fellow could be deposed and replaced!" Hsiang Yü remarked. Hsiang Liang clapped his hand over his nephew's mouth. "Don't speak such nonsense," he cautioned, "or we and all our family will be executed!" After this incident Hsiang Liang looked with wonder at his nephew.[6]

Hsiang Yü's spontaneous expression, "This fellow could be deposed and replaced," speaks of his ambition to replace the powerful First Emperor of Ch'in. In like manner, Liu Pang, who later became Emperor Kao-tsu of the Han, expressed a similar ambition:

> Kao-tsu was often sent on corvée labor to [the capital city of] Hsien-yang and happened to have an opportunity to see the First Emperor of Ch'in. When he saw him he sighed and said, "Ah, this is the way I should be."[7]

Like Hsiang Yü, Liu Pang was not intimidated by the awe-inspiring display of the First Emperor of Ch'in. Instead, he was inspired to cherish the ambition of becoming an emperor himself: "Ah, this is the way I should be."

Ssu-ma Ch'ien's profound insight into human character makes him the most admired historian in the history of China. His images of "self-made" emperor Liu Pang and Liu's rival, Hsiang Yü, have become archetypes of all dynastic contenders in historical times. In historical novels, almost all dynastic contenders share Liu Pang's and Hsiang Yü's ambition. Fascinated by the idea of being the Son of Heaven and encouraged by the historical precedent of a self-made emperor, the ambitious men in historical times trod on the heels of Liu Pang and Hsiang Yü in their perpetual struggles for power and fame. It is interesting to note that while there are numerous dynastic contenders in historical novels, few colorful and memorable characters emerge from this group. The reasons are twofold. Historically speaking, the dynastic game was played under the unwritten rule derived from the imperial institution itself. Those who succeeded became emperors and those who failed were merely labeled bandits. Dichotomized by this "emperor versus bandits" tradition, a general stereotyped pattern developed: the victor is glorified and the vanquished condemned. This stereotyped treatment of the winners and the defeated was further conditioned by the conventional belief in predestination (i.e., Heaven determines the final outcome of all historical struggles). Under such circumstances it is understandable that, with few exceptions, the defeated — those unsuccessful contenders who failed to receive support from Heaven — generally did not receive much attention. On the other hand, images of victors are also handicapped by their fixed imperial roles in history. Restricted by all the taboos and prerogatives surrounding the throne, novelists had little room for imagination. Besides, there was too much treachery and bloodshed surrounding the acquisition of the throne to make the victors truly lovable heroes.

Among all dynastic contenders in historical novels, the well-known victors are the founders of the four longest dynasties: Liu Pang, Kao-tsu of the Han; Li Shih-min, T'ai-tsung of the T'ang; Chao K'uang-yin, T'ai-tsu of the Sung; and Chu Yuan-chang, T'ai-tsu of the Ming. Although they all are central figures in novels dealing with the founding of their respective dynasties, they are not always the shining heroes in these novels. For example, in the novel dealing with the founding of the Han, *Hsi-Han*, the image of Chang Liang (d. 189 B.C.), Liu Pang's chief adviser, is far more colorful and memorable than that of the founding emperor himself. In novels dealing with the founding of the T'ang, the heroic image of the warrior Ch'in Shu-pao (fl. early seventh century) outshines that of Li Shih-min, the future emperor. As a matter of fact, the novel *Sui-shih*, which features Ch'in Shu-pao as the leading hero, is far superior to the *T'ang-shu*, another novel of the same theme that features Li Shih-min as the leading character.[8] In novels dealing with the foundings of the Sung and the Ming, *Nan-Sung* and *Ying-lieh chuan* respectively, the two founders, Chao K'uang-yin and Chu Yuan-chang, are central figures. The *Nan-Sung* tells how Chao K'uang-yin, in the latter half of the Five Dynasties (907–959), led by events of his day, rose to power and finally united the divided country. The *Ying-lieh chuan* tells how Chu Yuan-chang, in the scramble for power during the waning years of the Mongol Yuan (1280–1368) dynasty, sought and reached the highest office through conscious efforts to recruit men of talent for his cause. In both novels, the superior qualities of Chao K'uang-yin and Chu Yuan-chang over their rivals are exaggerated and their "acts of treason" against their own former overlords are easily justified. There is no doubt that the novelists regard both of them as heroes, for no other characters (from these two novels) emerge as greater heroes. But since both novels are mediocre works, the heroic images of Chao K'uang-yin and Chu Yuan-chang cannot rank among the best in popular fiction.

In contrast with the many "heroic" victors, only two of the numerous unsuccessful dynastic contenders are portrayed as heroes. They are Hsiang Yü and Liu Pei. As mentioned before, Hsiang Yü's image in history was largely shaped by Ssu-ma Ch'ien, who portrays him as a tragic hero with fatalistic, self-defeating shortcomings. Praising him for surpassing others in ability and spirit, Ssu-ma Ch'ien sums up Hsiang Yü's achievement as follows:

> When the rule of Ch'in was maladministered and Ch'en She started his revolt, local heroes and leaders arose like bees, struggling with each other for power in numbers too great to be counted. Hsiang Yü did not have so much as an inch of territory to begin with, but by taking advantage of the times he raised himself in the space of three years from a commoner in the fields to the position of commander of five armies of feudal lords. He overthrew the Ch'in, divided up the empire, and parceled it out in fiefs to the various kings and marquises; but all power of government proceeded from Hsiang Yü and he was hailed as a "Dictator King." Though he was not able to hold his position in the end [and died a peaceful death], yet from ancient times to the present there has never before been such a man![9]

Although Hsiang Yü overthrew the Ch'in and made himself the Dictator King of the Western Ch'u, his success proved temporary. The main cause for his failure, according to Ssu-ma Ch'ien, was his obstinacy:

> He was obstinate in his own opinions and did not abide by established ways. He thought to make himself a dictator, hoping to conquer and rule the empire by force. Yet within five years he was dead and his kingdom lost. He met death at Tung-ch'eng, but even at that time he did not wake to or accept responsibility for his errors. He was wrong.

"It is Heaven," he declared, "which has destroyed me, and no fault of mine in the use of arms!" Was he not indeed deluded![10]

Apparently Ssu-ma Ch'ien regards the fall of Hsiang Yü as the result of Hsiang Yü's own faults. He greatly deplores that Hsiang Yü "did not wake to or accept responsibility for his errors" even at the time of his death. On three occasions in the *Shih-chi*, Ssu-ma Ch'ien repeats Hsiang Yü's overwhelming delusion that either Heaven had destroyed him or the times were against him.[11] And Ssu-ma Ch'ien makes it very clear to his readers that he thinks quite the opposite. This emphatic denial of intervention from Heaven causing the downfall of Hsiang Yü is in contrast to Ssu-ma Ch'ien's reflections on the rise of Liu Pang, the victor, whom he regards as "the work of Heaven":

Surely this was the work of Heaven! Who but a great sage would be worthy to receive the Mandate of Heaven and become emperor?[12]

Compared with the formality of the complimentary address Ssu-ma Ch'ien gave to Liu Pang, his criticism of Hsiang Yü is genuine and heartfelt. This criticism, together with his vivid description of Hsiang Yü's heroic death, shows the historian's strong sentiment toward a defeated hero. Through the influence of this strong sentiment, Hsiang Yü's image in history was shaped.

The novel *Hsi-Han*, which tells fictional accounts of the Ch'u-Han dynastic war, generally follows the major historical events outlined in the *Shih-chi*. While the historian's sentiment toward Hsiang-Yü is subtle, the novelist is emphatically sympathetic. The stories about how Hsiang Yü bade farewell to his beautiful Lady Yü and his famous horse Dapple are good examples. Although the *Shih-chi* provides basic materials for both stories, it mentions neither Lady Yü's suicide nor Dapple's jumping into the river to drown. Both accounts were an essential part of the Hsiang Yü legend in popular fictions and dramas. In the novel *Hsi-Han*, as well as in the *Shih-chi*, the famous farewell scene is told like this: When the last moment came, Hsiang Yü, who was encircled by Liu Pang's army, bade farewell to the beautiful Lady Yü, who enjoyed his favor and followed wherever he went. He composed his immortal poem, which he sang to her in passionate sorrow:

My strength plucked up the hill,
My might shadowed the world,

> But the times were against me,
> And Dapple runs no more,
> When Dapple runs no more,
> What then can I do?
> Ah, Yü, my Yü
> What will your fate be?[13]

In the novel, Lady Yü killed herself afterward to show Hsiang Yü both her devotion to him and her determination not to serve two masters, but in the *Shih-chi*, Ssu-ma Ch'ien does not tell his readers what happened to her. According to Ssu-ma Ch'ien, after Hsiang Yü composed his song:

> He sang the song several times through, and Lady Yü joined her voice with his. Tears streamed down his face, while all those about him wept and were unable to lift their eyes from the ground. Then he mounted his horse and, with some eight hundred brave horsemen under his banner, rode into the night, burst through the encirclement to the south, and galloped away.[14]

Again, in the story about Hsiang Yü's horse, the novel differs from the *Shih-chi* only in details. In the novel, as well as in the *Shih-chi*, when Hsiang Yü reached Tung-ch'eng he had only twenty-eight horsemen with him, while Liu Pang's cavalry pursuing him numbered several thousand. Still fighting bravely, Hsiang Yü and his horsemen broke through the enemy's encirclements many times, cut down their leaders, and severed their banners. Finally, they reached Wu-chiang. The village head of Wu-chiang, who was waiting with a boat on the bank of the river, urged Hsiang Yü to make haste and cross over. He told Hsiang Yü he was the only one who had a boat, so that when Liu Pang's men arrived they would have no way to get across. Hsiang Yü refused to board the boat; his reason was as follows:

> Once, with eight thousand sons from the land east of the river, I crossed over and marched west, but today not a single man of them returns. Although their fathers and brothers east of the river should take pity on me and make me their king, how could I bear to face them again? Though they said nothing of it, could I help but feel shame in my heart?[15]

He then gave the village head his horse since he could not bear to kill him. While the *Shih-chi* does not say anything more about the fate of the horse, the novel adds that the horse too, like Lady Yü, refused to be separated from his master and jumped into the river and was drowned.[16] Then the novel follows the *Shih-chi* closely in describing Hsiang Yü's death scene. It tells how Hsiang Yü, with his back to the river, ordered all his men to dismount and proceed on foot, and with their short swords to engage in hand-to-hand combat with the enemy. According to this account Hsiang Yü alone killed several hundred of the Han men until, having suffered a dozen wounds, he decided to kill himself. And even when Hsiang Yü decided to kill himself, he did it in his own grand style. The following is *Shih-chi*'s description of Hsiang Yü's suicide scene, copied in the novel:

> Looking about him, he spied the Han cavalry marshal Lü Ma-t'ung. "Are you not my old friend?" he asked. Lü Ma-t'ung turned about and instructing Wang I, said, "That's King Hsiang!" "I have heard that Han has offered a reward of a thousand catties of gold and a fief of ten thousand households for my head," said Hsiang Yü. "I will do you the favor!" And with this he cut his own throat and died.[17]

Ssu-ma Ch'ien's unforgettable portrayal of Hsiang Yü must have left a tremendous impact on people's minds. Ever since he wrote the *Shih-chi*, the historical image of Hsiang Yü has been shaped by his portrayal, and this heroic image was copied again and again in popular fiction and drama. No new major stories were developed about Hsiang Yü in either traditional fiction or drama. No imaginative writers seem able to create a more memorable Hsiang Yü than the one described by the historian Ssu-ma Ch'ien.

In addition to Hsiang Yü, the other well-known unsuccessful dynastic contender is Liu Pei. As one of the protagonists of the famous novel *San-kuo*, Liu Pei's image in people's minds is largely shaped by the novel. As pointed out in our discussion of dynastic legitimacy, Liu Pei's image in the *San-kuo* is that of a sage-king or benevolent ruler whose ostensible ambition was to overthrow the illegitimate reign of Ts'ao Ts'ao and to restore the legitimate Han imperial house. However, the novel also makes it clear that Liu Pei is not a naive performer of good deeds. On the contrary, he is described as a man with a sagacious mind and a master of maneuvering who always knows the right thing to say at the right moment. We will give two examples to elaborate on this point.

In the famous episode "Ts'ao Ts'ao Discusses Heroes" in the *San-kuo*,[18] the story tells that while Liu Pei held a post at the Han Court and was honored as uncle of the emperor, Ts'ao Ts'ao, then the prime minister, tried to find out if Liu Pei was a man of dynastic ambition. One day Ts'ao Ts'ao invited Liu Pei to his house to have wine with him. After a goblet of wine, they sat down to a confidential talk. Discussing all the possible heroes of the day, Ts'ao Ts'ao pointed his finger at his guest and then at himself saying, "The only heroes in this world are you and I." Having heard this, Liu Pei gasped and the spoon and chopsticks rattled to the floor, for he thought Ts'ao Ts'ao had some suspicions toward him. Just at that moment the storm burst with a tremendous peal of thunder and rush of rain. Liu Pei stooped down to recover the fallen articles, saying, "What a shock! And it was quite close." "What, are you afraid of thunder?" said Ts'ao Ts'ao. Thus pretending that he was startled by the thunder — a sign of cowardice — Liu Pei convinced Ts'ao Ts'ao of his inability to cherish such lofty designs as building an empire for himself.

Another example is the episode in which the brave Chao Yun (d. 229) rescues Liu Pei's son. After Chao Yun risked his life to save the child, he presented the child to his father, Liu Pei. The following scene from the *San-kuo* describing Liu Pei's reaction is truly revealing:

> "Happily, Sir, your son is unhurt," said Chao as he drew him [the child] forth and presented him in both hands.

> Yuan-te [Liu Pei] took the child but threw it aside angrily, saying, "To preserve that suckling I very nearly lost a great general."

> Chao Yun picked up the child again and, weeping, said, "Were I ground to powder I could not prove my gratitude."[19]

Such was the way Liu Pei won over his men's hearts. He acted as if he valued his general's life more than the life of his son. This unusual ability to say the right thing at the right moment made him an astute leader.

But Liu Pei's image as a benevolent ruler was mostly built up by his ability to attract the able and the learned. It is interesting to point out that unlike Hsiang Yü, whose image was largely shaped by Ssu-ma Ch'ien's *Shih-chi*, Liu Pei's image in the *San-kuo* was mostly formed by the professional oral tradition discussed before. As the *San-kuo* legends grew and grew, Liu Pei's status in history also grew, and stories about his relations with his advisers and warriors became the paradigms for others to follow. The fact that the common people accepted Liu Pei and his advisers and warriors as their heroes suggests that they identified with the values of the *San-kuo*. As pointed out earlier in discussing the dynastic legitimacy, in the *San-kuo* Liu Pei is regarded as the legitimate successor of the Han. And this attitude is different from the Official History, *San-kuo chih*, upon which the novel was based; according to the *San-kuo chih*, Ts'ao Ts'ao was the legitimate successor of the Han, not Liu Pei.

As always happened in history, when people assumed a defiant attitude toward an establishment, they sought help from an older tradition. In order to establish Liu Pei's legitimacy, they molded him after the image of the ancient sage-king, and the first criterion of the sage-king is his ability and willingness to recruit the able and the virtuous. It becomes clear that there was a two-way search underlining a dynasty-building drama: the search for the able and the learned on the part of the emperor-aspirant and the search for a worthy lord on the part of the majority of ambitious men who aspired to help a benevolent sage-king to build a new dynasty.

Historically speaking, the concept of searching for the able and the virtuous stems from the ancient belief that government should be ruled by men of worth. In the *Shu-ching* (Book of History) the legends of abdication of the ancient sage-kings Yao and Shun are mentioned. We are told that both Yao and Shun did make men of worth their successors. In the *Lun-yü*, the account of how Yao commanded Shun to be the king and how Shun commanded Yü to be the king is reminiscent of the *Shu-ching*.[20] By the time of the Warring States (403−221 B.C.), the concept of honoring the able and the virtuous had been gradually developed into various theories among scholars of different schools of thought. In some of their philosophical discourses, for example, the *Meng-tzu*, the *Mo-tzu*, and the *Han Fei-tzu*, the accounts of King Yao's and King Shun's abdication were given a detailed and vigorous discussion.[21] The sagehood of Yao and Shun is shown in the clear choice they made between hereditary legitimacy and individual merit. We are told that both Yao and Shun made men of merit their successors instead of their own sons. Even in the anarchical *Chuang-tzu*, which rejects politics and debunks all the ancient heroes, the legend that King Yao ceded the empire to Shun, not his son, is mentioned on several occasions. Only in *Chuang-tzu* is King Yao sarcastically referred to as an "unkind" father because he did not make his own son his successor.[22] Clearly, the ideal of honoring the able and the virtuous has been a prominent theme shared by the major schools of thought in China since ancient times. In the next chapter, when we discuss the ethical values and sociopolitical order reflected in Ming historical novels, we will present these legends through the eyes of historical novelists and will examine their explanations about how kingship became hereditary in the Hsia dynasty.

As kingship became hereditary, the application of this principle of honoring men of merit was transferred to the selection of ministers. Thus "thirst for men of merit" (*ch'iu-hsien jo-k'o*) became one of the yardsticks for a sage-king. In historical novels this idea is popularized in the famous episode "The Three Visits to the Recluse" from the novel *San-kuo*, which tells how Liu Pei, an emperor-aspirant, humbled himself three times before the scholar-recluse Chu-ko Liang (181–243) to ask the latter to leave his retreat and to help him restore the crumbling Han empire. The importance of this episode lies in the fact that as one of the early novels in the field, the *San-kuo* is the first to define the relationship between the emperor-aspirant and his adviser. The key words here are *three visits*, which represent sincerity on the part of Liu Pei. Although the historical *three visits* episode mentioned in Chu-ko Liang's own memorial is not a fictional invention, the genius of the novelist lies in his supplying the fascinating details of the visits to dramatize the historical events. Further, he created an ideal relationship that has kindled the interest and imagination of his readers for generations.

To its credit, the novel creates a flesh and blood Liu Pei, a man of great compassion. Following is the parting scene between Liu Pei and his first adviser Hsu Shu, which reveals much about Liu Pei, the man:

> Yuan-te [Liu Pei] could not bring himself to part from Hsu Shu. He escorted him a little further, and yet a little further, till Shu said, "I will not trouble you, O Princely one, to come further. Let us say our farewell here." Yuan-te dismounted, took Hsu Shu by the hands. . . .
> But the last goodbyes were said and when the traveller had gone, Yuan-te stood gazing after the little party and watched it slowly disappear. At the last glimpse he broke into lamentation: "He is gone. What shall I do?" One of the trees shut out the travellers from his sight and he testily pointed at it, saying, "Would that I could cut down every tree in the countryside." "Why?" said the men. "Because they hinder my sight of Hsu Yuan-chih."[23]

Such was the profound affection Liu Pei held for Hsu Shu, his friend and adviser. Naturally when Hsu Shu recommended the scholar-recluse Chu-ko Liang to Liu Pei, saying, "if you win him, it will be like the Chou dynasty winning Lü Wang, or the Han gaining Chang Liang,"[24] Liu Pei was impressed and wanted to meet this extraordinary man.

Having used Hsu Shu's wholehearted recommendation vouching for Chu-ko Liang's abilities, the novelist then sets up a series of intriguing tests for Liu Pei, testing whether or not he has the makings of a worthy lord. As the story is unraveled, Liu Pei passes all the tests with flying colors. He is so humble, so patient, so eager, so sincere in seeking advice from others. At the same time he was ever so firm in his belief that he is a Liu, scion of the Han, bound to right the ruling house and bring order back to the world.

Despite Liu Pei's determination to have a heart-to-heart talk with Chu-ko Liang, the scholar-recluse is very reluctant to meet with the emperor-aspirant. The following dialogues describe Chu-ko Liang's first reaction when their mutual friend Hsu Shu tells him that he has been recommended to Liu Pei:

> Asked why he [Hsu Shu] had come, he replied: "I wished to serve Liu Pei of Yü-chou but my mother has been imprisoned by Ts'ao Ts'ao, and he has sent to call me. Therefore, I have to leave Liu Pei. At the moment of parting I recommended you to him. He is coming to you at once to offer his respect. I hope you will not shunt him aside but will consent to use your great talents to help him. What a blessing that would be." K'ung-ming [Chu-ko Liang] froze. "And you mean to make me the victim of your sacrificial feast?" Saying no more, he flicked his sleeves and left the room.[25]

Chu-ko Liang was annoyed with Hsu Shu because he thought Hsu was his friend and should respect his wish to lead a secluded life. Besides, there was a common belief among the recluses that it was impossible to bring disorder to an end once the cycle started. The novelist employs Ts'ui Chou-p'ing, another of Chu-ko Liang's good friends and a recluse, to explain this view to Liu Pei. Ts'ui met Liu Pei on Liu's way home from his first unsuccessful visit to Chu-ko Liang:

> Chou-p'ing smiled: "My lord, you are bent on bringing disorder to an end. But from ancient times, periods of civic order and disorder have alternated.... Again the shield and the spear are all around us.

It is a moment of transition back to disorder, and things cannot be abruptly brought to a conclusion. And if you would have Kung-ming redirect the Heavens and the Earth to compensate for destiny, I am afraid it will not be easy — a futile expense of mind and body. I'm sure you know that 'Who adapts to Heaven shall know content; who contravenes Heaven shall toil in vain,' and that 'None can deduct from the Reckoning; none can force what is fated.'"[26]

That the task of the unification of China under Liu Pei is compared to "redirect the Heavens and the Earth to compensate for destiny" represents the novelist's point of view. In fact, the religious theme of predetermination (which will be discussed in detail later) is one of the central themes of the *San-kuo*: it was the predestinate will of Heaven that Liu Pei and his group should fail. According to the novel, Chu-ko Liang, the smartest among the recluses, must also have shared Ts'ui's view that the unification of China under Liu Pei was an impossible dream. But the historical meeting between Liu Pei and Chu-ko Liang, which finally took place on Liu's third visit, changed everything. After a long talk with Liu, Chu-ko Liang was profoundly impressed and deeply moved by Liu's sincerity, and he consented to try unification for a *chih-chi* (one who knows me, or who shares the dream with me). This sense of *chih-chi* laid a foundation of enduring trust between Liu and Chu-ko Liang, and this trust defines the special relationship between the two men in the novel. All his life, according to the novel, Liu Pei respected his adviser and treated him as his mentor. Chu-ko Liang, on the other hand, was loyal to his lord all his life and never forgot the three visits — the symbol of sincerity and humility on the part of the lord — that started his life career as an imperial adviser. Note here the use of "three," which was a mystical numeral in the traditional Chinese mind. Three symbolizes "myriad," an immense number.[27] Whenever one's sincerity (one's heart) is in question, three is the number to observe. In all ceremonial rites, for example, one is required to make obeisance three times.

The Three Visits story in the novel *San-kuo* reinforced the traditional belief that a sage-king would try his best to seek the able and virtuous to serve the country. Many later historical novels repeated this theme. One example is the I Yin story in the novel *Yu-Hsia chih-chuan* (*Yu-Hsia* hereafter), which tells how the Prince of Shang (later King T'ang of the Shang dynasty, r. ca. 1600 – ca. 1588 B.C.) three times sent special messengers to enlist the able I Yin as minister.[28] Another example is the *Ying-lieh chuan*, a novel about the founding of the Ming dynasty, which actually attributes Chu Yuan-chang's success to his policy of *chao-hsien na-shih* (to recruit the able and the virtuous and to receive the learned).[29] Throughout the novel, the author stresses that it was Chu Yuan-chang who took the initiative in enlisting the able and the learned during his dynasty-building campaigns. According to the novel, when Chu Yuan-chang was engaged in military campaigns to unify the country, he never failed to look for talent in others. Wherever he went, he always asked for the able and the learned in the area and sent for them. In order to emphasize Chu's effort, the novel sometimes twists historical accounts to suit this purpose. Consider the Official History *Ming-shih* as an example. In the biography of Hsu Ta (1329−83), it was Hsu who took the initiative in joining Chu's force. According to the biography, Hsu himself went to see Chu and joined his force when Chu was still serving in Kuo Tzu-hsing's army.[30] In the novel, the story is completely different. Here we are told that Chu humbled himself before Hsu (by visiting Hsu in person) to seek his service.[31] Again, in stories about how Chu Yuan-chang recruited Li Shan-ch'ang (1314−90), Feng Sheng (fl. mid−fourteenth century), and T'ao An (1315−71), the novel tells that it was Chu who heard about these men and sent for them,[32] while according to biographical accounts in the *Ming-shih*, the initiatives came from these men: Li Shan-ch'ang presented himself to Chu when Chu occupied Hsu-yang (modern Ho-fei, Anhwei); T'ao An presented himself to Chu when Chu took T'ai-ping (modern Tang-t'u, Anhwei); Feng Sheng and his older brother, Feng Kuo-yung, presented themselves before Chu when Chu took Miao-shan.[33]

The fictional elaboration of Chu Yuan-chang's search for the able and the talented reveals the popularity of the stereotyped image of sage-kings. However, the readiness of people's belief in sage-kings cannot conceal the historical reality that there were plenty of men of talent but very few sage-kings. In historical novels, the scarcity of sage-kings is in contrast to the numerousness of men of talent whose yearning for worthy lords became the source of inspiration for many imaginative writers. Moreover, since there were few worthy lords, emphasis was placed on the unfortunate fate of those men of talent who served unworthy lords. This sympathy for those who served an unworthy lord captured the tragic sense of the imaginative mind.

Following are two examples that illustrate how people felt about choosing an unworthy lord.

First, we will examine the story about the above-mentioned Hsu Shu and his mother in the novel *San-kuo*. Hsu Shu was serving as Liu Pei's adviser when he received a forged letter in the handwriting of his mother, who was a captive of Ts'ao Ts'ao. In the letter, Hsu Shu was asked to go to the capital where his mother was in prison and to submit himself to Ts'ao Ts'ao. Hsu Shu was fooled by the letter and he, being an obedient son, hastened to the capital to submit to Ts'ao Ts'ao in order to release his mother from imprisonment. After presenting himself to Ts'ao Ts'ao, he asked to see his mother. The following passage describes the reunion of mother and son:

> Hsu Shu then took his leave and hastened to his mother's dwelling. Weeping with emotion he made his obeisance to her at the door of her room.

> But she was greatly surprised to see him and said, "What have you come here for?" "I was at Hsin-Yeh, in the service of Liu of Yü-chou when I received your letter. I came immediately." His mother suddenly grew very angry. Striking the table she cried, "You shameful and degenerate son! For years you have drifted about the country. I thought you had made some progress in your study, but you are worse than you were before. You are a student and know the books. You must then know that loyalty and filial piety are often opposed. Did you not recognize in Ts'ao Ts'ao a traitor, a man who flouts his king and insults his superiors? Liu Pei is virtuous and upright as all the world knows. Moreover, he is of the royal House of Han and when you were with him you were serving a fitting master. Now on the strength of a scrap of forged writing, with no attempt at any inquiry, you have left the light and plunged into darkness and earned a disgraceful reputation. Truly you are stupid! How can I bear to look on you? You have besmirched the fair name of your forefathers and are of no use in the world."

> The son remained bowed to the earth, not daring to lift his eyes while his mother delivered this vilifying tirade. Then she rose and left the room. In a little while, one of the servants came out to say: "The old Madame has hanged herself." Hsu Shu rushed in to try to save her, but was too late.[34]

Mother Hsu decided to hang herself because she dreaded to think of what would happen to her son who, in her words, "left the light and plunged into darkness and earned a disgraceful reputation." To her, Liu Pei was a fitting master, and Ts'ao Ts'ao a traitor. To leave a fitting master to join a traitor's camp was unbearable for her, and it disgraced the family. Thus she killed herself to impress on her son his wrongdoing. All his life, Hsu Shu never forgot his mother's last words and never formed any plan for Ts'ao Ts'ao, even though he was listed as Ts'ao Ts'ao's adviser. (He had already pledged his support to Ts'ao Ts'ao before his mother killed herself.)[35]

While Hsu Shu was a victim of circumstance, there were men who by choice committed to an unworthy lord. The story of T'ien Feng in the same novel (*San-kuo*) is an example. T'ien Feng was Yuan Shao's adviser who was thrown into prison in the later part of his career because his advice displeased Yuan Shao. Finally, after his defeat by Ts'ao Ts'ao at Kuan-tu (in modern Chung-mu Hsien, Honan), Yuan Shao realized his mistake of not heeding T'ien Feng's advice. But even when he was in a remorseful mood, he still could not help listening to slander:

> The next day, Yuan Shao mounted his horse for the return journey. As he was about to start, he was met by another adviser, Feng Chi, and his reinforcements. Shao said to Feng Chi, "I suffered this defeat because I didn't listen to T'ien Feng. I am now going back, but I am ashamed to face him." Feng Chi therefore took the opportunity to slander T'ien Feng. "While in prison Feng heard of my lord's defeat and he clapped his hands and laughed, 'Precisely as I have predicted.'" Yuan Shao was highly incensed. "How dare a mere scholar make fun of me? I must kill him." He then gave a messenger his personal sword and ordered him to leave for Chi-chou immediately and kill T'ien Feng in prison.[36]

T'ien Feng was not surprised at the fatal order; he was expecting it when he heard of Yuan Shao's defeat. He only blamed himself for having not been able to choose a worthy lord. His last words were most revealing:

> Stupid indeed is he who, born into this world with all his talent and ambition, has chosen to serve an unworthy lord. Today I die, but I deserve no pity.[37]

He then killed himself in prison.

There were numerous men like T'ien Feng in imperial China —

men who had talent and ambition but who either by fate or by circumstance had chosen to serve an unworthy lord. Their misfortune was an
ironic testimony of history to a value system in which government
service took precedence over all other career possibilities. Since the
system endorsed the concept of "I am the State," there was little
distinction between personal service to one's lord and public service to
one's country. Moreover, there was no legal protection of the subject
against the tyranny of his lord. As a result, one who served an unworthy
lord was doomed to ill fortune no matter how hard he tried to serve his
country.

While there were numerous unfortunate men who served unworthy
lords and ended their lives in failure, there were a memorable few who
were trusted by their lords and succeeded, at least in part, in carrying
out the great undertaking of building a new dynasty. Among them the
most celebrated were I Yin (eighteenth century B.C., a semimythical
figure) of the Shang, who assisted and guided his lord, T'ang, in
overthrowing the tyrant King Chieh of the Hsia; Lü Shang (or Chiang
Shang in popular fiction from his original surname Chiang, fl. late
eleventh and early twelfth centuries B.C.) of the Chou, who assisted and
guided his lord, King Wu, in defeating the tyrant King Chou of the
Shang; Chang Liang (d. 189 B.C.) of the Han, who assisted Liu Pang in
defeating Hsiang Yü and in founding the Han dynasty; Chu-ko Liang
(181−243) of the Three Kingdoms period, who assisted and guided his
lord, Liu Pei, in founding the Shu kingdom during the chaos of the
collapse of the Han empire; and Liu Chi (1311−75) of the Ming, who
guided his lord, Chu Yuan-chang, in founding the Ming dynasty. These
men were the most celebrated imperial advisers in Chinese history.
Although each of them had his own career and unique position in
history, as imperial advisers they shared a few things in common. They
were all idealized and exaggerated in their role as adviser, as shown by
their superhuman images exalted both in the moralistic historical writings
and in widespread popular legends and literature. This superhuman
image has two sides, the orthodox and the popular. Although both the
orthodox and popular images are products of the cumulative process of
various historical models and traditional stereotypes, the former stresses
the merits of an ideal imperial adviser in traditional thought, and the
latter emphasizes the vulgarization of the two distinct qualities of an
imperial adviser's career — astuteness in political wrangling and genius

in military maneuvering. Before we discuss the themes that deal with imperial advisers in historical novels, we will first examine briefly the orthodox image of these imperial advisers.

According to the high ideals of the Confucian ideology, imperial advisers were all learned men who cherished the noble aspiration of ordering the state and caring for the welfare of the people. They were content with a simple and obscure life when opportunities to serve the state were not available to them. When the "true sage-kings" humbled themselves to request their services, however, the advisers all abandoned their seclusion and served their lords with loyalty and dedication. Such was the case with I Yin, Chiang Shang, Chu-ko Liang, and Liu Chi. All accepted their lords' calling and came out of seclusion. Together with Chang Liang of the Han, these five advisers embody all the traditional virtues of a public servant. I Yin exemplified the virtue of political courage. After his lord King T'ang's death, I Yin served T'ai-chia, the heir apparent. When T'ai-chia proved incapable of ruling the kingdom, I Yin deposed him to take personal command, but restored his lord's authority after T'ai-chia had rescinded his past misdeeds.[38] Chiang Shang exemplified the virtue of perseverance. He had waited until he was eighty years old to serve a sage-king, but he did assist and guide his lord in the founding of a new dynasty, the Chou.[39] Chang Liang exemplified the virtue of retiring after meritorious service. After carrying out the great undertaking of building the Han dynasty, he decided to give up his titles and position and went into retirement. In doing this he exalted the image of a statesman who had no personal interest in gaining power and influence once his noble dream had been fulfilled.[40] Chu-ko Liang exemplified the virtue of ardent dedication, which is best described by his now famous words: *"Chü-kung chin-ts'ui, ssu erh hou i."* (Bowed down I exhaust my energy in the public service; only with death does my course end.) His unforgettable "Memorial on the Expedition [to the North]" (*Ch'u-shih piao*), which is by itself a literary classic, bears testimony to his unswerving loyalty and ardent dedication.[41] Finally, Liu Chi exemplified the tragedy of an outspoken statesman serving under a despotic emperor. As a man of integrity, he often spoke to his lord without reserve. His candor was well received and appreciated by his lord during the course of building the empire, but it became a source of trouble after his lord became emperor. Furthermore, his critical remarks about his colleagues made him many enemies in court, who slandered him whenever possible. Even after his retirement, he was still a target of their attacks and was eventually poisoned to death by one of them.[42]

These historical models became the archetypes for the imperial advisers in historical novels. Five historical novels tell fictional stories about these five model advisers: I Yin in the *Yu-Hsia*, Chiang Shang in the *Feng-shen*, Chang Liang in the *Hsi-Han*, Chu-ko Liang in the *San-kuo*, and Liu Chi in the *Ying-lieh chuan*. In all of these novels the importance of these advisers is greatly enhanced. They are portrayed as men with extraordinary abilities and credited with the founding of a new dynasty. They conceived strategic ideas and mapped out detailed military plans while their lords appeared to have constantly depended on their advice. Consider Chang Liang as an example. In the novel *Hsi-Han*, Chang Liang's decisive role in helping Liu Pang to win the Ch'u-Han War is enhanced. The novel follows closely the Standard Histories *Shih-chi* and *Han-shu* in describing Chang Liang's career. It tells how, on a number of occasions when his lord, Liu Pang, found himself in grave difficulties, Chang Liang always figured a way out for him. The novel adds, however, two meritorious services to Chang Liang's record. Thus, according to the novel, it was Chang Liang who first persuaded Han Hsin (d. 196 B.C.) that Liu Pang was the "true king."[43] The importance of Han Hsin to Liu Pang cannot be exaggerated because according to both the *Han-shu* and the *Shih-chi*, Liu Pang himself once said of Han Hsin, "In leading an army of a million men, achieving success with every battle and victory with every attack, I cannot come up to Han Hsin."[44] But there is no single reference in either the *Shih-chi* or the *Han-shu* to suggest Chang Liang's role in persuading Han Hsin to change sides. Apparently this is one of the "imaginary details" that were so often added by the novelist "to supplement omission to history." Secondly, according to the novel, it was Chang Liang who devised psychological warfare to break down the morale of Hsiang Yü's army by teaching the Han soldiers (who surrounded Hsiang Yü's army) to sing the songs of the Ch'u (the native land of Hsiang Yü and his soldiers) in the night. Having been misled by the songs of the Ch'u and thinking that the Han had already conquered the Ch'u, according to the novel, the majority of Hsiang Yü's generals and soldiers fled before the enemy.[45] Both the *Shih-chi* and the *Han-shu* make no mention of Chang Liang's role in this psychological warfare and merely record without explanation the fact that "in the night Hsiang Yü heard the Han armies all about him singing the songs of the Ch'u."[46] The novelist's intention is obvious: he wants his readers to believe that Chang Liang was responsible for every important strategy that won victory for the Han over the Ch'u.

However, we should note that the *Hsi-Han*, as a historical novel, closely follows the Official Histories *Shih-chi* and *Han-shu*. Although the importance of Chang Liang's role as adviser is enhanced in the novel, his official image remains generally intact. Even Chang Liang's connection with the Taoists is not an exaggeration in the novel. Following the *Shih-chi* closely, the novel *Hsi-Han* tells the story of how Chang Liang received a book on statecraft and military tactics from a mysterious old man named Huang-shih-kung (Master Yellow Stone, a legendary Taoist immortal) after the latter had tested Chang's patience and perseverance three times.[47] Here the emphasis is on Chang's patience and perseverance. Next let us consider the story about Chang Liang's decision "to join Ch'ih-sung-tzu (Master of the Red Pine, a legendary Taoist hermit) in immortal sport."[48] Although some imagined details are added (for example, the novelist invents an interesting philosophical conversation between Chang Liang and his son to show that Chang's retirement was initiated by his cautiousness), these details only represent the novelist's theory of political retirement. Throughout the entire novel, Chang Liang's success is attributed to his political sagacity and tactical ingenuity. None of the unusual qualities of a popular Taoist type of adviser, such as Taoist magic and occult power, are ascribed to Chang Liang in the *Hsi-Han*.

While the orthodox images of Chang Liang and I Yin remain intact in both the novels *Hsi-Han* and *Yu-Hsia*, the images of Chiang Shang, Chu-ko Liang, and Liu Chi have undergone considerable changes in the novels *Feng-shen*, *San-kuo*, and *Ying-lieh chuan*, respectively. In these novels not only has the importance of their role as advisers been stressed, but the qualities of their careers have also been transformed. As imperial advisers, they all were portrayed as men with supernatural power (masters of astrology) who could foretell future happenings by studying the stars and other aspects of the sky, and who also had the magic power to perform all sorts of miracles such as arousing the wind to defeat enemies. For example, in the novel *San-kuo*, Chu-ko Liang's Confucian statesman image is overshadowed by his overall popular image as a Taoist adviser who knows fate and the intentions of Heaven and who excels in Taoist magic. The novel exaggerates his ability to devise military strategies and makes him an ever-victorious strategist in every battle he fights. Since the *San-kuo* is the most influential historical novel in traditional times, it is only natural that Chu-ko Liang, the Taoist magician, became the archetype of all imperial advisers in later novels. However, the *San-kuo* still preserves all the outstanding qualities of Chu-ko Liang as a dedicated and selfless Confucian minister as revealed, for instance, in Liu Pei's memorable deathbed scene in the episode "Memorial on the Expedition," and in Chu-ko's own death scene.

In contrast with the *San-kuo*, the *Feng-shen* and the *Ying-lieh chuan* are less serious about being truthful to history. In the *Ying-lieh chuan*, Liu Chi, the Confucian intellectual and statesman who was caught in an age of dynastic transition, is almost nonexistent. Instead, his entry into the novel is through the legend of a white ape who is said to have delivered Chang Liang's divine book to Liu Chi. Later on, Liu Chi subdued this same white ape when it was causing trouble for a young girl.[49] These two episodes set the tone for the novel, which proceeds to emphasize Liu Chi's occult powers, his ability to read celestial portents, and to foretell future events. The novel portrays Liu Chi as a mysterious figure of occult powers who perceives the emergence of a "true king," alluding to the rise of Chu Yuan-chang, founder of the Ming dynasty. Although the Standard History *Ming-Shih* also recognizes Liu Chi's ability to presage future happenings, the popular image of him as a prophetic man was formulated in the novel.[50] Only occasionally does Liu Chi's image as a Confucian statesman shine through the pages of the novel. For example, the novel follows official histories in telling the story about Liu Chi's defending of Li Shan-ch'ang (the prime minister at the time) before Emperor T'ai-tsu. Speaking his mind against the emperor's wish, Liu Chi urged T'ai-tsu to keep Li Shan-ch'ang as prime minister in spite of the fact that Li had attempted several times in the past to ruin Liu Chi's career.[51] This episode shows how Liu Chi put the welfare of the country ahead of his personal resentment of the prime minister.

As far as subject matter is concerned, historical events are still principal in the *Ying-lieh chuan*, but they become secondary in the novel *Feng-shen*, in which the historical Shang-Chou dynastic war is transformed into a fictional account of the predestined investiture of gods. Chiang Shang, the chief adviser to King Wu of the Chou in founding the Chou dynasty, is featured in the novel as a mythical figure who possesses supernatural powers and Taoist magic. According to the novel, Chiang Shang was the man designated by the leaders of the celestial hierarchy to carry out the predestined investiture of gods. All participants in the Shang-Chou dynastic war, warriors and transcendent genies of both camps, were on the list of the gods to be invested. Thus, in the popular tradition, Chiang Shang was regarded as having exercised authority over the spirits of the unseen universe and was respected as the god of gods.

Historically speaking, there is not much biographical information about Chiang Shang, although one may find occasional references about him in many historical texts.[52] Known by the name of Lü Shang (because his ancestor was once awarded a fief at Lü), he was the mentor to King Wen and King Wu of the Chou, according to the *Shih-chi*.[53] Later, as chief adviser, he helped King Wu to defeat King Chou of the Shang. He was thoroughly conversant in statecraft and military tactics, asserted the *Shih-chi*, and was regarded as the mastermind who aided King Wen and King Wu in building the Chou dynasty. He was further credited with having written a treatise on the art of war called *Liu-t'ao* (Six Military Tactics), which established his authority on that subject. Capitalizing on his reputation as a master of military tactics, the novel *Feng-shen* has popularized Chiang Shang's entire military career and transformed him into a demigod figure equipped with supernatural powers.

In spite of the different roles played by the imperial advisers in the dynasty-building historical drama, one theme constantly recurs in the historical novels: the close rapport between the adviser and his lord. The sovereign's humble manner in requesting the service of the wise man, and his perfect trust given to this man afterward, have been carried to an even greater extent in the novels than was the case in actual history. The advisers, on the other hand, place service to their lords more on a personal basis than on the abstract principles of orthodox ethics and moral obligations. The deep sense of gratitude shown by the adviser toward his lord for the latter's being "the one who recognizes me" (*chih-yin*) has also been carried to a greater extreme in the novels than was the case historically. This sense of gratitude and a sense of mission form the two central themes in the treatment of advisers in historical novels.

Next to advisers, the most important talents the emperor-aspirants sought were those of warriors (*wu-chiang*), men who excelled in martial arts and who were the actual fighters on the battlefield. They not only appeared in all dynastic romances, but became the most celebrated heroes in historical novels, e.g., Han Hsin in the *Hsi-Han*; Kuan Yü (d. 219), Chang Fei (d. 220), and Chao Yün in the *San-kuo*; Li Ts'un-hsiao (d. 894) and Wang Yen-chang (fl. late ninth and early tenth centuries) in the *Ts'an-T'ang*; Ch'in Shu-pao, Ch'eng Yao-chin (fl. early seventh century), and Shan Hsiung-hsin (fl. early seventh century) in the *Sui-shih*; Yang Yeh (d. 986) and his seven sons and grandson Yang Tsung-pao (d. 1074) in the *Pei-Sung Yang-chia-chiang* (*Yang-chia-chiang* hereafter); Li K'uei, Lu Chih-shen, and Wu Sung in *Shui-hu*; and Yueh Fei (1103–41) in the *Ta-Sung*. These warriors took part in all sorts of military campaigns. They were fighting either in the wars between states contending for the unification of the empire, or in expeditions against invading barbarian troops, or in the suppression of rebel forces. They all showed meritorious service for their lords and their country and hence have become shining military heroes in people's minds.

Similar to the imperial advisers, warriors in popular fiction have been made to conform to certain formalized concepts of behavior, and their images share some common stereotyped attributes. Table 7 presents the most common traits ascribed to the warriors in popular fiction. These traits represent general images of the warriors and can serve as a basis for the analysis of their traditional models. Table 8 gives examples of popular warriors in historical novels and checks them against the attributes listed in table 7. The fact that most of the warriors fit these descriptions attests the existence of a common stereotype.

However, several observations should be made in regard to the popular image of warriors. First, as with all general rules, there are exceptions. For example, there are exceptions even to the most common attribute, awe-inspiring appearance (A,1). A notable case is Li Ts'un-hsiao, the main hero of the novel *Ts'an-T'ang*. Portrayed as the most distinguished warrior in his time, with unmatched physical strength and incomparable martial arts, Li is described in the novel as a man "less than five feet, thin and emaciated like a stick, and with a sickening countenance."[54] This fragile appearance, contrary to the conventional description of warriors, which is usually "six feet or seven feet in height with enormous girth and a voice like thunder," only adds surprising effect to the narratives; it does not change the basic image of

TABLE 7. Common Attributes of Popular Warriors

A. *Unusual Physical Strength and Incomparable Martial Arts*
   1. Awe-inspiring appearance and majestic features
   2. Excellence in martial arts
   3. Outstanding commandership
   4. Mighty physical strength

B. *Fearlessness*
   1. A dauntless, fearless spirit
   2. Heedlessness of consequences
   3. An unyielding fighter
      a. Never skulking when going into battle
      b. Never willing to surrender to the enemy
   4. Looking upon death as going home

C. *Power of Endurance*
   1. Endurance of pain
      a. Enduring a great physical pain without flinching
      b. Enduring corporal punishment without uttering one cry
   2. Ability to take humiliation in order to achieve a far-reaching goal
   3. Facing death with dignity and serenity
   4. Smiling in the face of adversity

D. *Selflessness*
   1. Always ready to lay down their own lives for friends
   2. Impulsive generosity
   3. Loyalty to their lords (or leaders) and their country
   4. Reciprocating favors to friends and taking revenge on enemies

E. *Asceticism and Other Behavioral Attributes*
   1. Showing little interest in women
   2. Never hesitating to fight against the rich or the powerful in order to correct injustices
   3. Outspoken bluntness and volcanic temper
   4. Eating and drinking to excess
   5. Showing filial piety to parents, especially widowed mothers

the warrior—Li is still a military superman in every way except his appearance.

The second observation about the popular image of warriors is that the existence of certain common stereotypes does not prevent the warriors from being interesting and multifarious. There are many unforgettable incidents that reflect the colorful lives and diverse career courses of the warrior-heroes in historical novels. These incidents illustrate the unique character of each individual warrior.[55] It is through

TABLE 8.   Examples of Warriors

Warrior	Novel	Warrior's Attributes as Listed in Table 7
Han Hsin	*Hsi-Han*	A,1−3; B,1; C,2−3; D,4; E,1
Kuan Yü	*San-kuo*	A,1−2,4; B,1−4; C,1a; D,1, 3−4; E,1−3
Chang Fei	*San-kuo*	A,1−2,4; B,1−4; C,1b; D,1−4; E,1−4
Chao Yün	*San-kuo*	A,1−2; B,1,3−4; C,1b; D,1,3−4; E,1−2
Ch'eng Yao-chin	*Sui-shih*	A,1−2,4; B,1−4; C,1b; D,1,3−4; E,1,3−5
Ch'in Shu-pao	*Sui-shih*	A,1−2,4; B,1−4; C,1b,4; D,1−4; E,1,2,5
Shan Hsiung-hsin	*Sui-shih*	A,1−2,4; B,1−4; C,1b,3; D,1−4; E,1,2
Li Ts'un-hsiao	*Ts'an-T'ang*	A,2,4; B,1−4; C,1b,3; D,3; E,1
Wang Yen-chang	*Ts'an-T'ang*	A,1−2,4; B,1,3−4; C,3; D,3; E,1
Yang Yeh	*Yang-chia-chiang*	A,1−2; B,1−4; C,3; D,3; E,1
Yueh Fei	*Ta-Sung*	A,1−4; B,1,3−4; C,3−4; D,3; E,1−2
Lu Chih-shen	*Shui-hu*	A,1−2,4; B,1−4; C,1b,3; D,1−2,4; E,1−4
Wu Sung	*Shui-hu*	A,1−2,4; B,1−4; C,1b,3; D,1−2,4; E,1−4
Li K'uei	*Shui-hu*	A,1−2,4; B,1−4; C,1b,3; D,1−2,4; E,1−5

these individualized incidents in historical novels that the warriors are remembered. For example, Han Hsin of the novel *Hsi-Han*, the outstanding general of Liu Pang, is remembered as a man who has the strength of will to endure humiliation (C,2). In order to avoid an unnecessary fight, young Han Hsin, before he became Liu Pang's general, crawled between the legs of a village rascal, thus acquiring a notorious reputation for cowardice.[56] However, at the end he proved to the world that a great man fights only great battles, not petty ones.

Kuan Yü of the novel *San-kuo* is remembered as a dauntless, fearless warrior (B,1) through several famous stories such as his going alone to a meeting in the enemy's camp, facing possible ambush, armed only with a single long-handled knife. His endurance of pain

(C,1a) is also a legend. Suffering from a poisoned arrow wound in the arm, Kuan Yü accepted his surgeon's decision to cut open his arm and scrape the bone; the bloody operation was performed during a game of Go (*Wei-ch'i*) and Kuan Yü continued talking and playing the game as if nothing were happening.[57] Chang Fei of the same novel is remembered as a courageous warrior in the famous episode of the Ch'ang-pan Bridge, where he was left behind to cover the retreat of Liu Pei. Riding on his horse at the end of the bridge, Chang Fei alone faced the approaching troops of Ts'ao Ts'ao. At the sight of the enemy, he shouted defiantly, "Here is Chang I-te from Yen! Who wants to fight to the death with me?" Overwhelmed by Chang's awe-inspiring appearance and reputation as a fierce fighter, and suspicious of being ambushed, Ts'ao's troops fled.[58] Chao Yun, another unforgettable hero of the *San-kuo*, is immortalized through the episode of "a solitary Chao Yun [who] galloped through the enemy's encirclement to save the life of his young master."[59]

In the novel *Yang-chia-chiang*, Yang Yeh's heroic image is forever associated with the fictional account of his committing suicide by Li Ling's memorial tablet, an image that represents the spirit of "better to die than to surrender to the enemy" (B,3b).[60] In the novel *Ta-Sung*, Yueh Fei's patriotism (D,3) is symbolized by the legend of the four tattooed characters on his back: "*ching-chung pao-kuo*" (serve the country with unswerving loyalty).[61] Even the popular theme of killing tigers singlehandedly with bare hands, proof of a warrior's unusual physical strength (A,4), illustrates interesting and different stories each time it is used, as shown by tiger-killing stories about Li K'uei, Wu Sung, and Li Ts'un-hsiao in the novels *Shui-hu* and *Ts'an-T'ang*.[62]

The third observation about the warriors' image is that these common attributes also may help us to understand the force of conventional beliefs in the stereotyping of warriors. Consider the trait of showing little interest in women (E,1) as an example. Following the traditional *yin-yang* (the negative and the positive) theory, in which the female is considered the negative element and the male the positive element in nature, as well as the belief in the importance of preserving and cultivating one's vitality, the warriors believed their training in martial arts to be incompatible with other claims on their energy. Such opinions and beliefs were seldom voiced or elaborated on by the heroes themselves. Rather they were accepted matter-of-factly by the novelists in their comments or explanations. For example, in the novel

Shui-hu, after the story about Sung Chiang's unfaithful mistress, Yen P'o-hsi, is told, the novelist offers the following explanation:

> Well, Sung Chiang was a real man whose main interest was skill with weapons. The love of women was to him a thing of no great importance. But P'o-hsi being a woman as unstable as water, was eighteen or nineteen years old and was in bloom of youth. She was quite dissatisfied with Sung Chiang.[63]

Another time, the author comments on Sung Chiang's fewer visits to his mistress, Yen P'o-hsi:

> But Sung Chiang was a real man who did not hold lust for women in his heart, and so he did not go more often than once in a half month or once in ten days.[64]

In this matter-of-fact way the novelist accepts this conventional belief among the warriors as self-evident truth. This belief that a real man (*ta-chang-fu*) does not hold lust for women explains the notable absence of women in stories about the lives and careers of warriors. As a general rule, women are seldom mentioned unless they cause trouble, such as becoming unfaithful, as in Yen P'o-hsi's case. Thus, unless specified to the contrary, we ascribe trait E,1 to the warriors in Ming novels.[65] But there is one interesting contrast. Emperors and emperor-aspirants who are warriors are excluded from this rule. For instance, both Liu Pang and Hsiang Yü are warriors in their own right but they are fond of women. According to the novel *Hsi-Han*, before Liu Pang becomes a contender for the throne, he is said to be fond of wine and women, and Hsiang Yü is said to have his Lady Yü with him wherever he goes. Apparently emperors or emperor-aspirants followed a different rule: one possible explanation is that they were allowed to indulge in women in order to insure the succession by prolific procreation.

A few words more must be said here with regard to other well-accepted conventional beliefs that mold the popular images of warriors. Besides showing little interest in women, the warriors were often described as not hesitating to fight against the rich and the powerful in order to correct injustices (E,2), outspoken bluntness and volcanic temper (E,3), eating and drinking to excess (E,4), and showing filial piety to parents, especially widowed mothers (E,5). In depicting these behavioral traits, the novelists never attempted to make a moral issue of them. Instead they wrote about the traits in a matter-of-course fashion and used them mainly to add color to their stories. Even the virtue of filial piety, the cornerstone of Confucian ethics, was not treated as a major theme, as loyalty and righteousness were, but was used to emphasize the intense sincerity of the heroes in contrast to their rough temperament. Notable examples are Ch'eng Yao-chin and Li K'uei. Both were described as men of volcanic temper and outspoken bluntness, but both showed childlike affection toward their widowed mothers.

The fourth observation about the warriors' popular image is that the common attributes of the warriors (shown in table 7) reveal the dominance of popular heroism in the tradition of folk literature. We call it popular heroism because it does not represent the orthodox Confucian values in the established modes, but rather their popular effusion. This is manifested in the popular warriors in historical novels who are, in most cases, plebian heroes reflecting the popular taste and interest of a largely unreflective audience. Even the famous Kuan Yü, the paragon of warriors and the official God of War since the Yuan dynasty, was portrayed in the *San-kuo* as a flesh and blood plebian hero, not as an apotheosis of loyalty and righteousness. Following is an example of a plebian hero who was not worshiped as a flawless god but was adored for both his virtues and shortcomings.

Nicknamed "the tattooed priest," Lu Chih-shen of the novel *Shui-hu* is one of the most favorite characters among the common people. His martial-looking (A,1) appearance, according to the *Shui-hu*, was consistent with the popular image of a warrior:

> He had large ears, a straight nose and a broad mouth. A full beard framed his round face. He was six feet tall and had a girth of ten spans.[66]

His physical strength was awe inspiring (A,4) and was well demonstrated when he pulled a big willow tree out by the roots:

> Chih-shen looked [at the tree] for a moment, then walked to the front of the tree. He took off his cassock, put down his right hand, bent far over and grasped the upper trunk with his left hand. Then suddenly he straightened his back and pulled the whole willow tree out by its roots.[67]

The novelist comments on this unusual display of strength through a bystander's exclamation: "If a man had not a thousand times ten thousand catties [a Chinese unit of weight] of strength in him, how could he pull a tree up by the roots?" Then the novelist quotes Lu Chih-shen himself, who considered his own physical strength as not being worth mentioning in comparison with his military skills: "And what cursed great matter is this? Tomorrow I will show you my military feats and the tricks I have with my weapons."[68] Since Lu Chih-shen takes pride in his military skills while downgrading his mighty physical strength, the novelist leaves Lu's excellence in martial arts (A,2) to his readers' imagination without giving detailed descriptions of them.

There are two categories of stories about Lu Chih-shen in the *Shui-hu*. One tells personal stories about Lu Chih-shen's early life and the other tells stories about his chivalric deeds. The personal stories reveal the temperament of the man, such as his volcanic temper, outspoken bluntness, excessive eating and drinking, and lack of interest in women (E,1,3–4). The stories about how Lu Chih-shen, in a drunken quarrel, made a mighty turmoil on the Five-Crested Mountain, or about how he greatly disturbed the Peach Flower Village are examples of this category.[69] The chivalric stories testify to his fearlessness (B) and selflessness (D). Almost all the traits listed in table 7 under these two headings (B,1–4; D,1–2,4) fit the descriptions of Lu Chih-shen very well. The stories about how he helped out the poor Old Man Chin and his daughter who were being exploited by a local magnate, and how he saved the life of his friend Lin Ch'ung from two bearers of dispatch ordered by the powerful Grand Commandant of the Imperial Guard are examples of his chivalric deeds.[70] Finally, while none of these stories tell directly about his power of endurance (C), given his dauntless and fearless image throughout the novel, it seems unlikely that he would show any sign of weakness if he had to endure corporal punishment (C,1b). Besides, the story about his calm acceptance and preparation for his own death reveals his inner strength (C,3).[71]

The fifth and final observation in regard to the popular image of warriors in historical novels involves the conventional references to their weapons when first introduced to the readers. These weapons were used to individualize each warrior. The following passage in the novel *Shui-hu* is a typical example:

Now in the lair on Mount Shao-hua, the three bandit chiefs were holding a conference. The leader, Chu Wu, the Miraculous Strategist who was from Ting-yuan District, could fight with a sword in each hand. Although his skill was not perfected, he was shrewd in battle tactics and was a clever strategist. The second bandit chief was called Ch'en Ta, who was originally from Yeh-ch'eng District and was skillful in the use of a steel-tipped spear. The third bandit chief was a P'u-chou man from the district of Hsieh-liang, and he used a long-handled knife.[72]

In the same vein, weapons were also described in the *San-kuo* when the three major heroes first met. The novelist depicts how the three felt drawn to each other instantly, became sworn brothers, and pledged to devote their lives to a military career. Then he describes their preparations for military equipment as follows:

After the two guests had taken their leave, armorers were summoned to forge weapons. For Yuan-te [Liu Pei] they made a double sword; for Yun-ch'ang [Kuan Yü] a long-handled, curved blade called "Black Dragon" or "Cold Beauty," which weighed eighty-two catties, and for Chang Fei, a fourteen-foot steel spear. Each too had a helmet and a full armour.[73]

The weapons are carefully individualized and become an inseparable part of the warrior's heroic image. As mentioned before, Kuan Yü's prowess is remembered in the famous episode of his going alone to a meeting in the enemy's camp and facing a possible ambush. He was described as bringing with him only his long-handled knife.[74] Chang Fei's heroic image is forever remembered in the unforgettable episode of the Ch'ang-pan Bridge where he alone stopped the enemy troops in pursuit. He was described as riding alone on his horse at the end of the bridge with his long steel spear in one hand.[75]

A few words more must be said here with regard to weapons. The wide variety of weapons in traditional times made it possible for novelists to use weapons to individualize the warriors. The frequently mentioned "eighteen subjects of military arts" in historical novels indicates the wide choice. Moreover, there was a strong presumption that warriors who excelled in martial arts knew all eighteen subjects. For example, in the *Shui-hu*, when young Shih Chin asked the former instructor of the Imperial Guard, Wang Chin, to be his teacher, he asked to be taught the eighteen subjects of military arts. Wang Chin did help him to master all eighteen subjects in less than a year. (Shih Chin had studied martial arts ever since he was a little boy.) These eighteen subjects, according to *Shui-hu*, consist of the lance, the hammer, the bow, the crossbow, the jingal, the iron whip, the iron truncheon, the two-edged sword, the chain, the whip, the ax, the battle-ax, the *ko* halbert, the *chi* halbert, the shield, the cudgel, the spear, and the rake.[76]

These eighteen weapons, however, did not represent the actual arms of the times. For example, the historical setting of *Shui-hu* was the Northern Sung dynasty, but some items in the above-mentioned list, such as the ancient *ko* halbert and the *chi* halbert, were no longer used as combat weapons in that period.[77] Moreover, the knife, especially the long-handled one, which was not mentioned on the list, was one of the important weapons of the Sung period.[78] Thus, the eighteen subjects of military arts did not represent the actual combat weapons of the times and seem to be used by historical storytellers to represent the totality of martial arts training. Nevertheless, the fact remains that there was a wide variety of weapons in traditional times.

Having discussed the popular image of warriors in historical novels, we now turn our attention to another unique theme regarding their fates. Although their fates varied under different circumstances—for example, Ch'in Shu-pao was well rewarded after the founding of the T'ang, while Han Hsin was persecuted after the founding of the Han—the general conception about their fates is best expressed by the popular proverb "*Chiao-t'u ssu, tsou-kou p'eng*" (The hunting dogs will be killed when the rabbits are all killed off). This conception reflects a long trend of popular sympathy toward military heroes in imperial China. In chapter 2, "The Pattern of History," we have already discussed why militarism has become a major theme in historical novels, stressing the common belief that wars are inevitable. Here we shall try to discuss the same question from the point of view of the warriors, placing more stress on the grievances of the warriors that aroused popular sympathy. However, in order not to exaggerate the grievance factor, it is important to realize that this theme of "Kill the hunting dog" was quite subdued and low-key. For example, in the novel *Hsi-Han* the persecution of the meritorious general Han Hsin, who helped found the dynasty, was largely blamed on Empress Lü.[79]

Although conventional practice was to make the emperor's wife (or concubines) take all the blame, it shows the effect of tuning down the significance of the persecutions, since women in general were regarded as inferior to men and untrustworthy, according to conventional standards. Again in the novel *Ts'an-T'ang*, the persecution of the meritorious warrior Li Ts'un-hsiao was blamed on K'ang Chün-li and Li Ts'un-hsin, two evil and jealous fellow-warriors in Prince Chin's camp, who plotted to execute Li Ts'un-hsiao on a false pretext. In order to play down the injustice Li Ts'un-hsiao received, the novelist goes further to suggest that it was Heaven's will that Li Ts'un-hsiao should leave the world and return to Heaven. No one could kill Li Ts'un-hsiao, the novelist maintains, since he was formerly the Spirit of Iron and Stone in the Heaven. In the execution field, Li Ts'un-hsiao would not submit to being killed until a messenger from Heaven appeared in the air and told him that it was Heaven's will that he come back to his former post.[80]

While Han Hsin's and Li Ts'un-hsiao's persecutions are played down in the *Hsi-Han* and the *Ts'an-T'ang* respectively, there are other novels that take a stronger position on the issue of kiling the meritorious warriors. The notable example is the novel *Yang-chia-fu shih-tai chung-yung t'ung-su yen-i* (The Saga of the Yang Family, *Yang-chia-fu* hereafter). In this story, the deep-seated bitter feelings of the Yang warriors are directly aimed at the reigning Sung imperial court. For generations the Yang family produced, so says the story, many courageous generals and warriors, but most of them died either on the battlefield or at the hands of evil ministers in court. Finally, the warriors became fed up with the Sung regime. Led by Yang Kung-cheng and Yang Huai-Yü, the Yang family decided to abandon the country and retired to the T'ai-hang Mountains.[81] When the court sent a prince to the T'ai-hang Mountains to ask the Yangs back, Yang Huai-Yü's answer was that they would rather die in the mountains than go back. In his explanation, Yang Huai-Yü first told the prince the family history of martyrdom; then he concluded:

> When the emperor was not enlightened, he gave ear to court ministers who were men of letters and had his trust, but the warriors [like us] were away from the court and had no way to reach him. Whenever a slander was uttered against us, our lives were immediately endangered because at that time the emperors hardly took into account our hardship and suffering on the battlefield and gave us any special

consideration. These were the facts, not excuses made up by us to fool your highness![82]

Here Yang Huai-Yü speaks not only for the Yang warriors, but also for the military officers who resented the fact that the control of the government was in the hands of civil officials. This was especially true in Sung times when the country was constantly under the threat of foreign invasions and the government was divided over the issue of war or peace. Generally speaking, the military generals favored war against foreign invaders while civil officers favored peace negotiation. Public opinion and sympathy were with the military generals, a fact that probably helped produce many legendary military heroes in historical fiction and drama. With the popularity of military heroes growing, the idea of achieving fame through military service also spread. Moreover, this idea of achieving fame through military service appealed more to the common people than did the idea of achieving fame through civil service or other cultural and moral achievements.[83] This idea also justifiably explains why detailed descriptions of martial arts and military campaigns occupy a major part of historical novels.

Although the majority of stories in historical novels are about ambitious heroes who have made themselves known in history through their moral examples or performance in public services, there are stories about people who took a different attitude toward ambition. Among the various unconventional approaches, the most notable are those taken by the recluses. Originally the recluse was one who renounced the world and hid himself in the wilderness. However, there were various types of recluses during different periods of Chinese history. The earliest reported recluses were two righteous men named Po Yi and Shu Ch'i of the twelfth century B.C., of whom the *Shih-chi* gives a terse account.[84] Po Yi and Shu Ch'i were the elder and younger sons of the ruler of Ku-chu (in modern Hopei and Jehol) in Shang times. Their father wished to set up Shu Ch'i as his heir but, when the father died, Shu-Ch'i yielded in favor of Po Yi, his elder brother. Po Yi replied that it had been their father's wish that Shu Ch'i should inherit the throne, and so he departed from the state. Shu Ch'i likewise, being unwilling to accept the throne, went away and the people of the state set up the middle brother as the new ruler. At this time Po Yi and Shu Ch'i heard that Ch'ang (King Wen), the chief of the West, was good at looking after old people, and they decided to go to the

West. But when they went there, they found that Ch'ang was already dead and his son, King Wu, was marching east to attack the ruler of the Shang dynasty. They tried to stop King Wu from marching east, but without success. After this, King Wu conquered and pacified the people of the Shang and the world honored the house of Chou as its lord. But Po Yi and Shu Ch'i were filled with outrage and considered it unrighteous to eat the grain of Chou. They fled and hid on Shou-yang Mountain, where they starved to death. To Po Yi and Shu Ch'i, the act of reclusion was a gesture of defiance. They were men of moral integrity and were praised highly by Confucius. They set a moral example for the later generations of Confucian recluses who took the act of reclusion as a gesture of protest against political corruption and tyranny, or against alien rule of China. In the world of popular literature, especially historical fiction and drama, these recluses are the most familiar ones.

In addition to the protestant recluses, there were those who took the act of withdrawal as a gesture of nonconformity. They kept themselves apart from the world of affairs because they abhorred the current state of affairs and viewed them as beyond remedy. Their attitude was best demonstrated by Chieh-ni, a recluse in the time of Confucius who thought scornfully of Confucius for trying to change the world. According to the *Analects of Confucius*, which records an indirect encounter between Confucius and Chieh-ni, Chieh-ni commented on Confucius to Tzu-lu, a leading disciple of Confucius, after he learned that Tzu-lu was a follower of Confucius:

> Under Heaven there is none that is not swept along by the same flood. Such is the world and who can change it? As for you, instead of following one who flees from this man and that, you would do better to follow one who shuns this whole generation of man.[85]

When Tzu-lu told Confucius what Chieh-ni said, Confucius sighed ruefully and made his famous remark:

> One cannot herd with birds and beasts. If I am not to be a man among other men, then what am I to be? If the Way prevailed under Heaven, I should not be trying to alter things.[86]

This philosophy of "to be a man among other men" is in contrast to what he said of the recluse who "herds with birds and beasts," and it is the essence of the Confucian philosophy of public service. On the other hand, the act of withdrawal as represented by Chieh-ni and his friend is not an isolated incident, but is related to the Taoist concept of noninvolvement that came into prominence during the period of the Warring States. This Taoist philosophy of noninvolvement, the traditional antithesis to Confucian and Legalist philosophies of public service, has been periodically popular among intellectuals, especially the literati, who at times were ill at ease with the hustling and bustling world of ambitious heroes.

While the ancient concepts of reclusion continued to grow and expand, new ideas and concepts were introduced and developed as China emerged from feudal states to a united empire. Among the new ideas and concepts stimulating the thought of reclusion, the most influential were the Buddhist concept of withdrawal from life, and the growing love of nature. Although Buddhism itself was a foreign religion at that time, the Buddhist practice of withdrawal from life appealed to indigenous recluses and reinforced the earlier tradition of retiring from world affairs. Moreover, the choice of mountaintops and spots of natural beauty for Buddhist temples and monasteries furthered the growing love of nature. As a result, the practice of withdrawal from world affairs and the love of nature reinforced each other. Thus, the concept of reclusion became one of the major undercurrents in Chinese thought. The prominence of this concept is reflected in historical writings: Fifteen of the twenty-five Standard Histories contain sections devoted to biographies of the recluses.[87]

In historical novels, the concept of reclusion is equally visible. The recluse, although never assuming a major role, has appeared in almost every historical scene. Generally speaking, the popularity of the philosophy of reclusion coincided with times of war and disorder, when people realized that there was little they could do to order the state and the society. In the novel *San-kuo*, for example, before Chu-ko Liang joined Liu Pei's group, he and his younger brother, Chu-ko Chün, had lived a reclusive life in Nan-yang in the waning years of the Han dynasty. They tilled their field and regarded themselves as recluses. To quote Chu-ko Liang directly from his famous memorial, *Ch'u-shih piao*:

> I was originally a private citizen, a farmer in Nanyang, concerned only to secure personal safety in a troubled age and not seeking fame

among the contending nobles. His late Majesty, overlooking the commonness of my origin, condescended to seek me thrice in my humble cot and consult me on the trend of events. His magnanimity affected me deeply, and I consented to do my utmost for him.[88]

It is interesting to note how the novelist interprets Chu-ko Liang's giving up of his early reclusive life to become an imperial advisor. In a poem about the phoenix and the scholar, the novelist compares his ideal scholar (here he refers to Chu-ko Liang) to the noble phoenix. The major points of the poem can be paraphrased as follows: As the phoenix flies high and perches on a *wu-tung* tree, the scholar is hidden until his lord appears; while he is awaiting his day, he tills his land and is well content with expressing his feelings by reading books, playing the lute, and roaming the woods.[89] According to the novelist, Chu-ko Liang "hid till his lord appeared," waiting to serve a worthy lord.

Different from Chu-ko Liang were his friends Shih Kuang-yuan and Meng Kung-wei, two true recluses who called themselves "idle folk of the wilds" and sang:

> Let's drown our sorrows in the cup,
>   Be happy while we may
> Let those who wish run after fame
>   that is to last for aye.[90]

As for the true recluses, they were too wise to get involved with a futile attempt. That is why Ssu-ma Hui, another of Chu-ko Liang's recluse friends, said the following words when he met Liu Pei:

Though the "Sleeping Dragon" [Chu-ko Liang's nickname] has found his lord, he has not been born at the right time. It is a pity.[91]

Here, the expression "has not been born at the right time" is the Chinese way of saying "futile attempt."

Since most protagonists of the historical novels are fame-seekers, the Taoist recluses were often introduced to provide a sardonic commentary on the contending world of fame-obsessed heroes. Moreover, their lifestyle of *laissez-aller* brings back the nostalgia of the utopian Golden Age of remote antiquity, a nostalgia that most Chinese intellectuals share in their longing for a simple, nontangled life. The most elaborate example of this nostalgia is in the historical novel *P'an-ku*, in which many classical myths about ancient kings are retold in vernacular language. Since mythology is not the subject of our study, we shall not repeat the contents of the myths, but shall only point out some ideal lifestyles described in this novel. Following are two examples:

> See how people lived [during the time of mythical Jen-huang shih]: When they were thirsty, they drank water from clear springs; when they were hungry, they picked shoots from wood stumps to eat. In hot days, they gestured to each other and gathered in shade; in cold days, they tasted the snow together in joy. They ate and drank according to natural products; they enjoyed sexual relations freely without paying attention to any artificial discrimination. They did not fight one another, nor did they engage in oral quarrels. They lived peacefully without government and school; and they shared happiness together with their king.[92]

Again, in another passage, we find similar lines:

> [During the time of the mythical Tung-hu shih] people walking in the road never picked up things lost by others; the lost items were left in the road so that the owner could always come back and find them. Those who farmed always had plenty of food. They need not store their crops every day, only leave them in the field, but no one would steal them overnight. When they were happy, they naturally sang together and laughed together; they never slandered or slighted others. When they were sad, they grieved alone and sobbed in solitude; they never cried aloud to disturb others. So Tung-hu said to himself: This world was truly pure and moral! If I were to teach people to realize the existence of "we" and "they," that was to teach them to cultivate a calculated mind. So he took no action and the state was governed. People were allowed to become uncultivated while the customs which had been handed down were observed. Everything was pleasant and harmonious.[93]

The utopia described in the novel is a world free of government, school, or any kind of social, political, or ethical order. Comparing it with the ideal state of Chuang Tzu, one of the two great exponents of the Taoist school of thought, we find a striking similarity between the two. The following passage from the book *Chuang-tzu* is an example:

> In the age of Shen Nung, the people lay down peaceful and easy, woke up wide-eyed and blank. They know their mothers but not their fathers, and lived side by side with the elk and the deer. They plowed

for their food, wove their clothing, and had no thought in their hearts of harming one another. This was Perfect Virtue at its height.[94]

The Taoist attitude of passivity, of yielding, of doing nothing that is forced, unnatural, or purposive is a sharp contrast to the Confucian scheme of values. The essence of this philosophy lies in its total elimination of human ambition that is the driving force for all fame-obsessed Confucian and Legalist activists in history. However, judging from the basically passive and unrealistic tone of this Taoist utopian scheme, the novelist is obviously not attempting to offer a positive alternative to his readers. He merely suggests that the root of human unhappiness is human ambition, which is not an inherent quality in man, but is adopted through education and ideological inculcation.

To sum up this chapter, we can conclude that during the sixteenth and seventeenth centuries when historical novels were flourishing, the heroes that dominated the central stage of the historical dramas were the empire-builders — the dynastic contenders, their advisers, and warriors. Of the three categories of "immortalities" in the scale of traditional values, meritorious public service, the second category in order of importance, was ranked above moral virtues and words. People seemed to be fascinated by the idea of the making of an emperor; the once lofty Mandate of Heaven became a convenient verdict in the hands of the "kingmakers." Moreover, the popular heroes, the emperor-aspirants, and their followers, all shared one interest in common: they were all interested in military arts or strategies. This interest in the military is a sharp contrast to the disparagement of the military in the Confucian system of values.

However, this interest in the military, which also reflects other Chinese traditions such as Legalism, is balanced by repeated appeal for moral restraints from Confucian writers. It is virtue, the Confucian writers insist (in the novels), not military might, that unifies the country and brings peace to the world. They used the slogan "A good victory is won by bravery; a better victory is won by wisdom; but the best victory is won by benevolence" to express their belief in the power of persuasion. But the fact remains that every dynasty in history was founded by the sword.

Thus it was the sword, the symbol of the armed forces, that became the center of the historical world. To cope with this reality, the novelists, who were writers of all ranks and classes, resorted to various compromises. In their attempts to portray their heroes in history, they used a variety of source materials and borrowed many devices from different traditions. The role of the Taoist recluses described in the *San-kuo* is one example of these devices: in the novel the recluses are used to provide critical commentaries on those fame-obsessed Confucian and Legalist activists in history. Another important device is to adapt religious concepts, such as the Buddhist idea of predestination, to interpret the roles played by some tragic heroes in the historical novels, and to provide answers for the many difficult "why" questions.

Chapter 4

Ethical Values and
Sociopolitical Order

Kindness on the part of the father, and filial duty on
that of the son; gentleness on the part of the elder
brother, and obedience on that of the younger;
righteousness on the part of the husband, and
submission on that of the wife; thoughtfulness on the
part of the elders and deference on that of juniors;
with benevolence on the part of the ruler, and loyalty
on that of the minister.

— Li-chi

In the areas of ethical values and sociopolitical order, the dominant influence in Ming times was the orthodox teaching of Neo-Confucianism — the Chu Hsi school of Confucianism — which provided the ideological frameworks for the Ming state and society. Within the Confucian traditions, unorthodox schools of thought existed; of these the Wang Yang-ming school of Confucianism was the most influential in the late Ming. Earlier, in our discussion of the general setting in the Introduction, I discussed two important cultural movements related to this study: the popularization movement and the vernacular literature movement. Both were influenced by Wang Yang-ming's followers and sympathizers. These two movements are very important to this study because the subject of this study, the historical novel, is part of these movements which stimulated and accelerated the process of interaction between the elite and popular cultures.

Since we have examined the theories and development of vernacular literature in some detail, in this chapter we will first take a closer look at the popularization movement that shared the ideal of transmitting knowledge to the masses. Then we will compare the dominant ethical ideas and values in orthodox Confucian teaching with those in the novels to see if there are similarities or contrasts. As pointed out earlier, the sixteenth century was the period of the rise and growth of an urban culture of great diversity and refinement in China. The increasing urbanization (occasioned by the expansion of commerce and industry), together with wide availability of educational opportunities, generated new interests and enthusiasm in cultural activities.[1] Moreover, while economic affluence prepared the ground by raising the general level of subsistence and enabling more people to participate in the cultural life of the nation, there were vigorous and conscientious efforts among concerned scholars who truly believed in transmitting education to the masses. Wang Ken, of the T'ai-chou school of thought, the famous radical wing of the Wang Yang-ming school, was a leader of this "mass" movement. Believing that every man could be a sage, Wang Ken inspired many followers who viewed it as their mission to awaken the masses. As a result, popular lecturers of this radical school flourished and spread throughout the land, carrying with them their zealous efforts to promote education among the masses. It was not a mere coincidence that private and semiprivate academies began to blossom during the period when this radical school thrived.[2]

The enthusiastic response the popular lecturers drew was tremendous; everywhere they went, people flocked to hear them. Both Li Chih and later Huang Tsung-hsi wrote accounts of these popular lecturers' activities, giving vivid and unforgettable descriptions of the mass gatherings. For example, Huang Tsung-hsi depicted Han Chen's public lectures in this way:

> Farmers, craftsmen, and merchants amounting to more than a thousand, they all came to study under him. In the autumn, during the slack season for farming operation, he traveled to villages after villages, gathering all students and discussing philosophy with them. [Wherever he gathered a crowd,] the sound of book-chanting was spontaneous; one started [something] at the front, and the others picked them up at the back.[3]

In Li Chih's description of Lo Ju-fang's (1515—88) public lectures, the audience was said to have been even larger than that of Han Chen's. People in every walk of life came to listen to Lo Ju-fang; they included women, youth, old fishermen, office clerks, scholars, retired officials, and local ruffians.[4] This picture clearly tells of a downward penetration of the cultural activities to the lower levels of society. Moreover, the wide range of people attracted to these gatherings reflected not only the ability to inspire people among these popular lecturers, but also a vigorous interest in cultural activities among the lower classes of society. This cultural interest among the common people and the widening of popular participation in cultural activities in the late Ming society are significant. Note that Lo Ju-fang was a contemporary of at least three productive historical novelists: Hsiung Ta-mu (fl. 1552), Chen Wei (fl. 1573), and Yü Shao-yü (fl. 1550s and 1560s) have all been discussed previously.

We see that from the viewpoint of shortening the distance between the well-educated elite and the less-educated or unlettered common people, the vernacular literature movement served the same role as the popularization movement of the radical philosophers. In contrast, here the vehicle for the advancement of the movement was not philosophical discussion (*chiang-hsueh*) but vernacular fiction and drama. Thus the aspirations of the historical novelists — editing, compiling, or rewriting their novels for both the educated as well as the uneducated — were essentially not much different from those of popular lecturers who aspired to bring Confucianism to all people.

Furthermore, although the historical novelists generally structured their historical world through models provided by the elitist historians, they also learned from the radical philosophers to challenge the "authority" by referring to "older texts" or "original texts." In addition, the novelists seemed to have one advantage on their side: they had much more source material at their disposal. The tremendous amount of historical materials and the wide variety of their antecedent literature offered the writers endless possibilities to present their stories and points of view.

A final note is needed before we return to the topic of ethical values and sociopolitical order. In our discussion of Confucian ideas and values, we use only the Four Books and the Five Classics as the authoritative texts in the Confucian traditions. Whenever possible, we stay away from controversial issues and concentrate on the basic concepts. Following are some brief descriptions of Confucian ethical values; they serve as the backdrop for our thematic discussion.

The base of Confucian social morality is a framework of moral obligations designated to regulate the relations of humanity. As the individual was never considered other than part of mankind as a whole, the ethics that regulate the standards of conduct and moral judgment emphasize the hope for a common happiness in society. There are five cardinal human relationships, according to the Confucian scheme: between father and son, sovereign and ministers, husband and wife, brothers, and friends. The moral principles dealing with these relationships are sociopolitically oriented; they are derived from the major Confucian concern about the government of men. Believing that men could be governed, if everyone loved his parents and treated his elders with deference, both Confucius and Mencius singled out filial piety and fraternal submission as the root of true virtues.[5] Confucius first pointed out the importance of proper relations among men in his reply to Duke Ching of the Ch'i (r. 547−490 B.C.), who asked the Master about government: "There is government, when the prince is prince, and the minister is minister; when the father is father, and the son is son." At another time, when Duke Ting of the Lu (r. 509−495 B.C.) asked how a prince should employ his ministers and how ministers should serve their prince, Confucius replied more specifically: "A prince should employ his ministers according to the rules of propriety; ministers should serve their prince with faithfulness."[6] However, Confucius did not theorize his ideas about the relations of humanity, Mencius did. Based on the framework of five human relationships, Mencius ruled as follows: "Between father and son, there should be affection; between sovereign and ministers, righteousness; between husband and wife, attention to their separate functions; between old and young, a proper order; and between friends, fidelity."[7] By the time the *Li-chi* (Book of Rites) was written, moral obligations assigned to the different roles the individual played in the society were well defined. There are ten moral obligations governing the five human relationships listed in the *Li-chi*:

> Kindness on the part of the father, and filial duty on that of the son; gentleness on the part of the elder brother, and obedience on that of the younger; righteousness on the part of the husband, and submission on that of the wife; thoughtfulness on the part of the elders and deference on that of juniors; with benevolence on the part of the ruler, and loyalty on that of the minister.[8]

Thus, theoretically speaking, the cultivation of Confucian virtues should abide by a reciprocal principle: The emperor should be benevolent on his part, and the minister should be loyal in return; the father should be kind and the son, dutiful; the husband should be righteous and the wife, submissive; the elder brother should be gentle and the younger brother, obedient; the elders should be thoughtful and the juniors, deferent. But in reality the traditional society never observed this reciprocal principle. Instead, the authoritarian principle of "three bonds" (*san-kang*) was observed. Of the five human relationships, according to the dogma of the three bonds, three are of vital importance: between sovereign and subject, father and son, husband and wife. The original reciprocal principle was changed to an absolute dogma: The minister should be absolutely loyal to the emperor, even when the emperor was not benevolent; the same is true with both the son and the wife. The son should absolutely obey his father, and the wife, her husband.

As the long unification of the Han empire saw the growth of Confucianism, the prolonged period of disunity following the collapse of the Han empire saw the growth of Taoism and Buddhism. By the Sung period, the reconsolidation of the Sung empire renewed faith in Confucianism — the Neo-Confucianism — as the spiritual support for the imperial political order. From then on, with the exception of the Yuan period, Neo-Confucianism was the state orthodoxy. And the absolutist dogma of the three bonds was the dominant ideology for both the state and the society. With this background in mind, we now turn to the historical novels.

We will start with Tso Ju's story. In Feng Meng-lung's *Hsin lieh-kuo*, there is a story about an upright minister named Tso Ju in the court of King Hsuan (r. 827–782 B.C.) of the Chou. King Hsuan was angry with one of his ministers, Tu Pai. In a sudden flare-up, he ordered the execution of Tu Pai. At this time Tso Ju was also present, and he pleaded for Tu Pai's life. This made King Hsuan even more furious:

> "You speak for your friend against my order. This means that you value friendship more than your prince's wish," said King Hsuan. Tso Ju replied: "If your Majesty is right and my friend Tu Pai is wrong, I should obey your order. Now Tu Pai did not commit any crime that deserves a death penalty. If your Majesty go ahead to kill him, the whole world will view you, my lord, as being unjust. If I, as your minister, do not point out your wrong judgment, then the whole world will view me as being unloyal. If you, my lord, feel that you have to put Tu Pai to death, please put me to death with him too."[9]

But King Hsuan was not impressed by Tso Ju's sincerity: "For me to put Tu Pai to death is like pulling out a weed. Do not say any more." And he ordered the guard to execute Tu Pai at once. So the guards carried out his order to have Tu Pai executed right away. Tso Ju went home and killed himself with a knife. The story ends with the following praise:

> What an outspoken Confucian minister Tso Ju was! Not afraid of angering his king he spoke his mind. He stood by his friend when the friend was right. He pointed out the fact when his king was wrong. He valued his integrity more than his position and his friendship more than his life. History will always honor his outspoken loyalty and righteousness.[10]

Tso Ju's story has three interesting aspects: First, of the five human relations, two are involved here: the ruler-subject relationship and the relationship between friends. Significantly, the novelist seems to ignore the usual primacy given to the ruler-subject relationship, which tends to exemplify a hierarchical sociopolitical order. Instead, he emphasizes a relationship of equality between friends. In the story, Tso Ju was praised for valuing "his friendship more than his life." Second, when Tso Ju's integrity as a minister is praised, it seems nothing new at first glance; Tso Ju did only what a loyal Confucian minister was supposed to do. The duty of a loyal minister is to remonstrate, at the risk of his own life, his lord's wrong-doing, according to conventional Confucian values. However, in the novel, Tso Ju not only did his job by trying to prevent the king from making a serious mistake, he committed suicide after the king had ignored his advice and had executed his friend Tu Pai. Tso Ju's suicide was an act of protest. In so doing, he not only impressed upon King Hsuan the enormity of the king's wrongdoing, he also upheld the dignity of the individual minister who refused to submit himself to the tyranny of an unjust king. Third, Tso Ju's name cannot be found in *Shih-chi*, or *Tso-chuan*, or *Kuo-yü*, the historical classics of the period. But *Kuo-yü* does mention Tu Pai in one important sentence: "[The ghost of] Tu Pai shot [an arrow] at King Hsuan; this was [the beginning of] the decline of the Chou."[11] An authoritative note explains the above quote as follows: According to the *Chou Ch'un-ch'iu* (The Annals of the Chou), King Hsuan unjustly sentenced Tu Pai to death. Three years later the ghost of Tu Pai came back to haunt the king and caused King Hsuan's death.[12] In other words, the decline of the Chou, according to the *Kuo-yü*, started with King Hsuan, who unjustly sentenced Tu Pai, one of his ministers, to death. This seems to be the clue to the Tso Ju story.

Since Tso Ju was not mentioned in standard historical works, Feng Meng-Lung, the novelist, molded the character according to his own imagination. Thus the different emphases and approaches the novelist used regarding Tso Ju are revealing; they reflect the novelist's point of view and represent one seventeenth century writer's opinions. Although it is not for us to decide to what extent these opinions reflect the signs of the times, the important point is that opinions existed in Feng's mind when the novel was written.

Our second example is Yueh Fei (1103–41), the famous Southern Sung general whose stories became very popular during Ming times. So many stories have been written about the tragic death of this patriot in both drama and fiction that his life has become a myth in people's minds. Many factors contributed to Yueh Fei's transformation from a historical figure into legend and myth.[13] The most important ones are: first, the growing sentiment of patriotism that was a result of military conflicts between the Han Chinese and the invading "barbarian" forces during the long period from the Southern Sung through Mongol Yuan to Ming times; second, the active official support as shown in the Official History (the *Sung-shih*), which even falsified documentation to glorify Yueh Fie; and third, the general Confucian sanction that was evident by Yueh Fei's image created by the literati as a Confucian general whose moral strength and literary talent were as outstanding as his military prowess. Thus by Ming times, Yueh Fei's stature in history had reached its height as the standard-bearer of loyalty and patriotism.

Various versions of Yueh Fei's stories can be found in historical novels; at least four versions were written in Ming times.[14] The central themes of these novels are basically the same; they are about Yueh Fei's heroic resistance against the Chin (Jurchen) invasions in the early years of the Southern Sung and the injustice he suffered from the incompetent and selfish Sung court, which was eventually responsible for his execution under a false pretext given by jealous and corrupt ministers. For example, consider Hsiung Ta-mu's *Ta-Sung*, one of the earlier versions, among novels about Yueh Fei.

In *Ta-Sung* Yueh Fei's loyalty is characterized by the four-character motto tattooed on his back: *ching-chung pao-kuo* (serve the country with unswerving loyalty). The novelist believes these words were Yueh Fei's motto, as he constantly reminds his readers. Following are three examples of Yueh Fei's motto. The novelist first tells about the origin of these words. During the Ching-k'ang period (1126–27), the country was in turmoil caused by invading barbarian forces. The Sung armies were weak and could not stop the enemy, so the barbarians came and went as they pleased, devastating everything in their way. The country was disrupted and disorder prevailed. As a result, many strong and venturesome men joined bandits in the mountains. In Yueh Fei's village there was also talk of escape to the mountains to join the bandits. But Yueh Fei stopped this talk, according to the novel, by asking someone to tattoo his motto, the four-character *ching-chung pao-kuo*, on his back:

> During Ching-k'ang period, the nomads on horseback [who invaded the country] were everywhere. The Sung soldiers flinched from the enemy and scattered. In the village some strong and venturesome men came to consult Yueh Fei [on what to do about the dangerous situation]. They suggested that they could all escape to the mountains to join the bandits. Fei was appalled at the suggestion. He told them: "It is unthinkable that a soldierly man does not wish to leave a good name in history but wants to be a thief and robber and lead a wrongful life." To show his determination not to follow the evil path of life, he asked someone to tattoo four big characters on his back: *ching-chung pao-kuo*. Hereafter, whenever people came to ask him [to join the bandits], he showed them the tattoo on his back. As a result, most of the strong and venturesome men [in his village] did not join the bandits.[15]

Note the choice Yueh Fei put before his fellow villagers. He was asking them to make a choice between joining the bandits and enlisting in the army. This was the same choice that faced most peasants in times of war and disorder in imperial China. Yueh Fei himself enlisted in the army when he was only twenty years old, according to his biography.[16] Although he did not stay there long and returned home when his father (a farmer) died, he always considered himself a soldier. That was why he had the four characters meaning "serve the country with unswerving loyalty" tattooed on his back. Shortly after he acquired the tattoo, he enlisted in the Sung army again, according to the novel.

Yueh Fei did very well in the army, and distinguished himself by his courage and military skill. However, his determination to serve the country caused a dilemma when he received ill-advised orders. When he had just repelled the invading Jurchens and was about to pursue them, he received imperial decrees ordering him to give up his plans and to retreat to a place named Chu-hsien chen (southwest of modern Kaifeng, Honan). He knew this was the only opportunity for him to destroy the Jurchens, yet he also knew that he should obey the imperial decree. The country should defeat the enemy once and for all, but it would be a disloyal act to defy an imperial decree. After Yueh Fei received twelve imperial decrees in one day to order him to retreat, he obeyed reluctantly, according to the novel.

Yueh Fei took his anti-Jurchen stand when he showed his reluctance to obey orders to retreat. This was against the wish of the Sung Court, represented by the Prime Minister Ch'in Kuei (1090–1155), who advocated negotiating for peace with the Jurchens. Later, Ch'in Kuei and his parties accused Yueh Fei and his son, Yueh Yun, of treason and put them in the prison of the Grand Court of Judicial Review. According to the story, Yueh Fei was ordered to write his affidavit to the Grand Court. Instead, he wrote an account of his military career, detailing all the battles he had fought. After finishing his writing, he tore off his clothes and showed his back to the chief minister of the Grand Court of Judicial Review, Chou San-wei:

> Chou San-wei saw that there were four black tattooed characters, *ching-chung pao-kuo*, which were cut deeply into the skin.... All who witnessed the scene hid their faces, and tears too ran down from Chou San-wei's cheek.[17]

This is the second time that the novelist refers to the four tattooed characters to dramatize the old soldier's unswerving loyalty to his country.

Even though Ch'in Kuei could not find Yueh Fei and Yueh Yun guilty of any of the accusations, he still ordered their execution. Yueh Fei was put to death by strangulation. Days later, Yueh Fei's wife came to find Yueh Fei's corpse. The novelist describes the scene as follows:

> [She] saw that [the dead] Grand General Yueh had not changed and still looked very much alive. She then loosened the rope off on his neck and took off his blood-red clothes. When the clothes were off, she could still distinctly see the four tattooed words *ching-chung pao-kuo* in spite of all the blood-stained scars [from torture].[18]

This is the third time the author reminds his readers of Yueh Fei's tattooed words. Yueh Fei was dead; he was cruelly executed, yet in his countrymen's memory he will always be "very much alive."

We should note that the story of the tattooed *ching-chung pao-kuo* was not the novelist's creation. Earlier, in a brief description of Yueh Fei's trial, the Standard History of the Sung reported the fact that these four characters were tattooed on Yueh Fei's back.[19] However, the attitude of the period shows itself in the way the motto is presented: Serve the country with unswerving loyalty; the emphasis is on the *country* (*kuo*). Throughout the novel, whenever the author mentions *loyalty* (*chung*), he never connects it with the sovereign (*chün*). The emphasis is on the country, not the sovereign. It is true that in imperial Ming times, there was no difference between the country and the sovereign as far as the conventional concept of loyalty was concerned. The emperor was the state. But it was a different situation if there was a conflict of interest between the country and the imperial government. According to the novel, Yueh Fei was caught in such a difficult situation. The novelist, as well as his contemporaries, was well aware of Yueh Fei's dilemma because the same dilemma was faced by a great Ming patriot, Yü Ch'ien (1398–1457), and should still have been fresh in their memories. Yü Ch'ien was condemned to death by decapitation as a traitor because his loyalty to the country was higher than his personal loyalty to his emperor. In the next chapter when we discuss the imperial institution we will examine Yü Ch'ien's tragedy in greater detail.

Besides the virtue of loyalty, the most celebrated virtue in historical novels is *i* (righteousness). Here the concept of *i* was used in a broad sense: It means not only the conventional Confucian concept of *i* in the sense of propriety and righteous conduct, but also the popular concept of *i*, such as justice, brotherhood, and selfless friendship. Generally speaking, the Confucian concept of *i* was applied to the educated elite and the popular concept of *i* to the common people. Since most of the protagonists in historical novels come from the common folk, the emphasis on justice, brotherhood, and selfless friendship is understandable.

Consider the concept of *i* in the novel *San-kuo*. The episode of "Brotherhood Sworn in the Garden of Peaches" (*T'ao-yuan chieh-i*) in the *San-kuo* is one of the best-known stories among the Chinese, and this sworn brotherhood has been so well entrenched in the popular mind that it has become a source of inspiration for popular heroism.

The famous oath of the peach garden tells the essence of this heroism. It reads as follows:

> We three, Liu Pei, Kuan Yü, and Chang Fei, though of different families, swear brotherhood, and promise mutual help to one end. We will rescue each other in difficulty, we will aid each other in danger. We swear to serve the state and save the people. We ask not the same day of birth but we seek to die together. May Heaven, the all-ruling, and Earth, the all-producing, read our hearts, and if we turn aside from righteousness or forget kindliness may Heaven and man smite us.[20]

The two objectives of this solemn oath, to serve the country and to seek to die together, represent the central themes of the *San-kuo*. The former upholds the virtue of loyalty, the latter, that of *i*. In our discussion of the concept of dynastic legitimacy, we have already examined the strong pro-Han — that is, loyal to the Han — moral conviction of the *San-kuo*. It is for this noble cause of restoring the legitimate Han regime that these three sworn brothers swear to seek to die together. And according to the novel, they all keep their oath: they are loyal to the Han cause to the end; they rescue each other in numerous difficult situations; they aid each other in many dangers; and finally, they actually could be described as seeking to die together. When Kuan Yü died in 219, both Liu Pei and Chang Fei turned into men of passion; in their reckless acts of vengeance, they instigated their own deaths.[21]

Significantly, the *San-kuo* upholds the friendship among the three sworn brothers as the noblest among all human relations. The novel views the relationship between friends as more important than the relationship between sovereign and subject, the number one "bond" among men in the prevailing Confucian ideology. Liu Pei, afterall, was the ruler of the Shu, and both Kuan Yü and Chang Fei were in fact his subjects. Of course, they had sworn brotherhood before Liu Pei was enthroned. Nevertheless, their relationship had not changed after Liu Pei became king, according to the novel, and they remained loyal to each other toward the very end. Although the common people accepted the image of an absolute monarch, they were not entirely satisfied with this situation. Their hearts yearned for a more beautiful and more meaningful relationship, which they found in the *San-kuo*. That is why the novel was so popular and why the theme of "sworn brotherhood" was so captivating. Almost all the historical novels adopt this theme.

Another novel, the *Shui-hu*, tells of Sung Chiang and his band of outlaws who flourished briefly during Hui-tsung's reign (1101–25) of the northern Sung dynasty.[22] The celebrated virtues are loyalty and selfless friendship, as professed by the two catchwords *chung* and *i* that precede the title of the novel. Although there are several versions and numerous editions of the novel (with slightly varied titles and contents), the title *Chung-i Shui-hu chuan* is used most often.[23] Traditionally, *chung-i* is interpreted literally as "loyal and righteous," two adjectives that describe the *Shui-hu* bandit-heroes. The famous Ming critic Li Chih especially emphasized these two qualities — loyalty and righteousness — and pointed them out in his introductory note to the novel.[24] According to Li Chih, loyalty and righteousness were the two principles that guided the 108 bandit-heroes: They showed loyalty in their service to the country and they showed righteousness in their dealings with friends. However, opinions on Sung Chiang and his Liang-shan band have long been divided since their stories were put into written forms. The two representatives in traditional times were Li Chih and Chin Sheng-t'an (1610?–61), whose views of Sung Chiang and his band are poles apart: Li Chih viewed them as loyal and righteous men, whereas Chin Sheng-t'an viewed them as plain bandits. We will discuss Chin Sheng-t'an's view later when we discuss Sung Chiang's concept of loyalty. In the meantime, we need only to point out that no matter how the *Shui-hu* band is considered, the concept of *chung-i* is generally accepted and treated as a moral issue. But this attitude was recently challenged by some *Shui-hu* scholars in China who view *chung-i* as a political issue representing the Sung nationalism against alien Chin forces. They cited many examples to support their view that *chung-i* meant Chung-i chün (The Army of the Loyal and the Righteous), which represented the peasant rebel forces of the antiforeign (Jurchen) movement in the late Northern Sung dynasty.[25] According to them, *chung-i* in the novel *Shui-hu* revealed the original connection between the peasant revolts and the anti-Chin resistance movement, which died out after the establishment of the Southern Sung regime. When the oral legends of *Shui-hu* stories were put into written form, the original anti-Chin sentiment in *chung-i* was lost and replaced with the Confucian concept of loyalty and righteousness. Since our following discussion is based only on the factual narration of the novel, which reflects little or no anti-Chin sentiment,[26] we shall still discuss *chung-i* in the context of moral commitments. However these oral legends of *Shui-hu* are very important because they explain why in China *Shui-hu* stories have been generally viewed as "historical."

As pointed out before, the catchwords *chung-i*, loyalty and righteousness, are the two central themes of the novel. While *loyalty* follows the Confucian concept of loyalty to one's country and sovereign, *righteousness* is largely the popular idea of selfless friendship connected together with *i* (justice) in *"shu-ts'ai chang-i"* (to give generously and show devotion to justice). We shall first discuss the concept of loyalty versus the concept of selfless friendship as exemplified by Sung Chiang and Li K'uei. In a later chapter on the themes of social and economic grievances, we shall discuss *i* (justice) in *"shu-ts'ai chang-i."*

In the novel, Sung Chiang, the leader of the band, is identified as the symbol of loyalty. In chapter 42, the author specifically made clear that the principle of loyalty is given to Sung Chiang by a goddess named Chiu-t'ien hsuan-nü (The Goddess of the Ninth Heaven), who appeared to him in a dream and delivered three heavenly books to him:

"Star Lord," said the goddess, "we have given you three Heavenly Books. You should hereby uphold justice for Heaven. Show complete loyalty to and do justice for the emperor. As officials serve the country, take care of the people, and do away with the wrong and direct them to the right. Never forget this."[27]

Note also in the same passage that the novelist first introduces the concept of *t'i-t'ien hsing-Tao* (uphold justice for Heaven) that is to be adopted by the Shui-hu band as their standard banner. When Sung Chiang became the leader (in chap. 60), the first thing he did was to change the name of the meeting place from Chü-i T'ing (The Hall of Righteousness) to Chung-i T'ang (the Hall of Loyalty and Righteousness).[28] Before Sung Chiang became the band leader, the moral principle among the band had been the heroic code of *i* that stressed reciprocity: to return favors to friends and to take revenge on enemies. That is why they named their meeting place the Hall of Righteousness. When Sung Chiang became the leader, he introduced the concept of loyalty to the band. He also talked constantly about honorable surrender to the imperial government in exchange for amnesty.

Sung Chiang's wish for amnesty was against the wishes of many of his bandit-brothers, notably Li K'uei, Lu Chih-shen, and Wu Sung, who distrusted the corrupt officials of the imperial court. The scene of commotion caused by Sung Chiang's suggestion of honorable surrender in chapter 71 is an example.[29] But, in the end, they all followed their leader Sung Chiang's wish for surrender in exchange for amnesty. There is a difference between Sung Chiang's concept of loyalty and that of his bandit-brothers: To Li K'uei and others, Sung Chiang—the symbol of friendship—is the object of their loyalty. Since Sung Chiang had bestowed many favors on them in earlier days, he won their hearts and loyalty. Thus, unconsciously they felt they had to reciprocate his favors, even with their own lives. The best example is Li K'uei. Ever hot-tempered, he once offended Sung Chiang when he spoke against Sung Chiang's suggestion of honorable surrender. In a rage of anger Sung Chiang ordered Li K'uei executed, but the bandit-soldiers were all afraid of Li K'uei and dared not even go near him. Li K'uei said the following to them:

> You people are afraid that I would resist the order. But I won't complain if my brother (Sung Chiang) wants me to die; I won't show any resentment even if he wants to hack me to pieces. Him I obey, though I am not even afraid of Heaven.[30]

Li K'uei was not executed that time, but he eventually died at Sung Chiang's hand at a much later date, after the band had surrendered to the Sung Court and had rendered many meritorious military services to the Sung regime. When Sung Chiang discovered he had been poisoned by some evil court officials and was about to die, he sent for Li K'uei immediately. Knowing Li K'uei's devotion, Sung Chiang was afraid that Li K'uei would take revenge after his death, and thus damage the reputation of the Shui-hu band. Without telling Li K'uei anything about his being poisoned, Sung Chiang set up a plan to poison Li K'uei as well. After Li K'uei had drunk the poisoned wine, Sung Chiang then told him the whole story.

> As Sung Chiang was talking, he could not help himself weeping and sobbing. Li K'uei, too, wept, as he replied, "Enough, enough, enough! In life I serve you, and in death I'll simply be an attendant-ghost in your command."[31]

Making no protest or complaint, Li K'uei's response to Sung Chiang rings with the true eloquence of unswerving devotion.

Compared to Li K'uei's selfless friendship, Sung Chiang follows a different kind of duty. He considers loyalty to the emperor as the most important element in life. He tells Li K'uei:

> All my life, I have abode by two resolutions: loyalty and righteousness. I have never compromised on these two principles with myself. Today the Court sends me the poisoned wine to order my death even though I am innocent of any wrongdoing. I would rather let the Court betray me than betray the Court. But I am afraid that after I die you might take revenge on the Court and rebel against the government, thereby destroying the honorable reputation of all our brothers of Liang-shan-po, who have vowed to do justice for Heaven and have abode by the two principles of loyalty and righteousness. Therefore I sent for you [to prevent you from wrongdoing]. The wine you drank yesterday was poisoned. But the poison is the slow kind, and you definitely will die when you go back to Yun-chou. After you die, please come to join me here [as ghosts].[32]

The difference between Sung Chiang's loyalty and Li K'uei's selfless friendship lies in the difference between orthodox Confucian teaching and popular heroism. Unlike Li K'uei, who was a jailer before joining the bandits, Sung Chiang was an educated clerk for the magistrate in Yun-ch'eng District (modern Yun-ch'eng District, Shantung) before he was forced by circumstance to flee and join the band of bandits.[33] Although by interest and temperament he excelled in martial arts and inclined to chivalrous conduct, by profession he was a low-ranking bureaucrat who received a Confucian education. When he told Li K'uei that he would rather let the court betray him than betray the court, he was thinking of himself as a loyal subject of the imperial court. As a loyal subject, he would ask himself only what he could do for the imperial court, regardless of what the court had done to him. However, when Sung Chiang, without any hesitation, poisons Li K'uei in the name of loyalty, this act becomes less convincing than the idea itself.[34] Few people would doubt Li K'uei's devotion to Sung Chiang, but many people might question the self-righteousness of Sung Chiang. As a matter of fact, many critics were finding fault with the character of Sung Chiang. The Ch'ing critic Chin Sheng-t'an was one example.

In his popular annotated seventy-chapter edition of the *Shui-hu*, Chin Sheng-t'an makes clear that to him Sung Chiang was nothing but a scheming hypocrite who always maneuvered for personal power and gain.[35] In this shortened version of the novel, Chin Sheng-t'an revised the text of its first seventy-one chapters, changed the first chapter into a prologue, renumbered subsequent chapters, and ended the novel at the grand gathering of all the 108 bandit-heroes at Mount Liang. In order to stress his point that all bandits should be punished, Chin Sheng-t'an deliberately concluded the novel with the episode "The Nightmare," his own creation. In this episode, Lu Chün-i had a dream right after the 108 bandit-heroes' grand gathering: He dreamed that he and all his brother-bandits were beheaded. The implication is obvious: All bandits are doomed to ill fortune. Although it is generally accepted that Chin Sheng-t'an fabricated the short version of *Shui-hu* in order to discredit the bandit-heroes, especially Sung Chiang, ironically, the popularity of Chin's version in Ch'ing times actually helped to popularize the *Shui-hu* legends, and three English versions were based chiefly on this short version.[36]

However, in our thematic discussion we use the longer version of *Shui-hu*, which was based upon the most complete edition, the Yang Ting-chien's (fl. late sixteenth to early seventeenth centuries) edition of the 120-chapter text.[37] According to this version, all bandit-heroes received their amnesty as Sung Chiang wished, and were incorporated into the Sung imperial army. There they fulfilled their duties of serving the country by participating in a series of military campaigns against the invading enemies from abroad and against other rebellious forces at home. The campaigns were successful, though the last one proved to be rather costly, and more than half the band of heroes died in the course of the campaign. Those who survived became further dispersed, and the novel ends tragically with the death of the two leaders, Sung Chiang and Lu Chün-i, caused by the treachery of wicked courtiers, and the death of Li K'uei, Wu Yung, and Hua Jung. Wu and Hua, like Li K'uei, are martyrs to friendship; they hanged themselves on the trees in front of Sung Chiang and Li K'uei's graves. Thus, at the end, the bandit-heroes proved to the world that they are men of *chung* and of *i*, that they have kept their vows to serve the country and to die for friendship.

With loyalty and righteousness the most celebrated ethical values in historical novels, the next question concerns benevolence. Is benevolence also a dominant theme in the novels? According to Confucian ethics, the sovereign, at least in theory, should be benevolent in order for his subjects to be loyal and righteous. In fact, Mencius's most eloquent and convincing account about what a benevolent ruler should do was known to every educated Chinese in Ming times.[38] But in the historical novels, with the exception of Liu Pei (who is, however, an "unsuccessful" dynastic contender), we find no representative of the benevolent ruler after Mencius's model. Instead, we find the ancient sage-kings as the inspiration for molding an ideal sovereign. Since the sage-kings are known only through their legendary abdication stories, the emphasis is on how they, with the interest of the public in mind, abdicated the throne in favor of able and virtuous successors, not how they, as benevolent kings, ruled their kingdoms.

Consider the novel *P'an-ku*. According to this novel, during the period of the ancient sage-kings, the society was an egalitarian and simple society in which public spirit ruled all under Heaven. In this ideal society leaders were chosen for their virtue, wisdom, and ability to lead. The story about the abdication of King Yao (trad. 2356–2256 B.C.) in favor of Shun, represents this ideal in the novel.[39] The story goes that King Yao was looking for men of virtue and talent to succeed him when he became old. He ruled out his own son Tan Chu because the latter was incompetent. After a long search, a blind man's son, Shun, was recommended for his virtue, wisdom, and ability to lead. Living with his father, stepmother, and a half-brother, Shun was known as a dutiful son and a devoted brother in his village. Many times Shun's stepmother and half-brother convinced his father to murder him, but Shun managed to keep himself alive and still be able to be pious and kind to his parents and brother. When he was a farmer in the field, other farmers would not quarrel because of his moral example. He was a fisherman once, and when he was fishing, all his fellow fishermen learned to be polite to each other. After King Yao heard all these good things about Shun, he sent for him immediately. Impressed by Shun's manners and answers, King Yao married his two daughters to Shun and sent them back to Shun's village. After observing Shun's good influence upon his daughters for years, King Yao then assigned to Shun various governmental responsibilities, which Shun performed very well. Satisfied with both his virtue and ability, King Yao was convinced that Shun was the right man for the country, and then asked him to take over the government. Shun was in charge of the government for twenty-eight years before King Yao's death. After King Yao died, Shun retired from the government in order to prepare the way for

Yao's son Tan Chu to take over, but the people did not wish Tan Chu to be their king. They did not go to Tan Chu's court to pay their respects; they did not go to Tan Chu to praise him; and they did not go to Tan Chu to seek his counsel and opinions about their affairs. Instead, they all went to Shun. This mandate from the people made Shun decide to ascend the throne and become King Shun.[40] Here, the public spirit of King Shun is also noticeable. He never took the people's consent for granted: After having governed the country for twenty-eight years, he was still prepared to turn the government over to another, if that was the people's wish.

The essence of the abdication story of King Yao lies in the public spirit that was shared by all concerned. To King Yao, his first and last concern was the welfare of the people; to him, the best guarantee he could find to safeguard the welfare of the people was finding an able and virtuous new leader to succeed him. He tried diligently until he finally found the right man; once he found the right man he gave up his power entirely without hesitation. For twenty-eight years, King Yao lived contentedly while Shun governed the country. This public spirit is a great contrast to the later imperial institution of succession on the basis of family inheritance, which viewed the country as the private property of a royal house.

The second example, the story of King Shun's (trad. 2255–2206 B.C.) abdication in favor of his minister Yü, elaborates the same ideal. According to the novel, *Yu-Hsia*, King Shun appointed Yü to regulate the rivers and water courses, which had caused floods since King Yao's days. Yü did a good job on this assignment and regulated all the rivers and water courses very well. King Shun was so pleased that he appointed Yü as *Ta-ssu-k'ung* (Minister of Works) to head the government. Satisfied with Yu's performance, King Shun then recommended Yü to Heaven and asked Yü to take over the throne. After King Shun abdicated, he went southward on an imperial tour of inspection and died there. Although Yü followed King Shun's historical example of retiring from the government, in order to make King Shun's son Shang Chün king, the people of the country let Yü know that they wanted Yü to be their king, not Shang Chün. With this mandate from the people, Yü succeeded to the throne and became King Yü (trad. 2205–2198 B.C.), the first king of the Hsia dynasty (trad. 2205–1767 B.C.).[41]

The examples of King Yao and King Shun tell the noble ideals of the ancient sage-kings, who upheld the public spirit by practicing it themselves. To them, kingship meant responsibility, and only the able and virtuous deserved to assume that responsibility. However, the tradition of abdication in favor of the able and virtuous could not carry on further after King Yü died even though King Yü wanted to uphold it. According to the novel, King Yü appointed Po I, his principal assistant during the tenure of his appointment of regulating watercourses, to be his successor. After King Yü died, Po I, following the traditional courtesy, turned the government over to the former king's son, Ch'i, and retired to Chi Shan. But this time things changed: The people did not follow Po I to Chi Shan. Instead, they wanted Ch'i to be their king because Ch'i was King Yü's son and also had a reputation of being able and virtuous. "Ch'i could not help accepting the mandate from the Heaven and succeeding the throne from his father. He became the king of the Hsia. This is the beginning of [the concept of] *chia t'ien-hsia* (attaining to the throne by inheritance)," the story concludes. As if not satisfied with his own statement, the novelist added:

> Actually, the Hsia did not start this practice of making son succeed father to the throne, [although as an institution, it was established by the Hsia]. Ever since the time of King Yen (trad. 2737–2698 B.C.) there were occasions when a son succeeded the throne from his father. But it was only by the time of the Hsia that the possessive nature of human beings prevailed and it took over the place of the public spirit. This was the natural development of things; even sages could not change it.[42]

The transition from the ideal system of abdication to a kingship system of inheritance must be of great concern to the novelist. On the one hand, he attributed the change (of the rules of succession) to the theory of "natural development." On the other, he pointed out the accidental nature of historical development: King Yü's son Ch'i happened to be a man of virtue and talent and that was why the inheritance system started from him. Stressing the superior quality of Ch'i, the novelist further inquired why the people of Hsia preferred Ch'i to Po I.[43] The people of Hsia held special affection for Ch'i because Ch'i reminded them of King Yü's dedication to his work, according to the novelist. Four days after Ch'i was born, Yü (at this time he was not king yet) left his wife and newborn son for his work of regulating watercourses, and he did not return home for years until his work was done. Thus, Yü exemplified the image of a hard-working leader who held his public duty above his private affairs, and Ch'i reminded the people of this image of Yü. Besides, Ch'i was well educated: He was raised by a very wise and virtuous mother and had learned about statecraft from his father at an early age, when Yü returned to King Shun's court and served in the government after he had regulated all watercourses within the boundaries. Compared with Ch'i's well-grounded education, Po I — an assistant to Yü in regulating flooding and a specialist in explosives — seemed too specialized to be a good statesman. Furthermore, the novelist pointed out that Po I had served King Yü for only seven years, a relatively short period compared with the longer time held by King Yü in serving King Shun and King Shun in serving King Yao. All these show the novelist's attempt to justify Ch'i's succession to the throne. In doing this, the novelist was stressing a point to his readers: that later generations observe Ch'i's example as the rightful succession to the throne and follow suit, but they seem only to remember that Ch'i was King Yü's son and forget about the important fact that Ch'i, too, was a man of ability and virtue.

Another example describing the changing attitude toward kingship in the Hsia dynasty is Hou I's story in the same novel, *Yu Hsia*. After King Ch'i (trad. 2197–2189 B.C.) died, his son T'ai-k'ang then succeeded to the throne. At the beginning of his reign, King T'ai-k'ang (trad. 2188–2160 B.C.) was not a diligent king and the country was in great disorder. At this time, in the neighboring state of Yu-ch'iung, there was an able and powerful ruler named Hou I. When Hou I learned of trouble in the Hsia, he marched his troops to the Hsia to restore order. Hou I was an ambitious man; he wanted to take over T'ai K'ang's place and become the king of the Hsia. But he had four wise and virtuous advisers who disagreed with him on this issue. They all told Hou I that a king could not be made by oneself; one had to wait to be called to the throne by the people. They advised him not to take advantage of the Hsia but to help King T'ai-k'ang to regain his control over the country. Hou I followed their advice. Later when King T'ai-k'ang died, upheavals emerged again in the Hsia; Hou I was thinking again of making himself the king of the Hsia, but his advisers still said no. They all told him that there were ways to win the support of the people and the most important one was to win over people's hearts. Once one had won over the people's hearts, then one would receive the Mandate of Heaven. Hou I was convinced by their reasoning. He then asked them: "But how can I win over the people's hearts?" The four wise men pointed out to him that the most popular thing to do at the very moment would be to send messengers to pay respects to Prince Chung-k'ang, the fifth son of King Ch'i, who was admired by all lords and chiefs under Heaven. Since Prince Chung-k'ang was still in his mourning period and was not in the country, whoever first sent messengers to invite him back to succeed to the throne would be admired by all. Hou I followed their advice and sent messengers to Chung-k'ang, who later became the next Hsia king (trad. 2159–2147 B.C.).[44]

With all his ambition and active participation in the events of the day, Hou I was never made king, in spite of his rightful course of action. The times changed and people's concept of kingship also changed, the novelist tells his readers. Contrary to what the wise men told Hou I, virtue and ability were no longer the criteria for selecting a king. By Hou I's time, royal blood increasingly became the most important factor in choosing a king. Hou I's story reveals that by his time people already preferred members of the royal house to outsiders as rightful successors to the throne. This is what the novelist called the "natural development of things."

That circumstances change with the times is the theme of Hou I's story, which reminds us of the teaching of Han Fei (ca. 280–238 B.C.), one of the influential Legalists in traditional times. In his famous treatise, "The Five Vermin," Han Fei observes the happenings of his day with the following remark: "It is because benevolence and righteousness served for ancient times, but no longer serve today. So I say that circumstances differ with the age." Since circumstances change according to the times, Han Fei proposed that "ways of dealing with them [should] change with the circumstances,"[45] a slogan that has been since identified with the Legalists' doctrine of change in imperial China.

As kingship became inherited, people turned their attention from the search for a benevolent sovereign to the selection of able ministers, and especially to that of the prime minister. They started to measure a sovereign's merits by his selection of ministers. In other words, a sovereign's ability to rule was judged by his ability to attract and select capable and virtuous men to his government. Consider the story of King T'ang (ca. 1600–ca. 1588 B.C.) as an example. In the novel *Yu Hsia*, there is a story about how the Prince of Shang (later King T'ang, the founder of the Shang dynasty) enlisted the able I Yin as his minister.[46] According to the story, the Prince of Shang sent three messengers successively to pay respect to a wise man named I Yin and to invite him to the Shang court. I Yin declined the prince's invitation the first two times. The third time, the prince planned to visit I Yin (ca. 1652–ca. 1601 B.C.) himself to show his sincerity, but he could not go because he had just received an order from King Chieh of the Hsia (ca. 1625–1601 B.C.) to join the Hsia army for an expedition. The Prince of Shang did not want to take part in King Chieh's expedition and he made an excuse, feigning illness. Although the prince himself did not go to visit I Yin (because of his pretense of illness), he sent a representative to see I Yin and to express his sincere wishes to consult with I Yin. I Yin was moved by the prince's sincerity and accepted his invitation. After seeing I Yin and listening to him, the Prince of Shang was impressed by I Yin's broad learning. From that time on, he treated I Yin as his teacher. With I Yin's help the Prince of Shang eventually consolidated his state and defeated the tyrannical King Chieh of the Hsia.[47]

This story of sending messengers three times to enlist I Yin's service is very much like the famous "Three Visits to the Recluse" of the *San-kuo*, in which Liu Pei pays three visits to Chu-ko Liang.[48] Since the *San-kuo* was published much earlier than the *Yu Hsia* and was much more popular, it seems very likely that the I Yin story was inspired by the Liu Pei and Chu-ko Liang story discussed earlier. Nevertheless, they all testified to the popularity of the ancient belief that a sage-king would do everything to seek the able and virtuous to serve the country.

However, as ability and virtue rarely come together in one person, the principle of honoring the able and virtuous gradually became a halfway political slogan that emphasized only the individual's ability to serve the country. At times this emphasis on an individual's ability even ran counter to conventional values such as loyalty and righteousness. The story of Pai-li Hsi's eventful political career in the novel *Lieh-kuo*, by Yü Shao-yü, is an example of how a Ming novelist used an ancient classical story to challenge contemporary conventional values. Pai-li Hsi (fl. 725–645 B.C.), a well-known historical figure in the Eastern Chou period, was a minister in the marquisate of Yü as the story begins.[49] In the year of 655 B.C., Duke Hsien of the Chin (r. 676–651 B.C.) planned to attack the state of Kuai, a neighboring state of the Yü. He first sent an envoy, Hsun Hsi, to the Yü to ask permission to let the Chin army pass through Yü's territory.[50] In order to obtain a favorable answer, the Chin envoy brought with him valuable presents from Duke Hsien of the Chin to the ruler of the Yü, the Marquis of Yü. The Marquis of Yü, being a greedy and shortsighted person, granted the Chin permission to let their army pass through the domain of the Yü. Kung Chih-ch'i, another minister in the Yü court, protested strongly against the marquis's decision. His reason was true and simple: The Yü and the Kuai were neighboring states and the fall of the Kuai would endanger the Yü. But the Marquis of Yü did not listen to him.

At this time, Pai-li Hsi was also in court, but knowing that whatever he said would not change his lord's mind, he kept silent. Instead, he then went to see Shun Hsi, the Chin envoy. Scolding Shun Hsi's attempt to bribe the Marquis of Yü to do injustice to the Kuai, Pai-li Hsi pointed out to Shun Hsi that he knew for certain that once the Chin army defeated the Kuai, it would attack the Yü. Shun Hsi was greatly surprised that Pai-li Hsi had foreseen his whole scheme. He did not deny it. The following dialogue between the two is most revealing:

> "The Marquis of Yü is a greedy and shortsighted man, that's why he did not listen to good advice. If we [the Chin] do not take your country now, some other country will sooner or later take it. You are an able and farsighted minister, why don't you leave the Yü [and look for an opportunity to serve a better lord]?" Hsun Hsi spoke bluntly. Pai-li Hsi wept and replied: "It is not that I do not know the end of the Yü is near. But I have served the country as a minister when it has been safe; I would not bear the thought of leaving the country when it is in danger. Would you give me some advice as to what I should do?" Hsun Hsi said: "Since you do not have the heart to leave the Yü, and the Marquis of Yü is a man who would not accept [good] adivce, why don't you pretend to be sick and retire from your post? At the fall of the Yü, you can leave the country," Pai-li Hsi thanked Hsun Hsi for his advice, and he immediately resigned from his post with the excuse of poor health.[51]

Shortly afterward, the Chin attacked the Yü as it had conquered the Kuai. At the fall of the Yü both the marquis and Pai-li Hsi were captured by the Chin soldiers. Shun Hsi, who was now the commander in chief of the Chin army, remembered Pai-li Hsi to Duke Hsien of the Chin. But Duke Hsien of the Chin obviously did not regard Pai-li Hsi highly, despite Shun Hsi's recommendation. For a short while afterward Pai-li Hsi was sent to the Ch'in by Duke Hsien as an envoy to accompany the princess of the Chin, who was to be married to the ruler of the Ch'in. Humiliated by this assignment, Pai-li Hsi fled the Ch'in.[52]

When the Earl of Ch'in, who married the Chin Princess, heard that Pai-li Hsi had fled the country, he did nothing. Then one of his generals, Kung-sun Chih, brought the subject to the Earl's attention:

"Pai-li Hsi is known to be a man of unusual wisdom. My lord should send someone after him," Kung-sun Chih said. The Earl of Ch'in smiled and said: "I heard that Hsi was a Yü minister. But the Yü was defeated and the Marquis of Yü died, and he was captured by the Chin and sent to us as an envoy to accompany the Chin princess. I cannot see what talent he possesses." Kung-sun Chih said: "Although Pai-li Hsi served the Marquis of Yü, he was not trusted by the marquis. When the Yü was conquered by the Chin, he was asked to serve the Chin. But the ruler of the Chin still could not recognize his real talent and that's why he was sent to us. This means that it is Heaven's will to have Pai-li Hsi sent to you, my lord. If my lord could really trust Hsi with state affairs, I am sure our country, the Ch'in, could achieve hegemony among all the feudal states." The Earl of Ch'in was still not convinced: "Even if Pai-li Hsi was a master of statecraft, he still was too old. How could he be useful [to us]?" Kung-sun Chih said: "In the past, when the Earl of the West [Hsi-po, that is, the later King Wen of the Chou] found Lü Shang at the bank of the Wei River, Lü was already over eighty years old. But with his help, the Chou dynasty [ca. 1027–256 B.C.] was firmly established, and Lü Shang was enfeoffed as a prince in Ch'i. For a great statesman, old age does not have [an] effect on his performance." Reluctantly, the Earl of Ch'in sent Kung-sun Chih to look for Pai-li Hsi.[53]

Eventually Pai-li Hsi became a minister of the Ch'in and helped to make the Ch'in a strong state, which laid the foundation for its eventual conquest of all feudal states of the Warring States period (403–221 B.C.) and the establishment of the first imperial dynasty of China.

The novel *Lieh-kuo*, was published during the reign of Wan-li (1573–1619) in the Late Ming. Although the basic plot of Pai-li Hsi's story was based on the *Tso-chuan* and the *Shih-chi*, the sentiment and interpretation of the story belong to the Ming novelist. A comparison between the novel and the *Shih-chi* regarding this special story reveals a basic difference: In the *Shih-chi* the historian Ssu-ma Ch'ien records only what happened in a factual way; in the novel, Yü Shao-yü elaborates his story with fictionalized details and actually praises Pai-li Hsi enthusiastically. In the context of Pai-li Hsi's handling of the episode of "the Chin request from the Yü of letting its invading army pass through the

Yü to invade the Kuai," the novelist praises him with the following verse:

> An unusual man indeed had an unusual career. His farsighted views can hardly be perceived by ordinary man. It is not that Pai-li Hsi had no wisdom and conscience, he knew that his lord could not accept advice.[54]

When the novelist praised Pai-li Hsi's career as "unusual," he was thinking of him as a contemporary. In Pai-li Hsi's day, what he did was not "unusual"; it was in Ming times when the values of personal loyalty to one's sovereign became predominant that Pai-li Hsi's pursuance of individual fulfillment stood out as being unusual. In the story, Pai-li Hsi did not advise the Marquis of Yü on the issue of permitting the Chin army to pass through his territory. Pai-li Hsi's justification for not speaking his mind to his lord, as any loyal Confucian minister should, is that he knew from past experiences that he could not change the marquis's mind. This justification seemed realistic because Kung Chih-ch'i, another minister of the Yü, had tried and had failed to change the marquis's mind. But the novelist does not stop there; he goes further to describe how Pai-li Hsi cared more about his own reputation than the fate of his state. The Yü ruler was greedy and shortsighted, so Pai-li Hsi gave up on him. Now he thought of himself; he did not want Hsun Hsi to think he was fooled by the Chin scheme. After listening to Pai-li Hsi, Hsun Hsi was indeed impressed by Hsi's farsightedness. Because of this conversation Hsun Hsi later recommended Pai-li Hsi to Duke Hsien of the Chin. As mentioned previously, during this conversation, Pai-li Hsi asked Hsun Hsi's advice on the coming disaster—that the Chin would attack the Yü in a short time—and he accepted Hsun Hsi's advice for immediate resignation from his post. This action, consulting with the enemy, could be viewed by traditional ethics as an act of treason. In Pai-li Hsi's time, the idea of personal loyalty to one's lord or one's state was not widely accepted; no one could blame him for what he did. However, praising him for his action is different from not blaming him. The novelist's compassion for Pai-li Hsi is obvious when he commented on him with the words: "His farsighted views can hardly be perceived by ordinary men." This compassion becomes more distinguishable when we compare the novel to the original history.

While the history merely tells the facts about Pai-li Hsi, the novel interprets the inner sensitive feelings of the man. About Pai-li Hsi's experiences with the Yü and the Chin, the standard history *Shih-chi* says simply:

On the fifth year, Duke Hsien of the Chin conquered the Yü and the Kuai and captured the ruler of the Yü and his minister Pai-li Hsi, as a result of Chin's bribing the Yü with jade and horses [so that its army could first attack the Kuai by passing through the Yü and conquered the Yü on the way back]. After having captured Pai-li Hsi, Duke Hsien sent [Pai-li Hsi] to the Ch'in to be an escort to accompany the princess of the Chin, bride-to-be of Duke Mu of the Ch'in. Pai-li Hsi then fled the Ch'in and left for Wan.[55]

But this brief record was turned into a long fictionalized account in the novel, which we have just briefly summarized. Significantly, in the last sentence of the *Shih-chi*, "Pai-li Hsi fled the Ch'in and left for Wan." Historian Ssu-ma Ch'ien did not explain why Pai-li Hsi fled the Ch'in, but the novelist did. According to the novel, having learned of his new assignment, Pai-li Hsi expressed his feelings as follows:

Pai-li Hsi sighed to himself: "I have the ability of ordering the world [but do not have the opportunity to do it]. I was a minister of the Yü. The Yü was conquered, and I came to the Chin court. But the Chin still did not use me as an official, and sent me to be an escort to accompany a bride-to-be princess to the Ch'in. I am over seventy years old. All my life I have not had the good fortune to serve a worthy lord to fulfill my noble aspiration of ordering the state and the society. How could I be an escort to a bride in my old age!" On the same night, he fled the city.[56]

According to the novelist, the humiliation of being underestimated and the frustration of not being able to fulfill his lifelong aspiration made Pai-li Hsi flee. This sympathy with one's pursuance of individual fulfillment not only represents the ancient value of honoring the able and the talented, but was also in complete accord with the original pursuance of Confucius and Mencius. (Both masters toured the feudal states in their respective times, looking for a worthy lord to serve.) That is why Mencius also praised Pai-li Hsi when he commented on Pai-li Hsi's career.[57] However, when the Neo-Confucianism was established as the orthodoxy of the state ideology in the Ming period, it lost the vigor and dynamism of the original Confucianism, and the orthodox ethics of "loyal subjects and filial sons" became predominant, as testified by the popular dictum: "A virtuous woman does not marry twice; a loyal subject does not serve two sovereigns."

Clearly, while Pai-li Hsi's story ignores the sovereign-subject relationship between Pai-li Hsi and his prince, the Marquis of Yü, the emphasis is on the importance of the individual's self-fulfillment, not the individual's loyalty to his lord. At times this pursuance of one's career and fulfillment runs counter to one's promises and other obligations, and success at all costs becomes the rule, turning son against father, brother against brother, friend against friend, and so forth. In historical novels there are many stories that center on these conflicts. For example, the novel *Sun P'ang tou-chih yen-i* (Wu-men hsiao-k'o [pseud.]; *Sun P'ang* hereafter), tells stories about two sworn brothers who become bitter enemies because one of them was blinded by ruthless ambition.

In the *Sun P'ang*, both the hero and the villain of the novel, Sun Pin (fl. fourth century B.C.) and P'ang Chüan (fl. fourth cent. B.C.) respectively, are men of talent; they both excel at martial arts and are masters of military strategy. The historical background of the story is the period of Warring States when every ambitious ruler of the sovereign state in the multistate system of the late Chou was struggling constantly for superiority. This was a golden era for those "men of talent" who were sought after everywhere by all ambitious princes and rulers. The basic plot of the novel follows the historical work of *Shih-chi*, but with one notable change: In the *Shih-chi*, Sun Pin was a native of the Ch'i state; in the novel, Sun Pin was from the Yen state.[58] However, both the *Shih-chi* and the novel acknowledge that Sun Pin was an offspring of the famous strategist Sun Wu (fl. 514–496 B.C.), of the Ch'un-chiu Period. The fact that the novelist changes Sun Pin's native land can be interpreted as either a careless mistake or as a deliberate effort to stress a common practice during the Warring States period—one does not have to serve one's own country. In the novel, Sun Pin serves as chief adviser in the Ch'i army instead of his native state of Yen. Sun Pin and P'ang Chüan were sworn brothers who studied military strategy under the strategist Master Kuei Ku on a mountain.[59] P'ang Chüan left the mountain first and became a general in the state of Wei. By the time Sun Pin left Master Kuei Ku's mountain, P'ang was already a power in the Wei court and had married a princess of the Wei.

Knowing in his heart that Sun Pin was much smarter than he, P'ang Chüan plotted against Sun Pin and had him thrown into a Wei prison. In order to disable Sun Pin, P'ang Chüan convinced the king of Wei to order Sun's ten toes cut off. Disabled as he was, Sun Pin managed to make himself known among the ambitious rulers of the larger sovereign states and was sought after by all the other larger states except the Wei. Finally, Sun Pin accepted Ch'i's offer and became the chief adviser in Ch'i's court. In a battle between the state of Wei and the state of Ch'i, Sun Pin defeated and captured P'ang Chüan. Ordering all of P'ang Chüan's toes cut off, Sun Pin then turned P'ang over to P'ang's other enemies, who killed him mercilessly. The novel ends with Sun Pin's retirement from the world following his revenge upon P'ang Chüan.

Popular as it was in traditional times, the novel *Sun P'ang* is a much cruder and more inferior work of fiction compared with other popular historical novels such as the *San-kuo*. Not only does it fall short in literary skill, it is also inferior in its treatment of subject matter. Regardless of its basic plot of history, the overwhelming impression the novel leaves is of a battle of wits between two characters who are masters of magic and military strategy. As the novelist centers his attention on magic and intrigue, the two protagonists become insignificant, and the historical significance of Sun Pin and P'ang Chüan are reduced to the stereotyped hero-versus-villain story line.

Nevertheless, the novel has been popular because it appeals to the simple and unsophisticated tastes of the populace. There are three reasons why it fascinates people. First, Sun Pin was a descendant of the famous military strategist Sun Wu. Second, Sun suffered injustice at the hands of his sworn brother P'ang who ordered, under false pretext, to have Sun's toes cut off. Third, the disabled hero came back to win a great victory and took revenge on his enemy. Note the hero-versus-villain story line that dramatized the evil nature of the villain. Although the *Sun P'ang* novel is an exaggerated example — Sun is all good and P'ang is all bad — the fact remains that almost all historical novels seem to fall into this story line in some way or other. Believing that all villains are evil by nature, the writers as well as their readers of Ming times seemed to share a conviction that all villains are past redemption. In a society in which ethics have always been more important than religion, the ethics that are known for promoting an ethos of self-sacrifice and dedication to the common good adopt a "black and white" dichotomous approach toward passing moral judgment. People are either good or bad, but never in between. One of the chief functions of the historical novels is, according to the novelists, passing these important final moral judgments on historical personages.

To conclude, as ethical values were the cornerstone of the social and political order, moral obligations that were designated to regulate the relations of humanity became the predominant concern of the individual and society. In historical novels this concern is clearly demonstrated by their writers' efforts to redefine or reinterpret the various established ethical values regarding the relationships between the individual and the sovereign, between the individual and the state, and between the individual and the society. The ideas and values examined in this chapter demonstrate the emphases and approaches of these writers. They are the ideas of

loyalty
righteousness
wang (being a true king)
public spirit
individual merit
justice
national security

All these ideas are promoted in the historical novels, and they gave rise to ideals that were goals to be sought, striven for, and realized by action on the part of the individual or on the part of organized society.

Of the ideas mentioned, loyalty generates two ideals in addition to the original "loyalty [to the sovereign] on the part of the minister": they are loyalty to the country and loyalty toward friends. The former lead to the ideal of patriotism and "nationalism"; the latter lead to the ideal of brotherhood and selfless friendship. In the case of righteousness, the emphases are also shifted from the moral principles that govern the relationship between the sovereign and minister to those that govern the relationship between the individual and the society, in other words the relationship among fellow men. Specifically, they mean three things in historical novels: the ideas (and ideals) of reciprocating favors, mutual appreciation, and sworn brotherhood. All three show elements characteristic of popular heroism.

The idea and ideal of *wang* (being a true king) are rooted in the concept of universal benevolence that was conceived as the totality of moral virtues in the Confucian scheme of values. Both *wang* and *wang-tao* (literally the kingly way, or the perfact way of the sage-king), symbolize the highest ideal of a benevolent government, and they figure prominently in historical novels. In chapter 5, "Ideals and Reality: The Despotic Imperial Institution," the ideals of *wang-tao* are discussed in great detail. Here we only discuss the idea of *wang*, referring to the relationship between the sovereign and the state. In the historical novels, the discussion of the role of a king emphasizes the public spirit of the ancient sage-kings, who took it upon themselves to promote the general welfare of the people through their efforts at honoring the good and wise and employing the able in their governments. This public spirit is amplified by the abdication stories of the legendary King Yao and King Shun who abdicated the throne to let the most qualified men take over the government. With these stories the writers of historical novels reinforce the ancient idea that the sovereign's moral obligation is to govern the country well.

The idea of individual merit derived from the principle of honoring the good and wise and employing the able, an ancient ideal of government that was advocated by all major schools of thought except Taoism in the pre-Chin era of ancient China. The original idea was to provide a guideline for the government regarding the recruitment of government service. In historical novels, the idea of individual merit is approached from a different direction. Here the emphasis is on the individual, instead of looking at things from the point of view of the government. From the individual's point of view, the senses of personal value and of self-fulfillment are most important. In their stories about historical personages, the writers of historical novels are very sympathetic to the individual's needs and sentiments. At times, they even went so far as to put the well-being of an individual ahead of the conventional values such as loyalty to one's king.

The idea of justice derives from the concept of *tao*, the Way or the Truth. In historical novels the emphases are twofold: historical justice in the context of making historical judgments and the universal justice in the context of "upholding the justice for Heaven." The former was influenced by the historians' tradition of "Praise and Blame"; the latter was influenced by a very special oral tradition of heroic tales that cherished the qualities of the ideal knight-errant such as honor, bravery, generosity, and protection of the weak.

The idea of national security is closely related to the idea of "a people." A multitude of persons forms a single people when they are united for a common purpose and are willing to cooperate in its pursuit. In the historical novels the common purpose, for which the Chinese people are united, is to defend the country against invading barbaric forces. Historically speaking, the growing sentiment of patriotism or "nationalism" was a result of military conflicts between the Han Chinese and the invading "barbarian" forces during the long period from the Southern Sung through Mongal Yuan to the Ming times. This growing sentiment of nationalism coincided with the militarism that represents the rising force of the popular heroism in the oral tradition of historical tales.

Finally, a closer examination reveals that among the prevailing ethical values presented in the historical novels, something "modern" was burgeoning. The sentiment of nationalism that gave rise to the concept of "a Chinese nation" is very strong, as reflected by the overwhelming popularity of patriotic military heroes, who in their heroic resistance to foreign invasion, lay emphasis on their unswerving loyalty to the country. At the same time, the elements of romanticism, individualism, and plebeianism, which drew attention to the needs and emotions of an individual, gave rise to the concept of "common man." This is reflected in the emphasis the writers put on the popular heroes' feelings and instincts, instead of the rationality and moral beliefs of their Confucian counterparts. Although the subsequent Ming-Ch'ing dynastic change in the second half of the seventeenth century bore witness to the reassertion of supremacy of the Confucian orthodox teaching (and the abatement of such modern ideas and beliefs), the elements of late Ming liberal culture did not fade out completely. They only became subterranean, waiting for the right moment to burgeon again.

Chapter 5

Ideals and Reality: The Despotic Imperial Institution

"How virtuous must a man be before he can become a
true King?" [asked King Hsuan of Ch'i.]
"He becomes a true King by bringing peace and order
to the people. This is something no one can stop."
— *Meng-tzu*

In the political sphere, conceptions of an ideal state have preoccupied
the Chinese mind ever since the classical era. While these conceptions
claimed the undivided attention of the scholarly world in traditional
times, they became a kind of political slogan used to express popular
effusion in the world of vernacular literature. Those cherished dreams,
the longing for sage-kings and benevolent rulers, the yearning for the
return of the lost public spirit exemplified by the sage-kings, and the
waiting for the realization of the grand peace and the great equality,
are in sharp contrast to cruel reality. In historical novels, the most
recurrent themes regarding contradiction between ideals and reality
are ones of political corruption, social and economic injustice, crimes
and violence, and above all, the abuse of imperial power.

We will first examine the dominant ideas. As the orthodox teaching
in Ming times, the Confucian ideal of a benevolent government first
expounded eloquently by Mencius, was read and memorized by every
educated Chinese at that time. Mencius said:

If you [the ruler] honour the good and wise and employ the able so
that outstanding men are in high position, then Gentlemen throughout
the Empire will be only too pleased to serve at your court. In the
marketplace, if goods are exempted when premises are taxed,
and premises exempted when the ground is taxed, then the traders
throughout the Empire will be only too pleased to store their goods in
your marketplace. If there is inspection but no duty at the border
stations, then the travelers throughout the Empire will be only too
pleased to go by way of your roads. If tillers help in the public fields

129

but pay no tax on the land, then farmers throughout the Empire will be only too pleased to till the land in your realm. If you abolish the levy in lieu of corvee and the levy in lieu of the planting of the mulberry, then all the people of the Empire will be only too pleased to come and settle in your state. If you can truly execute these five measures, the people of your neighboring states will look up to you as to their father and mother; and since man came into this world no one has succeeded in inciting children against their parents. In this way, you will have no match in the Empire. He who has no match in the Empire is a Heaven-appointed ruler, and it has never happened that such a man failed to become a true King.[1]

Four items in the above passage are relevant to our discussion. First, the concept of honoring the good and wise and employing the able was the most recurrent theme in political discourse in imperial times. This has already been discussed in previous chapters. Second, the five measures proposed by Mencius represent the Confucian concern for people's livelihood. Although measures discussed by Confucians of later generations varied, concern about people's welfare has always been a dominant theme. In other words, people's happiness, prosperity, and well-being are considered the cornerstone of a benevolent state. Third, in Confucian idealizations, bonds formed within the family are viewed as models for a variety of relationships between the individual and the state. When Mencius proposed that the ruler should take care of his subjects so that they could look up to the sovereign as to their father and mother, Mencius's emphasis was on the sovereign. Be benevolent, he seemed to tell the ruling princes, and that is the only way to be a true king. But when Confucianism was established as the orthodox teaching in imperial times, the emphasis shifted. People then were told that they should respect and obey the ruler as their father and mother, and this political indoctrination reinforced the moral indoctrination of Confucian ethics, which views filial piety as the root of true virtue. In popular fiction and drama, the stereotyped expression *fu-mu kuan* (the father and mother official), which refers to the magistrate in the local district, is significant. Since the magistrate as the head of local government represented the imperial power in the district, the phrase "the father and mother official" speaks well for the indoctrination of Confucian ethics. In historical novels in which the local magistrate never plays any important role, the term "father and mother official" does not often appear. But in other Ming fiction, for example the social and domestic novels and short stories, the presence of the magistrate is commonplace, and so is the use of this popular expression. Fourth, the concept of *wang*, being a true king, is rooted in the concept of universal benevolence that advocates concrete measures to bring material improvements to people's lives. Both *wang* and *wang-tao* (literally the kingly way, or the perfect way of the sage-king), symbolize the highest ideal of a benevolent government, and they figure prominently in historical novels, as will be demonstrated later in this chapter.

The eloquence of Mencius lies in his special touch of optimism. The following statement is a typical example:

> No man is devoid of a heart sensitive to the suffering of others. Such a sensitive heart was possessed by the ancient Sage Kings and this manifested itself in compassionate government. With such a sensitive heart behind compassionate government, it was as easy to rule the Empire as rolling it on your palm.[2]

Mencius's political philosophy was built on a firm conviction that human nature is good. He believed that all men possess the heart that distinguishes man from animals. According to Mencius, there are four incipient tendencies in the heart. These he calls "the heart of compassion," "the heart of shame," "the heart of courtesy and modesty," and "the heart of right and wrong."

> As far as what is genuinely in him is concerned, a man is capable of becoming good.... That is what I mean by good. As for his becoming bad, that is not the fault of his native endowment. The heart of compassion is possessed by all men alike; likewise the heart of shame, the heart of respect, and the heart of right and wrong. The heart of compassion pertains to benevolence, the heart of shame to dutifulness, the heart of respect to the observance of the rites, and the heart of right and wrong to wisdom. Benevolence, dutifulness, observance of the rites, and wisdom are not welded onto me from the outside; they are in me originally. Only this has never dawned on me. That is why it is said, "seek and you will find it; let go and you will lose it."[3]

According to Mencius, a man naturally has these incipient moral tendencies, but they are easily smothered and need a great deal of care and cultivation. The Confucian emphasis on education is based upon this belief that every man is capable of becoming good. And the goal of education is to bring out all the goodness inside oneself.

In the political sphere, Confucianism as the state orthodoxy provided support for the imperial political order. The emperor, as the
supreme ruler of this political order, was, according to the orthodox
teaching, automatically regarded as a sage, one who is divinely good
and intuitively wise, and therefore an infallible exponent of right
and wrong in human affairs. In Official Histories, as well as in all
official documents and writings, whenever the emperor is referred to
or addressed, the word *sheng* (sage, holy, holiness) is added: *Sheng-
shang*, *Sheng-chün*, and *Sheng-chu* all refer to the emperor, the holy
man; *Sheng-yü*, an imperial edict; *Sheng-ts'ai*, imperial decision;
Sheng-en, imperial clemency; *Sheng-chih*, the imperial decree; *Sheng-
ch'ao*, the present dynasty, the emperor. But in historical novels,
the image of the emperor is very different; here the official image of
a divine sage is overshadowed by the common images of *pao-chün*
(tyrannical ruler) or *hun-chün* (muddleheaded ruler). The contrast
between the ideal and reality was indeed tremendous.

Historically speaking, the Ming regime is one of the most despotic
regimes in Chinese history. The unprecedented concentration of power
in the hands of the emperor started with the founder of the dynasty,
Chu Yuan-chang, who put his prime minister, Hu Wei-yung, to death
in 1380 and abolished the office Hu held known as the *Chung-shu
sheng* (Central Secretariat). With this highest level of bureaucratic
administration abolished, the second level, that of the Six Ministries,
became directly responsible to the throne, and the emperor became his
own chief of administration as well as the sole source of administrative
authority. At the same time, the chief military office, the *Ta-tu-t'u fu*,
analogous to a general staff, was divided into five separate offices and
commanders were deprived of their military commands until specially
appointed by the throne through the civilian Ministry of War in time of
need. Finally, in this reorganization of administrative functions, the
Censorate was reorganized in the period 1380−82, giving it both greater
supervisory and censorial powers than it had ever possessed in the
past, and making it directly accountable to the throne, separate from
all other administrative channels. Thus, the Ming despotic government
placed the emperor as sole superior coordinator directly in control of
all governmental affairs.[4] The effective functioning of such government
depends upon the strong character and good ability of its rulers.
Unfortunately, in the whole history of the Ming dynasty, most emperors failed to meet this requirement.

In addition to the highly centralized system exalting the position of the emperor, there are other creations of Chu Yuan-chang's that characterized the Ming regime as a reign of terror. These means of exercising tyranny and terror included institutions for maintaining the gulf between the ruler and his bureaucracy; consciously applied terror for the purpose of intimidating the unreliable but indispensable scholar-official class; unspeakably cruel punishments and institution- alized humiliation of officials intended to keep them conscious of their insecurity; secret-service agencies beyond the reach of the law and answerable only to the throne; and a literary inquisition through which unsuspecting persons were made the object of the emperor's unpredictable wrath. Among all the vicious institutions of Chu's creation, two stand out as the most notorious features of the Ming government. First was the so-called *t'ing-chang* (beatings at court), administered by eunuchs with heavy clubs, in the presence of the court, to any official who incurred the emperor's displeasure. In later reigns these *t'ing-chang* were a chief means by which the eunuchs came to intimidate officialdom. Second was the so-called *chin-i-wei* (literally, brocaded uniform garrison), the imperial bodyguard in name, but in fact, a secret police organization that had the power to arrest a person, to incarcerate him for any length of time, and to inflict torture on him in order to prepare a case against him.[5]

The inherent despotic institutions changed from bad to worse in the waning years of the Ming empire. While the late Ming was a time of increasing economic prosperity, as mentioned earlier, it was also a time of symptoms of many kinds of social decline. One unmistakable sign of disintegration lay in the frequencies of rebellions recorded in local histories. The causes for rebellions were, more often than not, connected with famine that generally followed some kind of natural disaster such as flood or drought. The impoverishment of the rural countryside was caused by exploitation by the imperial household and landed proprietors, through the Ming phenomenon land annexation. The countryside seemed like a time bomb, ready to explode any time when natural disasters struck. Economic affluence was concentrated in urban centers only, while in the countryside the mass of people were in a state of daily struggle for survival. Although the social and economic grievances of the people were never addressed directly in historical novels, the degree of violence described in great details in the novels seems to reveal the intensity of the wrath of the people.

Another unmistakable sign of decline was the notorious eunuch rule that started to plague the Ming regime after its first century of efficient rule. The apogee of eunuch power was reached during the reign of Hsi-tsung (1621–27). What made eunuch rule particularly objectionable was that whenever it occurred, it was accompanied by nepotism and corruption. As often happened in history, whenever there was the eunuchs' clique, there were oppositions formed by antieunuch Confucian scholars. In the late Ming the most famous clique was called Tung-lin (named after an academy at Wu-hsi, Kiangsu). Their heroic struggles against the eunuch stirred up strong public opinions and thus helped to generate people's interest in the actions of government as well as people's awareness of these problems and their possible solutions.

In the vernacular fiction and drama of the late Ming, this interest in the affairs of the state is noticeable, as evidenced by a surge of interest in historical subjects. Since historical personages and past events are inextricably related to politics, the fact that both the writer and the playwright took an interest in historical subjects reflected their interest in politics. Furthermore, the spread of political consciousness fostered a critical attitude toward the government in general. In historical novels, this critical attitude is reflected in the various themes on which the novelists elaborated. The social evils, the political corruptions, the economic grievances — they are all explored by the writers of historical novels.

While the writers' opinions and concerns were "contemporary," the source materials they used were not. As pointed out before, most of the historical novels are based on some antecedent literary works that were composed by other writers and oral artists through a long period of evolutionary development. Thus many motifs and formulae from earlier oral traditions are preserved in these novels. Through these motifs and formulae the emotions and sentiments of the "unlettered but unaffected" common people make their impact.

With this sketch of background information, we now turn our attention to the major political themes in historical novels. First, consider the theme of corruption in the imperial government. A good example is the novel *Shui-hu*, which forcefully elaborates official injustice, on the one hand, and describes, on the other, the wrath of the oppressed as shown by a common hatred of the corrupt officials among outlaw-heroes who, at times, exhibited an outburst of uncontrolled violence. The novel deals with the corruption theme right from the beginning. After the prologue in which Commander Hung, in heedlessness, set free the spirits of the thirty-six stars of Heaven and seventy-two stars of Earth (altogether referring to the 108 bandit-heroes of the novel), the arch villain of the novel, Kao Ch'iu, is introduced.[6] This sets the tone of the novel. The rise of Kao Ch'iu reveals the essence of political corruption in imperial China. Kao Ch'iu, nicknamed Kao the Ball Kicker, was an idle, noisy, bragging, good-for-nothing fellow. He was hired by Prince Tuan because he could kick the ball (a ball filled with feathers that is kicked by the players) very skillfully. Once hired, he won the Prince's trust because he knew how to please his master. When Prince Tuan became emperor (Hui-tsung, r. 1101–25), Kao Ch'iu gained quick promotion as well. He was appointed Grand Commandant of the Imperial (Capital) Guard. The first thing he did then was to avenge himself upon an instructor of the Imperial Guard, Wang Ching, whose father, the former instructor, had once hurt Kao Ch'iu during a martial arts contest. This was the beginning of Kao Ch'iu's abuse of power, and it indicates that he was an evil man. Wang Ching's story is only the prologue to that of Lin Ch'ung, a major hero of the *Shui-hu*, who is also a victim in the hands of Kao Ch'iu.

Lin Ch'ung was an Instructor of the Imperial Guard who was relentlessly hounded by Kao Ch'iu. This time the story started with Kao Ch'iu's son, who desired Lin Ch'ung's beautiful wife. The young man fell sick because of his unfulfilled desire. Kao Ch'iu decided to do everything to see Lin Ch'ung dead so that his son could have Lin Ch'ung's wife. Lin Ch'ung suffered endless persecution and several narrow escapes from death, and finally was forced to flee to Liang Mountain to join the band of bandits. The stories about Lin Ch'ung are among the best and most detailed episodes in the novel. Set in the early part of the novel, in chapters 7 through 12, they create a strong impression of official injustice, thus making corruption a dominant theme of the novel.[7]

Besides being victims of official persecution, there are other desperate circumstances that force people to break the law. Lu Chih-shen's and Sung Chiang's stories are two examples. The story of how Lu Chih-shen killed the bully of Kuan-hsi (in modern Shensi), Cheng the Butcher, emphasizes the familiar image of a chivalrous hero who helps the poor and the weak to attack the rich and the powerful.[8] Lu

Chih-shen did not kill Cheng the Butcher intentionally; he only wanted to teach Cheng a lesson because Cheng took advantage of a poor old man named Chin and his helpless young daughter. Lu Chih-shen took the law into his own hands because the law did not protect the poor and the weak against the rich and the powerful. In his rage, he killed the rich butcher accidentally. In a similar accident, Sung Chiang killed his unfaithful mistress Yen P'o-hsi, who blackmailed him.[9] Yen P'o-hsi made Sung Chiang very angry, threatening to reveal Sung Chiang's friendship with Liang-shan outlaws, and he lost his temper and accidentally killed her.

Both Sung Chiang's and Lu Chih-shen's stories reveal more about the social and economic grievances of their time than of official wrongdoings. In Sung Chiang's case, his mistress Yen P'o-hsi was a victim of poverty. Her father was a poor singer whose sudden death left the mother and daughter with nothing. Sung Chiang took pity on them and took care of them. In return, Yen P'o-hsi was given by her mother to Sung Chiang as his mistress. They got along for a while until Yen P'o-hsi found a new lover; then everything fell apart. Finally, in a rage of anger, Sung Chiang killed her. In Lu Chih-shen's story, it was chivalry that led him to take the trouble to help the poor Old Man Chin and his daughter, who were exploited by the rich man Cheng the Butcher. Cheng first took an interest in the girl and coerced the old man into selling her as a concubine for *san-ch'ien kuan* (three thousand *kuan*; 1 *kuan* equates 1000-cash). He fabricated the contract for sale without really paying the old man any money. After taking the girl as a concubine for about three months, his wife found out. She got mad and threw the girl out, and the poor girl went back to her father. But that was not the end of their misfortune. Having uncovered the sale contract, Cheng's wife insisted on having the three thousand *kuan* back, ignoring the fact that Cheng had never fulfilled his contract duty to pay the money to Old Man Chin in the first place. Poor and obscure, Old Man Chin and his daughter could not fight the rich butcher and his wife, so they went to a tavern every day where the girl sang and the father collected money. Yet all the money they earned went to the butcher and his wife. For these poor people, three thousand *kuan* was a tremendous amount. Feeling that they still had a long way to go to pay the bully the money they did not owe, both father and daughter could not help sobbing. This sobbing scene in the tavern led Lu Chih-shen to meet them and learn their story.

In both Sung Chiang's and Lu Chih-shen's stories, the miserable life of the poor is shown, although the novelist's emphasis is on the chivalry of his heroes. Compared with the poor, the rich lived in a completely different world. In chapter 16, we have the story of how Governor Liang spent one hundred thousand *kuan* of cash in preparing a birthday gift for his father-in-law.[10] This great contrast between the poor and the rich reveals the tremendous social and economic grievances of the time: Old Man Chin sold his daughter for three thousand *kuan* of cash while Governor Liang spent one hundred thousand *kuan* of cash on gifts for only one birthday.

Connected with these social and economic grievances is another popular expression, *Shu-ts'ai chang-i* or *Chang-i shu-ts'ai* (to give generously and show devotion to justice), which is used to describe an underworld hero in the *Shui-hu*. The best example is Sung Chiang, whose nickname of "Chi-shih yü" (the Opportune Rain) is an attribute of his generosity. Looking lightly on money, Sung Chiang always helps those in need and thus earns a great reputation in the community of "popular heroes." We will again consider him and Li K'uei as examples. When he first met Li K'uei, he heard that Li K'uei needed ten ounces of silver, which he gave without hesitation. His generosity immediately won over Li K'uei's heart:

> When Li K'uei had this silver he thought to himself, "It is not often that I meet such a one as Elder Brother Sung Chiang. He never met me before, but he lends me ten ounces of silver! He is truly generous and he certainly deserves his reputation for righteousness and generosity."[11]

Thus, when Li K'uei first met Sung Chiang, his first impression was the expression, *chang-i shu-ts'ai*. Again, in chapter 15, when Wu Yung exhorted the three Yuan brothers to join the robber band headed by Ch'ao Kai, he told them that Ch'ao Kai was a man of *Chang-i shu-ts'ai*.[12] Obviously the virtue of generosity represents the basic criterion of a real hero and is the magnet that attracted the heroes to each other. We will consider still another example to stress this point. When Lu Chih-shen first met Shih Chin and Li Chung (chap. 3), he was impressed with Shih Chin's generosity and disgusted at Li Chung's stinginess. The following scene describes Lu's character quite well. It took place in the tavern where Lu and his two new acquaintances met the old man Chin and his daughter. After the old man had told them his story, Lu immediately decided to help him out.

> Then he [Lu Chih-shen] said, "Old fellow, come here! I will give you some money for travel. Tomorrow go back to the Eastern Capital — how is that?"... Then he felt on his person and brought out five ounces and more of silver and put it on the table, and he looked at Shih Chin and said, "I have not brought much silver with me today. Do you have any to lend me? I will repay you tomorrow." Shih Chin said, "What small matter is this that I should seek repayment!" From his bundle he took out a ten-ounce piece of silver and put it on the table and Lu Ta [Lu Chih-shen] looked at it and then at Li Chung and he said, "You lend a little to me, too!" Then Li Chung took out from his girdle something over two ounces of silver. When Lu Ta saw it he thought it too little and he said to himself, "What a stingy fellow too!" He gave fifteen ounces of the silver to the old man and he commanded him, saying, "You two, father and daughter, take this for your travel expenses...." Old Man Chin and his daughter knocked their heads on the ground before him and thanked him. Lu Ta then took the two ounces of silver and threw it back to Li Chung.[13]

Lu Chih-shen threw the two ounces of silver back to Li Chung because he thought the latter was stingy. And this impulsive gesture spoke well of Lu Chih-shen. He was, by instinct, a "good fellow" (*hao-han*) of *chang-i shu-ts'ai* and could not stand any sign of stinginess.

To take a close look at the novel *Shui-hu*, the term *chang-i* (literally, to enforce justice) always connects with *shu-ts'ai* (to give money away generously). This means that the popular concept of *i* has something to do with the spirit of free spending and generosity. In a poverty-stricken society in which the mass of people were in a state of daily struggle for survival, the heroes who gave away money generously were worshiped as gods. Ostensibly, all the heroes could easily be "bought" by money; Li K'uei received only ten ounces of silver from Sung Chiang, and his heart belonged to Sung Chiang immediately. But money is not the only thing that counts. To those simple and rugged fellows, money was only a symbol. When Sung Chiang lent Li K'uei the money at their first meeting, he also conveyed a warm feeling of trust to Li K'uei. This trust is important among the rugged heroes; it is what most of them have yearned for all their lives. The characteristic of this yearning is best expressed by the Yuan brother (in *Shui-hu*, chap. 15) who declared: "We will sell this hot blood of ours to the man who appreciates its worth."[14]

Although the yearning to be appreciated is typical of heroes, the fact remains that money (or its equivalent, such as jewels and other valuables) did play a decisive role. It is not only the reputation of Ch'ao Kai, but also the one hundred thousand *kuan* of cash worth of birthday gifts that attracted the above-mentioned Yuan brothers to join the band of bandits. One modern scholar, Professor Sa Meng-wu, once suggested that the original moral principle of the band of bandits at Liang Mountain was very practical and simple: to reciprocate favors to friends and to take revenge on enemies.[15] This popular principle of righteousness, which had been carried out in terms of materialistic reciprocation, was different from the Confucian moral principle introduced to the Liang-shan band by Sung Chiang.[16] This materialistic reciprocation reflected the general attitude of the mass of people, who tended to connect the idea of enforcing justice with the idea of distributing wealth. Thus the expression *chang-i shu-ts'ai* did, to a certain degree, reveal the general social and economic grievances of the time.

While the social, economic, and political grievances of the people are exposed in the novel *Shui-hu*, this does not mean that the author advocated wholeheartedly the principle of the people's right to revolt against corrupt government. In the latter part of the novel, the dominant theme is the outlaws' wish to be granted amnesty. The tragedy of these bandit-heroes lay in their dilemma. On one hand, they were rebels who protested a corrupt government. They upheld the flag: *t'i-T'ien hsing-Tao* (uphold justice for Heaven). They felt that they were justified in revolting against evil officials. On the other hand, these bandit-heroes resented the very act of rebellion and wished that they could be granted amnesty, so that they could return to being law-abiding citizens again. This attitude is represented by their leaders, Sung Chiang and Lu Chün-i, who were brought up in the tradition of Confucian ethics that emphasized the five cardinal human relationships, especially the one between rulers and subjects. Their dilemma — the right to revolt and the wish to be granted amnesty — eventually led the bandits to tragedy. At the end of the novel, they were all suppressed and their leaders were killed by court officials.

Another notable aspect of the *Shui-hu* is its accounts of violence. The general impression one gathers from the novel is of its heroes' simple heroism, stressing such qualities as generosity, chivalry, excellence in martial arts, and abstinence. However, one cannot help sensing a smug, primitive masculine grandeur in the description of the heroes' physical encounters with their enemies. There are some calculated acts of cannibalism and impetuous massacres in the novel that actually smack of sensationalism. For example, in chapter 31, Wu Sung is described as an indiscriminate killer who, in his passion for vengeance, killed fourteen or fifteen people, of whom only three were his enemies and the rest all innocent bystanders.[17] The fact that the novelist gives the massacre scene his most vivid and detailed effort shows his talent for realistic imagination and also reveals his unconscious appeal to sensationalism. This appeal to sensationalism is repeated so many times in the novel that it sometimes appears to reach a degree of sadism, such as the scenes of Li K'uei's executing Huang Wen-ping (chap. 41) and Yang Hsiung's lynching of his wife, P'an Ch'iao-yun (chap. 46).[18] In both scenes the victims were tortured to death with extreme cruelty. Again, in chapter 50, after the village of Hu had paid its allegiance to the Liang-shan band, Li K'uei, in his exuberant mood of killing, killed the whole house of the Hu, leaving no one alive.[19]

For a careful and conscientious reader the fact of many ruthless and senseless killings in the novel is disturbing.[20] Although tortures and murders are also commonplace in the Official Histories, the perpetrators of such sadism are nearly always implicitly condemned. But in the novel *Shui-hu*, the story is different. Since the novelist unambiguously sides with the heroes in all their actions, without realizing it he gives his readers the impression of his approval of these killings and violence. Exactly because of this endorsement of savagery and sadism, some critics of *Shui-hu* (for example the famous commentator Chin Sheng-t'an) view it as a dangerous book for the general reader, especially younger people. For a student of history, this endorsement of gang morality and atrocity reflects the wrath of people who felt so helplessly trapped by the social, economic, and political injustices of their time that they welcomed any form of protest, and actually helped to make the bandit legends grow.

Significantly, although the corruption theme is one of the dominant keynotes in the novel *Shui-hu*, the novelist never tackled it in depth. The four arch villains of the novel, Kao Ch'iu, Ts'ai Ching, T'ung Kuan, and Yang Chien, who symbolized corruption and weakness in national life, are such stereotyped evil officials that we cannot tell one's wrongdoing from the other's. Such treatment of corrupt officials is typical in traditional fiction and drama, especially in historical novels and plays. In almost every historical play and novel, the villains can be named. Ts'ao Ts'ao and his associates in all *San-kuo* stories, Ch'in Kuei and his associates in all Yueh Fei stories, P'an Jen-mei and his associates in all the *Yang chia-chiang* stories, are some of the famous ones. Coming into consideration here is the "heroes versus villains" formula that views history as a perpetual struggle between evil-minded villains and upright heroes. This formula also illustrates the basic simple nature of popular tales; for in all historical novels, there is a distinctive black-and-white, dichotomized value scheme that is characteristic of folk legends.

While the "heroes versus villains" formula was adopted by all historical novels, the treatment of heroes was different from that of villains. In dealing with heroes, the novelists used the method of supplying incidents to illustrate the characters. Consequently, there are many moving stories about the heroic deeds of these colorful heroes. In the last two chapters, we have discussed in great detail the various categories of heroes in historical novels, such as the dynastic contenders, the imperial advisers, the warriors, the Confucian statesmen, the patriotic generals, and the chivalrous heroes of the underworld. In the case of the villains, since their role is a supporting role — they represent the counterpart of heroes — they were categorically denounced by the novelists and were painted as totally negative so that the virtues of the heroes could stand out clearly. As a result, the villains are generally less interesting and more stereotyped. Nevertheless, they also fall into some loose categories, such as corrupt officials, deceitful ministers, powerful generals, transgressive eunuchs, licentious women, and bad emperors. Each category was in some way connected with the abuse of power under the Ming despotic political system. As we continue our discussion on corruption and related themes, these roles will become apparent.

Returning to the central issue dealing with government corruption, the roots were in the imperial institution. In almost every historical novel the abuse of imperial power (in various degrees) is shown. When the emperor was strong, the abuse of power came directly from the emperor himself; when the emperor was weak, the abuse came from those pretenders who used the name of the emperor to satisfy their own selfish desires. In the novels dealing with the histories of the Ming empire, the most familiar pretenders are the notorious eunuchs. Take, for example, Feng Meng-lung's novel *Wang Yang-ming ch'u-shen chin-luan lu* (*Wang Yang-ming* hereafter).

In this novel, the hero is the well-known philosopher Wang Shou-jen (styled Yang-ming), the founder of the school of Yang-ming thought. The central theme of this novel is the retelling of Wang Yang-ming's brilliant career in government service. Two critical events highlighted Wang's turbulent political career and both reveal the vulnerability of the imperial system under the dominance of the imperial favorites, especially the eunuchs. In 1506, the reigning emperor, Wu-tsung (r. 1506−21), was only fifteen years old, and the empire fell into a situation in which the eunuch Liu Chin dominated the government. A supervising censor in Nanking, Tai Hsien led a group in a joint memorial criticizing the powerful eunuch. Liu Chin was angry and had them thrown into prison. Wang, who was then secretary of a bureau in the Ministry of War, immediately presented a memorial in their defense. As a result, he was imprisoned and after suffering a beating of forty strokes (in the court), was banished to northwestern Kweichow to become head of the Lung-ch'ang dispatch station.[21] Thus, at the age of thirty-four, Wang became known as a courageous Confucian official who was not intimidated by the powerful and who dared to protest an unjust decision.

The second critical event happened in 1519 after Wang had suppressed the revolt of Prince Ning (Chu Ch'en-hao, d. 1521). Having captured the rebellious prince, he encountered difficulties with the imperial court. At that time, Emperor Wu-tsung, who styled himself as the Generalissmo, was leading an imperial expedition to the south on the pretext that the remaining rebels had to be eliminated. Actually, the emperor (who was instigated by his favorites) undertook the expedition with the hope that he and his coterie might claim credit for the victory and handle the rebellious prince themselves. Reporting earlier on the rebellion, Wang had advised the emperor not to leave the capital. Now he dispatched a special memorial urging the emperor to halt his expedition, but he failed. The expedition was charged to several imperial favorites: Hsu T'ai as the Vice General, Chang Chung (a eunuch) as the Superintendent of Military Affairs, and Liu Hui as the Left Commissioner-in-Chief. Upon receiving news of Wang's victory, they sent a messenger to Wang and urged him to deliver Prince Ning to them. Wang refused to obey this order and became their enemy. They slandered Wang before the emperor, accusing him of having originally plotted rebellion with Prince Ning. It was only with the help and protection of another influential eunuch, Chang Yung, that they did not succeed in ruining Wang. Chang Yung, who in earlier times was instrumental in getting rid of the evil eunuch Liu Chin, thus winning Wang's respect, was able to persuade Wang to turn the prisoner over to him and give, in a new report, Hsu Tai, Chang Chung, and others full credit for the victory. This ended the crisis for Wang, who was then made governor of Kiangsi.[22]

In retelling Wang's stories, the novel disputes the accusations that Wang originally had some understanding with Prince Ning and fought him only after he had concluded that the latter would fail or because imperial armies were on the way. These accusations were made by Wang's enemies, according to the novel. Later when the Official History was composed (in early Ch'ing), Wang was cleared of blame: Wang's official biography states clearly that these accusations were made by Wang's enemies. While the Official History tells of Wang's suppression of the revolt in a few paragraphs, the novel elaborates and gives a long fictional account, allowing Wang full credit for the victory. Both history and the novel, however, report the fact that, although Wang was not made a victim of malicious slanders, his student, Chi Yuan-heng (d. 1521), was. According to both the Standard History and the novel, Wang had been in contact with Prince Ning prior to his revolt in the summer of 1519. He received Liu Yang-cheng, the prince's aide, who ostensibly came to invite Wang to lecture. Instead of accepting the invitation, Wang sent his student, Chi Yuan-heng, to the prince to dissuade him from rebelling. Because of this connection Chi was accused of plotting rebellion with Prince Ning. In spite of Wang's repeated pleas, Chi was thrown into prison together with his wife and two daughters. It was not until 1521, when Emperor Wu-tsung died and Chu Hou-ts'ung, a fourteen-year-old boy, ascended the throne, that Chi was given a new trial and acquitted. Five days after Chi's release, he died.[23]

These stories about Wang reveal two unstable factors in the imperial government: the emperor and the eunuch. The dominance of the eunuch in the imperial court is self-evident; even Wang made concessions to this. As to the emperor, the problem of a young emperor who ascended the throne at a tender age is also self-evident. In this instance it was inevitable that the imperial power was abused. Consider Emperor Shen-tsung (r. 1573–1619) as an example. He was only nine years old when he ascended the throne and was overwhelmed by the immense responsibilities. Even with good intentions and an excellent education, as a recent study shows, Emperor Shen-tsung did not stand much of a chance of being a good ruler under the existing institution.[24] In fact, the job was so complicated and demanding that only those born with the extraordinary qualities of a strong leader and shrewd administrator could become an outstanding emperor. The long history of imperial China attests this finding; there were indeed very few outstanding emperors.

Another example of novels dealing with the histories of the Ming empire is *Yü Shao-pao ts'ui-chung ch'üan-chuan* (*Yü Shao-pao* here-after), which deals with Yü Ch'ien's life. Yü Ch'ien was a statesman and a military man in the reign of Emperor Ying-tsung (r. 1436−49). In the summer of 1449 when the emperor who fell under the malign influence of the eunuch Wang Chen set out on his ill-fated campaign against the invading Mongols, Yü was Vice Minister of War and acting head of the Ministry. When the news of the capture of Emperor Ying-tsung by the Oirats arrived at the capital, there was a panic among the officials in the imperial court. Yü, according to both the Official History and the novel, is said to have played a decisive role in the plan to proclaim the regent as the new emperor, in order to stabilize the critical situation as well as to deprive the Oirat leader, Esen, of the prestige of keeping a Chinese emperor as his prisoner.[25] With the installation of a new ruler, the imperial captive lost his former value, and Esen was no longer in a position to exploit his prisoner as a means of political pressure on China.

Because Yü believed that it was in the best interest of the country to keep the imperial government stable under a new emperor (Tai-tsung, r. 1450−56), he refuted the plan that risked everything in order to recover Emperor Ying-tsung. Consequently, upon the restoration of the latter (in 1457), Yü was at once arrested and indicted for high treason. On February 16, 1457, he was publicly executed. The ex-tremely unjust penalty Yü Ch'ien suffered reveals the basic nature of political despotism in imperial China. Like the tragedy of Yueh Fei, it again raises the same profound question: What could an upright official do when the imperial power was abused? The answer is absolutely nothing. There was absolutely nothing anyone could do when the emperor, who held absolute power of life and death over his subjects, wanted to abuse his authority. Since the throne represented absolute power, it became the center of constant power struggles. Since power tends to corrupt, the imperial power was constantly in danger of being abused.[26]

The Confucian theory of the Mandate of Heaven for benevolent rulers was intended to check this despotism and, as mentioned before, was based upon the ancient doctrine of the Mandate of Heaven. According to this theory, a prince, in addition to holding princely status and privileges, must also fulfill the various obligations entailed by his princely status, such as caring for the welfare of his people. Failing to do this, a prince (or ruler) would lose the Mandate of Heaven and disqualify himself as a prince. Upon this theoretical basis, founders of both the Shang and Chou dynasties justified their revolts against tyrannical feudal lords. This is Mencius's theory of the people's right to revolt against a tyrannical prince.[27]

However, this Confucian theory of the Mandate of Heaven for benevolent rulers rested entirely on moral sanctions that were not effective in imperial China. Instead of checking the imperial power, it actually enhanced the inherent despotism of the system by backing up the emperor with a divine mandate. Nevertheless, the ideal of benevolent rulers had been deeply rooted in the Chinese mind since the late second century B.C. through the established orthodoxy of Confucian education. Connected with this ideal of benevolent ruler or sage-king is the concept of the perfect Way of the sage-kings mentioned before. In the historical novels, the ideals of a benevolent ruler and the perfect Way of the sage-kings are also very visible.

Consider the historical novel *Ying-lieh chuan* as an example. When the emperor-aspirant Chu Yuan-chang visited Hsu Ta (1329—83), a man recommended for his mastery over Confucian statecraft and military strategy, he asked Hsu Ta for the best course to follow if he wished to unify the country and bring peace to the world. Hsu Ta smiled and said:

> It is virtue, not military might that unifies the country and brings peace to the world. If you would foresake ruthless killing and adopt benevolence and virtue as your guidance, you will succeed in bringing peace to the world.[28]

Hsu Ta was, no doubt, elaborating Mencius's theory of *wang-tai*. Later, when he was asked about which military strategy should be used, he evaded the details of strategy but continued to stress the same general principle:

> A good victory is won by bravery; a better victory is won by wisdom; but the best victory is won by benevolence. These three things, benevolence, wisdom, and bravery, are the essentials for a military general.[29]

By casting Hsu Ta as a noble and humane general, the novelist's attempt to create an idealized Confucian general is self-evident. This idealized Confucian general is a familiar image of military hero in historical novels.

In another historical novel, the *Nan-Sung*, the Confucian general Ts'ao Pin's story is a further good example. Ts'ao Pin (930–99) was a grand marshal of the Sung founding emperor, T'ai-tsu (r. 960–76). When Ts'ao Pin's southward-bound expedition army approached the capital of southern T'ang (937–75) at Nanking (in 975), its ruler, Li Yü (937–75), consulted with his advisers and decided to surrender. Li Yü then ordered a white flag to be raised on the city wall. The news of Li Yü's gesture of surrender reached Ts'ao Pin. Suddenly Ts-ao Pin announced that he was not feeling well and could not attend his daily meeting with his field marshals. All the field marshals came to inquire after his health. Ts'ao Pin then told them: "My illness could not be cured by medicine. The only thing that would cure me is that there will be no killing when our army enters into the city." All the generals answered at once: "If you, commander-in-chief, so desire, we all will obey." So they all burned incense and pledged themselves to abide by their promise of no killing. The next day Ts'ao Pin ordered all field marshals to lead their troops into the city. And the novelist concluded the story as follows: "So the Sung army entered the city peacefully without a single killing or looting. The people of the city were all pleased."[30] This episode tells of Ts'ao Pin's shining image as a true Confucian general who believed in the basic principle of benevolence. But the fact that he had to pretend he was ill to impress upon his subordinates his desire not to kill innocent people testifies to the common practice of massacre and looting that accompanied the victorious troops who marched into fallen cities.

This Confucian ideal of benevolence was in contrast to the cruel reality in many historical novels. We will take the *San-kuo* as an example. In chapter 8, there is a passage describing the wanton cruelties of Tung Cho (d. A.D. 192), the powerful general of the Han court:

> One day, [Tung] Cho was leaving [the city Ch'ang-an] through the Gate Heng. All the officials of the court came to Gate Heng to see him off. Cho spread a great feast for all those assembled to see him off. While the party was in progress there arrived a large number of malcontents from the north who had voluntarily surrendered. Cho had them brought before him as he sat at a table [and meted out to them wanton cruelties]. The hands of this one were lopped off, the feet of that; one had his eyes gouged out; another lost his tongue. Some were boiled to death. Shrieks of agony arose to the very heavens and the courtiers were faint with terror, but Cho ate and drank, chatted and smiled as if nothing was going on.[31]

The insanity of persecution that was displayed by Tung Cho in his torture of prisoners of war who "had voluntarily surrendered" testifies to the horror people suffered under the lawless autocratic regime. Prisoners of war were not the only victims of senseless killings. Sometimes the whole population of a district was under the threat of senseless massacre. For example, in chapter 10 of the *San-kuo*, there is the episode describing Ts'ao Ts'ao's wrath over his father's murder near Hsu-chou and how he swore to sweep Hsu-chou "off the face of the earth." When his friend Ch'en Kung reminded him that the people of Hsu-chou were innocent of crime and to slay them would be very wrong, Ts'ao would not listen. Instead, he marched his army of revenge toward Hsu-chou, laying waste wherever he passed and desecrating cemeteries.[32] Again, in chapter 13, we find a similar description of the armies of Li Ts'ui and Kuo Ssu: "Wherever they went they left destruction behind them."[33]

The episodes mentioned above are only samples of the cruelties described in historical novels. They reveal the great discrepancy between the ideal Confucian benevolent government and the actual practice of the day. Although the novelists denounce these crimes and cruelties, they hardly touch the root of these evils. The fact that power corrupts was the root of all these outrageous behaviors. Instead of asking how to check the corrupted power, the novelists generally seemed to be satisfied with the simple conclusion that these crimes and cruelties were committed by evil men. This attitude is especially apparent in the general treatment of bad emperors in historical novels.

Using virtue and ability as criteria, there are at least four categories of emperors in traditional China: the able and benevolent; the able but tyrannical; the benevolent but incompetent; and the tyrannical and incompetent. However, in historical novels, there seem to be only two kinds: the virtuous and the virtueless. The former measure up to the Confucian ideal of *hsiu-te ch'in-cheng* (cultivating virtue and laboring with diligence over administration of the government); these are the good emperors. The latter neglect both moral cultivation and the administration of government; these are the bad emperors.

The archetypal bad emperors in history were King Chieh of the Hsia dynasty and King Chou of the Shang dynasty, who were often singled out in Confucian classics as examples of tyrants. Since both were the last rulers of their respective dynasties, the image of the last ruler of a dynasty became that of a tyrant. In historical novels, this tyrannical last-ruler image of Chieh and Chou was greatly exaggerated, fictionalized, and eventually, stereotyped. They became models of bad emperors, incorporating all the vices of an evil ruler. The best example is in the novel *Feng-shen*, which describes King Chou as a man lacking in personal virtues, who was so licentious and self-indulgent that he neglected all his obligations, such as attending to government business and taking care of the welfare of the people. To make things worse, King Chou was bewitched by the beautiful but evil Tan Chi, who corrupted his mind and was the cause of the dynasty's fall. It should be pointed out that, although the Standard History, in this case the *Shih-chi*, also singles out Tan Chi's name as King Chou's favorite and states flatly that Chou always listened to Tan Chi,[34] Chou is still treated as a man capable of making his own decisions. In other words, King Chou was a tyrant according to the *Shih-chi*, while in the *Feng-shen* King Chou was often referred to as *hun-chün*, the muddleheaded ruler who could not tell right from wrong.

There is a difference between a tyrant and a muddleheaded ruler: the tyrant knows what he is doing and the muddleheaded ruler does not. To take the famous Pi Kan's story as an example, both history and fiction agree that King Chou of the Shang killed his prime minister, Pi Kan, but they disagree on why and how. According to the *Shih-chi*, Pi Kan was next of kin to the royal family and also a prime minister. As a man of impeccable moral integrity, he felt it was a minister's duty to remonstrate with his king about the latter's wrongdoings. His persistent remonstration finally angered King Chou, who said, "I heard that a sage has seven holes in his heart," and ordered Pi Kan's heart be cut out to see whether or not it had seven holes.[35] According to the *Feng-shen*, however, it was not King Chou, but Tan Chi, who was responsible for Pi Kan's death. In the novel, Tan Chi was an evil fox-fairy who was transformed from a fox to a beautiful woman. When Pi Kan, the prime minister and royal uncle of King Chou, found out Tan Chi's real identity, he was worried. Instead of telling King Chou about Tan Chi's fox-fairy origin, he tried to scare Tan Chi away by killing many of her fox-fairy relatives. Determined to take revenge on Pi Kan, Tan Chi first fixed up King Chou with one of her friends, a pheasant-fairy who also transformed into a beautiful woman. Then Tan Chi pretended to be very ill. King Chou worried about Tan Chi's illness and he asked the pheasant-fairy what he could do to make Tan Chi well again. He was then told that a slice of Pi Kan's heart, if made into soup, could cure Tan Chi's fatal disease. As if he did not know the implication of taking a slice of heart from a human body, King Chou ordered Pi Kan to donate a piece of his heart in order to save Tan Chi's life. When Pi Kan protested that this would mean taking away his own life, King Chou replied: "Uncle, you are wrong. All I ask is only one piece of your heart; what harm would it do? Please say no more."[36] Throughout the novel, King Chou is cast in the same mold. There are many stories dealing with King Chou's tyrannies, but these were all initiated by Tan Chi. These stories, which dominate the first quarter of the *Feng-shen*, tell how King Chou, with Tan Chi's help, drew the wrath of Heaven upon the Shang dynasty.[37] It was this wrath of Heaven that revoked King Chou's mandate to rule, according to the novel.

Two other novels follow this same approach to the evil last ruler of the dynasty. The *Yu-Hsia* and the *Lieh-kuo* treat King Chieh and King Yu (r. 781−169 B.C.; the last ruler of the Western Chou dynasty) in similar fashion. Both are described as muddleheaded rulers lacking in personal virtues. Depraved by lust, both failed to attend to government business. Like King Chou in the *Feng-shen*, they were also bewitched by troublemakers. In the case of King Chieh (in the *Yu-Hsia*), it was his favorite concubine, Mo Hsi, who made him lose his head. In the case of King Yu (in *Lieh-kuo*), it was Pao Ssu who caused the downfall of the Western Chou dynasty.[38]

A few words must be said here with regard to the roles of licentious women in historical novels. Tan Chi, Mo Hsi, and Pao Ssu are all cast as stereotyped vicious women. Like all categories of villains, the licentious woman was created to present a contrast between virtuous heroes who resisted them and the virtueless villains who yielded to them. Representing the lusts of the flesh, these women bring forward an illustration that lust (for women) is disaster-prone and must be curbed. This explains partly why warrior-heroes have to "show no interest toward women," while villains like Chou, Chieh, and Yu yield to their temptation.

We should note that although Tan Chi, Mo Hsi, and Pao Ssu were all concubines of kings, the category of bad women is not confined to them. For example, in the novel *Shui-hu*, the unfaithful wives, who were described as temptresses, licentious, and debauched, constitute a unique category of "vicious women." The most notorious representative is P'an Chin-lien, wife of Wu Sung's elder brother, Wu Ta, who first tried to tempt Wu Sung (one of the leading heroes in the *Shih-hu*) to commit adultery with her. Failing to achieve that, she later committed adultery with another man (the famous Hsi-men Ch'ing) and murdered her own husband, Wu Ta, when Wu Sung was not in town. Returning from a trip, Wu Sung was stunned by news of his brother's sudden death. After thorough investigation, he discovered the truth and took revenge on P'an Chin-lien and her lover, killing them. There are five chapters dealing with the antecedents and the consequence of Wu Sung's killing of P'an Chin-lien in the *Shui-hu*.[39] Through its most vivid and detailed description, the *Shui-hu* presents P'an Chin-lien as one of the most unforgettable characters in the novel. Unlike the *Feng-shen* stories about Tan Chi, whose cruelty and sadism are incredible, the *Shui-hu* stories about P'an Chin-lien deal with a flesh and blood, life-sized human being whose crimes are much easier to comprehend. This means that in describing characters the *Shui-hu*, a novel about the more recent past, is far more realistic than the *Feng-shen*, a novel about remote antiquity. In fact the artistic achievement of the *Shui-hu* lies in its descriptive power that shows a strong inclination for psychological realism. The stories about P'an Chin-lien are only examples. However, the treatment of women in the *Shui-hu* is significant because the *Shui-hu* is one of the earliest and most popular novels in China. In historical novels, it sets the tone for the general treatment of the so-called bad women.[40]

As P'an Chin-lien represents the most notorious example of a licentious woman in historical novels, Emperor Yang (r. 605–18) of the Sui dynasty (589—618) represents that of the evil last emperor of a dynasty. In the long imperial period since the Ch'in and Han dynasties, the most notorious example of an extravagant and corrupt monarch in the world of popular fiction is the Emperor Yang of the Sui. There are many fictional accounts dealing with Emperor Yang; among them is the popular novel *Sui Yang-ti yen-shih* (Ch'i-tung yeh-jen [pseud.]; *Sui Yang-ti* hereafter). Centered on Emperor Yang's private life, especially his relations with women, the novel emphasizes the emperor's self-indulgence and licentiousness as the main causes of his downfall. In the prelude to the novel, the novelist sums up the main theme: The story is about a "gay and profligate son of Heaven" who lost his country because of his indulgence in a pleasure-seeking lifestyle.[41] Throughout the novel, the vices of the evil last emperors are elaborated, with particular emphasis on sexual license. The force of traditional models in the stereotyping of Emperor Yang is obvious if we compare Emperor Yang to King Chieh and King Chou, the two earliest representatives of the type. All the behavioral attributes of Chou and Chieh can serve as a basis for the analysis of Emperor Yang.[42]

At the end of the novel *Sui Yang-ti*, Emperor Yang was killed by treacherous officials after he saw, with his own eyes, his eleven-year-old son killed. His wives and palaces were all taken over. The novelist describes in detail the last days of Emperor Yang with disgust and contempt, and the novel concludes with the burning of Emperor Yang's palace, Mi-lou, by Li Shih-min, later Emperor T'ai-tsung of the T'ang dynasty: "The fire [that burned the Palace Mi-lou] lasted for months," the novelist notes, pointing his finger again at Emperor Yang's spectacular extravagance.[43]

Compared with Emperor Yang of the Sui, Emperor Ch'ung-chen (r. 1628—44), the last ruler of the Ming, was treated with great sympathy. Many fictional accounts deal with Emperor Ch'ung-chen's tragic death. Among the historical novels, the *Chiao Ch'uang* is an interesting example. While Emperor Yang was held responsible for the misgovernment of his empire, Emperor Ch'ung-chen was not. When Emperor Ch'ung-chen succeeded the throne in 1627, the condition of the Ming regime was already deteriorating. Although he promptly put down the notorious eunuch, Wei Chung-hsien (1568—1627) (who was responsible for corrupting the imperial government during the reign of Emperor Hsi-tsung [r. 1621—27]), Emperor Ch'ung-chen could not stop the spreading evil influence of party strife and political intrigues that characterized Wei Chung-hsien's rule and eventually led to the Ming's downfall. Nevertheless, the emperor's prompt action toward Wei Chung-hsien won over people's hearts; they were convinced that Emperor Ch'ung-chen desired to rule well. This faith in the emperor's desire to rule well was further enhanced by the latter's tragic death that made him a martyr. Ever since the fall of the Ming, public sympathy has always been on the side of Emperor Ch'ung-chen; it was not the emperor's fault that he lost his empire, it was the fault of his ministers and generals. The novel *Chiao Ch'uang* demonstrates this public sympathy.

This novel deals with the rise and fall of Li Tzu-ch'eng (1605−45). Its climax comes at the death of Emperor Ch'ung-chen when Li Tzu-ch'eng's rebel army enters Peking in April, 1644. Throughout the novel, it is made clear that Ming officials and generals were considered responsible for the upheaval caused by the rebels. At the beginning of the novel, the Ming regime under Emperor Ch'ung-chen is compared to a very weak man recovering from a serious illness (referring to the powerful eunuch Wei Chung-hsien's tyrannical rule).[44] If there had been able and virtuous ministers in court at this time there would have been better chances for a restoration of the country. Unfortunately, the corrupting influence of Wei Chung-hsien produced a generation of incompetent and perfunctory officials who were so intimidated by the rich and powerful that they cultivated an ostrichlike attitude of doing and seeing nothing.

The spread of the local uprisings is an example. According to the novelist, the rebel force was actually very small at the beginning: "If local officials could give their full attention to suppress them, destroying them would be as easy as blowing out the flame of a lamp."[45] But the perfunctory local officials were remiss in their duties. The story about Li Yen (in chap. 1) is a case in point.[46] Li Yen was a virtuous young gentleman who always gave away money generously to people in need. It was because of his generosity that other rich men in the area disliked him. These men conspired with the local magistrate to throw Li Yen into prison. When word about Li Yen's arrest spread, the people of the district became very angry. They rose to revolt against the local authority and killed the magistrate. After learning of the killing of the magistrate, Li Yen had no choice but to lead the people to join the rebel Li Tzu-ch'eng's force.[47]

While Li Yen's story tells the growing strength of the rebels, it also reveals the distressful social and economic conditions that were the causes of widespread uprisings in the country. Finally, the rebel Li Tzu-ch'eng advanced on Peking (in chap. 2 of the novel). When news of Li's advance reached Peking, the capital was in great confusion and panic. The treasury was empty, the garrison was too poorly staffed to man the walls, and the ministers were anxious to secure their lots. Li Tzu-ch'eng's advance was scarcely opposed, as the eunuch-commanders of cities and forts were all hastening to surrender. On the day before Peking's fall, the nineteenth day of the third month of the seventeenth year of Ch'ung-chen (April 25, 1644), according to the novel, the emperor personally struck the bell (for the court to assemble) at dawn, but no one came. Knowing that there was nothing he could do to save his empire, the emperor decided to kill himself. With great compassion, the novelist describes how the emperor met his own death with dignity and courage. He first slew Lady Yuan, who fell to the ground after the rope she used to hang herself broke. He attempted, and accomplished with great pain, the slaying of his daughter, the eldest princess, who was only fifteen years old. And finally he hanged himself. Before he did, the emperor wrote a last decree:

> It has been seventeen years since we ascended the throne. [Poor in Virtue] We have incurred the wrath of Heaven. Three times the barbarians invaded the land and the rebels are now approaching the Capital. All these are caused by our ministers who misled us. Our corpses can be dismembered [after we die]. All ministers can be slain. But do not destroy the royal ancestral temple and do not hurt a single one of the people![48]

Here, the Emperor blamed himself and his ministers for the fall of the empire. He did not ask that he and his ministers be forgiven, but he did ask that his ancestors and his people be spared. This respect for the ancestors and care for the welfare of the people make Emperor Ch'ung-chen stand out from other "last emperors" in people's minds. Moreover, his final act of suicide proves to the world that he lived as an emperor and died as an emperor. There is a great contrast between the death of Emperor Yang of the Sui, who died as a helpless villain, and the death of Emperor Ch'ung-chen, who died as a noble sovereign. Since the emperor is the absolute authority on earth, no one can kill him except himself, theoretically speaking. When Emperor Yang did not have the courage to take his own life, he forfeited his princely status in the eye of the people, because he did not live up to the expectations of the Son of Heaven.

The novel *Chiao Ch'uang* has ten chapters. Emperor Ch'ung-chen's death is described in the second chapter. The rest of the novel centers on random stories and material dealing with "loyal subjects," which include both common people and officials during the last days of the Ming. The central theme of the novel is summed up by the opening statement of the preface, which quotes two popular dictums as follows: "Those who are responsible for the death of one's father and sovereign are irreconcilable enemies, with whom one cannot live together under the same sky," and "Those who are not in the government do not propose [how to run the country]."[49] The second quote, which cultivates a "follow the leader" mentality, actually strengthens the first quote, which stresses personal loyalty to the sovereign. Based on these beliefs, General Wu San-kuei (1612–78), who asked for assistance from the Manchu to chase the rebels away from Peking, was regarded as a national hero despite the fact that the Manchus, having entered Peking, refused to retreat, took over the Ming government, and established an alien regime in China. The following passage illustrates the people's sentiment when the Manchus helped General Wu chase the rebels away and avenge the emperor's death.

> On the twelfth day, news came to Peking that General Wu won a victory over the rebels and the bandits had fled far away. All literati and people in the city raised their hands over their foreheads [a gesture of "thank Heaven"] and said: "Although we suffered devastation, fortunately, our former Emperor's death is avenged, and the Ch'uang bandits are defeated. That's all that we have wished for. What is there to regret!"[50]

According to the above quotation from the novel, even when the capital — Peking — was conquered by the alien Manchus, the people felt no regrets because their former emperor's death was avenged. Three observations can be made regarding this emphasis on avenging the emperor's death at any cost. First, it is very possible that the writer was among the Ming Chinese who hated Li Tzu-ch'eng and what he stood for — a ruthless bandit who tortured people for the sake of collecting money and other wealth — more than they resented the

Manchus. Second, the novel was written in 1645 after the fall of Peking. At this time South China was still under the control of the Emperor Hung-kuang of the Southern Ming. Therefore it was possible that some Ming people still felt that the Manchurian occupation was a temporary situation. Besides, the Manchus claimed that they were not fighting against the Ming regime, that they came to help avenge the Ming emperor's death, and that they chased away the bandits. Third, the emphasis on avenging the emperor's death reveals the mentality of some Ming people whose blind loyalty to the sovereign made them incapable of distinguishing between loyalty to the emperor and loyalty to the country, because the Manchus did choose to remain permanently once they entered Peking.

Finally, a few words more must be said in regard to the downfall of the Ming dynasty. During the Ming-Ch'ing transitional period, the search for the causes of the downfall of the Ming was very intense among contemporary scholars, writers, and playwrights. On the one hand, serious thinkers and scholars were engaging in penetrating and soul-searching analyses, and some even came to criticize the imperial institution; indeed, this was the first time in Chinese history that the imperial institution became a target of severe criticism. On the other hand, writers and playwrights of popular literature were also very much involved with the subject of the downfall of the empire. One of the recurrent themes in fiction and drama on the evils of Ming government is the corrupting influence of the imperial favorites who gained easy access to the emperor. In fact, some of the most celebrated works were written on this theme.[51]

In traditional fiction and drama, although the eunuchs were looked upon as one of the chief factors responsible for the Ming's fall, no attempt was made to analyze the eunuch system. Instead, each was treated individually as an evil person who just happened to be a eunuch. As villains, they were categorically denounced; however, sometimes they were condemned vehemently and at other times they were treated with good humor. For example, in one of Li Yü's (1611–80) plays, the *Yü sao-t'ou* (the Jade Pin), the powerful eunuch, Liu Ching, in Emperor Wu-tsung's reign, was humorously referred to as "the standing emperor," in contrast with Emperor Wu-tsung, who was referred to as "the sitting emperor."[52] In the novel *Chiao Ch'uang*, the corrupting influence of the powerful eunuch Wei Chung-hsien was singled out at the beginning of the novel as the cause of the general deterioration of the government leading to the fall of the Ming. But the novelist saw only the individual villain Wei Chung-hsien, not the system the eunuch represented. And he seemed satisfied with ending the discussion by condemning Wei Chung-hsien.

To conclude, in areas related to governmental affairs, historical novels expose corruption and injustice in imperial government; describe social and economic grievances of the people; criticize licentious and extravagant lives of the tyrannical rulers; and depict both actual and imaginary crimes and violence in every stratum of society. In reconstructing these stories, the novelists follow the "villains versus heroes" formula that views history as a perpetual struggle between evil-minded villains and upright heroes. Since there have always been, and always will be, evil persons in the world, it is inevitable that evils in history repeat themselves. Among the man-made disasters in history, war and its ensuing evils were most terrible because they involved great loss of human life. It was, it is, and it will always be, according to the novelists, up to the heroes to bring peace and order to the world. These heroes are what Mencius called "true Kings" when he expounded his ideal of good government to King Hsuan of Ch'i:

> "How virtuous must a man be before he can become a true King?" [asked King Hsuan of Ch'i]. "He becomes a true King by bringing peace and order to the people. This is something no one can stop."[53]

The essence of good government thus boils down to only one thing: bringing peace and order to the people. This simple ideal did not sound very ambitious to Mencius, as the average agrarian kingdom in his day was quite small and relatively controllable. But it sounded lofty in Ming times when the empire was large, loosely organized, and ridden by all sorts of local upheavals, regional rebellions, and foreign invasions. In historical novels the yearning for peace and order is in contrast to the historical realities.

Chapter 6

The Cosmic and Religious Order

Life, death and transmigration, these are to revolve
without end. The retribution for sins and grievances
committed in a previous existence will never stop. I
feel great compassion for them [humankind].
— *Feng-shen yen-i*

The cosmic and religious order described in traditional novels reflects a
complex system of religious attitudes, beliefs, and practices in imperial
China. Characterized by the blending and interpenetration of classical
polytheism, Confucianism, Buddhism, and religious Taoism, the system
of authorities of this cosmic order was very complex. On the one hand,
it was patterned after the mundane imperial government, with the celestial diety of classical religion as the supreme administrative authority
of Heaven, Earth, and the Underworld. In this aspect, it revealed the
most significant characteristic of this system — its "this-worldliness" —
that was typical of Chinese thought. On the other hand, there were the
Buddhist sages and Taoist patriarchs whose final authorities in the
religious realms were juxtaposed with the celestial hierarchies of classical
deities. The influence of Buddhist and Taoist paradises was tremendous, especially the former, in regard to the concept of cosmos. Compared to the Chinese concept of Heaven and Earth, Indian Buddhists
envisaged a cosmos of incomprehensibly enormous dimensions where,
across equally enormous temporal and spatial distances, all creatures
were connected in all directions by the threads of karma. In popular
literature, in which Buddhist and Taoist traditions fused with Confucian
and classical traditions, the cosmic and religious order has been kept
alive to bear testimony to the assimilative power of a people.

The cosmic and religious order as seen in the vernacular fiction
confirms the overwhelming impression of the so-called three teachings
(*san-chiao*) in traditional times. During its long process of evolution
from the Sung to the Ming dynasties, vernacular fiction was exposed to
the influences of both Buddhist literature from India and the indigenous

157

Taoist literature. It was also during the Sung-Ming period that the culmination of full-blown syncretism of Confucianism, Buddhism, and religious Taoism occurred. Naturally, the reconciliation of the Three Teachings, which included all manner of borrowing, influence, and unconscious debts, is reflected in the vernacular fiction. Before we discuss religious ideas and beliefs in Ming historical novels, we will take a closer look at the history and development of the Three Teachings movement.

Historically, three major stages mark the development of the traditional religions. First, the consolidation of the Former Han dynasty, after the short-lived first empire (the Ch'in dynasty, 221–207 B.C.), saw the theological systematization of the classical religion that played a predominant role in political life and the organization of the state. Second, the decline of the Han empire and the prolonged period of disunity following the collapse of the empire saw the rise and growth of religious Taoism and Buddhism competing for dominance both against the classical religion and against the state. Third, the full reconsolidation of the Confucian state in the Sung dynasty saw a spiritual unification under Confucianism, which was reasserted as the orthodoxy of the state. From then on, government control over religion was stabilized, and from the fusion of Confucianism and the traditional religions emerged the positive religious beliefs and practices instrumental in the secular life of traditional society. As a result, the religions in the late Ming acquired a unique syncretic nature. It is this syncretic system of traditional religions that we will deal with when we discuss the cosmic and religious order revealed through the historical novels. Following is a brief account of the basic tenets of this syncretic faith in traditional China and their significant historical development.[1]

The classical religion contained four elements: ancestor worship; the worship of Heaven, Earth, and a subordinate system of naturalistic deities; divination; and sacrifice. Although these classical beliefs played an intimate role in political life and the organization of the state in the pre-Ch'in (classical) period, it was not until the Yin-Yang (Cosmologist) School of the Han that they were gradually molded into theological systematization.[2] Based on classical beliefs in the regulatory power of Heaven and Earth, the Cosmologists theorized that all human events were predetermined by the set of forces of Yin-Yang (negative and positive forces) and the Five Elements (metal, wood, water, fire, and earth). The forces of Yin-yang and the Five Elements were, according to this theory, connected with the movement of the stars in directing the mystical operation of time which, in turn, determined the nature of human events. There were many mystical explanations for the relationship between the Way of Heaven and human affairs; the explanation (belief) that the succession of dynastic powers was predetermined by the rotation of the Five Elements—the Five-Phase Cosmology—was the most well-known explanation. Not only were the affairs of the state thought to be predetermined by the Yin-Yang forces and the rotation of the Five Elements, but the intimate life of the people was thought to be predetermined by them as well. The theory of the Yin-Yang forces and the Five-Phase Cosmology provided a link between the supernatural basis of the affairs of the state and the intimate life of the people, thus strengthening the classical belief in the regulatory power of Heaven and Earth to predetermine the course of all events. Moreover, the unification of the Han empire exerted a universalizing influence on the many local religious traditions. Local spirits and deities were incorporated into a central system under a belief in the supremacy of Heaven and its related naturalistic forces. The political implications of this worship of Heaven were tremendous since the emperor, the Son of Heaven, was regarded as the representative of Heaven, the only one who could perform the ancient religious ritual of making sacrifice to Heaven. While the Mandate of Heaven symbolized, since the Chou, the legitimacy claimed by every dynastic power and widely accepted by the common people, this divine sanction of imperial power was one of the factors that blended the classical religion thoroughly with the imperial institution of the Han.

The Han empire saw not only the theological systematization of the classical religion, but also the establishment of Confucianism as the state orthodoxy. The importance of the establishment of Confucian orthodoxy lies in the official recognition of its moral authority over religion and ethics, which indirectly encourages the Confucian to take an active interest in religious ideas. In addition to earlier Confucian support of, and ethical elaboration on, the practices of sacrifice, divination, and ancestor worship, the Confucians in Han times also developed a theory called "Interaction between Heaven and Man" (*T'ien-jen kan-ying*). This theory was a corollary to the classical cult of Heaven. According to Tung Chung-shu (179–104 B.C.), the most famous Confucian exponent of this theory, the world of man and the world of nature operate as a harmonious whole:

Therefore when the human world is well governed and the people are at peace, or when the will [of the ruler] is equable and his character is correct, then the transforming influences of Heaven and Earth operate in a state of perfection and among the myriad things only the finest are produced. But when the human world is in disorder and the people become perverse, or when the [ruler's] will is depraved and his character is rebellious, then the transforming influences of Heaven and Earth suffer injury, so that their (*yin* and *yang*) ethers generate visitations and harm arises.[3]

According to this theory, an intimate relationship exists between Heaven and man. Therefore the occurrence of unharmonious and abnormal events in the human world inevitably stirs Heaven to manifest corresponding abnormal phenomena in the natural world. Such phenomena are variously known as *tsai* (portents) or *i* (catastrophe or unusual event).

The creatures of Heaven and Earth at times display unusual changes and these are called catastrophes. Lesser ones are called ominous portents. The portents always come first and are followed by catastrophes. Portents are Heaven's warnings, catastrophes are Heaven's threats. Heaven first sends warnings, and if men do not understand, then it sends catastrophes to awe them. This is what the *Book of Poetry* means when it says: "We tremble at the awe and fearfulness of Heaven!" The genesis of all such portents and catastrophes is a direct result of errors in the state.[4]

This belief in the portentous significance of unusual or freakish occurrences in the natural world formed the basis for the Han theory that evil actions or misgovernment in high places incite dislocations in the natural order, causing the appearance of comets, eclipses, drought, floods, earthquakes, etc. Thus, Heaven represents not merely a powerful but a morally meaningful body of forces, operating on ethical principles that are fully binding on man as an integral part of the universe. This Confucian theory of Interaction between Heaven and Man reveals how the ethics of the Confucian doctrine derive their sacred and awe-inspiring quality from the classical religion. As the theory of the Interaction between Heaven and Man was institutionalized into a guiding political concept, the classical religion in the Han became well blended with Confucianism as the orthodoxy of the state.

As the long unification of the Han empire saw the growth of

classical religion, the prolonged period of disunity following the collapse of the Han empire saw the growth of Taoism and Buddhism. Historical records show that Buddhism and Taoism began to flourish during the declining years of the Later Han when the imperial orders were disintegrating and the people's faith in the celestial power of the classical religion and Confucianism was shaken. The fact that the rise of Buddhism and religious Taoism coincided with the structural and ideological breakdown of Chinese society reveals both the strength of the new religions and the limitation of the Confucian orthodoxy. It explains the conflict that underlay the two significant phenomena in the history and development of these religions: attempts at armed rebellion on the side of religions and religious persecutions on the side of the state. From the declining years of the Later Han to the full reconsolidation of the Confucian state in the Sung, Buddhism and Taoism competed with each other for dominance, both against the classical religion and against the state. There were many recorded attempts at armed rebellion by either Buddhists or Taoists, as well as recorded persecutions of either Buddhists or Taoists. However, it was also during this period that these two religions became intimately diffused into secular social institutions. By the Sung period, the reassertion of Confucianism helped to renew faith in the classical religion as the spiritual support for the imperial political order. From then on, government control over religion was stabilized; religions (in diffused form) became the social and political instruments of the state. The fates of Buddhism and Taoism depended, to a large extent, upon the disposition or caprices of the emperors, upon their willingness to attack or to support them.

With the government control over the various religions stabilized, competition among them lessened. The interpenetration of Taoism and Buddhism, which existed in the early stage of their development, accelerated. Many common beliefs and ideas were shared by these two religions. The theory of karma, which was originally a Buddhist idea, was adopted by Taoism, while the idea of the evolution of Heaven and Earth, a Taoist idea, was absorbed by Buddhism. Other shared beliefs include the immortality of the soul, the transmigration of souls, belief in the existence of paradise and hell, opposition to killing (any living things), and the belief in the redemption of sin through accumulative good deeds. These shared ideas and beliefs attest the assimilative process of a syncretic system. Nevertheless, as an individual religion, popular Buddhism, characterized by its "pity for all creatures," remained distinctly different from religious Taoism, characterized by its magical cult and "cultivation of divinity and immortality."

As the classical religion was assimilated by Confucianism, so were Buddhism and Taoism. The Buddhist fusion with Confucianism was persistent. One significant development was the rise of lay Buddhism in the late Ming. The fact that it was no longer necessary to renounce societal and familial ties to become a Buddhist was revealing. A close examination of Buddhist morality books reveals that the sinicized Buddhism put as much emphasis on civil virtue and filial piety as on compassion and wisdom.[5] The Taoist fusion with Confucianism was equally indelible. Taoist ideas of cultivation provide a good example: The Confucians in Ming times had become so accustomed to these Taoist ideas that it would hardly occur to them that such ideas were foreign to Confucianism. However, systematic modern study affirms their Taoist origin.[6]

With this general introduction to the historical background of the syncretic system of traditional religions, we turn to a specific discussion of cosmological thought. In the *Ming Shih-lu* (Veritable Records of the Ming), the basic source for the later Official History of the Ming, the influence of traditional correlative cosmology is self-evident.[7] In the *Ming Shih-lu*, there are detailed records of astronomical phenomena as well as all kinds of abnormal phenomena and catastrophies in the natural world and they all were interpreted as the signs of and messages from Heaven. Applications of traditional correlative cosmology clearly flourished throughout the Ming era. However, significant developments relating to cosmological ideas emerged in the waning years of the Ming empire. These developments are reflected in the Official History, the *Ming-shih*, compiled in the early Ch'ing.

In the *Ming-shih* there are three chapters on astronomy and three chapters on Five-Phase Cosmology. In the astronomical chapters, European ideas and contributions are recognized. For example, prominent Jesuit missionaries, Matteo Ricci (1552–1610) and Johann Adam Schall van Bell (1592–1666), are mentioned and western astronomy and calendaric calculations are given credit for supervising the construction of important astronomical instruments and correcting the calendar. The western theory that the earth is round is officialy recognized, citing the fact that the ancients had had a similar theory a long time ago. There were three cosmological schools regarding the structure of heavens in ancient China. One, the school of *Hun-t'ien* (the spherical heavens) shared similar ideas with the Europeans. According to the theory of the spherical heavens, the heavens resemble an egg, while the earth is like the yolk within it, and is situated alone in the heavens.[8]

The Jesuit introduction of western science and technology into seventeenth-century China had come at a most opportune moment; it accelerated the trends of the late Ming and early Ch'ing cosmological criticism that was part of a dynamic intellectual movement in the early Ch'ing period. The partial acceptance of western ideas in the *Ming-shih* serves to indicate the presence of certain critical elements in the prevalent and seemingly unreceptive correlative thought.[9] But in popular fiction in which the religious world views of the Three Teachings prevail, no sign of these developments can be detected.

Another significant aspect concerns the religious rituals observed by the imperial Ming court. Their importance cannot be over-emphasized, because they defined the functions of an emperor. In the chapters on rites in the *Ming-shih*, all the traditional rituals are observed. Consider the religious rituals of making sacrifices. There were particular events in which the emperor performed the religious rituals of making sacrifices. Specified by the code of rites, the emperor sacrificed to Heaven, to Earth, to imperial ancestors, to the gods of the soil and harvests, and to the deities of the mountains and rivers. Comparing these rites with those recorded in the *Han-shu*, written by Pan Ku (32–92 A.D.), it is clear that in the sphere of ritual observance, the force of tradition was prevalent.[10]

Finally, we come to the prevailing religious world views of the Three Teachings in Ming times. The belief in the essential harmony of the Three Teachings was a characteristic of Chinese religious life for centuries before the Ming.[11] But it was Chu Yuan-chang, the founding emperor of the Ming empire, who gave imperial sanction to the Three Teachings syncretism by declaring that Confucianism, Buddhism, and Taoism are of one essence.[12] Historically speaking, the sixteenth century was a period in which notions about the "combined practice of the Three Teachings" and the "unity of the Three Teachings" became popular. Scholars who were advocates of Three Teachings syncretism were quick to quote Chu Yuan-chang's words to support their syncretic point of view. Yang Ch'i-yuan (1547–99), Kuan chih-tao (1536–1608), and Li Chih were notable examples. Yang Ch'i-yuan, who managed to place first in the metropolitan civil service examinations, set a precedent for using Ch'an Buddhist ideas in the examination papers. In his anthology of Chu Yuan-chang's writings, Yang also included the important essay "On The Three Teachings." Kuan Chih-tao, a *chinshih* degree holder, also echoed Chu Yuan-chang's view that the following of the moral teaching in the Buddhist *Heart sutra* (*Hsin-ching*) could benefit all people. Li Chih, the influential radical thinker of the late Ming, actually quoted Chu Yuan-chang to uphold his belief in "one *Tao* for all ages."[13]

As this tendency grew, it affected the maintenance of the contemporary official orthodoxy. Ku Yen-wu (1613−82), a leading early Ch'ing critic of late Ming thought, observed that the civil service examination under the Ming even allowed the candidates to elaborate Ch'an Buddhist and Taoist ideas.[14] With the assimilation of the ideas of Ch'an Buddhism and Taoism, the content of Ming Neo-Confucianism changed. New trends of thought made their appearance on the Ming scenes.

In the area of popular religion, the most significant development was the cult of Three Teachings, which prevailed among the syncretists in the late Ming. Consider Lin Chao-en's (1517−98) cult of the "Three-in-One Doctrine" (*San-i chiao*), for example.[15] Lin established a religious organization that was devoted to the practice of combining the Three Teachings into one. Believing that the three teachings were originally one, as they were all manifestations of the Way, he taught his followers how to integrate Taoism and Buddhism into Neo-Confucianism. In so doing, he not only adopted the ideas and practices of both Buddhism and Taoism, but also asserted the basic social and ethical values of Neo-Confucianism. In typical Confucian fashion, Lin was addressed as the Master (*hsien-sheng*) of the Three Teachings, not as the Patriarch (*chiao-chu*) of the Three Teachings. Basing themselves in Lin's home town of P'u-t'ien, Fukien, Lin and his followers traveled extensively in southeast China, recruiting members along the road, erecting shrines for religious worship, and disseminating collections of Lin's writings to promote his ideas.

Lin Chao-en exemplified a Confucian's attempt to unite the three teachings in a single homogenous moral teaching in the late Ming. Through his openness to ideas and practices from Buddhism and Taoism, he adopted in his teachings both Taoist and Buddhist forms of spiritual and physical cultivations, such as healing techniques, meditative disciplines, alchemical interpretations of the *I-ching* (Book of Changes), and mystical speculations. However, in his own mind, he regarded himself as a Confucian teaching the only true and all-encompassing Way. Thus he not only absorbed the ideas and practices of both Buddhism and Taoism, he also adapted them to his Confucian worldview.

While Confucian scholars showed more interest in the philosophical aspects of the Three Teachings, popular writers described the religious and supernatural aspects of the Three Teachings. The first striking impression is that in vernacular novels, the compositions of the Three Teachings vary, an indication of the lack of precise clarification of the religious issues in the writers' minds. Consider the novel *Feng-shen*, which deals with the Shang-Chou dynastic war. The dominant religious idea in the *Feng-shen* is the concept of *San-chiao* (Three Religions or Three Teachings), although the components of the Three Teachings vary even within the novel itself. In chapter 5, the idea of the Three Teachings refers to Shan-chiao (The Promulgating Sect of the Religious Taoism), Chieh-chiao (The Intercepting Sect of the Religious Taoism), and Confucianism.[16] In chapter 15, the Three Teachings refers to the three categories of the members of the celestial hierarchy, i.e., Shan-chiao, Chieh-chiao, and jen-tao (humankind).[17] In chapter 47, it refers to Taoism, Buddhism, and Confucianism.[18] In chapters 72 and 77, the term *San-chiao* is mentioned in connection with a conference among the three Taoist patriarchs, the Yuan-shih t'ien-tsun (The Patriarch of the Promulgating Sect), the T'ung-t'ien chiao-chu (The Patriarch of the Intercepting Sect), and Lao Tzu, the borrowed Patriarch of Taoism. Judging from the context, the term *san-chiao* in the last instance seems to refer to the three patriarchs themselves rather than to the Three Religions.[19] But in chapters 78, 83, and 84, the term *San-chiao* clearly refers to the Promulgating Sect, the Intercepting Sect, and Buddhism.[20] A modern scholar, Liu Ts'un-yan, an authority on the *Feng-shen*, offers the following explanation for these confusing phenomena. According to him, though the author of the *Feng-shen* might have planned that the Promulgating Sect, the Intercepting Sect, and the Buddhist sages from the West would form the Three Schools of Teaching and their patriarchs would be the sages of the Three Religions, in his subconsciousness he could not help keeping the conception that Confucianism, Buddhism, and Taoism are the Three Schools of Teaching under Heaven.[21]

We should point out here that elements of the classical religion are present in the *Feng-shen* too. In the prelude to chapter 15, the novelist gives a brief introduction to the background of his story. In his description of the cosmic order, he mentions the existence of the Sovereign on High in the Vast Heaven (Hao-t'ien shang-ti).[22] In the *Feng-shen*, the Sovereign on High in the Vast Heaven seems to be a believer in the Taoist philosophy of noninvolvement. During the long and fierce Shang-Chou dynastic war involving two Taoist sects and the Buddhist patriarchs, the Sovereign on High does not intervene in the struggle, nor makes himself heard to either side. In the absence of the regulatory power of Heaven, the cosmic and religious order in the *Feng-shen* is apt to collapse. The result is the grand scale of magic warfare depicted in the *Feng-shen*, which reveals Buddhist and Taoist influences as well as the predominant feature of the magic cults in traditional Chinese religions.[23]

The magic warfare in the *Feng-shen* reflects the tremendous influence of magic on the popular mind. Since the main function of magic lies in its being a supernatural sanctioning agent for the religion, the relation of magic to religion is not as a source of moral ideas but rather as a source of superstitious beliefs. As the *Feng-shen* was one of the early full-length novels — it was published after the famous *San-kuo* and *Shui-hu* but earlier than the *Hsi-yu chi* and others[24] — its exemplariness is understandable. This explains partly why there are so many descriptions of warfare in the world of vernacular fiction in traditional China.

Let us consider another historical novel as an example. In the *Shui-hu*, the three dominant religions are the classical religion, the religious Taoism, and Buddhism. Generally speaking, the complex system of authorities in the cosmic order in the *Shui-hu* was patterned after the traditional temporal imperial government, with the Jade Emperor (*Yü-huang ta-ti* or *Yü-ti*) as the supreme administrative authority of Heaven and Earth. That the Jade Emperor of Heaven was in charge of supervising the mundane imperial government was made very clear in the beginning of the *Shui-hu*. In the prelude to the novel, the novelist tells some legendary tales about the founding of the Sung dynasty. He first refers to the founding Emperor T'ai-tsu of Sung as "the God of Thunder and Lightning" and then refers to the Emperor Jen-tsung (r. 1022–63) as follows:

> Now this Emperor Jen-tsung was in truth the Barefoot God from Heaven and when he was born a mortal baby he wept without ceasing night and day.[25]

In order to comfort baby Jen-tsung, who was awed by the tremendous responsibility of kingship, the Jade Emperor of Heaven sent two stars to aid the emperor:

> And truly was it that the Jade Emperor of Heaven dispatched two stars from the Propitious Constellation to serve the future emperor. The civil affairs star became Pao Chen, prefect of Kaifeng and a senior member of the Dragon Diagram Academy. The Military affairs star became Ti Ch'ing, the great general who led an expedition against the Kingdom of Western Hsia.[26]

Here the novelist identifies the two Sung historical figures and legendary heroes Pao Chen, as "the civil affairs star," and Ti Ch'ing, "the military affairs star." As to the leader of the bandit-heroes in the novel, Sung Chiang, he too was sent to this earth by the Jade Emperor. We will discuss Sung Chiang later when we discuss the idea of the incarnation of stars and evil spirits.

Although the Jade Emperor represents the popularized celestial deity of classical religion, other religions such as religious Taoism and Buddhism also feature prominently in the *Shui-hu*. In the prelude of the novel, the novelist tells the story about Marshal Hung, who was sent by Emperor Jen-tsung to invite the Divine Teacher, the patriarch of Taoism, to go to the Eastern Capital and conduct a great prayer service in order to drive away the plague that had struck the land. At the end of the story, we are told that

> the Divine Teacher held a great prayer service in the Imperial Park for seven days and seven nights and distributed many charms. Now the sick are cured and the plague is completely gone.[27]

The belief that the Divine Teacher did have the power to cure the sick and stop the plague testifies the tremendous prestige the Taoist patriarch had over the imperial court. There was no question that religious Taoism was an influential religion in Sung times.

The third important religion mentioned in the *Shui-hu* is Buddhism, especially the Buddhist order at the Five-Crested Mountain (or the sacred Mount Wu-tai where the Wen Shu Buddha used to meditate). In chapter 90, after the campaign against the Liao, Sung Chiang and his Liang-shan brothers offered homage to the abbot at the monastery

at Mount Wu-tai. (Keep in mind that this was the monastery where Lu
Chih-shen had shaved his hair and become a monk before he joined
the Liang-shan band.) The following is the abbot's prayer, which he
chanted in the temple on Mount Wu-tai:

> Holding a stick of smoldering incense, he (Abbot Chih-chen) offered
> a prayer. "With this incense, I humbly wish ten thousand years to the
> emperor, with the empress at his side, and a thousand autumns to the
> prince. May the imperial children flourish and the officials rise con-
> stantly in rank. Let there be peace throughout the land, and may the
> people be happy at their labors."
> The abbot took another stick of incense. "May our patrons be at
> ease in body and mind, live for a thousand circuits of the sun, and
> their fame last forever."
> Taking a third stick, the abbot intoned: "May the country be
> peaceful and the people serene for years to come, the five grains
> abundant, the three teachings glorious, with calm on all four sides,
> and everything exactly as wished."[28]

Of the three parts of the prayer, the last part is the most significant
because the prelate had the whole country in his mind: "May the
country be peaceful, the five grains abundant, and the three teachings
glorious," he prayed.

What were the three teachings the abbot referred to? The three
teachings were, presumably, Confucianism, Buddhism, and Taoism.
As mentioned before, the official notion of the Three Teachings was so
ingrained in people's minds in Ming times that whenever the term *three
teachings* was mentioned, people automatically thought of Confucianism,
Buddhism, and Taoism. However, it should be pointed out that as the
orthodoxy of the state, Confucianism had blended in well with the
classical religion ever since Han times. In other words, the three
religions in *Shui-hu* are classical religion, Buddhism, and religious
Taoism.

As in the *Shui-hu*, the complex system of the celestial authorities
in the cosmic order parallels the hierarchical Confucian order of imperial
government; in other historical novels, the celestial authorities in the
cosmic order are the same, although the names vary. Sometimes it was
called *Hao-t'ien shang-ti* (the Sovereign on High in the Vast Heavens),
sometimes it was just called Heaven. In novels of popularized chronicle
style, for example, the *San-kuo* and *Hsi-Han*, the writers were serious
about history, and they tried to stay away from most gods and spirits in

order to tell stories within the limit of "authenticity." In these novels, religious ideas and beliefs have more subtle expression, for example, through ancient astrology, the divination of the supposed influences of the stars and planets on human affairs and terrestrial events by their positions and aspects. Next we will discuss common religious ideas and beliefs that have surfaced through vernacular novels.

Among the many religious ideas and beliefs, the most dominant ones are fatalism, predestination, transmigration, moral retribution, ancestor worship, the worship of Heaven, and the idea of the evolution of Heaven and Earth. These were reflected in almost every aspect of Chinese life, from the top political structure and military campaigns to such domestic affairs as marriage arrangements between families. Since all these beliefs were of an eclectic nature, and since there were no strongly organized congregations in traditional China, extensive religious beliefs permeated into every level of secular institutions. Thus we find, through popular fiction, a panorama of religious life including practices such as sacrifice, divination, alchemy, astrology, geomancy, and physiognomy, together with the long-established religious practice of ancient polytheism and ancestor worship. Although all these were recorded at random in popular literature, their recurrent appearances reveal their subconscious hold on the popular mind. Following are some of the most recurrent themes related to religious ideas and beliefs in historical novels.

The dominant religious theme in historical novels is the inscrutable workings of Heaven or, in other words, the belief in predestination. In almost every dynastic novel, the founding of a new dynasty replacing an old one is believed to be predetermined by fate. For example, there are several historical novels about the legendary story of how the founder of the Chou dynasty defeated the last king of the Shang dynasty.[29] Most of the stories agree with the fact that the last king of the Shang was a tyrant and that the first king of the Chou was a sage-king, and furthermore, they all seem to share a superstitious belief that everything was predetermined by fate and that man was not responsible for what happened in history. The best example is the above-mentioned *Feng-shen*, which incorporated at least two other versions of the historical stories about the Shang-Chou dynastic war. The novel *Feng-shen* tells how the first king of the Chou dynasty defeated the last king of the Shang dynasty and how the warriors and transcendent genii of both camps, killed in the Shang-Chou war, were removed to Heaven and deified. According to the novel, the war between the Shang and Chou groups in history was not caused by human factors but by the predestined investiture of the gods.

Another example of predestination in historical novels can be found in the many legendary and mythological stories about the births of the dynastic founders who were believed to have been sent from heaven. There are stories of these founding emperors being born with unusual signs and omens and growing up with an extraordinary endowment of talents. In our earlier discussion of dynastic legitimacy and divine sovereignty, we have already discussed these birth myths.

Not only were the fates of great men predestined, but the common people, too, sometimes felt their fates predetermined by the inscrutable workings of Heaven. This belief in the predestination of the human lot was keenly felt when people realized that they had no control over their own lives or deaths. Thus, we usually find that fatalism looms over the death scenes described in historical novels. The famous episode of "The Death of Yang Yeh by the Li Ling Stele" in the *Yang-chia-chiang* is an example. In the story, the Sung General Yang Yeh was trapped by the scheming Sung minister Pan Jen-mei, who deliberately withheld reinforcements when they were expected. As a result, Yang Yeh was defeated by the invading Liao army and was trapped in the valley of Ch'en-chia ku. While Yang Yeh and his troops were treading in the valley of the shadow of death, he suddenly saw a stone stele (a carved slab) with three characters *Li Ling Pei* (Li Ling Stele) inscribed on it.

> Yeh thought to himself: "Li Ling of the Han was not loyal to the Han, what is this stele for?" He then told his troops: "I can no longer protect you; here is the place I have to die for my country. You all should take care of yourselves from now on." Having said these words, he threw down his gold helmet and exclaimed: "Heaven! Heaven! Please witness my loyalty to my country." He then struck himself to death on the stone stele.[30]

This episode of "Death at the Li Ling Stele" is very popular in both historical novels and plays, and it has established Yang Yeh's reputation as a courageous hero who died for his country. Yang Yeh's martyrdom contrasts with the Han general Li Ling (ca. 134–74 B.C.) who surrendered to the Hsiung-nu when defeated. However, Li Ling's case was a controversial one even during his day. For example, the historian Ssu-ma Ch'ien of the Former Han was sympathetic with Li Ling, and it was because of his defense of Li Ling's loyalty that he suffered a terrible penalty of mutilation. Nevertheless, the fact that Li Ling did surrender (regardless of his motive) made him a traitor among the simple-minded people, such as the brave old general Yang Yeh. It was because Yang Yeh did not want to repeat Li Ling's story that he killed himself to avoid being captured by barbarians.[31]

But why did he kill himself by the Li Ling Stele? It seems that the stone stele represented Yang Yeh's conscience. When Yang was defeated and trapped in the Ch'en-chia ku, he was desperate and troubled. Then the appearance of the stele reminded him of his commitment to his country. That is why he said to himself: "Li Ling of the Han was not loyal to the Han, what is the stele [in memory of him] for?" To Yang Yeh, this stele was a sign from Heaven. It was Heaven's will that he should die as a martyr and be remembered forever as a loyal hero who died for his country. The novelist makes it very clear that to Yang Yeh, the stele was for him; the stele reminded him not to repeat Li Ling's mistake. Indeed, to the simple-minded old soldier, fate, Heaven's will, and his own conscience all mean one thing.

Another example is the episode about the death of Chu-ko Liang (styled K'ung-ming) in the novel *San-kuo*. It runs as follows:

Ill as he was, K'ung-ming that night went forth from his tent to scan the heavens and study the stars. They filled him with fear. He returned and said to Chiang Wei, "My life may end at any moment."

"Why do you say such a thing?"

"Just now in the San-t'ai constellation the roving star was twice as bright as usual, while the fixed stars were darkened; the supporting stars were also obscure. With such an aspect I know my fate."

"If the aspect be as malignant as you say, why not pray in order to avert it?" replied Chiang.

"I am in the habit of praying," replied K'ung-ming, "but I know not the will of Heaven. However, prepare me forty-nine men and let each have a black flag. Dress them in black and place them outside my tent. Then I will from within my tent invoke the Seven Stars of the North. If my masterlamp remains alight for seven days, then is my life to be prolonged. If the lamp go out, then I am to die...."

It was the sixth night of K'ung-ming's prayers, and the lamp of his fate still burned brightly. He began to feel a secret joy. Presently Chiang Wei entered and watched the ceremonies.

Suddenly a great shouting was heard outside, and immediately Wei Yen dashed in, crying, "The Wei soldiers are upon us!" In his haste he had knocked over and extinguished the Lamp of Fate.

K'ung-ming threw down the sword and sighed, saying, "Life and death are foreordained; no prayers can alter them."[32]

Here the emphasis that life and death are foreordained and that no human power can alter them represents not only the deep sense of sadness and helplessness of Chu-ko Liang, it also speaks for many of the tragic heroes in history who failed to fulfill their dreams.

The superstition of identifying a man's fate with a star relates to the ancient astrology that also plays an important role in the military campaigns of the historical novels. In almost every historical novel the men in charge of military campaigns were men like Chu-ko Liang, who were supposedly masters of astrology, as well as Taoist magicians who had the magic to perform miracles of every sort. In the novel *San-kuo*, Ssu-ma I (178−251) of the Wei (220−65), one of Chu-ko Liang's chief opponents, was also a master of astrology. When Chu-ko Liang was ill, Ssu-ma I suspected it. The following passage tells what was happening in Ssu-ma I's camp when Chu-ko Liang was ill:

Ssu-ma I remained still on the defensive. One night as he sat gazing up at the sky and studying its aspect he suddenly turned to Hsia-kuo Pa, saying joyfully, "A leadership star has just lost position; surely K'ung-ming [Chu-ko Liang] is ill and will soon die. Take a reconnoitering party to the Wu-chang Plain and find out. If you see signs of confusion in the Shu camp and the Shu soldiers do not come out to fight, it means that K'ung-ming is ill, and I shall take the occasion to smite hard."[33]

This passage provides the familiar picture of a battlefield in which the commanders-in-chief on both sides spend their nights gazing up at the sky and studying its aspect. The implication is clear: It is Heaven or fate that decides the outcome of the battle, as well as historical events; men are not responsible for what happens. When the stars were darkened in the sky, who on the earth has power to do anything about it? When a man's fate or the fate of a dynasty is foreordained, there is nothing anyone can do to alter it. The novelist concludes his stories about Chu-ko Liang's death, quoting the words of the great T'ang poet Tu Fu (712–70), an admirer of Chu-ko Liang, as follows:

> The fates forbade that Han should be restored,
> War-worn and weary, yet he steadfast stood.[34]

Thus, Chu-ko Liang's fight against fate is a heart-warming story about humanity: "Heroes since have ever grieved for him."

Relating to the concept of fatalism was a supernatural belief that many unusual men were stars who had descended to the earth. This idea that stars descended to the earth and turned into men of extraordinary power had deep roots in the popular mind. Not only were emperors identified with gods or stars, but statesmen and great warriors, as well as notorious bandits, could also be identified with stars.

In the prelude to the novel *Shui-hu*, the novelist creates the story of Commander Hung who, in heedlessness, freed the guilty spirits of thirty-six stars of Heaven and seventy-two stars of Earth. He indicates that the 108 bandit-heroes of the novel were incarnations of these devilish stars.[35] In chapter 42, the novelist reinstates this theory of incarnation by inserting the episode of Sung Chiang's receiving of the divine books from a goddess, the Goddess of Nine Heavens. In the story, the goddess commanded Sung Chiang as follows:

> The Jade Emperor, because the evil in your heart is not yet cut off, and because the way of virtue you have not yet completed, has now punished you by sending you to this earth. But in no great while you shall return to the halls of the gods and there must be no smallest point then in which you fail, for if when you die your soul cannot ascend into Heaven and must descend into Hell even I may not save you.[36]

The Goddess told Sung Chiang that he was once the Lord of Stars before he had been punished and sent to the mundane world by the Jade Emperor of Heaven. Now he needed to acquire a store of good deeds and redeem his sins before he would be allowed to return to Heaven.

In addition to the belief in the incarnation of stars and the superstition of identifying a man's fate with a star, there are other features in the historical novels that are related to the basic concept of pre-destination. Consider the stories of *chan-cheng chao-ch'in* (proposing marriage on the battlefield) as examples: using "marriage by destiny" as a convenient rationale, these stories are usually comical episodes. There are two types of *chan-cheng chao-ch'in*, those initiated by the lady-warriors and those either arranged by a third person or initiated by a comic hero. In the first type, the heroines were always the superior lady-warriors (*nü-chiang*) who defeated young and handsome braves and then proposed to marry them. The popular example is the story of Mu Kuei-ying and Yang Tsung-pao in the historical novel *Yang-chia-chiang*.[37] In the story, Mu Kuei-ying was a superior lady-warrior who defeated and captured the young and handsome Yang Tsung-pao. After having captured him, she fell in love with him and proposed to marry him. There are many heroines of the Mu Kuei-ying type in the world of popular literature, especially in the later Ch'ing historical novels about the T'ang and the S'ung periods.[38] These stereotyped lady-warriors, who excelled at martial arts but always fell helplessly for the young and handsome heroes, are in contrast to the ideal lady of the traditional society who was shy and gentle and never dreamed of proposing marriage herself to any man. In the second type of proposing marriage on the battlefield stories, it is the man who takes the initiative. Here the comical nature of these stories is even more obvious, for either the heroes are comical characters, or the couple about to be married is a comical pair. Take Wang Ai-hu's story in the *Shui-hu* as an example: nicknamed Wang the Dwarf Tiger, this comical character, as arranged by Sung Chiang, was to marry Hu San-niang, nicknamed Ten-foot Green Snake, a lady-warrior and newly acquired captive of the Liang-shan band.[39] It seems that no one in the novel notices the odd match — a dwarf and a ten-foot-tall girl. Everyone praised Sung Chiang's act. The novelist described it matter-of-factly:

> Thus Sung Chiang took it upon himself to give the Green Snake to Wang the Dwarf Tiger for a wife, and all acclaimed Sung Chiang as a good and noble man, and on that day again a feast was made for congratulations.[40]

But for the reader, the contrast is all too obvious and comical. We should mention in passing that the insertion of comical episodes in the historical novels reveals the influence of the tradition of the storytellers who viewed it as part of their profession to entertain their audience. Such comicality was later carried to a degree of vulgarity, such as the episode about Yü-ch'ih Kung's "proposing marriage on the battlefield" to Lady Black in the Ch'ing edition of the novel *Shuo T'ang*, of which we find no counterpart in the Ming novels.[41]

All these proposing marriage on the battlefield stories share two things in common. First, they all rely on a superstitious belief in marriage by destiny. Second, they offer no satisfactory explanation about why there were so many lady-warriors in a male-dominated Confucian society, although in some stories the novelist did offer a simple explanation: They simply described the lady-warriors as barbarian princesses. The belief in marriage by destiny was universally accepted in traditional China. It had something to do with the traditional social custom of marriage by parental arrangements. In a society in which marriage was negotiated on the basis of the family's need, not on that of individual choice, personal tragedies and frustrations were bound to happen. While the prevailing Confucian value system guarded this marital institution, the helplessly trapped individuals had no place to turn except to the religious explanation of predestination. On the other hand, while the belief in marriage by destiny released some of the helpless frustration resulting from traditional marriage arrangements, it also served as a ready justification for unusual circumstances such as proposing marriages on battlefields. In the historical novels, where the belief in the predestination of the human lot predominates, marriage by destiny is just another example of the general attitude of "submitting to Providence" (*t'ing-t'ien yu-ming*), a characteristic of an agrarian culture that was the background of all traditional novels.

While belief in fatalism, predestination, and the inscrutable workings of Heaven reveals a generally passive attitude toward life, belief in transmigration of souls, moral retribution, and the theory of karma offers some positive prospects in the next life. Influenced by both Buddhism and Taoism, these related ideas and beliefs are based on an assumption that the soul is immortal. Since transmigration means the passage of a soul at death into another body, the presumption is that life and death are in a continual succession of beginnings and endings. This cyclic concept of life and death as a continual succession of beginnings and endings was very important in traditional religious thought, for it not only raised a hope of salvation in the next life, it also released some of the anger and anxiety caused by injustice in this

life. Related to this concept of transmigration is the theory of moral
retribution. Asserting that goodness has a good recompense and evil
has an evil recompense, the retribution theory emphasized moral cultivation and accumulation of good deeds. Although there are differences
in details about what constitutes the so-called moral cultivation and
meritorious deeds between Buddhism and Taoism, there is no major
difference in the principle of moral retribution. In principle, according
to this theory, man has no control over his fate in this life because he
has to pay for his sins and grievances committed in the previous life.
But if he works very hard to cultivate his personal virtues and to
accumulate enough good deeds in this life, he can expect a better fate
in the next life.

In historical novels in which historical justice was supposedly
sought, the retribution theory is often applied to remedy injustice.
There are stories dealing with the rewards of good deeds and there are
stories dealing with retribution for evil. Generally speaking, the former
are not as noticeable as the latter, which emphasize undoing the
injustice one historical personage did to another. For example, the
injustice received by Yueh Fei from Ch'in Kuai was a popular subject
for moral retribution. In the novel *Ta-Sung*, in which Yueh Fei's
story is told, the retribution theme is most evident in the concluding
chapter.[42] Emphasizing that evil has an evil recompense, Ch'in Kuai
and his wife, who were responsible for Yueh Fei's death, were made to
pay for their sins. They were not only tortured to death by ghosts and
spirits, according to the novel, they were also sentenced to hell to
endure severe punishment with other villains in history. After three
years in purgatory, the novel continues, they would be incarnated
in the form of animals such as a dog, cow, hog, or sheep to be eaten
by humankind. Then they would remain as animals in the kalpa
transmigration.[43]

The retribution theory was very popular among the forerunners of
historical novels, the *p'ing-hua* (the popular tales). Consider the *San-
kuo-chih p'ing-hua* as an example. In its prologue, the historical events
of Emperor Kao-tzu's (Liu Pang of the Han) killing of his three
meritorious generals, Han Hsin, Ying Pu, and P'eng Yueh, were used
as an example to elaborate the retribution theory. According to this
theory, since Liu Pang and his wife, Empress Lü, were unjust to their
three generals, they were later incarnated as Emperor Hsien and

Empress Fu of the Later Han and were killed by the order of Ts'ao Ts'ao, who was supposedly transmigrated from Han Hsin. And the Han empire, which was founded by Liu Pang, was divided into three kingdoms: the Wei, the Wu, and the Shu. The Wei was headed by Ts'ao Ts'ao who, as mentioned before, was transmigrated from Han Hsin; the Wu was headed by Sun Ch'üan, transmigrated from Ying Pu; and the Shu was headed by Liu Pei, transmigrated from P'eng Yueh.[44] By interpreting the division of the Three Kingdoms (the period of Three Kingdoms) as the result of divine retribution, the *San-kuo-chih p'ing-hua* conveys a simple conviction of the existence of historical justice.

When the Three Kingdoms stories were collected into a novel, this early retribution theory was dropped. In the novel *San-kuo*, there is no mention of the transmigrations of souls from Han Hsin, Ying Pu, and P'eng Yueh to Ts'ao Ts'ao, Sun Ch'üan, and Liu Pei, respectively. However, this retribution story was preserved in short story form. For example, in the collection of *Yü-shih ming-yen*, we have the short story "Nao yin-ssu Ssu-ma Mao tuan yü," which is very similar to the prologue in *San-kuo-chih p'ing-hua*.[45] As a matter of fact, moral retribution is a dominant theme in short stories and social and domestic novels in Ming times, although in the area of historical novels, it is not a dominant theme.

In addition to the retribution theory, the Taoist concept of viewing life and death as a continual succession of beginnings and endings also pervades the historical novels, together with the idea of the deliverance of the dead, which had a Buddhist origin. The best example is the novel *Feng-shen*, which assimilates both Buddhist and Taoist thought. As mentioned before, although the *Feng-shen* is a novel about the historical Shang-Chou dynastic war, its central theme is the investiture of the gods. According to the *Feng-shen*, the Shang-Chou dynastic war was instrumental in carrying out the predestined investiture of the gods, prearranged among the celestial hierarchies; those who died in the Shang-Chou war were the ones to be invested. The belief that when a meritorious man dies, he can be removed to Heaven and deified was a tradition long before the writing of the *Feng-shen*. But since meritorious men are, by nature, not of the same quality, their destinies after death should also be different. In the *Feng-shen* those who were to be invested were divided into three classes:

> [T]hose whose nature is high and who could be transformed into immortals, those of inferior nature, who would be invested as deities, those whose cultivation is low, who would remain as humankind, in the kalpa of transmigration. This is the evolution of Heaven and Earth.[46]

In other words, there are three possibilities waiting for the chosen ones: to be granted rebirth, to be invested as deities, and to be transformed into immortals. These possibilities, which are decided by the nature and cultivation of the chosen ones, indicated the order of the evolution, that is, from rebirth (returning to Earth as humankind) to deities (being removed to Heaven as deities) to immortals (deliverance from life, death, and transmigration), the highest order.

As for the fate of the great mass of the people, there is no immediate relief in sight. In the sacred mandate issued by Yuan-shih t'ien-tsun (Celestial Honoured Primordial), which was read to the souls of the dead by the Marshal Chiang Shang (the leading hero of the *Feng-shen*) on the Feng-shen T'ai (Tower for Investiture of the Gods), they are reminded of the common fate of humankind as follows:

> Life, death and transmigration, these are to revolve without end. The retribution for sins and grievances committed in a previous existence would never stop. I feel great compassion for them.[47]

The idea of the investiture of the gods in the *Feng-shen* reminds us of the belief in the practice of meritorious deliverance of the dead, which was shared by both the Buddhist and Taoist coenobites in Ming times. Emphasizing the deliverance from life, death, and transmigration as the final salvation, the two intervals — to be granted a return to earth or to be invested as deities and removed to heaven — were looked upon as part of the Earth-Heaven evolution granted only by the grace of the celestial hierarchies. Thus, in the final analysis, the movers of the universe were still the celestial hierarchies who controlled the dynamic force in the universe.

In conclusion, the common attitudes and general religious assumptions reflected in popular fiction are interesting in two aspects. First, they reveal the pervasive impact of the syncretism of the Three Teachings on all levels of the religious imagination. What is intellectually significant is not the synthesis of worldviews, but the creative interaction of the three traditions — Confucianism, Buddhism, and Taoism. The religious ideas fired the Chinese literary imagination; they appealed to the Chinese on all levels. Consider the concept of the inscrutable workings of Heaven. It is the dominant religious theme of the novel *San-kuo*; the novel ascribes Liu Pei and Chu-ko Liang's failure to rebuild the Han empire to fate. For the well-educated, the *San-kuo* is a profound tragedy; it symbolizes all unfulfilled dreams and ambitions in life. The Ming literati who were well-versed in the Confucian ideal of achieving "sageliness within and kingliness without" (*nei-sheng wai-wang*) and the Machiavellian application of Taoist principles of "to be" and "not to be" found great relief in the Buddhist gospel of compassion and predestination. They accepted the interpretation of fate. For the less educated, the senses of failure and unfulfillment did not touch them that much; they accepted the inscrutable workings of Heaven calmly and matter-of-factly. But they loved *San-kuo*, they loved all those intriguing stories, all those colorful and unforgettable heroes and villains. Besides, many of them truly believed in fate. In fact, the early popular narrative, the *San-kuo chih p'ing-hua*, which emphasizes the moral retribution theme, reflects its appeal to the popular taste.

Second, the influence of correlative cosmology in historical novels is manifested in the commonly accepted belief that the affairs of the state, as well as the intimate life of the people, are correlative with the naturalistic forces of heaven. The assimilation of Buddhist and Taoist elements into the classical religion multiplied the superstitious ideas related to this faith. While the influence of correlative cosmology in the Late Ming was increased by the teachings associated with the syncretic Three Teachings movement of the era, the cosmological criticism in the early Ch'ing could be viewed as a sort of reaction against the full-blown syncretism. Many factors contributed to this cosmological criticism. One was the late Ming to early Ch'ing assimilation of cosmologically subversive technical and empirical studies into the mainstream of Confucian scholarship.[48] But none of these critical cosmological ideas are to be found in popular fiction, especially the historical novels. Clearly, in popular fiction, remnants of old views tended to persist much longer and more vigorously.

Chapter 7

Conclusion: The Interplay between Elite and Popular Traditions

Heaven shows the way of the spirits by the four
seasons that never fail, [and the people look up to
Heaven]. The sages devised guidance by the way of
the Spirits, and [people in the] empire look up to the
sages.

I-ching

The sixteenth and seventeenth centuries witnessed the economic
affluence that was attested by the rise and growth of an urban culture
of great diversity and refinement in China. Almost simultaneous with
the rise of urban culture were the developments of a new vernacular
literature and a cultural movement of popularizing learning for all
people. The historical novel, which had first made its appearance in
the book market in the early sixteenth century and flourished throughout the seventeenth century, embodied these two exuberant movements.
On the one hand, it was undertaken with the expressed purpose of
popularizing and elucidating the profound and difficult Official Histories
to all people. On the other hand, it was also a literary undertaking,
adapting other unofficial historical sources and oral and fictitious
materials, thus opening the door to the influence of the folk stream in
literature.

Having incorporated, through a period of evolutionary developments, the various oral and antecedent narrative materials, the writers
of historical novels acted as mediators between the elite and the popular cultures. Thus the ideas and images that emerged in the novels
reflect a long period of dynamic interaction between the elite and
popular traditions. Furthermore, these historical novels, which cover
most of the legendary and historical periods of China up to the Southern
Ming reigns (1645–61), present a "historical world" that was shared by
the two most popular entertainments in the traditional times, the professional storytelling and the musical drama of all kinds. Together they

181

provide a body of generally accepted popular assumptions and attitudes that commands immediate emotional and inarticulate assent among their Chinese audiences.

As the historical novel was undertaken with an explicit purpose of popularizing and elucidating history for all people, it appealed to the popular taste of the time. The sensation, emotion, volition, and thought reflected in historical novels are, as demonstrated by the dominant motifs and images of heroes and villains discussed in previous chapters, more closely related to the ideals of the common people than to what the sages and philosophers taught.[1] The historical novels tend to describe problems and phenomena but do not get into the hearts or the roots of these problems. For instance, some of the salient aspect of Ming thought such as the new humanitarian view of the self, stressing the actual nature of men, especially his physical life and concrete needs, was never seriously dealt with in historical novels.[2] Concepts such as the image of licentious women were not deeply explored in the historical novels. However, such concerns are present, ready to be picked up by other writers who found a different literary genre — for example, the genre of social and domestic novels — for developing them. The stories about the licentious P'an Chin-lien, a minor character in the historical novel *Shui-hu*, is an example. From a minor character in *Shui-hu*, P'an becomes one of the leading characters in the famous novel *Chin P'ing Mei* (The Adventurous Story of Hsi-men and His Six Wives), which examines the social degeneracy and personal corruption and, at the same time, gives a truthful and penetrating picture of life as it was at the Ming time.[3]

Adapted to ordinary intelligence or taste, historical novels generally avoided controversial and heretical opinions. The key issues that concerned their writers, and the attitudes and concepts the writers developed to deal with these issues, are often clear-cut; they remind us of the primacy of ethical and political consideration in the traditional Chinese mind. In this conclusion, we will sum up our findings from three different perspectives. First, we take a look at the major intellectual themes in historical novels. As pointed out before, the elements of the elite and popular traditions were in a process of changing and regrouping in history. The two traditions have long affected each other and continued to do so. In the case of Ming historical novels, the interplay of the two traditions has a special bearing on their major themes.

Thematically speaking, there are five categories of major themes in historical novels representing the worldviews and the basic values in imperial China. The first category deals with the dominant motif of the dynasty-building contest. The central issues are two seemingly conflicting value systems, the elite's classical theory of divine sovereignty and the nonelite's challenging theory of popular revolt by force of arms. The former centers upon such time-honored concepts as the Mandate of Heaven, divine birth, the sage-king, and the dynastic legitimacy, all of which support the theory of heaven-derived imperial sovereignty. The latter centers upon heroism and militarism that regard "righteous revolts" by force of arms as the driving force of history. Since both the emperor's claim of the Mandate of Heaven and the rebel claims of supernatural patronage (also a form of blessings from Heaven) fall back on the same source — the ancient folk belief in the potency of the supernatural — each submits to the de facto recognition that whoever wins gets Heaven's blessings.

Another outstanding belief stimulating the motif of dynastic cycle is the classical conception of an ideal state, the ultimate Great Harmony (*ta-t'ung*), or Grand Peace of Great Equality that is invariably associated with the ideals of equality, peace, order, and unity. The Chinese have, ever since ancient times, waited for the arrival of an ideal age of grand peace or for a return to the legendary Age of Sage-Kings, so they regard all kinds of war and disorder as being merely transitory, and have never given up hope for peace and unification in spite of the recurrence of chaos and disruption in history. Thus, the Ming Chinese, who came thousands of years after their ancestors had built an empire in their land, had history on their side when they thought of their empire as the only empire under heaven. Dynasties came and went, but the empire that had survived all perils in history would continue its cyclic course, or so they believed.

Closely related to the prospect of an ideal state is the classical belief in a sage-king. People were, we are told by the historical novelists, forever waiting for a sage-king who could bring peace and order to the world. In fact, the novelists often refer to the ideal state as sage-king. Here again, the *sage* concept was as vague as the concept of an ideal state. The key attributes of a sage, such as benevolence, righteousness, and dedication, tell very little about the relationship between the sage and the ideal state, just as the abstract words *peace, order, unity*, and *equality* tell very little about the contents of an ideal government.

Nevertheless, judging from the frequency with which historical novelists refer to the ideal state as the sage-king, it is clear that, to them, the emperor was the state. This personalization of politics characterizes the Chinese worldview.

The second category of major themes concerns human ambition. Among the three areas of activity in which one could achieve fame and glory in traditional times, the most glamourous ambition was, according to the historical novels, meritorious service to the state. Since the founding of a new dynasty was regarded as unifying the country and bringing peace and order to the people, it was considered to be one of the most meritorious services to the country. And the protagonists of the historical novels are, for the most part, people involved in the making of new dynasties: the dynastic contenders, including both the victor and the vanquished, their advisors, and their warriors. These four groups of fictionalized historical personages are the popularized heroes whose model behavior and common attributes have exerted tremendous influence on the populace. In spite of their different roles, they share two things in common: they are all men of humble origin — commoners — and they all have achieved fame and glory. Their examples implanted in people's minds the powerful suggestion that birth was no longer the mark of kingship, aristocracy, or any kind of distinction. The so-called roaming bandits (*liu-k'ou*) at the end of the Ming dynasty attest the pervasive influence of the dynasty-building examples: all the rebel leaders proclaimed themselves kings. The frequent occurrences of armed rebellions in Ming times, which are recorded matter-of-factly in the Official Histories, suggest that the socioeconomic and socio-political structure of the Ming empire was collapsing. The historical novelists were, without realizing it, actually advocating and promoting the popular revolts by force of arms.

While historical novels popularized the idea that kings and nobles are made, not born, they also presented alternative examples including total elimination of human ambition. A sharp contrast to the human motivation to achieve fame and glory is the idea of withdrawal from world affairs and the philosophical attitude of noninvolvement that rejects politics and debunks emotional propaganda. There were many kinds of recluses in traditional societies. Some took the act of being a recluse as a gesture of protest or defiance against tyranny, political corruption, or unacceptable alien rule. Some took it as a gesture of nonconformity and some took it as a religious gesture of withdrawal from secular life. In historical novels, although the recluses seldom assume a major role, they are often introduced to provide a sardonic commentary on the contending world of the fame-obsessed heroes. Moreover, the return-to-nature lifestyles of the recluses bring back the nostalgia for the Utopian Golden Age, a nostalgia that most people share during times of war and disorder in their longing for a simple life. Thus, the two attitudes — the Confucian and Legalist's philosophy of public service and the Taoist and Buddhist's calling of withdrawal from the life of this world — although conflicting with each other in their basic values, coexist in the historical world. In fact, they could be seen as complementing each other in the sense that together they shed light on human motivation in traditional times.

The third category of major themes deals with the sociopolitical order and its ethical values. On the surface, although the basic Confucian didactic tunes have not been changed, there are strong undercurrents of new attitudes beneath the seemingly familiar themes. Many of the elements of late Ming popular culture are reflected here: the romanticizing of militarism, the emergence of the ethnic issue in the presence of barbarian invasions, the openness to religious syncretism, the call for a return to the teachings of the ancient sages, the vital concern with historical justice, and the strong affirmation of popular heroism in its emphasis on selfless friendship. The most significant development regarding ethical values is the emphasis on the relationship between friends. Among the five cardinal human relationships in the Confucian scheme of values, the one between friends is the only one that offers an individual the opportunity of choosing. In Confucian society, an individual had no say about almost everything that concerned him, including his spouse, but he had the opportunity to choose his friends, or at least he felt he had some control in that area. It was not coincidence that in both cultures, the elite and popular, emphasis was placed on the relationship between friends. For example, Li Chih and Ho Hsin-yin, two influential radical thinkers of the late Ming, harangued about the importance of the relationship between friends.[4] In fiction and drama, many of the popular heroes echo this same sentiment. This was a small cry for freedom, a yearning to be liberated from the bondage of human relationships and the responsibilities that come with them. This was the beginning of the evolution of modern man.

A few more words are necessary here on the issue of the rise of modern man. Traditional Confucian culture had centered upon rational man, whose harmonious relationship with nature and whose moral self-control were expected to create the good society. This rational man, the pillar of the good society, was expected to be not only morally perfect but also a dedicated, selfless public servant whose highest goal in life was to serve his country in the best way he could. However, the cultural and socioeconomic changes of the late Ming — caused by the expansion of commerce and industry, increasing urbanization, and the growth of an urban culture of great diversity and refinement — were replacing that rational man with a more dangerous and mercurial urban man. This urban man, or modern man, was not merely a rational creature but a human being of feeling and instinct, as portrayed so vividly in the works of late Ming literati. Yet it was precisely this emphasis on feeling and instinct that was ascribed as the cause of the moral decline of the late Ming society by its early Ch'ing Confucian critics. This explains why the early Ch'ing intelligentsia were so preoccupied with their criticism of the literati of the late Ming. It also explains why there was such an urgent and sincere call to return to the orthodox Neo-Confucian teachings among the early Ch'ing thinkers and scholars.

The fourth category of major themes concerns the discrepancy between political ideals and the realities that manifest themselves in the areas of bureaucratic corruption, social and economic injustice, crime and violence, and, above all, the despotic imperial institution. In reconstructing historical stories dealing with these themes, writers of historical novels generally follow a basic formula that reflects the simple nature of these historical tales. It was a "heroes versus villains" formula that views history as a perpetual struggle between the villains and the upright heroes. It is true that the stories leave one with the impression of the heroes' simple heroism stressing qualities such as generosity, chivalry, excellence in martial arts, and abstinence. It is equally true that there are vivid and detailed accounts of torture and atrocities that reveal the writers' unconscious appetites for gross and violent stimulants. This desire becomes alarming when one encounters a great many ruthless and senseless killings in the novels.

Such killings are disturbing because they are not committed by the villains alone; they are also committed by the heroes, who in their exuberant spirit of revenge exhibit uncontrollable wrath in relentless killings. Evidence of rampant violence reflected in the historical novels compels the historian to take a hard look at the self-image of Chinese civilization traditionally held by the Chinese literati themselves. Contrary to the general image of a contented and peace-loving people, the Chinese in Ming times seemed to be violent and restless in many ways. They were violent and restless because they were helplessly trapped by the social, economic, and political injustices of their time. They were constantly in the dark about how to fight the villains who committed crimes against them, and they were also in the dark about how to check the corrupted power that inflicted inhuman persecutions upon them. Moreover, their Confucian leaders could not help them with their empty promise of benevolent government; even their beloved heroes were, at times, prone to bloodshed, violent impulse, and excessive cruelty. For them, the only hope was Heaven, and they had no choice but to trust their fate in the inscrutable workings of Heaven.

This note of despair leads us to the last category of our major themes, the category that concerns the cosmic and religious order in historical novels. The dominant motifs here, besides the belief in the predestination of the human lot, are the retribution theory, the theory of the transmigration of the soul, and the theory of the evolution of Heaven and Earth. Reflecting the syncretic nature of the traditional religions, these religious ideas and superstitions reveal the special blending and interpenetration of the classical religion, Buddhism, and religious Taoism. Since these religions have diffused intimately into the imperial-Confucian social and political institutions, they do represent a generally accepted religious order in traditional times.

This syncretic system of traditional religions was further characterized by two unique traits: magic cults and mythological lores. Based on beliefs in supernatural agencies, magic cults are primitive superstitious practices that predominated in the traditional religious sphere. They reflect the psychology of the people who longed for miracles or any form of psychological relief. People wanted to believe in the mysterious workings of the supernatural because, in this realm at least, they thought they had a chance of receiving justice, while in the human world, they had no chance at all. In the historical novels dominated by military romances, magic plays an important role in military campaigns; the fact that almost all the imperial advisers or chiefs of staff excelled in both strategy and magic testifies to the popularity of magic in people's minds. Since magic works as a supernatural sanctioning agent for religion, it is a source of superstitious ideas, not a source of moral ideas. This relation helps to explain why religions could not compete with Confucian ethics for moral authority in traditional times.

Another source of religious ideas and beliefs was mythological lore, which was also source material for popular writers and storytellers. As mentioned before, the common people received a considerable part of their religious information by listening to stories and by reading mythological literature. As a result, popular fiction and storytelling were important verbal and literary vehicles for the dissemination of religious ideas. In our search for the popular conception of the cosmic order of the Ming period, we naturally turn our attention to the imaginary writings of that period.

There are varied cosmic orders in Ming fiction, but the basic conception is the same. The supreme administrative authority of the cosmic order in the novel is the Jade Emperor, a mythological figure, who reigns together with a host of subordinate naturalistic deities over Heaven, Earth, and the Underworld. Although both the Buddhist patriarch, Buddha, and the Taoist Lord Lao are respected as equals by the Jade Emperor in the novels, they do not share with the latter any of his administrative authority. Moreover, patterning the celestial hierarchies after the temporal imperial government reveals a this-worldly orientation that is even more striking when we think of the explosive expansion of the Buddhist cosmos. But this enormous Buddhist cosmos of thousands of worlds did not seem to have much effect on the Chinese mind, even though Buddhism was very popular in China. To the Chinese, the three dimensions of Heaven, Earth, and the Underworld, described in all sorts of mythological literature, define the boundaries of the Chinese cosmos. Instead of looking outward and searching for an expanded cosmos, they tended to look at this world, and to search for the unity of cosmological order and earthly events.

Next, we try to place the dominant motifs of historical novels in proper perspective. As pointed out in the Introduction, the historical novels represent the collective effort of both oral artists and educated writers; thus they reflect the influence of the common people in literature as well as the influence on the Chinese mind of the elite traditions. Since the novelists generally structured their historical world through models provided by the elitist historians, the trails of the interplay between the elite and the popular traditions can be observed by the novelists' different emphases on, and occasional departures from, the established values. In table 9, we compare the dominant motifs of the

TABLE 9. The Interplay between Elite and Popular Traditions

Prevailing Elite Ideas and Values	Ideas and Values Highlighted in the Novels
Tao as the Truth in *ta-Tao* (the great Way)	*Tao* as socioeconomic justice in *t'i-t'ien hsiang-Tao* (uphold justice for Heaven)
Jen as universal benevolence, an ethical and political idea	Emphasis on no killing; "the best (military) victory is won by benevolence"
I as an ethical and political idea; righteousness, defining the three bonds	*I* as a social virtue; social justice; Friendship (sworn brothers)
Chung as loyal to the sovereign	*Chung* as loyal to country, people, and friends
Hsiao as the root of true virtue, emphasis on filial piety to parents	Emphasis on filial piety to widowed mother
Wen (civil) over *wu* (military)	Militarism and martial spirit
Sheng-chün, a political cliché referring to the (present) emperor or emperor in general	*Pao-chün* (tyrannical ruler) and *hun-chün* (muddleheaded ruler) are often used to refer to the emperor in general
Ch'an-jang, a concept of yielding (yield to virtue); Yao (yielded to virtue) abdicated the throne in Shun's favor	The abdication stories of Yao and Shun, emphasizing the public spirit
Hereditary emperorship	"Only those who have vigorous troops and stout horses could be the Son of Heaven."
Dynastic wars	Righteous revolts
Vertical relationship; superior-inferior	Horizontal relationship; among friends
Particularistic and ascriptive family-blood	Universalistic and voluntary associations
Belief in hierarchy, emphasizing superior-inferior relations; one-sided demand on the part of the inferior	Emphasis on reciprocal relationship with mutual responsibilities
Arranged marriage	More free marriage: stories of *chan-cheng chao-ch'in* (propose marriage on battlefield)
Male superiority	Female highlighted: superior military skills and intellect; exemplary behavior (story about Hsu Shu's mother)
Friendship as the last in the five cardinal human relationships	Friendship greatly emphasized

novels with the prevalent Confucian values. Although I only list the different emphases to highlight the contrast, it goes without saying that there are large areas of overlap between the elite and popular traditions during their long process of mutual influence. In fact, the above-mentioned five categories of major themes already reveal part of the overlap.

The common attitudes and assumptions expressed in the historical novels tell us something about the popular mind-set of the Chinese people in traditional times. To put this in proper historical perspective, we need to examine two additional factors regarding the traditional Chinese experience. The first involves the general attitude toward temporal experience in historical novels, and the second, the phenomenon of hero worship that took the form of deifying departed distinguished men. Consider the general attitude toward temporal experience. According to the late Russian philosopher Nicholas Berdyaev (1874–1948), there are three basic categories for describing time: cosmic time, historical time, and existential time.[5] Cosmic time is nature's time and refers to the endless recurrence of things: night following day, season following season, the cycle of birth, growth, and decay. Historical time, however, refers not only to nature's time, but also to historical epochs known by memory and tradition. Cosmic and historical time are both objectified and both are subject to mathematical calculation. Existential time is a breakthrough of eternity into historical and cosmic time. It is subjective and inward and cannot be externalized mathematically. Though it is not exactly eternity, it participates in eternity. Every creative act of man is performed in existential time and projected in historical time.

Describing a universal temporal experience, Berdyaev's three categories of time shed light on the time-history concepts in our historical novels. These three forms of time are all present: the concept of cycle (cosmic time) emphasizes the endless recurrence of things including the imperial dynasties; the longing to be recorded in history (both historical and existential time) emphasizes both the concept of immortality and the concept of historical continuity; the concept of historical achievement stresses both the accomplishment and the significance of each historical epoch (existential and historical time); the concept of the unity of the cosmological order and earthly events reflects basic religious beliefs in the oneness of the universe, to mention only a few examples. Making no distinction between the time-sense and the historical-sense, the traditional Chinese took them both to be specific manifestations of their aspiration to be known to posterity. Believing that time-history would always have the last word on everything, they lived in these three forms of time all at once.

Our second observation involves the phenomenon of hero worship that reflected the psychology of the people. Hero worship in traditional China went beyond ordinary hero-worship in the modern sense. The Chinese masses, with hearty approval from the imperial government, actually worshipped their heroes as gods. They built temples and shrines for them; they made sacrifices to them; they prayed to them for help. And most important of all, they believed in their deified heroes' abilities to perform miracles. Coming into play here was the common belief that a man of unusual virtue or ability would become, after death, a spirit of extraordinary magic prowess, capable of performing a variety of miracles. The reputation of the prowess of his soul was enhanced by stories of his legendary capabilities in his lifetime, thus transforming him into a divine hero living on as an efficacious spirit overseeing the activities of the community. The nationwide worship of Kuan Yü, one of the leading heroes in the novel *San-kuo*, was an example.

Originating as one of the folk heroes in the Three Kingdoms period and popularized by the many Three Kingdoms stories and plays spreading over several centuries, the legend of this great warrior — symbol of loyalty, righteousness, and unmatched prowess — grew with history until it transformed him into a divine god. Two factors helped the popular cults of Kuan Yü to grow: one was the official sanction and glorification of his moral courage, and second, the mythological stories about his magic power. The moral glorification of Kuan Yü could be seen on various levels of thought and popular consciousness expressed in imperial edicts, memorials to the throne, inscriptions on monuments, local gazetteers, popular fiction and drama, popular educational works, and so forth. These explain the ethicopolitical nature of the official worship of Kuan Yü and his buildup into a universally accepted paragon of virtue. The widespread mythological stories about Kuan Yü's magic power show the magic aspects of the cult. These supernatural stories were important in inspiring people's faith in Kuan Yü the god, and they actually helped to keep the cult alive.[6]

In the historical novel *San-kuo*, although the cult of Kuan Yü is still in its early stage, stories about his heroic deeds and magic power are very colorful. Since we have already discussed Kuan Yü the warrior in previous chapters, we shall only address the supernatural tales in which he is viewed as a god or spirit. The deifying of Kuan Yü started right after he was killed. There were stories about how Lü Meng, who set traps to capture Kuan Yü, became possessed by the spirit of Kuan Yü and died mysteriously at a banquet given in celebration of Kuan Yü's defeat, and how Ts'ao Ts'ao was horrified by the head of Kuan Yü, which was placed in a box and sent to him by Sun Ch'üan.[7] Following are some details of the Ts'ao Ts'ao story that reveal the supernatural aspect of these stories, bearing in mind that both the novelist and his traditional readers believed in the story:

> Then he [Ts'ao Ts'ao] ordered the messenger to come in with the box, which was opened, and he looked upon the face of the dead [Kuan Yü]. The features had not changed; the face bore the same appearance as of old. Ts'ao Ts'ao smiled.

> "I hope you have been well since our last meeting, Yun-ch'ang," said Ts'ao Ts'ao.

> To his horror, the mouth opened, the eyes rolled and the long beard and hair stiffened. Ts'ao Ts'ao fell to the ground in a swoon.

> They rushed to him, but it was a long time before he recovered consciousness.

> "General Kuan is indeed a deity from heaven," he said.[8]

Continuing his stories about Kuan Yü, the novelist tells how the spirit of the great warrior did not dissipate into space but wandered through the void till it came to the famous Mount of the Jade Spring, where it was enlightened by a Buddhist priest on the subject of causal relation. Then the novelist concludes:

> After this appearance to the priest his [Kuan Yü's] spirit wandered hither and thither about the mountain, manifesting its sacred character and guarding the people. Impressed by his virtue, the inhabitants built a temple on the mountain of the Jade Spring, wherein they sacrificed at four seasons.[9]

The stories of Kuan Yü in *San-kuo* illustrate the evolution of hero worship in traditional times. There are all types of heroes in historical novels, including the martyrs, such as upright officials and patriotic generals; the empire-builders, such as the founding emperors and their counselors and warriors; and the outlaw heroes. For various reasons, these heroes distinguished themselves among their fellowmen: the martyrs, whose primary attributes are loyalty and courage, exhibit extra moral strength and great endurance; the founding emperors, whose primary attribute is a mysterious charisma, display godly appearance and noble conduct; the warriors and outlaw heroes, whose primary attributes are prowess and great physical strength, demonstrate powerful muscles that command instant respect; the counselor-strategists, whose primary attribute is intellectual strength, show not only intelligence but also supernatural power that enables them to interpret dreams, to deal with the other world, and to master the force of nature. It is because of these extraordinary powers — moral, divine, physical, magic, and intellectual — that they rose above their fellow men and became heroes.

Regardless of the different types of heroes, the basic elements of the apotheoses of departed heroes were the same: with or without divine rank they were worshiped as efficacious spirits; temples, shrines, or altars were built to honor them; sacrifices were offered to them; and prayers were addressed to them. It is interesting to note that although the heroes distinguished themselves during their lifetimes for a certain specific virtue or ability, these specific virtues or abilities became less significant after they were deified. In other words, once deified, they became all-round protective gods in people's minds, representing both general and specific values.

Another interesting aspect of the elevation of departed heroes to divine status in historical novels is the novelists' assumption that people were accustomed to seeing such things. As a matter of fact it is always "the people" or "the inhabitants" to whom the novelist refers as having the final word on the departed distinguished men. For example, in the novel *Shui-hu*, we are told matter-of-factly that after Sung Chiang died, "people" built a temple to worship him and offered sacrifices to him according to the seasons: "Whatever and whenever people prayed for help [in the Sung Chiang's temple], they got what they asked for."[10] Here, *people* seems to represent a kind of public vindication. Sung Chiang, the one-time bandit leader, was vindicated when his temple was erected. The significance of the apotheosis of Sung Chiang lies not in the fact that the novelist mentioned it, but in the fact that it was mentioned in such a casual and matter-of-fact way. Without giving any explanation, the novelist seems to assume that the apotheosis of a departed hero was the practice of the day.

Although the apotheosis of departed distinguished men is a common phenomenon in many cultures, few can match its extensive development in China, as evidenced by the fact that almost every community in traditional China had temples (or shrines or altars) to worship their deified heroes, as pointed out in a modern study.[11] The cult of deified heroes represents a unique characteristic of Chinese religious life. From the point of view of popular religion, this cult represents the supernatural element that has been an outstanding mark of Chinese religious life. From the point of view of popular ethicopolitical cults, it also attests the traditional Confucian emphasis on exemplary principles that initiated the use of hero worship as a means of social control.[12]

Thus, in the Official Histories, as well as in historical novels, we find a Confucian "theology" that runs as a connecting thread through the various popular minds. This Confucian theology is the theory of *shen-tao she-chiao* (to devise guidance by the way of the spirits) that can be found in an early commentary on the ancient classic, *I-ching* (The Book of Changes):

> Heaven shows the way of the spirits by the four seasons that never fail, [and the people look up to Heaven]. The sages devised guidance by the way of the spirits, and the [people in the] empire look up to the sages [too].[13]

Although this positive attitude of "to devise guidance by the way of the spirits" seems inconsistent with Confucius's evasive and agnostic attitudes toward religion,[14] the fact that *shen-tao she-chiao* was widely quoted in traditional discussions on religion shows its effectiveness. Here lies one of the problems of founders and followers: How do the interpretations of the followers relate to the original teachings of the founders? It seems obvious that Confucian followers generally took the liberty of interpreting the principle of *shen-tao she-chiao* as they saw fit.

The *shen-tao she-chiao* is also a very common phenomenon in many cultures, for in a broad sense all religions could be viewed as a method "to devise guidance by the way of the gods"[15] to lead people away from fear and wrongdoing. However, this rationale was further enhanced in China by the authoritarian Confucian ideology that divided people into two classes: those who rule and those who are ruled. As long as there were those who are ruled, the need for "devising guidance" existed. The Confucian metaphor of "the wind and the grass" is an example: It was believed that the nature of the governing elite is that of the wind, while the nature of the governed masses is that of grass — when the wind blows, the grass must bend. With this mentality, hero-worship — as an institutionalized system of moral values, political dogma, religious beliefs and practices — will always be used as an instrument of social control for the ruling class. That is why *shen-tao she-chiao* had endured more than two thousand years together with the imperial institution. Thus, contrary to a once-popular opinion that China was a country whose people were not bound by religious beliefs, in the world of popular literature we find a China that is full of strong and pervasive religious influence.[16] The most significant phenomena of these religious influences are the popular ethicopolitical cults that represent large-scale hero-worship in the form of the apotheosis of departed heroes. Since these deified heroes were worshiped for their exemplary behaviors, they became the most visible part of the grand scheme of *shen-tao she-chiao*, to devise political and societal guidance by the way of deifying heroes.

Finally, as in all other cultures and histories, the great men or heroes played a critical role in the history of imperial China.[17] They were not only the makers of history, but also became, after death, the model of behavioral emulation for later generations and, by virtue of their deification, the performers of supernatural miracles and objects of religious worship. In the end, these heroes became legendary and mythological figures in the syncretic religious system of imperial China, and as such became the instruments of moral indoctrination and political and social control. Perhaps as much by design as by natural development, these deified heroes — almost all of them can be found in historical novels — became part of a Confucian theocratic system in imperial China, the powerful source of the popular literary imagination, and the most representative indictor of the traditional Chinese mind.

Notes

Chapter 1

1. Although Western scholars do not always share the same definition of the historical novel, it is generally agreed that "the historical novel arose at the beginning of the nineteenth century" (Georg Lukacs) and that Sir Walter Scott was the "pioneer" (Helen Cam), the "inventor" (Brander Matthews), and "the founder" (Lion Feuchtwanger) of the genre. For details see, among others, Georg Lukacs, *The Historical Novel*, trans. Hannah and Stanley Mitchell (London: Merlin Press, 1962), pp. 17–63, esp. p. 19; Helen Cam, *Historical Novel* (London: Historical Association, 1961), pp. 1–19, esp. p. 5; Brander Matthews, *The Historical Novel and Other Essays* (New York: Charles Scribner's Sons, 1901), pp. 3–28, esp. p. 8; and Lion Feuchtwanger, *The House of Desdemona*, trans. Harold A. Basilius (Detroit: Wayne State University Press, 1963), pp. 44–80, esp. p. 44. For a detailed study of Scott's novels, see John H. Raleigh, "What Scott Meant to the Victorians," in *Time, Place, and Idea: Essays on the Novel* (Carbondale: Southern Illinois University Press, 1968), pp. 96–125. For discussion of the development of recent historical novels, see John Tebbel, *Fact and Fiction: Problems of the Historical Novelist* (Lansing: Historical Society of Michigan, 1962), pp. 1–12; and John Voelker, *About the Historical Novel* (Lansing: Historical Society of Michigan, 1970), pp. 1–9.
2. The origin of Chinese vernacular fiction is a complex issue. The availability of Sung sources helped scholars trace its beginning to the professional storytelling during the Sung period. For a discussion on the tradition of professional storytelling and its influence over vernacular fictions, see, among others, Hsu Shih-nien, *Ku-tien hsiao-shu lun-chi* (Shanghai: Shang-hai ch'u-pan kung-ssu, 1955), pp. 157–234; Lo Yeh, "Hsiao-shuo k'ai-p'i," in *Tsui-weng t'an-lu* (Shanghai: Ku-tien wen-hsueh ch'u-pan she, 1957), pp. 3–5; Li Hsiao-ts'ang, *Sung Yuan chi-i tsa-k'ao* (Shanghai: Shang-tsa ch'u-pan-she, 1953), pp. 71–94; Lu Hsun, *Chung-kuo hsiao-shuo shih-lueh* (Hong Kong: Chin-tai t'u shu kung-ssu, 1965), pp. 81–89; Sun K'ai-ti, *Su-chiang shuo-hua yü po-hua hsiao-shuo* (Peking: Tso-chia ch'u-pan she, 1956), pp. 1–30; T'an Cheng-pi, *Hua-pen yü ku-chü* (Shanghai: Ku-tien wen-hsueh ch'u-pan she, 1957), pp. 2–12; Yeh Te-chün, *Sung Yuan Ming chiang-ch'ang wen-hsueh* (Shanghai: Chung-hua shu-chü, 1959), pp.

1−9; Wu Hsiao-ju, *Chung-kuo hsiao-shuo chiang-hua chi ch'i-t'a* (Shanghai: Ku-tien wen-hsuen ch'u-pan she, 1956), pp. 17−28; Jaroslav Průšek, *The Origin and the Authors of the Hua-pen* (Prague: Orient Institute, Academia, 1967), pp. 15−30, 91−104; P. D. Hanan, "The Early Chinese Short Story, a Critical Theory in Outline," *HJAS* 27 (1967): 168−207; P. D. Hanan, "The Authorship of Some *Ku-chin hsiao-shuo* Stories," *HJAS* 29 (1969): 190−200; P. D. Hanan, "Sung and Yuan Vernacular Fiction: A Critique of Modern Methods of Dating," *HJAS* 30 (1970): 159−84; W. L. Idema, "Storytelling and the Short Story in China," *T'oung Pao* 59 (1973): 1−67; W. L. Idema, "Some Remarks and Speculations Concerning *p'ing-hua*," *T'oung Pao* 60 (1974): 121−72; and Y. W. Ma, "The Beginnings of Professional Storytelling in China: A Critique of Current Theories and Evidence," in *Etudes d'historie et de litérature chinoises offertes au Professeur Jaroslav Průšek* (Paris, 1976), pp. 227−45.

3. Generally speaking, Ming historical novels are grouped into two cognate categories that, according to Cheng Chen-to, are termed *chiang-shih* (historical narration) and *ying-hsiung ch'uan-ch'i* (heroic tales of marvels). See Cheng Chen-to, [*Ch'a-tu-pen*] *Chung-kuo wen-hsueh shih* (Hong Kong: Ku-wen shu-chü, n.d.), vol. 4, pp. 699−726. In his article "The Military Romance: A Genre of Chinese Fiction," C. T. Hsia also divides the traditional historical novels into two categories, the "popular chronicle" and the "military romance." The former refers to those that approximate the spirit and form of a popular chronicle; the latter refers to those that, despite their celebration of historical personages and events, make no pretensions to be serious history. Compared with Cheng's classification, Hsia's military romances generally fit in with Cheng's heroic tales of marvels, and Hsia's popular chronicles fit in with Cheng's historical narrations. But Hsia did not discuss only in generalities as Cheng did; he went further to examine the various elements and features of the genre. For details, see C. T. Hsia, "The Military Romance: A Genre of Chinese Fiction," in *Studies in Chinese Literary Genres*, ed. Cyril Birch (Berkeley: University of California Press, 1974), pp. 339−90.

4. In their book *The Growth of Literature*, a comparative study of the literary genres, H. M. and N. K. Chadwick term the Homeric epic as part of heroic literature (poetry and saga), which is the oldest literature in Western cultures. The Chinese historical novel, although an entirely different genre, shares some of the features of heroic literature. For a comparative study of heroic literature, especially the characteristics of heroic stories, see H. M. and N. K. Chadwick, *The Growth of Literature*, vols. 1 and 2 (Cambridge: Cambridge University Press, 1932, 1936), 1:1−95, 133−98; 2:77−100, 360−73, 487−95, 666−76. For a contemporary discussion of the relation and distinction between the Homeric epic and the modern novel, see Ian Watt's "Fielding and the Epic Theory of the Novel," in *The Rise of the Novel: Studies in Defoe, Richardson and Fielding* (Berkeley: University of California Press, 1964), pp. 239−59. Jaroslav Průšek, however, viewing the Western conception that "history is some sort of stream, a

continuous flow" as "the epic mode of expression," contends that European historiography (under the influence of Greek literature and historiography) has resembled epic works while in China "epics have no place in the artistic prose (*wen-chang*)." For an interesting discussion on the divergent approaches to historical phenomena in Greece and in China, see Jaroslav Průšek, *Chinese History and Literature* (Prague: Orient Institute, Academia, 1970), pp. 17–34. For a general discussion of the fundamental divergencies that differentiate Chinese and Western conceptions of historical writing, see Charles S. Gardner, *Chinese Traditional Historiography* (Cambridge: Harvard University Press, 1961), pp. 69–78, 86–105. For a comparison of the historiography of ancient China with that of Greece and Rome, see Burton Watson, *Early Chinese Literature* (New York: Columbia University Press, 1962), pp. 109–114.

5. With a few exceptions, such as the mythological stories about Creation, legends of ancient sage-kings, and tales about notorious "bad last-emperors," Ming historical novels as a whole are preoccupied with warfare. Most protagonists in these novels are military heroes engaged in all sorts of campaigns such as dynastic wars, expeditions against foreign invasions, and suppressions of domestic unrest. In chapter 2, the heroism and militarism, which are emphasized in historical novels in their writers' interpretations of the patterns of history, are evidence of this preoccupation. Again, in chapter 3, the driving force behind history is dynasty-building ambition that is inseparable from perpetual warfare in history. For a comparative study of the predominant role played by warfare in heroic stories in other cultures, see H. M. and N. K. Chadwick, *The Growth of Literature*, 1:64–95; 2:77–100, 360–73, 487–95, 666–76. For a criticism of the warfare feature of Homeric epics, see William Blake, "On Homer's Poetry" (ca. 1820), in *Poetry and Prose of William Blake*, ed. Geoffrey Keynes (London; Nonesuch Library, 1956), pp. 582–83. Blake denounced the features of warfare in Homer's epics as evil influences that "desolate Europe with wars." One could raise a similar issue of evil influence with the feature of "violence" in Ming historical novels. For example, the famous Ch'ing critic Chin Sheng-t'an viewed the novel *Shui-hu* as a dangerous book for the general reader, especially young people because *Shui-hu* promotes violence and rebellion.

6. Cheng Chen-to referred to the *San-kuo-chih t'ung-su yen-i* as the first *an-chien* novel. Here *an-chien* means "according to the history" — referring mainly to Ch'en Shou's *San-kuo chih* (History of the Three Kingdoms) and related sources, since the novel is supposedly an elaboration of Ch'en Shou's historical work. In other cases, such as *Sui T'ang yen-i* (the edition with added commentary by Hsu Wen-ch'ang), *an-chien* seems to refer to the various added chronological statements at the beginning of the novel and at the beginning of each *chüan*. Sometimes these "chronological statements" were not written by the novelists but were added by publishers of later periods. See Cheng Chen-to, *Chung-kuo wen-hsueh yen-chiu* (reprint, Hong Kong: Ku-wen shu-chü, 1970), 1:190–91, 211–18. Generally speak-

ing, writers and publishers of Ming historical novels often include some sort of historical statement (usually chronological) in their novels. The various *an-chien* phrases added to the main titles seem to emphasize these historical references.

Originally *chien* stood for the *T'ung-chien*, the abbreviation of Ssu-ma Kuang's *Tzu-chih t'ung-chien*, which is the most important historical opus since the *Shih-chi* of Ssu-ma Ch'ien. Although the novel was based on the Standard History *San-kuo chih*, it adapted the annalistic approach of *T'ung-chien*, listing the events considered worth mentioning in chronological order. For detailed discussion of the history and characters of the compilation of the novel, see, among others, Ch'en Chou-ch'ang, "*San-kuo-chih t'ung-su yen-i* hsing-ch'eng kuo-ch'eng lun-lueh," in *San-kuo yen-i yen-chiu chi* (Cheng-tu: Sze-chwan She-hui k'o-hsueh yuan, 1983), pp. 306–25; Chang Kuo-kuang, "*San-kuo-chih t'ung-su yen-i* ch'eng-shu yü Ming chung-yeh pien," in *San-kuo yen-i yen-chiu chi*, pp. 266–79; Wang Li-ch'i, "Lo Kuan-chung yü *San-kuo-chih t'ung-su yen-i*," in *San-kuo yen-i yen-chiu chi*, pp. 240–65; and Ou-yang Chien, "Shih lun *San-kuo-chih t'ung-su yen-i* ti ch'eng-shu nien-tai," in *San-kuo yen-i yen-chiu chi*, pp. 280–95.

It should be pointed out that on the critical issue of dynastic legitimacy, the novel does not follow Ssu-ma Kuang in his assigning the Wei as the rightful succession to the Han. In the novel, the Shu, instead of the Wei, was the legitimate regime after the Han fell. For a detailed discussion of this issue, see chapter 2.

7. In the late Ming it was the fashion among scholars to compile chronological accounts of histories following the example of Chu Hsi's (1130–1200) *Tzu-chih t'ung-chien kang-mu*. They were called *kang-chien*, such as Wang Shih-chen's (1526–1590) *Kang-chien*, Yuan Huang's (1533–1606) *Kang-chien pu*, Chou Ching-hsien's (fl. sixteenth century) *Hsu-pien kang-mu fa-ming*, and so forth. Since the second half of the sixteenth century, the prosperous printing center, Chien-yang Bookstore, which published some *kang-chien* types of history books, also revised and published many historical novels. It was probably for the purpose of enhancing the commercial values of these novels that various *an-chien* phrases were incorporated in their titles.

Another notable feature of these historical novels is the historical poems. In the 1592 edition of the *San-kuo* there are more than seventy historical poems, all written by Chou Ching-hsien. See Liu Hsiu-yeh's discussion of the 1592 edition of the novel in his book *Ku-tien hsiao-shuo hsi-ch'u ts'ung-k'ao* (Peking: Tso-chia ch'u-pan she, 1958), pp. 65–67. Liu also points out that it was this same Chou Ching-hsien whose historical treatises were widely adapted by various *Kang-chien* history books published by the Chien-yang Bookstore. For a detailed discussion of Chou Ching-hsien's and others' historical poems (in historical novels), see Cheng Chen-to, *Chung-kuo wen-hsueh yen-chiu*, 1:218–23.

Finally, as a passing note, I would like to point out that among the four dynastic novels of the pre-Ch'in period, two have the phrase *an-chien* incorporated in their titles. They are *P'an-ku chih T'ang Yü chuan* and *Yu-*

Hsia chih-chuan. Here *an-chien* stands for "historical text." See original publisher Yü Chi-yueh's note at the end of the *P'an-ku chih T'ang Yü chuan* (*chüan* 2, p. 43b). Judging from the use of the same format and the authorship attributed to these two novels, they probably were published by the same publisher at about the same time, although Yü Chi-yueh's note did not appear in *Yu-Hsia chih-chuan.* The other two pre-Ch'in dynastic novels *Ch'un-chiu lieh-kuo chuan* and *Tung-Chou lieh-kuo chih,* which do not have the phrase *an-chien* incorporated in their titles, actually claim their sources more specifically: the former adds a statement at the beginning of each *chüan* claiming *Tso-chuan* as its source; the latter adds a prefatory note at the beginning of the novel claiming many historical texts such as *Shih-chi, Tso-chuan, Kuo-yü, Chan-kuo ts'e,* and *Wu-Yueh ch'un-ch'iu* as its sources.

8. See Hsiung Ta-mu's preface to his own novel *Ta-Sung chung-hsing t'ung-su yen-i* (8 *chüan,* Ming Wan-li edition), *chüan* 1, pp. 1a−3b, esp. 2a. Yuan Yü-ling and Ch'en Wei shared Hsiung's view: See Yuan Yü-ling, "Sui-shih i-wen hsu" in *Sui-shih i-wen* (Taipei: Yu-shih yueh-k'an she, 1975), pp. 1−4, esp. 1; Ch'en Wei's preface to *Hsi-Han yen-i* is quoted by Sun K'ai-ti in his *Jih-pen Tung-ching so-chien Chung-kuo hsiao-shuo shu-mu* (Peking: Jen-min wen-hsueh, 1958), p. 55. In Hsiu Jan-tzu's (whose real name is Chang Shang-te) "Introduction" to the novel *San-kuo,* he uses the term *yü-i hsin-shih* (to supplement the authentic history) to describe the function of historical novels. For the complete text of the introduction, see *San-kuo-chih t'ung-su yen-i* (Chin-ling Chou Yueh-chiao edition, printed 1591), pp. 1a−4b.

9. The most well-known example was the noted Ch'ing scholar Chang Hsueh-ch'eng who cited the confusion of facts and fiction as his reason for disliking the famous historical novel *San-kuo-chih t'ung-su yen-i.* According to Chang, it is confusing because "seventy percent of the novel is facts and the rest fiction." For Chang's remark, see Chang Hsueh-ch'eng, *Ping-ch'en cha-chi* in *Chu-hsueh-hsuan ts'ung-shu,* comp. Liu Shih-heng (Taipei, 1970), 16:63b. For the same reason Li Tzu-ming, another Ch'ing scholar, expresses his strong dislike for the *San-kuo* in his diary. Li's remarks are quoted by K'ung Ling-ching, *Chung-kuo hsiao-shuo shih-liao* (Shanghai: Ku-tien wen-hsuen ch'u-pan she, 1957), p. 37. In Ming times, Hu Yin-ling's unfavorable opinion of the *San-kuo* is also clear; see Hu Yin-ling, *Shao-shih shan-fang pi-ts'ung* (Shanghai: Chung-hua shu-chü, 1964), 2:571.

10. Many modern scholars question this assumption. Wu Han's study "li-shih chung ti hsiao-shuo" (The Fiction in History) is an example to illustrate this point. In his study of the *Ming-shih* (The History of the Ming Dynasty), Wu Han found numerous "fiction" works that could be easily grouped into the various types of traditional fiction. Since all these "fiction" works are recorded in the *Ming-shih,* Wu Han points out, and since they are in essence no different from other Ming fiction, it is obvious that history and fiction in traditional times overlapped as a means for recording past experiences. Wu Han's comparison of the "fiction" in the Standard History

to other Ming fiction makes it clear that the intrinsic authenticity of the Standard History is not beyond doubt. For details of Wu's findings, see his article "Li-shih chung ti hsiao-shuo," in *Chung-kuo wen-hsueh yen-chiu* (Hong Kong: Lung men shu-tien, 1964), pp. 1201–17. Note that Wu Han was an eminent historian on Ming history.

In his long article, "Towards a Critical Theory of Chinese Narrative," Andrew Plaks discusses the extensive overlapping of historical and fictional narratives; for details see *Chinese Narrative: Critical and Theoretical Essays*, ed. by Andrew H. Plaks (Princeton, N.J.: Princeton University Press, 1977), pp. 309–52, esp. pp. 311–20.

11. Yung-yü-tzu, "*Ch'üan-hsiang San-kuo-chih t'ung-su yen-i* hsu" in *San-kuo-chih t'ung-su yen-i* (Microfilm copy made in 1955 of the original 1522 edition in Naikaku Bunko, Japan), pp. 5a–7b. After examining the general background and comparing earlier sources of the novel *San-kuo*, Sun K'ai-ti pointed out some of the novel's historical factual errors and contradictions. According to Sun K'ai-ti, the novelist had done less extensive historical research than people assumed; see Sun K'ai-ti, *Ts'ang-chou chi* (Peking: Chung-hua shu-chü, 1965), 1:109–20, esp. 116–17. However, in Cheng Chen-to's study of the evolution of the *San-kuo*, he stresses the increasing historical research of the later versions of the novel, compared to its early version of storytellers' text; see Cheng Chen-to, "*San-kuo chih yen-i* ti yen-hua" in *Chung-kuo wen-hsueh yen-chiu*, 1:166–239. C. T. Hsia, in his critical study of the classic Chinese novel, points out that the *San-kuo* was carrying forward the historiographical tradition of Ssu-ma Chien and Ssu-ma Kuang; see C. T. Hsia, "The Romance of the Three Kingdoms" in *The Classic Chinese Novel* (New York: Columbia University Press, 1968), pp. 34–74. Winston Yang, in his study of the use of Ch'en Shou's Standard History as a source of the *San-kuo*, demonstrates the relationship between the History and the novel; see Winston Yang, "The Literary Transformation of Historical Figures in the *San-kuo chih yen-i*," in *Critical Essays on Chinese Fiction*, ed. Winston Yang and Curtis Adkins (Hong Kong: Chinese University Press, 1980), pp. 47–84.

12. Feng Meng-lung, "Fan-li" (Explanatory Notes), in *Hsin lieh-kuo chih* (reprint, Taipei, 1981), 1:1a–3a. See also Ch'ien Ching-fang, *Hsiao-shuo ts'ung-k'ao* (Shanghai: Ku-tien wen-hsueh ch'u-pan she, 1958), pp. 8–17, esp. p. 8.

13. Liu Chao-yu, "Hsu lu" (Preface), in *Tung Hsi Chin yen-i* (Taipei: Chung-yang t'u-shu kuan, 1970), 1:1–4.

14. In Y. W. Ma's discussion of the historical novels, he made a point to exclude the novel *Shui-hu* because in *Shui-hu*, according to Ma, "the element of historical authenticity is too slim to form an identifiable core." See Y. W. Ma, "The Chinese Historical Novel: An Outline of Themes and Contexts," *Journal of Asian Studies* 34, no. 2 (February 1975): 277–94, esp. 278. In C. T. Hsia's "The Military Romance" mentioned above, he lists *Shui-hu* among military romances of the historical novel. Note also that Lu Hsun lists the *Shui-hu* among works of *chiang-shih* (historical

narratives) and Sun K'ai-ti places *Shui-hu* under the *hsia-yung* (chivalry) category of *shuo kung-an* (literally, cases on magistrates' table).

In Richard G. Irwin's study of the *Shui-hu*, he contends that the *Shui-hu* story is an "original creation" and that it "has developed from popular legend uninfluenced by historical fact." See Richard G. Irwin, *The Evolution of a Chinese Novel* (Cambridge: Harvard University Press, 1966), pp. 9−22. Yen Tun-i, however, suggests that *Shui-hu* legends are about the army of the Loyal and Righteous in the late Northern Sung period. See Yen Tun-i, *Shui-hu chuan ti yen-pien* (Peking: Tso-chia ch'u-pan she, 1957), pp. 31−32. Shu-yü [Phillip] Sun in his recent book, following the lead taken by Yen Tun-i, Wang Li-ch'i, Chang Cheng-lang, and others, devotes a long chapter relating the Liang-shan bandit-heroes with the mass anti-Chin (Jurchens) military activities during the Southern Sung times; see Sun Shu-yü, *Shui-hu chuan te lai-li, hsin-tai, yü i-shu* (Taipei: Shih-pao wen-hua ch'u-pan shih-yeh, 1981), pp. 47−140. For Wang Li-ch'i's and Chang Cheng-lang's articles on the *Shui-hu* and the Army of the Loyal and Righteous, see the collection of works on the *Shui-hu* in the *Shui-hu yen-chiu lun-wen chi* (Peking: Tso-chia ch'u-pan she, 1957), pp. 61−76, esp. 62; pp. 207−23, esp. 217−23.

15. Pan Ku, *Han-shu* (Peking: Chung-hua shu-chü, 1964), 6:1744−45.

16. *Lun-yü* in *Lun-yü i-chu*, edited and annotated by Yang po-chün (Peking: Chung-hua shu-chü, 1965), p. 116; see also Chu Hsi, *Ssu-shu chang-chü chi-chu* (Peking: Chung-hua shu-chü, 1983), p. 123. For English translation, see D. C. Lau, *The Analects* (Harmondsworth, England: Penguin Books, 1979), p. 106; Arthur Waley, *The Analects of Confucius* (New York: Vintage Books, 1938), p. 153. Note the original Chinese characters for the term *rustics* are *yeh-jen*, and those for the term *gentlemen* are *chün-tzu*. Here I follow the late Professor Fu Ssu-nien's interpretation that *yeh-jen* referred to the villagers who resided in the countryside while *chün-tzu* referred to the aristocrats who resided in the city; see Fu ssu-nien, "Chou tung-feng yü Yin i-min," in *Fu Meng-chen hsien-sheng chi* (Taipei: Tai-wan ta-hsueh, 1952), 4:28.

17. Ch'ang-sun Wu-chi et al., *Sui-shu ching-chi chih* (Shanghai: Shang-wu yin-shu kuan, 1955), *chüan* 2, pp. 39−70.

18. Ibid., pp. 49, 60.

19. Kan Pao, "*Sou-shen chi* hsu" in *Chung-kuo li-tai hsiao-shuo hsu pa hsuan chu*, ed. Ts'eng Tsu-yin et al. (Hsien-ning: Ch'ang-chiang wen-i ch'u-pan she, 1982), pp. 7−10; also compare "*Sou-shen chi* hsu" in *Chung-kuo li-tai hsiao-shuo lun-chu hsuan*, ed. Huang Lin and Han T'ung-wen (Nan-ch'ang: Chiang-hsi jen-min ch'u-pan she, 1982), pp. 20−22.

20. Ko Hung, "*Hsi-ching tsa-chi* pa" in *Chung-kuo li-tai hsiao-shuo hsu pa hsuan chu*, ed. Ts'eng Tsu-yin et al., p. 1.

21. Liu Hsu, et al., comps., *T'ang-shu ching-chi i-wen he-chih* (Shanghai: Shang-wu yin-shu kuan, 1956), pp. 94, 117.

22. T'o T'o et al., *Sung-shih i-wen chih, pu, fu-pien* (Shanghai: Shang-wu yin-shu kuan, 1957), pp. 53, 119.

23. Actually the blurring of the boundaries between history and *hsiao-shuo* continued to Ch'ing times. The book *Mu t'ien-tzu chuan* (The Travels of King Mu) is an example illustrating this point. It was not until the compilation of the *Ssu-ku ch'uan-shu tsung-mu ti-yao* (An Annotated Catalogue of the Complete Library of the Four Treasures, compiled 1773—1872) that *Mu t'ien-tzu chuan*, which was formerly classified as *ch'i-chü chu* (diaries of activity and repose) under History, was reclassified under *hsiao-shuo* as tales of marvels. Admitting that they altered time-honored convention, the editors of this annotated catalogue, Chi Yun (1724—1805) and others, wrote a special note to explain their position. They pointed out that *Mu t'ien-tzu chuan* had conventionally been classified as *ch'i-chü chu* of King Mu simply because it narrates the western travel of King Mu in the form of a chronicle. However, these travel accounts are, in substance, sheer fantasy and cannot be verified. If they were counted as authentic, the concept of history would be confused and the rules of history broken. Therefore, the editors concluded, it seems only appropriate that they should be put down as *hsiao-shuo* even though in so doing the time-honored convention should be altered. For the full text of the editors' annotation, see Chi Yun et al., *Ssu-ku ch'üan-shu tsung-mu t'i-yao* (Shanghai, 1934; reprint, Taipei, 1971), p. 2940. For a brief summary of all studies dealing with whether *Mu t'ien-tzu chuan* is "history" or "forgery," see Chang Hsin-ch'eng, *Wei-shu t'ung-k'ao* (Shanghai: Shang-wu yin-shu kuan, 1954), 1:514—20.

24. For P'ei Sung-chih's most detailed commentaries on the *History of Three Kingdoms*, see Ch'en Shou, *San-kuo chih*, 5 vols. (Shanghai: Ch'ung-hua shu-chü, 1964). For additional information about P'ei Sung-chih and his commentary, see "Ch'u-pan shuo-ming" (Explanatory Note), 1:1—7, esp. 2—4; and "Shang *San-kuo chih chu* piao" (Memoir on the Commentary of the *History of the Three Kingdoms*), 5:1471—72; both in Ch'en Shou, *San-kuo chih*.

25. Hsiung Ta-mu, "Preface," in *Ta-Sung chung-hsing t'ung-su yen-i*, pp. 1a—3b. For discussion of another novel by Hsiung Ta-mu, the *Nan Sung chuan*, see W. L. Idema, "Novels about the Founding of the Sung Dynasty," *Sung Studies Newsletter*, no. 9 (June 1974): 2—9.

26. Hsiung Ta-mu, *Pei-Sung chih-chuan t'ung-su yen-i t'i-p'ing*, chüan 1, p. 1a, in *Nan-Pei-Sung Ch'üan-chuan*.

27. Sun K'ai-ti, *Jih-pen Tung-ching so-chien Chung-kuo hsiao-shuo shu-mu* (reprint, Peking: Jeh-min Wen-hsueh ch'u-pan she, 1981), pp. 114—20, esp. 117—18: "Hsu Tung-ch'uang shih-fan chuan."

28. The complete text of Chen Wei's preface is quoted by Sun K'ai-ti in his *Jih-pen Tung-ching so-chien Chung-kuo hsiao-shuo shu-mu*, p. 55. In the preface Chen Wei reassures his genuine respect for Ssu-ma Ch'ien's *Shih-chi* but admits that his novel does not follow the Standard History word for word.

29. Yuan Yü-ling, "*Sui-shih i-wen hsu*" (Preface to the *Sui-shih i-wen*) in *Sui-shih i-wen*, pp. 1—4, esp. 1.

30. Hu Wan-ch'uan, "*Hsin lieh-kuo-chih* ti chieh-shao" (Introduction to the New Records of the States) in *Hsin lieh-kuo-chih*, by Feng Meng-lung (Taipei: Lien-ching ch'u-pan shih-yeh kung-ssu, 1981), 1:1−9.

31. Chang Cheng-lang, "Chiang-shih yü yung-shih shih," *Chung-yang yen-chiu yuan li-shih yü-yen yen-chiu so chi-k'an*, no. 10 (1948): 601−45, esp. pp. 605−11. Chang suggests that *p'ing-hua* evolved from a special style of *yung-shih shih* (poems on historical subjects) in the late T'ang and Five Dynasties. According to Chang Cheng-lang, such poems were used as popular schoolbooks during the Sung dynasty. The poems were arranged chronologically and each poem was followed by an explanation taken from a variety of historical works. This explains why there are so many poems quoted in both *p'ing-hua* and historical novels. For a list of these *p'ing-hua*, see Sun K'ai-ti's bibliography of popular Chinese fiction, *Chung-kuo t'ung-su hsiao-shuo shu-mu* (Hong Kong: Shih-yung shu-chü, 1967; rev. ed., Peking: Jen-min wen-hsueh ch'u-pan she, 1982), *chüan* 1, pp. 1−2.

32. The earliest extant written version of the *Shui-hu* legend can be found in Section Four of *Hsuan-ho i-shih*. For an English translation of its text, see Richard G. Irwin, *The Evolution of a Chinese Novel*, pp. 26−31. For a different English translation of the text of the *Hsuan-ho i-shih*, see William D. Hennessey, tr., *Proclaiming Harmony* (Ann Arbor: Center for Chinese Studies, University of Michigan, 1981), pp. 51−58. Following a different lead, W. L. Idema, in his discussion on Hsiung Ta-mu's novel *Ta-Sung chung-hsing t'ung-su yen-i*, points out that Hsiung, too, utilized the *Hsuan-ho i-shih* extensively. For details, see W. L. Idema, *Chinese Vernacular Fiction* (Leiden: E. J. Brill, 1974), p. 108.

33. Having made a detailed comparison between the contents of the novel *San-kuo* and the *San-kuo-chih p'ing-hua*, Sun K'ai-ti concluded that all important episodes of the novel could also be found in the *p'ing-hua*. See Sun K'ai-ti, "*San-kuo-chih p'ing-hua* yü *San-kuo-chih t'ung-su yen-i*," in *Ts'ang-chou chi*, 1:109−20, esp. pp. 111−13. For a summary of the *San-kuo-chih p'ing-hua* and a general discussion of its characteristics, see Cheng Chen-to, "*San-kuo-chih yen-i* te yen-hua," in *Chung-kuo wen-hsueh yen-chiu*, 1:171−90. The edition I use is a recent edition of *San-kuo-chih p'ing-hua*, published by Chung-hua Bookstore in Shanghai in 1959. There are two recent studies in English mentioning the relationship between the novel *San-kuo* and the *San-kuo-chih p'ing-hua*. They present two views: According to W. L. Idema, Lo Kuan-chung wrote his *San-kuo* following the outline of the *San-kuo-chih p'ing-hua* and occasionally uses its text. See W. L. Idema, *Chinese Vernacular Fiction*, p. 104. However, Winston Yang, in his study of the novel *San-kuo*, emphatically points out that the novel, as represented by its earliest surviving Chia-ching edition, "was not derived from or based on the *p'ing-hua* version; it was entirely a new creation." See Winston Yang, "The Use of the *San-kuo-chih* as a Source of the *San-kuo-chih yen-i*" (Ph.D. diss., Stanford University, 1971, microfilm), pp. 86−87.

34. W. L. Idema regards the *Wu-tai-shih p'ing-hua* as "one of the main sources" of the *Nan Sung chih-chuan*. For detailed information, see W. L. Idema, *Chinese Vernacular Fiction*, pp. 109—12.
35. Liu Ts'un-yan, "Yuan Chih-chih-pen *ch'üan hsiang Wu-wang fa-Chou p'ing-hua*, Ming-ken-pen *Lieh-kuo chih-chuan* chüan i yü *Feng-shen yen-i* chih kuan-hsi," *Hsin-ya hsueh-pao* 4, no. 1 (August 1959): 401—42.
36. Liu Hsien-t'ing, *Kuang-yang tsa-chi* (Peking: Chung-hua shu-chü, 1957), pp. 106—7. In the same essay, Liu proclaims that if there were a sage-king, he would have "used" fiction and drama to help him to rule the country. Liu's unusually strong endorsement reflects the achievement of the ver-nacular literature. For the significant meaning of Liu's strong endorsement, see Chang Hsueh-lun [Shelley] "Li Yü hsi-ch'ü hsiao-shuo chung so fan-ying ti ssu-hsiang," *Ta-lu tsa-chih* 50, no. 2 (February 1975): 4—35, esp. 8—10.
37. Shelley Hsueh-lun Chang, "Intellectual and Social Themes in Ming Fiction and Drama," *Chine ancienne*, in *Actes du XXIXe Congress international des orientalistes* (Paris: L'Asiatheque, 1977), pp. 31—36.
38. There are five Sung works describing the sights of Sung capitals that include a section on the popular entertainers (storytellers included) to be found in the city's bazaars. They were bound together into one book entitled *Tung-ching meng-hua lu (wai ssu-chung)* by Meng Yuan-lao et al. (Shanghai: Chung-hua shu-chü, 1962).
39. See Nai Te-weng's *Tu-ch'eng chi-sheng* in *Tung-ching meng-hua lu (wai ssu-chung)*, p. 98. As to the various interpretations regarding the descriptions of different branches of storytellers' art in *Tu-ch'eng chi-shen*, see Wang Ku-lu, "Nan-Sung shuo-hua jen ssu-chia ti fen-fa," appendix in *Erh-k'o p'o-an ching-ch'i* (Shanghai: Ku-tien wen-hsueh ch'u-pan she, 1957), 2:805—12.
40. Nai Te-weng, *Tu-ch'eng chi-sheng*, pp. 8—9; English translation, see John Bishop, *The Colloquial Short Story in China* (Cambridge: Harvard University Press, 1965), p. 8.
41. For detailed information about these two Three Kingdoms stories, see I Su, "T'an T'ang-tai te San-kuo ku-shih," in *Wen-hsueh i-ch'an tseng-k'an*, 10 (1962):117—26; reprinted in Chou Shao-liang, *Shao-liang ts'ung-kao* (Chi-nan: Ch'i-lu shu-she, 1984), pp. 223—33.
42. *San-kuo yen-i* (Peking: Tso-chia ch'u-pan she, 1953), 1:327; 2:866—68.
43. In his book *Tung-ching meng-hua lu*, describing the sights of the Northern Sung capital, Meng Yuan-lao (fl. 1126—47) includes a section on a popular entertainer to be found in the city bazaars. He mentions a special school of storytellers specializing in Three Kingdoms stories. See *Tung ching meng-hua lu*, pp. 29—30.
44. Su Tung-p'o, *Chih lin*, chüan 6, in *Pi-chi hsiao-shuo ta-kuan* (reprint, Taipei: Hsin-hsing shu-chü, 1973), 2:799—829, esp. 814.
45. The pro-Shu (Liu Pei) against Wei (Ts'ao Ts'ao) sentiment of the novel *San-kuo* will be discussed in detail in chapter 2.
46. Chou Mi, *Wu-lin chiu-shih* in *Tung-ching meng hua lu (wai ssu-chung)*,

Meng Yuan-lao et al., p. 454. For other Southern Sung works that make mention of Sung storytellers specializing in historical stories, see, in the same collection, Nei Te-weng's *Tu-ch'eng chi-sheng* (pp. 95–98), Hsi-hu lao-jen's *Hsi-hu lao-jen fan-sheng lu* (p. 123), and Wu Tzu-mu's *Meng liang lu* (pp. 310–11).

47. For numerous titles of Yuan dramas, see, among others, Chung Ssu-ch'eng's *Lu kuei pu* (1330), Chia Chung-ming's *Lu kuei-pu hsu-pien* (1422), and Chu Ch'üan's *T'ai-ho cheng-yin pu* (1398). The edition I use is a collection of five works published in 1959 under the title *Lu-kuei pu (wai ssu-chung)*, by Chung Ssu-ch'eng et al. (Shanghai: Chung-hua shu-chü, 1959), pp. 8–44, 64–93, 102–14, 135–55, 357–74.

48. The pioneering works regarding the relationship between the *San-kuo* and the *San-kuo shih p'ing-hua* are Sun K'ai-ti's and Cheng Chen-to's. See Sun K'ai-ti, *Ts'ang-chou chi*, 1:109–20; Cheng Chen-to, *Chung-kuo wen-hsueh yen-chiu*, 1:169–239. However, there are new studies that shed light on the evolution of the *San-kuo*. These studies revise some of Sun's and Cheng's opinions. For bibliographical information on these studies, see note 6 above, which gives four of them, all appearing in a collection entitled *San-kuo yen-i yen-chiu chi*.

49. In his discussion of two cultural traditions in Europe, Peter Burke observed that the elite participated in the little tradition, but the common people did not participate in the great tradition. The reason was that the great tradition was transmitted formally at schools and universities that were not open to all, and the common people were excluded. Thus he called it a "closed" tradition. The little tradition, on the other hand, was transmitted informally. It was open to all, like the church, the tavern, and the market-place, where so many of the performances occurred. For the elite, the great tradition was serious, the little tradition was play. But in China, the great tradition was not a closed tradition. There had been conscientious efforts of bringing the common people to participate in the great tradition in imperial time. The Confucian great Way and the small Way, as we just pointed out, was a two-way street. For example, the Confucian idea of education was, at least in theory, open to all. Even the civil service examinations were, in principle, open to all "good" people.

The interaction between the elite and popular traditions has fluctuated from time to time in imperial China. It is one of the major themes of this study that the late Ming was a period that saw vigorous interactions between the two cultures. The writers and playwrights of the late Ming vernacular literature, some of them (especially the playwrights) belonged to the elite themselves, were largely the mediators who stood in between the two cultures, and promoted interaction.

Burke, however, raises a question about the model of the two cultural traditions: It fails to distinguish different groups within the "people." But Burke was talking about Europe where not only the great tradition was a "closed" one, but "the upper classes gradually withdrew from participation in the little tradition in the course of the seventeenth and eighteenth centuries." In China, the situation was different. In China the upper classes did not withdraw from participation in the little tradition, and the door was never completely shut for the common people to participate in the great tradition. As long as the two-way street still existed and the people were divided into two groups — the governing elite and the governed masses — the two cultural traditions model is still a useful model.

David Johnson, in his recent article, "Communication, Class, and Consciousness in Late Imperial China," attempts to distinguish different groups within the Ming-Ch'ing society. He suggests nine social groups based on three educational levels — classically educated, literate, and illiterate — and three sociopolitical statuses — legally privileged, self-sufficient, and dependent. Based on these two sets of criteria, nine combinations were formed, which include the "classically educated and legally privileged" as the first social group and the "illiterate and dependent" as the last social group. See David Johnson, "Communication, Class, and Consciousness in Late Imperial China," in *Popular Culture in Late Imperial China*, ed. David Johnson, Andrew J. Nathan, and Evelyn S. Rawski (Berkeley: University of California Press, 1985), pp. 34—72.

50. For a general reference in English of the history and development of Chinese vernacular fiction, see, among others, Yang Hsien-yi and Gladys Yang, trans., *A Brief History of Chinese Fiction*, by Lu Hsun (Peking: Foreign Language Press, 1959), pp. 1—9; C. T. Hsia, *The Classic Chinese Novel*, pp. 1—33; John L. Bishop, *The Colloquial Short Story in China*, pp. 1—12; Ch'en Shou-yi, *Chinese Literature* (New York: Ronald Press, 1961), pp. 479—97; H. C. Chang, trans., *Chinese Literature: Popular Fiction and Drama* (Edinburgh: Edinburgh University Press, 1973), pp. 1—21; P. D. Hanan, *The Chinese Vernacular Story* (Cambridge: Harvard University Press, 1981), pp. 1—27; P. D. Hanan, *The Chinese Short Stories: Studies in Dating, Authorship, and Composition* (Cambridge: Harvard University Press, 1973), pp. 18—32, 212—14; P. D. Hanan, "The Development of Fiction and Drama," in *The Legacy of China* (London: Oxford University Press, 1964), pp. 115—43; P. D. Hanan, "A Landmark of Chinese Novel," in *The Far East: China and Japan* (Toronto: University of Toronto Press, 1961), pp. 325—35; Liu Wu-chi, *An Introduction to Chinese Literature* (Bloomington: Indiana University Press, 1966), pp. 195—212, 228—46; Jaroslav Průšek, "Researches into the Beginning of the Chinese Popular Novel," *Archiv Orientalni* 11 (1938—39): 91—132; 23 (1955): 620—22; Jaroslav Průšek, "The Beginnings of Popular Chinese Literature; Urban Centres—The Cradle of Popular Fiction," *Archiv Orientalni* 36 (1968): 67—115; and W. L. Idema, *Chinese Vernacular Fiction*, pp. ix—lxiv.

51. The interpretation of this passage follows Chu Hsi's commentary, which was the standard interpretation of the Confucian Classics in Ming times. Here Chu Hsi emphasized Confucius's humble attitude toward the ancients. However, it should be pointed out that Chu Hsi's commentary, like any other commentary, reflects only one school of thought; it does not necessarily precisely reflect the original meaning of Confucius's remark. Compare Chu

Hsi's commentary with that of Yang Po-chün's; see Chu Hsi's *Ssu-shu chang-chü chi-chu* (*chüan* 4) and Yang Po-chün's *Lun-yü i-chu* (p. 71). Both works are cited in note 16, above. The English translation follows with minor changes. Arthur Waley's *The Analects of Confucius*, p. 123. See also D. C. Lau, *The Analects*, p. 86.

52. For discussion of *hsiao-shuo* and its classification in Ming times, see Hu Yin-ling, *Shao-shih shan-fang pi-ts'ung*, 2:371–81, esp. 374. Note that Hu Yin-ling classified *hsiao-shuo* into six categories. For a general survey of Ming novels, see, among others, Lu Hsun, *Chung-kuo hsiao-shuo shih-lueh* (1930; reprint, Hong Kong: Chin-tai t'u-shun kung-ssu, 1965), pp. 97–155; Lu Hsun, *Chung-kuo hsiao-shuo te li-shih pien-ch'ien* (Hong Kong: Chin-tai t'u-shu kung-ssu, 1965), pp. 27–32; Cheng Chen-to, [*Ch'a-t'u pen*] *Chung-kuo wen-hsueh shih*, 4:699–726, 909–26; Cheng Chen-to, *Chung-kuo wen-hsueh yen-chiu*, 1:101–479; Sun K'ai-tu, *Chung-kuo t'ung-su hsiao-shuo shu-mu*, pp. 23–210; Pei-ching ta-hsueh chung-wen hsi i-chiu-wu-wu chi, *Chung-kuo hsiao-shuo shih kao* (Peking: Jen-min wen-hsueh, 1960), pp. 145–291; Li Hui-ying, *Chung-kuo hsiao-shuo shih* (Hong Kong: Tung-ya shu-chü, 1970), pp. 154–89; Fan Yen-ch'iao, *Chung-kuo hsiao-shuo shih* (Suchou: Ch'iu-yeh she, 1927), pp. 124–50; Meng Yao, *Chung-kuo hsiao-shuo shih* (Taipei: Chuan-chi wen-hsueh she, 1969), 3:304–463; Kuo Ch'ang-ho, "Chia-jen ts'ai-tzu hsiao-shuo yen-chiu," *Wen-hsueh chi-k'an* 1, no. 1 (1 January 1934): 194–215; no. 2 (1 April 1934): 303–23; Liu Wu-chi, *An Introduction to Chinese Literature*, pp. 195–212, 228–46; Yang Hsien-yi and Gladys Yang, trans., *A Brief History of Chinese Fiction*, by Lu Hsuan, pp. 163–255; Li Tien-yi, *Chinese Fiction* (New Haven: Far Eastern Publications, Yale University, 1968), pp. 79–82; Ch'en Shou-yi, *Chinese Literature*, pp. 479–97; Robert E. Hegel, *The Novel in Seventeenth-Century China* (New York: Columbia University Press, 1981), pp. 235–53.

53. There are about fifty titles of historical novels (different editions of the same novel not included) by Ming authors in Sun K'ai-ti's bibliography. They surpass the combined total of other categories of Ming novels. See Sun K'ai-ti, *Chung-kuo t'ung-su hsiao-shuo shu-mu*, pp. 23–69, 115–97. See also *Chung-kuo hsiao-shuo shih-kao* (pp. 276–86) by the Department of Chinese Literature, Peking University (Pei-ching ta-hsueh chung-wen hsi i-chiu-wu-wu chi [Peking: Jen-min wen-hsueh, 1960]), which does not list all titles of Ming historical novels but does make mention of "more than twenty 'historical romances' (*li-shih yen-i*)" and "more than twenty 'heroic tales' (*ying-hsiung ch'uan-chi*)."

54. In composing this table, a few observations need to be pointed out. First, two novels listed in the table are classified under different genres by some scholars: the *Shui-hu* and the *Shang-Chou*. Since we have discussed the novel *Shui-hu* before (see also n. 14 above), we will not repeat it here. The novel *Shang-Chou lieh-kuo ch'üan-chuan* was classified under the category of supernatural tale by both Sun K'ai-ti and Lu Hsun, using its more well-known title *Feng-shen yen-i* (The Investiture of Gods). However, according to Liu Ts'un-yan, this novel is very closely related to two other popular

historical narratives: the *Wu-wang fa-Chou p'ing-hua* and the novel *Lieh-kuo*. For details of Liu's study, see his article cited in note 35 above. C. T. Hsia, in "The Military Romance: A Genre of Chinese Fiction," lists both the *Shui-hu* and the *Feng-shen* among military romances of historical novels; see esp. pp. 343, 354.

Second, the novel *Nan-Sung* listed in the table refers to the one compiled by Hsiung Ta-mu, not the novel *Fei-lung ch'üan-chuan* by Wu Hsuan of the Ch'ing dynasty. The editions I use are the Chin-wen t'ang and Hsiu-chai t'ang editions that are bound together with another Hsiung Ta-mu's novel *Pei-Sung Yang-chia chiang* with the combined title *Nan pei Sung ch'üan-chuan*. For the various editions of these two novels, see Sun K'ai-ti, *Jih-pen Tung-ching so-chien Chung-kuo hsiao-shuo shu-mu*, pp. 43−46.

Third, the novel *Pei-Sung* listed in the table refers to the novel compiled by Hsiung Ta-mu. For a different version of the saga of the Yang family, see Ch'in-huao mo-k'o (Chi Chen-lun), *Yang-chia fu shih-tai chung-yung yen-i chih-chuan* (facsimile ed., Taipei: National Central library, 1970).

55. For Huang Mo-hsi's brief description of the novel, see Sun K'ai-ti, *Chung-kuo t'ung-su hsiao-shuo shu-mu* (1982 rev. ed.), p. 64. Note that Sun K'ai-ti himself did not see the novel.

56. A detailed study of printing, literacy, and urbanization in late Ming China is given in Chun-shu Chang and Shelley Hsueh-lun Chang, *State, Society, and Literature in Seventeenth-century China*, chap. 2 (forthcoming). This book also examines modern studies on these issues in China, Japan, and the West, and hence I will not list here the literature on the subject. However, for a succinct summation in English of the economic and social developments of the late imperial period, see a recent article by Evelyn S. Rawski, "Economic and Social Foundations of Late Imperial Culture," in *Popular Culture in Late Imperial China*, pp. 3−33.

57. Besides the two historical novels *Hsin lieh-kuo chih* and *Wang Yang-ming ch'u-shen ching-luan lu*, Feng Meng-lung wrote another vernacular novel, the new *P'ing-yau chuan*, a revised and enlarged forty-chapter version of the old twenty-chapter *San-Sui p'ing-yao chuan* (The Tales of How the Three Sui Quelled the Demons' revolt). Although the *Hsin p'ing-yao chuan* eventually is ended with the suppression of Wang Tse's rebellion (in 1047), Wang Tse is not the protagonist of the novel. In fact the novel is about sorceress Hu Yung-erh (who later becomes Wang Tse's wife in the novel), Sheng Ku-ku, the Pellet monk, and their sorceries that traditionally belonged to the realm of supernatural tales. As to the protagonist of the novel, the sorceress Hu Yung-erh, there was no historical equivalent for her. Note that Sun K'ai-ti identified the novel as a supernatural tale while Lu Hsuan placed it under historical novel.

58. Besides his own historical novel, the *Sui-shih i-wen*, Yuan Yü-ling edited and revised two historical novels concerning the Han period, according to Robert Hegal's study, but these novels disappeared soon after their first edition. See Robert E. Hegel, *The Novel in Seventeenth-Century China*, pp. 60, 120−23, and 281 (n. 56).

59. Li Chih-chung, "Ming-tai k'o-shu shu-lueh" in *Wen-shih* (Peking: Chung-hua shu-chü, 1984), 23:127-58. In Li Tien-yi's article about Feng Meng-lung, he suggests that Feng either owned or was closely connected with a printing concern; see "Feng Meng-Lung," in *Dictionary of Ming Biography*, ed. L. Carrington Goodrich and Chao-ying Fang (New York: Columbia University Press, 1976), pp. 450-53.

60. Sun K'ai-ti, *Chung-kuo t'ung-su hsiao-shuo shu-mu*, p. 28.

61. See my "Li Yü" article in *Ta-lu tsa-chih* 50, no. 2 (February 1975): 4-35.

62. Lung Wen-pin, *Ming Hui-yao* (Taipei: Shih-chieh shu-chü, 1963), *chüan* 26, p. 418. See also *Ming-shih, chüan* 2, p. 21.

63. *Tung Hsi Han t'ung-su yen-i* (1612 edition), pp. 1a-3b.

64. For a discussion of the T'ai-chou group of the left wing Wang Yang-ming school of Confucianism, see the Introduction.

65. S. N. Eisenstadt, "Intellectuals and Tradition," in *Intellectuals and Tradition*, ed. S. N. Eisenstadt and S. R. Graubard (New York: Humanities Press, 1973), pp. 1-19, esp. 18. See also Edward Shils, "Intellectuals, Tradition, and the Traditions of Intellectuals: Some Preliminary Consideration" in *Intellectuals and Tradition*, pp. 21-34; George F. Foster, "What is Folk Culture?" *American Anthropologist* 55, no. 21 (1953): 159-73.

66. As pointed out earlier, although fiction reached a much wider audience than any other genre of literature in Ming and Ch'ing times, it was through the mass medium of professional storytelling that it reached the vast illiterate population. From the late Ming through the Ch'ing period, storytellers specializing in historical narration used historical novels as a basis for their works. Although the details of their stories differed from the original novels, the basic plot and major themes were seldom changed. For more information see, among others, Ch'en Ju-heng, "P'ing-hua yen-chiu," in *Shih-hsueh tsa-chih* 2, no. 5 (April 1931): 1-16, esp. 6-16; Ch'en Ju-heng, *Shuo-shu shih-hua* (Peking: Tso-chia ch'u-pan she, 1958), pp. 95-114, 130-70; Li Tou, *Yang-chou hua-fang lu* (Peking: Chung-hua shu-chü, 1960), pp. 207-8, 257-58; Yeh Te-chün, *Sung Yuan Ming chiang-ch'ang wen-hsueh*, pp. 39-42; K'ung Ling-ching, *Chung-kuo hsiao-shuo shih-liao*, pp. 188-89.

67. Chi Wen-fu, *Wan-Ming ssu-hsiang shih lun* (Ch'ung-ch'ing: Shang-wu yin-shu kuan, 1944), pp. 33-47; Jung Chao-tsu, *Ming-tai ssu-hsiang shih* (reprint, Taipei: K'ai-ming shu-tien, 1973), pp. 231-56; Huang Tsung-hsi, *Ming-ju hsueh-an* (Taipei: Shang-wu yin-shu kuan, 1965), 2:54-98; 3:1-18; 6:62-102; 7:1-78.

68. For discussion of the interaction of the elite and popular cultures, see my article cited in note 36 above.

69. Li Chih, *Fen-shu* (Peking: Chung-hua shu-chü, 1961), pp. 98-99. For discussion about Yang-ming's concept of *liang-chih*, see Julia Ching, *To Acquire Wisdom: The Way of Wang Yang-ming* (New York: Columbia University Press, 1976), pp. 107-24. For discussion of Wang Yang-ming and the T'ai-chou group, see Frederic Wakeman, "The Price of Autonomy: Intellectuals in Ming and Ch'ing politics," *Daedalus* 101 (Spring 1972):

35–70. For a discussion of the dominant trend of late Ming thought, see Wm. Theodore de Bary, "Individualism and Humanitarianism in Late Ming Thought," in *Self and Society in Ming Thought*, ed. Wm. Theodore de Bary (New York: Columbia University Press, 1970), pp. 145–247, esp. 188–225.

70. In his study of traditional fiction criticism, Yeh Lang praises Li Chih as representing the "true spirit of Chinese classic fiction criticism." See Yeh Lang, *Chung-kuo hsiao-shuo mei-hsueh* (Peking: Pei-ching ta-hsueh ch'u-pan she, 1982), pp. 1–21, esp. 12; 22–25; 289–97.

71. For a discussion of Yuan Hung-tao's evolutionary theory of literature, see Liu Ta-chieh, *Chung-kuo wen-hsueh fa-ta shih* (reprint, Taipei: Chung-hua shu-chü, 1966), pp. 304–9; see also Kuo shao-yü, *Chung-kuo wen-hsueh p'i-p'ing shih* (1934; reprint, Taipei: Shang-wu yin-shu kuan, 1970), 2:264–83.

72. See Yuan Hung-tao's preface to his brother's poems "Shu Hsiao-hsiu shih," in *Yuan Chung-lang ch'üan-chi* (Hong Kong: Kuang-chih shu-chü, n.d.), p. 6. See also Yuan Hung-tao's poem "T'ing Chu sheng shuo *Shui-hu chuan*," in the same book, p. 21.

73. For examples of tradesmen and peasants entering into the ruling bureaucracy, see Ping-ti Ho, *The Ladder of Success in Imperial China* (New York: Columbia University Press, 1964), pp. 73–79. For discussion of the production and distribution of popular publication in Ming China, see Tadao Sakai, "Confucianism and Popular Educational Works," in *Self and Society in Ming Thought*, pp. 331–66.

74. These two groups of materials seem to coincide with those termed by Stuart Hughes as "on the level of popular acceptance" and those dealing with "ethico-political" history. For an illuminating discussion of the nature and ways of writing intellectual history, see H. Stuart Hughes, *Consciousness and Society* (New York: Vintage Books, 1961), pp. 3–32.

75. For an interpretive analysis of the cultures, see Clifford Geertz, *The Interpretation of Culture* (New York: Basic Books, 1974), pp. 1–30. For an illuminating discussion on the subject of ideas and men, see Crane Brinton's invaluable study, *Ideas and Men: The Story of Western Thought* (Englewood Cliffs, N. J.: Prentice-Hall, 1963) pp. 1–21.

Chapter 2

1. *Meng-tzu*, annot. Chiang Po-ch'ien. In Shen Chih-fang ed. *Ssu-shu tu-pen* (Taipei: Ch'i-ming shu-chü, 1952), 1:174–75. For an English translation, see James Legge, trans., *The Works of Mencius* (reprint, Tokyo, 1936), p. 605; for a different translation, compare D. C. Lau, trans., *Mencius* (Harmondsworth, England: Penguin Books, 1970), p. 113.

2. Ssu-ma Ch'ien, *Shih-chi* (Peking: Chung-hua shu-chü, 1959), 2:393–94; for an English translation, see Burton Watson, trans., *Records of the Grand Historian of China* (New York: Columbia University Press, 1961), 1:118.

Note that both the *Meng-tzu* and the *Shih-chi* were circulated during the Han dynasty (202 B.C.–220 A.D.). The text of the *Meng-tzu*, as we have it, has come down to us through Chao Ch'i (d. A.D. 201), one of the earliest commentators on the *Meng-tzu*, and the only early commentator whose commentary has come down to us. The *Shih-chi* was written at the beginning of the first century B.C. Note also that during Han times, Chou Yen's theory of Yin-yang and the Five Elements, which stresses a cyclical process in all events in nature, became influential in Chinese thinking. This theory of Yin-yang and the Five Elements will be discussed in chapter 6.

3. *San-kuo yen-i* (Peking: Tso-chia ch'u-pan she, 1953), 1:1; [Ch'uan-tu hsiu-hsiang] *San-kuo yen-i*, commentary by Mao Tsung-kang (Huhohet: Nei-Meng-ku jen-min ch'u-pan she, 1981), 1:2. Note that the 1981 edition of *San-kuo* collated the Mao version with other editions and keeps all the original commentaries by Mao Tsung-kang; hereafter it will be referred to as "*San-kuo yen-i*, CC ed." The English translation follows Roberts; see Moss Roberts, *Three Kingdoms: China's Epic Drama* (New York: Pantheon Books, 1976), p. 3. For different English translations, see Ch'u Chai and Winberg Chai, trans. and eds., "*San-kuo yen-i*," in *A Treasury of Chinese Literature* (New York: Appleton-Century, 1965), pp. 192–210, esp. 194; C. H. Brewitt-Taylor, trans., *Romance of the Three Kingdoms* (Shanghai, 1925; reprint, Taipei: Ch'eng-wen Publishing Co., 1969), 1:1.

4. In general historians have emphasized one of three patterns: repetitive dynastic cycles, continuous development, and stagnation. For discussion of the different points of view regarding patterns of Chinese history, see John Meskill, ed., *The Pattern of Chinese History* (Boston: D. C. Heath and Co., 1965), which attempts to present an all-around collection of works representing different views among historians in ancient China, Western scholars, and modern Asian historians. For discussion on why there was no enduring disunity in the long history of imperial China, see Mark Elvin, *The Pattern of the Chinese Past* (Stanford, Calif.: Stanford University Press, 1973), pp. 17–22.

5. Arthur F. Wright, "On the Uses of Generalization in the Study of Chinese History," in *Generalization in the Writing of History*, ed. Louis Gottschalk, (Chicago: University of Chicago Press, 1963), pp. 36–58, esp. 41.

6. For detailed discussion of the original concept and later development of the theories of dynastic legitimacy, see Jao Tsung-i, *Chung-kuo shih-hsueh shang chih cheng-t'ung lun* (Hong Kong: Lung-mang shu-tien, 1979), pp. 1–59. Jao's book also provides a most comprehensive collection of historical sources on the subject of dynastic legitimacy written by Chinese scholars from ancient to modern times (see pp. 61–383).

7. Ping-ti Ho, *The Cradle of the East* (Hong Kong: Chinese University of Hong Kong, 1975), pp. 333–38. See also H. G. Creel, *The Origins of Statecraft in China* (Chicago: University of Chicago Press, 1970), pp. 81–100. While Creel believes that *T'ien* (Heaven) was an exclusive Chou god, Ho contends that *T'ien* as an alternative expression of *Ti* (God on High) must have existed in the Shang. Kwang-chih Chang, an archaeologist, has

a theory regarding the myth-making process in ancient China. Chang maintains there were three principal stages of myth making during the Shang and Chou. The first occurred during the Shang when origin myths, ancestral heroes, and natural deities were all diffused into overlapping territories. At that time *Shang-ti* was identified either with the ancestors in the abstract or with one particular legendary ancestor. The second stage took place in Western Chou when the world of the ancestors and that of the gods was divided. The king had the status of the Son of Heaven instead of identifying his ancestors with the gods or *Shang-ti*. The third stage was during the Eastern Chou when there was a sudden proliferation of myths about the birth of heroes, often referred to as ancestors. See Chang Kwang-chih, "Shang Chou shen-hua chih fen-lei," *Min-tsu hsueh yen-chiu suo chi-k'an*, no. 14, (1962):47–94.

8. These words of the "T'ai-shih" of the *Shu-ching* (The Book of History) were quoted by Mencius in *Meng-tzu*; see *Meng-tzu, Ssu-shu tu-pen* ed., 2:261. For an English translation, see James Legge, trans., *The Works of Mencius*, p. 709. Note that these words of "T'ai-shih" are quoted from *Meng-tzu* rather than *Shu-ching* because the twenty-eight authentic sections of *Shu-ching* do not include the controversial "T'ai-shih." For an introduction to the complicated problem of the authenticity of the *Shu-ching*, see Liang Ch'i-ch'ao, *Ku-shu cheng-wei chi ch'i nien-tai* (Peking: Chung-hua shu-chü, 1962), pp. 91–109, esp. 104–5 on "The Problem of "T'ai-shih."

9. Derk Bodde, "Comments on the Paper of Arthur F. Wright" in *Generalization in the Writing of History*, p. 60.

10. For the official history of the Three Kingdoms period, see Ch'en Shou, *San-kuo chih*; also Ssu-ma Kuang, *Tzu-chih t'ung-chien* (Peking: Ku-chi ch'u-pan she, 1957), *chüan* 69–78. For studies of the novel *San-kuo*, see, among others, Cheng Chen-to, "*San-kuo yen-i* te yen-hua," in *Chung-kuo wen-hsüeh yen-chiu*, 1:196–239; Sun Kai-ti, "*San-kuo chih p'ing-hua yu San-kuo chih chuan t'ung-su yen-i*," in *Ts'ang-chou chi*, 1:109–20; Hu Shih, "*San-kuo chih yen-i* hsü," *Hu Shih wen-ts'un* (reprint, Taipei: Yuan-tung tu-shu kung-ssu, 1971), 2:467–75; Chou Li-po, "T'an *San-kuo chih yen-i*," in *Chung-kuo ku-tien hsiao-shuo p'ing-lun chi* (Peking: Hsin-hua shu-tien, 1957), pp. 51–64; Wen Chi, "T'an *San-kuo yen-i*," in *Chung-kuo ku-tien hsiao-shuo chiang-hua* (reprint, Hong Kong: Shang-hai shu-tien, 1960), pp. 67–120; *San-kuo yen-i yen-chiu lun-wen chi* (Peking: Tso-chia ch'u-pan she, 1957); Lu Hsun, *Chung-kuo hsiao-shuo shih-lueh*, pp. 97–103; Chao Ts'ung, *Chung-kuo ssu ta hsiao-shuo chih yen-chiu* (Hong Kong: Yu-lien, 1964), pp. 98–140; C. T. Hsia, "The Romance of the Three Kingdoms," *The Classical Chinese Novel*, pp. 34–74; Liu Ts'un-yan, "Lo Kuan-chung and His Historical Romances," in *Critical Essays on Chinese Fiction*, ed. Winston Yang and Curtis Adkins, pp. 85–114, esp. 91–99; Roy Andrew Miller, "Introduction," in *Romance of the Three Kingdoms*, trans. C. H. Brewitt-Taylor, pp. v–xii.

11. Ch'en Shou, *San-kuo chih*, 1:1–115; 2:871–92; 5:1115–49.

12. Chu Hsi, in his "fan-li" redefining the legitimate dynasties, referred to Hsi Tso-ch'ih (fl. fourth century) and Cheng Tzu as the ones who extended the Han period to cover the entire period of the Shu. See Chu Hsi, "*Tzu-chih t'ung-chien kang-mu* fan-li," in *T'ung-chien Kang-mu* (Chin Chieh Shu Yeh Teh Chi, Chia-ch'ing Chia-tzu [1804] ed.), pp. 1a—35b, esp. 3a.

13. Ssu-ma Kuang, *Tzu-chih t'ung-chien, chüan* 69, pp. 2185—88.

14. Chu Hsi, "*Tzu-chih t'ung-chien kang-mu* fan-li," pp. 3a—3b.

15. Su Tung-p'o, *Chih lin, chüan* 6, in *Pi-chi hsiao-shuo ta-kuan* (reprint, Taipei, 1960), 2:799—829, esp. 814.

16. The thorny problem of authorship in the novel *San-kuo* is, as is the case with other early novels such as the *Shui-hu* and the *Feng-shen*, due to the lack of firsthand information about its putative author Lo Kuan-chung. While the authorship remains an unsolved issue, the consensus among literary critics and historians is as follows: (1) the Chia-ching or 1522 edition of the novel (the edition prefaced by Chiang Ta-ch'i [dated 1494] and Chang Shang-te [dated 1522]) is the earliest extant edition; and (2) based on this 1522 version of the novel, Mao Tsung-kang revised, commented upon, and produced the famous "Mao version" of the *San-kuo*. Ever since the first appearance of the Mao version of the book in about 1662, it has been the most popular edition of the novel. In this study, both the 1953 and 1981 editions of the novel are based on the Mao version. In fact, the popular modern editions of the *San-kuo*, which are available today almost everywhere in China and overseas, are basically the Mao version.

   As pointed out earlier, the pro-Shu and anti-Wei sentiment of the *San-kuo* stories was consistent and unequivocal throughout the long process of evolution of the novel. Although critics might approve or disapprove with this pro-Han anti-Wei position, they recognize it as an important theme of the novel. To give an example of how a modern Communist critic looks at the complicated problem of dynastic legitimacy in the novel *San-kuo*, see Liu Shih-te, "T'an *San-kuo-chih yen-i* chung te cheng-t'ung kuan-nien wen-ti," *Wen-hsueh yen-chiu chi-ken* 3 (September 1956): 174—94.

17. *San-kuo yen-i*, 1:169—70; also Brewitt-Taylor, 1:207—8.

18. *San-kuo yen-i*, 1:173; *San-kuo yen-i*, CC ed., 1:196. Brewitt-Taylor, p. 214. English translation follows Brewitt-Taylor's but with revision.

19. *San-kuo yen-i*, 1:205; *San-kuo yen-i*, CC ed., 1:235; also Brewitt-Taylor, 1:253—54.

20. *San-kuo yen-i*, 2:549—51; *San-kuo yen-i*, CC ed., 2:665—67; also Brewitt-Taylor, 2:64—67.

21. *San-kuo yen-i*, 1:97—98; *San-kuo yen-i*, CC ed., 1:108—9; also Brewitt-Taylor, 1:115—16.

22. *San-kuo yen-i*, 1:331; *San-kuo yen-i*, CC ed., 1:396; also Brewitt-Taylor, 1:418.

23. *San-kuo yen-i*, 1:340; *San-kuo yen-i*, CC ed., 2:407; also Brewitt-Taylor, 1:428.

24. *San-kuo yen-i*, 1:441; *San-kuo yen-i*, CC ed., 2:535; also Brewitt-Taylor,

1:558. English translation follows Brewitt-Taylor's, but with significant revision.

25. Chen Wei (fl. 1573), [*Hsin-k'e chien-hsiao ke p'i p'ing*] *Hsi-Han yen-i chuan* (*Tung-Hsi-Han t'ung-su yen-i*, microfilm copy, made in 1955, of the original Ming edition in Naikaku Bunko, Japan), *chüan* 1, p. 386.

26. Burton Watson, trans., *Records of the Grand Historian of China*, 1:77, 78. R. L. Riftin also points out certain portrayal characteristics of a sovereign that allow him to trace the mythic pre-ancestor to a dragon, a totem of the ancient Chinese tribes. He further observes that these portrayal characteristics were of great significance in ancient China for confirmation of validity of the hereditary power of succession and the foundation of a new dynasty. Riftin's book is written in Russian, only the "Summary" is in English; see R. L. Riftin, *Ot mifa k romanu* (From Myth to Novel: Evolution of Character Depiction in Chinese Classical Literature) (Moscow, 1979), pp. 352−58.

27. *Ying-lieh chuan*, ed. and annot. Chao Ching-shen and Tu Hao-ming (Shanghai: Shang-hai wen-hua ch'u-pan she, 1956), pp. 24−25.

28. For the official version of T'ai-tsu's birth myth, see Chang T'ing-yü (1670−1756) et al., *Ming-shih* (Taipei: Kuo-fang yen-chiu yuan, 1962), *chüan* 1, vol. 1, p. 1.

29. For the popular version of T'ai-tsu's birth myth, see [*Hsin-k'e huang-Ming K'ai-yün chi-lueh wu-kung ming shih*] *Ying-lieh chuan* (Microfilm copy of the original San-t'ai kuan edition in Naikaku Bunko, Japan), *chüan* 1, p. 16a.

30. Yuan Yü-ling, *Sui-shih i-wen* (Taipei: Yu-shih yueh-k'an she, 1975), pp. 2b−3a.

31. Hsiung Ta-mu, *T'ang-chuan yen-i* (Microfilm copy made in 1955 of the original 1619 edition in Naikaku Bunko, Japan), *chüan* 1, pp. 3a−3b; also compare Li Shih-min's birth myth in Yuan Yü-ling, *Sui-shih i-wen*, pp. 53a−53b.

32. Hsiung Ta-mu, *Nan-Sung chih-chuan t'ung-su yen-i t'i p'ing* (Microfilm copy made in 1955 of the original Shih-te t'ang edition in Naikaku Bunko, Japan), *chüan* 1, p. 6a (bound in *Nan Pei Sung ch'üan-chuan*). I have checked this microfilm copy with two editions of *Nan Pei Sung ch'üan-chuan* by Yen-shih shan-chiao (pseud.), and Chih-li ch'i-jen (pseud.), and find them generally similar in contents. The two editions I use are the 1913 Shanghai reprint edition (bound with *Pei-Sung Yang-chia chiang* in 8 vols.) and the 1866 T'ung-chih edition (also bound with *Pei-Sung Yang-chia chiang*, but in 6 vols.). For a detailed discussion on different editions of these two novels (commonly referred to as *Nan Pei liang-Sung chih-chuan*), see Sun K'ai-ti, *Jih-pen Tung-ching so-chien Chung-kuo hsiao-shuo shu-mu* (Peking: Jen-min wen-hsueh ch'u pan she, 1981), pp. 43−46.

33. In his discussion of Chinese despotism, F. W. Mote emphasizes its historical development. According to him, despotism was at its height in the Ming dynasty when terror became an institutionalized feature. The Ch'ing dynasty that inherited many features of Ming rule also inherited the element of

terror as a regular and functionally conceived component of government. However, the amount of terror used in the Ch'ing government sharply diminished. For reasons for these historical developments, see F. W. Mote, "The Growth of Chinese Despotism: A Critique of Wittfogel's Theory of Oriental Despotism as Applied to China," *Oriens Extremus* 8, no. 1 (August 1961): 1—41, esp. 18—29. See also Karl A. Wittfogel, *Oriental Despotism* (New Haven, Conn.: Yale University Press, 1957), pp. 101—36, esp. 101—8; 134—37.

34. *Ts'an-T'ang wu-tai-shih yen-i chuan* (Microfilm copy made by the Library of Congress of the original Ming edition in the Rare Books Collection of the National Peiping Library, 8 *chüan* in 6 vols.), *chüan* 1, p. 11a. It should be pointed out here that although the novel (*Ts'an-T'ang* hereafter) was published under the name of Lo Kuan-chung during Ming times, modern scholars have generally been skeptical of the authorship of this novel. Starting from Lu Hsun, the prevailing view is that although Lo Kuan-chung might have written a primitive version of the novel, it was rewritten so many times by later unknown Ming writers that the extant Ming edition of the novel could hardly be called a novel by Lo Kuan-chung. For references on the authorship of the novel see, among others, Lu Hsun, *Chung-kuo hsiao-shuo shih-lueh*, p. 99; Chao Ts'ung, *Chung-kuo ssu ta hsiao-shuo chih yen-chiu*, p. 117; Cheng chen-to [*Ch'a-t'u-pen*] *Chung-kuo wen-hsueh shih*, 4:720—21; Sun K'ai-ti, *Chung-kuo t'ung-su hsiao-shuo shu-mu*, pp. 47—48; C. T. Hsia, *The Classic Chinese Novel*, pp. 341—42; R. G. Irwin, *The Evolution of a Chinese Novel*, p. 49; Liu Ts'un-Yan, *Chinese Popular Fiction in Two London Libraries* (Hong Kong: Lung men Bookstore, 1967), pp. 266—67.

35. Early in 1923, Hsieh Wu-liang expounded a theory that Lo Kuan-chung, the putative author of the *San-kuo*, wrote his novels to promote "popular revolution" (*P'ing-min ke-ming*) against the alien Yuan dynasty. For details of Hsieh's theory, see Hsieh Wu-liang, *Lo Kuan-chung Yü Ma Chih-yuan* (Shanghai: Shang-wu yin-shu kuan, 1935), pp. 12—61, esp. 19.

36. *Ts'an-T'ang*, *chüan* 1, pp. 3b—10b.

37. *Ts'an-T'ang*, *chüan* 2, p. 3a: "An Ching-ssu mu-yang ta-hu"; *chüan* 3, pp. 1a—7b: "Li Ts'un-hsiao li-sha ssu-chiang."

38. For biographies of Li Ts'un-hsiao in the Official Histories, see Ou-yang Hsiu, *Wu-tai shih-chi* (reprint, Taipei: I-wen yin-shu kuan, 1955), *chüan* 36, pp. 12b—18a; Hsueh Chü-cheng, *Chiu Wu-tai shih* (reprint, Taipei: I-wen yin-shu kuan, 1955), *chüan* 53, pp. 2b—5a.

39. In the novel *Shui-hu* Li K'uei does propose to overturn the government and seize the throne. See *Shui-hu* (Hong Kong: Chung-hua shu-chü, 1970), 2:489; *Shui-hu chuan hui-p'ing pen* (Peking: Pei-ching ta-hsueh, 1981), 1:768; *Shui-hu chuan* (Peking: Jen-min wen-hsueh ch'u-pan she, 1975), 2:574; *I-pai erh-shih hui ti Shui-hu* (Hong Kong: Shang-wu yin-shu kuan, 1969), 1:678—79. C. T. Hsia contends that Li K'uei speaks for Sung Chiang's suppressed desire to become emperor. See C. T. Hsia, *The Classic Chinese Novel*, pp. 108—9.

A few words more must be said here with regard to the editions of the novel *Shui-hu*. Of the many versions of the novel, three major ones are used in this study: (1) The so-called 70 chapter Chin Sheng-t'an version (actually it contains 71 chapters), which was edited, shortened, and commented upon by Chin Sheng-t'an, has been the most popular version of the novel ever since it was published in 1641; (2) the 100 chapter Jung-yü t'ang version (commented upon by Yeh Chou, a Ming critic), which was popular in Ming-Ch'ing times for its alleged commentary by the most popular unconventional writer Li Chih; and (3) the 120 chapter Yuan Wu-yai version (really annotated by Li Chih), which is the most complete version of the novel. The Chung-hua edition of *Shui-hu* cited above is a modern edition based on the 70 chapter version (*Shui-hu* [70-chapter] hereafter); the *Shui-hu chuan hui-p'ing pen* cited above is a modern 70-chapter variorum edition (*Shui-hu* [70-chapter variorum] hereafter); the *Shui-hu chuan* is a modern edition based on the 100 chapter Jung-yü t'ang edition (*Shui-hu* [100-chapter] hereafter); and the *I-pai erh-shih hui ti Shui-hu* is a modern edition based on the 120 chapter version (*Shui-hu* [120-chapter] hereafter). Note that this 120 chapter Shang-Wu edition is a reprint of its 1929 edition prefaced by Hu Shih.

40. Ch'en She's name is Sheng; "She" is his style. While the name "Ch'en She" is used in *Shih-chi*, "Ch'en Sheng" is used in *Han-shu*. I follow *Shih-chi*. For his biographies, see Ssu-ma Chien, *Shih-chi*, 6:1949–65; Pan Ku, *Han-shu* (Peking: Chung-hua shu-chü, 1962), 7:1785–1826. See also Burton Watson, trans., *Records of the Grand Historian of China*, 1:19–33. Recently there have been many pamphlets of popular reading materials published in the People's Republic of China, among them one about Ch'en She and Wu Kuang; see Hung Shih-ti, *Ch'en Sheng, Wu Kuang* (Shanghai: Jen-min ch'u-pan-she, 1972).

41. *Shih-chi*, 6:1952. For the English translation, see Watson, 1:21.

42. *Shih-chi*, 6:1949. For the English translation, see Watson, 1:19.

43. *Shih-chi*, 6:1952. For the English translation, see Watson, 1:21.

44. Both *Shih-chih* and *Han-shu* single out Ch'en She as the man who began the uprising that eventually succeeded in overthrowing the Ch'in. For details, see *Shih-chi*, 6:1949–65; *Han-shu*, 7:1785–1826. In the People's Republic of China today, Ch'en She and Wu Kuang are lauded as "revolutionary leaders of the first peasant-revolution (in Chinese history)." See Hung Shih-ti, *Ch'en Sheng, Wu Kuang*, p. 48.

45. Chen Wei, *Hsi-Han yen-i*, Hong Kong ed., 1:14.

46. The commoner image of Ch'en She was expounded most eloquently by Chia I (201–169 B.C.), a famous scholar in early Han times. When Chia I discussed the history of the Ch'in dynasty and the reason for its downfall, he ascribed the downfall of the Ch'in to its failure to rule with humanity and righteousness. It is because of this failure that "a single commoner opposed it and its seven ancestral temples toppled, its ruler died by the hands of men, and it became the laughing stock of the world." Here "a single commoner" refers to Ch'en She, who was described by Chia I as a

man "born in a humble hut with tiny windows and a wattle door, a day laborer in the fields and a garrison conscript." For details of Chia I's essay on the faults of Ch'in, see *Shih-chi*, 6:1961—65. For the English translation of this text, see Watson, 1:30—33. Also compare *Han-shu*, 7:1821—25.

47. The view of history as "comprehensive mirror" for aid in government is best represented by the Sung historian Ssu-ma Kuang whose famous *T'ung-chien* (discussed in chap. 1) is a good example. Based on this *T'ung-chien*, Chu Hsi later wrote his *T'ung-chien Kang-mu* (also discussed in chap. 1) to reinforce the moral principle of "praise and blame" in history. The preface to this *Kang-mu* specifically points out that the work provides warnings for "future emperors and ministers." In other words, the purpose of writing history was to provide guidance for future generations. For details of this preface, see "Yu chih *T'ung-chien kang-mu* hsu" in *T'ung-chien Kang-mu* (1804 ed.), pp. 1a—8a, esp. 6b—7a.

Chapter 3

1. *Tso-chuan*: annot. Takezoe Kōkō, *Tso-chuan hui-chien* (reprint, Taipei, 1970), vol. 2, chap. 17, pp. 21a—21b; also annot. Wang Po-hsing, *Ch'un-ch'iu Tso-chuan tu-pen* (Hong Kong: Chung-hua shu-chü, 1965), p. 412.

2. Chang T'ing-yü et al., "Ming-shih mu-lu," in *Ming-shih*, 1:1—137, esp. 16—137; Wang Ao, *Ku-su chih* (reprint, Taipei: Hsueh-shen shu-chü, 1965), *chüan* 43—58. Note the inclusion of "Recluses" and "Buddhists and Taoists" in the list: While the *Ming-shih* does not have the category of "Buddhists and Taoists" and the *Ku-su chih* does not have the category of "Recluses," both are included because they are established classifications. For a brief illustration of the diversity in biographies of Chinese local histories and Official Histories, see, among others, Li T'ai-fen, *Fang-chih hsueh* (1935; reprint, Taipei, 1968), pp. 10—14, 91—92; Fu Chen-lun, *Chung-kuo fang-chih hsueh t'ung-lun* (reprint, Taipei, 1968), pp. 114, 124; Hsu Hao, *Nien-wu shih lun-kang* (reprint, Hong Kong, 1964), pp. 339—41.

3. Arthur Waley, trans., *The Analects of Confucius*, p. 197; see also Watson, *Records of the Grand Historian of China*, p. 14; *Lun-yü*, annot. Liu Pao-nan, *Lun-yü cheng-i* (Hong Kong: Chung-hua shu-chü, 1963), p. 342. For an illuminating analysis of the problem of value systems and personal behavior in Chinese history, see Arthur F. Wright, "Values, Roles and Personalities," in *Confucian Personalities*, ed. Arthur F. Wright and Dennis Twitchett (Stanford, Calif.: Stanford University Press, 1962), pp. 3—23, esp. 3—9.

4. Pan Ku, *Han-shu*, 9:2725—36, esp. 2733—35. English translation of Ssu-ma Ch'ien's letter to his friend Jen An follows Watson's, with revisions. See Watson, *Records of the Grand Historian of China*, 1:xii. For the dating of Ssu-ma Ch'ien's letter to Jen An, see Watson, *Ssu-ma Ch'ien, Grand Historian of China* (New York: Columbia University Press, 1958), pp. 194—98. For the background and story of Ssu-ma Ch'ien's tragic humili-

ation, see Watson, *Ssu-ma Ch'ien*, pp. 54—55, 60—62; Cheng Ho-sheng, *Ssu-ma Ch'ien nien-p'u* (Shanghai: Shang-wu yin-shu kuan, 1956), pp. 73—86; Li Ch'ang-chih, *Ssu-ma Ch'ien chih jen-ko yü feng-ko* (reprint, Hong Kong, 1963), pp. 130—43.

5. Arthur Waley, *The Analects of Confucius*, p. 227; see also *Lun-yü*, annot. Yang Po-Chun, *Lun-yü i-chu*, p. 209.

6. *Shih-chi*, 1:296. The English translation follows Watson's, with revisions. See Watson, *Records of the Grand Historian of China*, 1:38.

7. *Shih-chi*, 2:344. The English translation follows Watson's, with revisions. See *Records of the Grand Historian of China*, 1:78.

8. C. T. Hsia in his "Introduction" to the 1975 reprint of *Sui-shih i-wen* ranks the latter as one of the four best Ming novels; see Hsia Chih-ch'ing, "*Sui-shih i-wen* ch'ung-k'an hsu," in *Sui-shih i-wen* (reprint, Taipei: Yu-shih yueh-k'an she, 1975), pp. 1—20.

9. *Shih-chi*, 1:338—39. For the English translation, see Watson, *Records of the Grand Historian of China*, 1:73—74.

10. *Shih-chi*, 1:339. For the English translation, see Watson, 1:74.

11. *Shih-chi*, 1:333—36.

12. *Shih-chi*, 3:760. For the English translation, see Watson, 1:121.

13. *Shih-chi*, 1:333. For the English translation, see Watson, 1:70. The novel *Hsi-Han* generally follows *Shih-chi*; see Chen Wei's *Hsi-Han yen-i chuan*, (Tung Hsi Han t'ung-su yen-i), Chien-hsiao-ko edition, *chüan* 7, pp. 46b—52b: "Dictator King Bade Farewell to Lady Yü"; see also *Hsi-Han yen-i* (reprint, Hong Kong: Hsiang-chi shu-chü, n.d.), 2:63—65. I have checked this Hong Kong edition against that of the microfilm copy, the Chien-hsiao-ko edition of Chen Wei's *Hsi-Han yen-i chuan*. The Hong Kong edition is an "abridged" edition based on the Chien-hsiao-ko edition. It is "abridged" in the sense that all comments and quotations (mostly poems) of the original are expunged; the original text, however, remains intact. (The number of chapters is incorrectly given as 100 in the contents of the Chien-hsiao-ko edition. The correct number of chapters should be 101, which is the number listed in the Hong Kong edition.)

14. *Shih-chi*, 1:333—34. For the English translation, see Watson, 1:70—71.

15. *Shih-chi*, 1:336; see also Watson, 1:72.

16. Chen Wei, *Hsi-Han yen-i* (Hong Kong ed.), 2:65; see also the Chien-hsiao-ko edition, *chüan* 7, p. 55a.

17. Shih-chi, 1:336. The English translation follows Watson, with significant revisions. See Watson, 1:72—73. For the story in the novel, see the Chien-hsiao-ko edition, *chüan* 7, pp. 52a—58b.

18. *San-kuo yen-i*, 1:178—80; also Brewitt-Taylor, 1:219—21.

19. *San-kuo yen-i*, 1:349; *San-kuo yen-i*, CC ed., 2:419; for the English translation, see Brewitt-Taylor with minor changes, 1:440.

20. For the *Book of History*, see *Shu-ching chi chuan* (Taipei: Ch'i-ming shu-chü, 1952), pp. 3—5, 8, 12—14. For the *Analects of Confucius*, see *Lun-yü i-chu*, p. 214. Comparing the language of the account in *Lun-yü*

with that of the *Shu-ching*, the similarity of the wording is striking. It is very unlikely that this passage has much to do with Confucius except that it may constitute teaching material used in the Confucian School. See D. C. Lau, trans., *The Analects of Confucius*, p. 158.

21. *Meng-tzu*, see *Ssu-shu tu-pen* edition, pp. 247–48, 255–56, 258–62. *Mo-tzu*, annot. Sun I-jang, *Mo-tzu hsien-ku* (reprint, Taipei, 1965), 1:27–45. *Han Fei-tzu*, annot. Wang Hsien-shen, *Han Fei-tzu chi chieh* (Taipei: Shang-wu yin-shu kuan, 1956), 1:21–29.

22. *Chuang-tzu*, annot. Kuo Ch'ing-fan, *Chuang-tzu chi shih* (Taipei: Shih-chih shu-chü, 1962), pp. 22, 995–97.

23. *San-kuo yen-i*, CC ed., 1:359–60. English translation follows Brewitt-Taylor, p. 382.

24. *San-kuo yen-i*, CC ed., 1:360. Note that Lü Wang (i.e., Chiang Tzu-ya) and Chang Liang were the two most celebrated imperial advisers who helped found the Chou and the Han dynasties respectively. Both men will be discussed in detail later in this chapter.

25. *San-kuo yen-i*, CC ed., p. 361. The English translation follows Brewitt-Taylor, with minor revision; see Brewitt-Taylor, p. 384. See also Moss Roberts, p. 110.

26. *San-kuo yen-i*, CC ed., p. 367. The English translation follows Moss Roberts; see Roberts, p. 116.

27. "One" denotes "heaven"; "two" denotes "earth"; "three" denotes "all things" or myriad. In the *Book of the Changes*, it says "when there were heaven and earth, then afterwards and things were produced." See *I-ching*, Wu-ching tu-pen edition, p. 73; for English translation, see James Legge, *The I-Ching* (reprint, New York: Dover Publications, 1963), p. 433. In Lao Tzu's *Tao-te Ching*, it says that "the way begets one; one begets two; two begets three; three begets the myriad creatures." See *Lao Tzu*, annot. Wei Yuan, *Lao-tzu pen-i* (Hong Kong, 1964), p. 49; for English translation, see D. C. Lau, trans., *Tao Te Ching* (Harmondsworth, England: Penguin Books, 1963), p. 103.

28. Chung Hsing, *Yu-Hsia chih-chuan*, chüan 3, pp. 24a–36a. It is interesting to point out that both *Shih-chi* and *Meng-tzu* mention the story about how King T'ang sent special messengers to enlist I Yin's help. In *Shih-chi* it is said that King T'ang sent messengers five times to visit I Yin, while in *Meng-tzu*, it is three times. See *Shih-chi*, 1:94; *Meng-tzu*, see *Ssu-shu tu-pen* ed., 2:265.

29. For a discussion of different editions of the novel, see Chao Ching-shen's "Preface," in *Ying-lieh chuan*, ed. Chao Ching-shen and Tu Hao-ming, pp. 1–8.

30. Chang T'ing-yü et al., *Ming-shih*, 3:1586–92, esp. 1586.

31. Chao Ching-shen and Tu Hao-ming, eds., *Ying-lieh chuan*, pp. 48–52.

32. Ibid., pp. 44–45, 75–77.

33. For biographies of Li Shan-ch'ang, T'ao An, and Feng Sheng, see *Ming-shih*, 3:1615, 1635, 1718. However, the novel follows *Ming-shih* in stories of how Chu Yuan-chang sent Sun Yen to recruit Liu Chi, Chang I,

Yeh Shen, and Sung Lien; see *Ming-shih*, 3:1625–31; also 5:3245–46. As to stories in the novel of how Sun Yen recruited Liu, Chang, Yeh, and Sung, see *Ying-lieh chuan*, pp. 96–103.

34. *San-kuo yen-i*, 1:301–7, esp. 307. *San-kuo yen-i*, CC ed., pp. 350–64, esp. 364. The English translation follows Brewitt-Taylor, with revisions; see Brewitt-Taylor, 1:385–86.

35. *San-kuo yen-i*, 1:340; also Brewitt-Taylor, 1:428.

36. *San-kuo yen-i*, 1:261–62. The English translation follows Hsia; see C. T. Hsia, *The Classic Chinese Novel*, pp. 72–73; also compare Brewitt-Taylor, 1:325–26.

37. *San-kuo yen-i*, 1:261–62. The English translation follows Hsia. See C. T. Hsia, p. 73; also compare Brewitt-Taylor, 1:36.

38. For I Yin's biography, see *Shih-chi*, 1:94–99. Also compare Herbert A. Giles, *A Chinese Biographical Dictionary* (1898; reprint, Taipei, 1964), p. 352. For a modern evaluation of the biographical sources on the semi-mythical I Yin, see Ch'ü Wan-li, "*Shih-chi Yin-pen-chi* chi ch'i-t'a chi-lu chung so-tsai Yin-Shang shih-tai ti shih-shih," in *Bulletin of the College of Arts, National Taiwan University* 14 (November 1965): 87–118, esp. 110.

39. For Chiang Shang's biography, see *Shih-chi*, *chüan* 32, vol. 5, pp. 1477–81. Also compare Herbert A. Giles, *A Chinese Biographical Dictionary*, pp. 135–136.

40. For Chang Liang's biographies, see *Shih-chi*, 6:2033–49; *Han-Shu*, 7:2023–38. Also compare Herbert A. Giles, *A Chinese Biographical Dictionary*, pp. 33–34.

41. For Chu-ko Liang's biography, see Ch'en Shou, *San-kuo chih* 4:911–37, esp. 923–24. Also compare Chu-ko Liang, *Chu-ko Liang chi* (Peking: Chung-hua shu-chü, 1974), pp. 16–21. For Chu-ko Liang's own writings, see *Chu-ko Liang chi*, pp. 4–7.

42. For Liu Chi's biography, see *Ming-Shih*, 3:1625–31; also see Wang Hsin-i, *Liu Po-wen nien-p'u* (Shanghai: Shang-wu yin-shu kuan, 1936). For a modern study of Liu Chi, see Chan Hok-lam, *Liu Chi: Dual Image of a Chinese Imperial Adviser* (Ph.D. Diss., Princeton University, 1967).

43. Chen Wei, *Hsi-Han yen-i* (Hong Kong ed.), 1:50–52; also Chien-hsiao-ko edition, *chüan* 3, pp. 10b–15b.

44. *Shih-chi*, 2:381; *Han-shu*, 1:56. English translation follows Watson, with revision, 1:107.

45. *Hsi-Han yen-i* (Hong Kong ed.), 2:61–63; also see Chien-hsiao-ko edition, *chüan* 7, pp. 41b–46b.

46. *Shih-chi*, 1:333; *Han-shu*, 1:50.

47. *Shih-chi*, 6:2034–35. Note here again the mystical numeral *three*: Three times Master Yellow Stone tried Chang Liang's patience before he gave Chang the book on military tactics by Chiang Shang.

48. *Shih-chi*, 6:2048. For the story in the novel, see Chen Wei, *Hsi-Han yen-i chuan*, Chien-hsiao-ko p'i-p'ing edition, *chüan* 8, pp. 6b–12a.

49. *Ying-lieh chuan*, pp. 88–96.

50. Liu Chi's ability to presage future happenings is adopted in the *Ming-shih*,

which tells a story about how Liu Chi saved Chu Yuan-chang's life by urging the latter to change boats. Seconds later the original boat was bombarded by the enemy. For details of the story, see *Ming-shih*, 3:1625.

51. For details of the story, see *Ying-lieh chuan*, pp. 402–3. Also compare *Ming-shih*, 3:1626.

52. In a modern evaluation by Wei Chü-hsien of the historical sources of the novel *Feng-shen*, biographical data on Chiang Shang have been conveniently collected in one section. See Wei Chü-hsien, *Feng-shen-pang ku-shih t'an-yuan* (Kowloon: Wei-hsing yin-wu so, 1960), 1:55–64.

53. *Shih-chi*, 5:1477–81.

54. *Ts'an-T'ang*, *chüan* 2, p. 23b; *chüan* 3, p. 2a. Note that the original Chinese text for "five feet" is "Shen pu-man Ch'i Ch'ih" (less than seven *ch'ih* in height). According to the Chinese measurement, one "Han ch'ih" equals 9.13 inches; therefore "less than seven *ch'ih*" approximates five feet.

55. For those who are interested in the art of the novel, the relation between "character" and "incident" is best summed up by Henry James's famous saying: "What is character but the determination of incident? What is incident but the illustration of character?" See Henry James, "The Art of Fiction," in *The Future of the Novel* (New York: Vintage Books, 1956), pp. 3–27.

56. For the young Han Hsin's story in the novel, see *Hsi-Han yen-i*, 1:19.

57. For the details of Kuan Yü's two stories, see *San-kuo yen-i*, 2:545–49, 615–20.

58. *San-kuo yen-i*, 1:350. Note that "I-te" is Chang Fei's style, and "Yen" (in modern Hopei), the area where he came from.

59. *San-kuo yen-i*, 1:346–47.

60. Lo Fen, ed., *Yang-chia chiang yen-i* (Shanghai: Shang-hai wen-hua ch'u-pan she, 1956), p. 92. In chapter 6, Yang Yeh's death will be discussed in detail. For biographical information about Yang Yeh, see related notes in that chapter.

61. Hsiung Ta-mu, *Ta-Sung chung-hsing Yueh-wang chuan*, *chüan* 1, p. 32b; *chüan* 7, p. 35b; *chüan* 8, p. 7b. In chapter 4, Yueh Fei's patriotism will be discussed in detail.

62. For details of the story about Wu Sung's killing a tiger singlehandedly, see *Shui-hu* (70-chapter), pp. 257–64; *Shui-hu* (70-chapter variorum), pp. 419–29; *Shui-hu* (120-chapter), pp. 352–64. For the story about how Li K'uei killed four tigers with his bare hands, see *Shui-hu* (70-chapter), pp. 502–11; *Shui-hu* (70-chapter variorum), pp. 790–815; *Shui-hu* (120-chapter), pp. 696–717. For Li Ts'un-hsiao's tiger-killing story, see *Ts'an-T'ang*, *chüan* 2, p. 3a.

63. *Shui-hu* (70-chapter), p. 228; *Shui-hu* (70-chapter variorum), p. 374; *Shui-hu* (120-chapter), p. 311. For the English translation, see Pearl Buck, trans., *All Men Are Brothers* (New York: Grosset and Dunlap, 1937), p. 335; J. H. Jackson, trans., *Water Margin* (1937; reprint, Cambridge, 1976), p. 264; Sidney Shapiro, trans. and ed., *Outlaws of the Marsh* (Peking:

Foreign Language Press, 1981; Bloomington: Indiana University Press, 1981), p. 313. While Jackson skipped the Chinese term *hao-han* (real man), Buck translated it as "masculine fellow" and Shapiro, "chivalrous man."

64. *Shui-hu* (70-chapter), p. 228; *Shui-hu* (70-chapter variorum), p. 374; *Shui-hu* (120-chapter), p. 312. For the English translation, compare Buck's (p. 336) with Jackson's (p. 264) and Shapiro's (p. 313).

65. This rule applies only to Ming historical novels; it does not apply to Ch'ing historical novels. For example, in the novel *Shuo-T'ang*, an early Ch'ing version about the founding of the T'ang dynasty, both Ch'eng Yao-chin and Yü-ch'ih Kung cannot be described as "warriors showing little interest in women"; certain episodes show their interest in women. See Ch'en Ju-heng, ed., *Shuo T'ang* (Shanghai: Chung-hua shu-chü, 1959; reprint, Hong Kong: Kwang-chih shu-chü, n.d.), chaps. 52, 53, pp. 268–76.

66. *Shui-hu* (70-chapter), pp. 86–87; *Shui-hu* (120-chapter), p. 113. The English translation follows Shapiro's (p. 46); see also Buck's (p. 51) and Jackson's (p. 22). Note that both Buck and Jackson mistakenly rendered the Chinese measurement *"ch'ih"* as "foot." As I mentioned before, 1 Han *ch'ih* equals 9.13 inches. Therefore, "eight *ch'ih*" approximates six feet, not eight feet.

67. *Shui-hu* (70-chapter), pp. 86–87; *Shui-hu* (70-chapter variorum) p. 161; *Shui-hu* (120-chapter), p. 113. The English translation follows Buck's with revisions; see Buck, pp. 124–125. See also Jackson, p. 69; Shapiro, p. 115. Both Jackson and Shapiro misread the original Chinese text in this case.

68. *Shui-hu* (70-chapter), p. 87; *Shui-hu* (120-chapter), p. 113. For the English translation, see Buck, p. 125.

69. *Shui-hu* (70-chapter), pp. 56–58, 62–70.

70. Ibid., pp. 36–42, 103–7.

71. *Shui-hu* (120-chapter), pp. 1811–17.

72. *Shui-hu* (70-chapter), p. 23; *Shui-hu* (70-chapter variorum), pp. 71–72; *Shui-hu* (120-chapter), p. 32. For the English translation, see Buck, pp. 35–36; Jackson, p. 14; Shapiro, p. 33.

73. *San-kuo yen-i*, 1:4. The English translation follows Brewitt-Taylor's with revisions. See Brewitt-Taylor, 1:6. Note that one catty equals one and one-third pound.

74. *San-kuo yen-i*, 2:547–49.

75. Ibid., 1:350.

76. *Shui-hu* (70-chapter), p. 21; *Shui-hu* (70-chapter variorum), p. 68; *Shui-hu* (120-chapter), p. 28. The English translation generally follows Jackson's, but with revision. See Jackson, pp. 11–12. Also compare Jackson's translation with Buck's, which names only seventeen weapons. Note that Shapiro skipped the names of all eighteen weapons; see Shapiro, p. 30.

77. The *ko* halbert was one of the most ancient weapons in China. Its active service lasted more than a millennium before it was finally abandoned during the Han dynasty. The *chi* halbert, which was combined from the *ko* and the *mao* (the spearhead), was the chief long-handled weapon during the Han dynasty. By the time of the Six Dynasties, the *chi* no longer

functioned as a battle weapon; it had become a kind of ceremonial apparatus. For the evolution of the *ko* and *chi* in the history of Chinese weapons, see Chou Wei, *Chung-kuo ping-ch'i shih-kao* (Peking: San-lien shu-tien, 1957), pp. 64–98, 207, 210.

78. Chou Wei, *Chung-kuo ping-ch'i shih-kao*, pp. 232–33. For an English account of the evolution of the *ko* and *chi*, see Li Chi, *The Beginnings of Chinese Civilizations* (Seattle: University of Washington Press, 1957), pp. 55–59.

79. Chen Wei, *Hsi-Han yen-i chuan*, Chien-hsiao-ko ed., *chüan* 8, pp. 23a–29a, esp. 26; also *Hsi-Han yen-i* (Hong Kong ed.), 2:81–82.

80. *Ts'an-T'ang*, *chüan* 5, pp. 17b–24a.

81. Ch'in-huai Mo-k'o [pseud.], *Yang-chia-fu shih-tai chung-yung yen-i chih-chuan* (facsimile ed., Taipei: Kuo-li chung-yang tu-shu kuan, 1970), 4:785–86.

82. Ibid.

83. Judging from the fact that the majority of military heroes are commoners, it seems clear that the easiest way to win fame for the commoners is military. Besides, there were other professions that required martial arts; for example, the profession of escort (*pao-piao*, guards who convoyed travelers along dangerous routes) flourished in Ming times, as evidenced by detailed descriptions of their activities in vernacular fiction.

84. *Shih-chi*, 7:2121–29; Watson, *Records of the Grand Historian of China*, pp. 11–15.

85. *Lun-yü cheng-i*, p. 392. For the English translation, see Waley, *The Analects of Confucius*, Book 18, pp. 219–20, esp. 220.

86. *Lun-yü i-chu*, p. 201. For the English translation, see Waley, *The Analects of Confucius*, Book 18, pp. 220.

87. If we only count the Official Histories that contain sections on the recluses, it should be fourteen, instead of fifteen as we have indicated. The extra one in our list is the *Shih-chi*, which does not contain a section on the recluses but has biographies of Po Yi and Shu Ch'i, the earliest recorded recluses in history. For a list of the other fourteen Official Histories, see Hsu Hao, *Nien-wu shih lun-kang*, pp. 339–41. It should be noted that local histories also have sections on the recluses. See, for example, *Ku-su chih*, section on *Yin-i* (hermits). For a modern study of the concept of the recluse, see Li Chi, "The Changing Concept of the Recluse in Chinese Literature," *HJAS* 24 (1962–63): 234–47.

88. *San-kuo yen-i*, 2:752; *San-kuo yen-i*, CC ed., 3:907; the English translation follows Brewitt-Taylor's with minor changes; see Brewitt-Taylor, 2:329.

89. *San-kuo yen-i*, 1:312; for the English translation, see Brewitt-Taylor, 1:393.

90. *San-kuo yen-i*, 1:311; for the English translation, see Brewitt-Taylor, 1:393.

91. *San-kuo yen-i*, 1:308; for the English translation, see Brewitt-Taylor's, 1:388.

92. Chung Hsing, ed., *P'an-ku chih T'ang Yü chuan*, pp. 9b–10a.

93. Ibid., pp. 16b–17a.

94. *Chuang-tzu chih shih*, 2:990–1015, esp. 995. For the English translation,

see Burton Watson, trans., *The Complete Works of Chuang-tzu* (New York: Columbia University Press, 1968), pp. 323–38, esp. 327.

Chapter 4

1. See the Introduction to this book, chap. 1, sec. V.

2. One of the main factors in the rise of academies was the burgeoning growth of philosophical schools in the sixteenth century. For an exposition of this thesis, see John Meskill, "Academies and Politics in the Ming Dynasty," in *Chinese Government in Ming Times: Seven Studies*, ed. Charles O. Hucker (New York: Columbia University Press, 1969), pp. 149–74. For an extended discussion of the mass movement of the radical philosophical schools in late Ming, see, among others, Chi Wen-fu, *Wan-Ming ssu-hsiang shih*, pp. 33–47; Jung Chao-tsu, *Ming-tai ssu-hsiang shih*, p. 231–56.

3. Huang Tsung-hsi, *Ming-ju hsueh-an*, 6:77. For Huang Tsung-hsi's accounts about other popular lecturers such as Wang Ken, Chu Shu, and Hsia T'ing-mei, see the same book, pp. 68, 76, and 77.

4. Li Chih, *Fen-shu*, p. 123.

5. In the *Analects of Confucius*, we find the following quotation about *jen*: "Filial piety (*hsiao*) and fraternal submission (*ti*), are they not the root of true virtues (*jen*)?" In *Meng-tzu*, Mencius said, "If only everyone loved his parents and treated his elders with deference, the world would be at peace." See *Lun-yü i-chu*, p. 2; *Meng-tzu*, *Ssu-shu tu-pen* edition, 2:200. The above English translations are based on those of James Legge and D. C. Lau, with minor revisions; see James Legge, trans., *The Confucian Analects*, vol. 1 of *The Chinese Classics* (1936; reprint, Hong Kong: Hong Kong University Press, 1960), p. 3; D. C. Lau, trans., *Mencius*, pp. 122–23.

6. For interpretations of Confucius's sayings, see *Lun-yü i-chu*, pp. 32, 135; for English translations of the two quotations, see Legge, trans., *The Confucian Analects*, pp. 29, 143, respectively. For different translations of the two passages, see Waley, trans., *The Analects of Confucius*, pp. 98–99, 166.

7. *Meng-tzu*, *Ssu-shu tu-pen* edition, p. 146. For English translation, see James Legge, trans., *The Works of Mencius* (reprint, Tokyo, 1936), p. 565. For a different translation, compare D. C. Lau, trans., *Mencius*, p. 102.

8. *Li-chi chin-chu chin-i*, annotated by Wang Meng-ou (Taipei: Shang-wu yin-shu kuan, 1969), 2:301–2. The English translation of *Li-chi* follows Legge's translation, but with minor revision. See James Legge, *Sacred Books of China* (reprint, Delhi: Matilal Banarsidass, 1966), pt. 3, pp. 379–80. The ten moral obligations listed in the *Li-chi* are very similar to those virtues mentioned by Yen-tzu in *Tso-chuan*. See *Tso-chuan*, *Wu-*

ching tu-pen edition (reprint, Taipei: Ch'i-ming shu-chü, 1952), 8:476. According to *Tso-chuan*, in the twenty-sixth year of the Duke of Chao, the Marquis of the Ch'i asked Yen-tzu about *li* (propriety). Yen-tzu replied: That the prince orders and the minister obeys, the father be kind and the son dutiful, the elder brother loving and the younger respectful, the husband be harmonious and the wife pliant, the mother-in-law be kind and the daughter-in-law submissive—these are things in propriety. That the prince in giving orders ordering nothing against the right, and the minister obeys without any duplicity; that the father be kind and at the same time instructive, and the son be dutiful and at the same time able to remonstrate; that the older brother, while loving, be friendly, and the younger, while respectful, be deferential; that the husband be righteous, while harmonious, and the wife be chaste, while pliant; that the mother-in-law be condescending, while kind, and the daughter-in-law be submissive and complaisant—these are excellent things in propriety. The above English translation of *Tso-chuan* follows Legge's but with revisions. See James Legge, *The Chinese Classics*, 5:718−19.

9. Feng Meng-lung, *Tung Chou lieh-kuo chih* (Peking: Tso-chia ch'u-pan she, 1955), 1:1−8, esp. 6−7. For a reproduction in facsimile of the original Ming edition of Feng's book, see Feng Meng-lung, *Hsin lieh-kuo chih* (Taipei: Lien-ching ch'u-pan shih-yeh kung-ssu, 1981), pp. 1−10, esp. 5−8.

10. Feng Meng-lung, *Hsin lieh-kuo chih*, p. 8.

11. *Kuo-yü* (Taipei: Shang-wu yin-shu kuan, 1956), 1:10; *Tso-chuan hui-chien*, 1:93−94; *Shih-chi*, 1:144−45.

12. *Kuo-yü*, 1:10.

13. For Yueh Fei's official biography, see T'o T'o, et al., *Sung-shih* (reprint, Peking: Chung-hua shu-chü, 1977), *chüan* 365, pp. 11375−98. For a critical analysis of three types of historical literature on the life and career of Yueh Fei, see Teng Kuang-ming, *Yueh Fei chuan* (rev. and enl. ed., Peking: Jen-min ch'u-pan she, 1983), pp. 432−51. For a study of Yueh Fei in English, see James T. C. Liu, "Yueh Fei—An Analysis in Historiography and Intellectual History," *Chinese Scholar*, no. 2 (September 1971), pp. 43−58; Hellmust Wilhelm, "From Myth to Myth: The Case of Yueh Fei's Biography," in *Confucian Personalities*, edited by Arthur Wright and Dennis Twitchett (Stanford: Stanford University Press, 1962), pp. 156−57.

14. Cheng Chen-to, "Yueh chuan te yen-hua," in *Chung-kuo wen-hsueh lun chi*, 1:360−68.

15. Hsiung Ta-mu, *Ta-Sung chung-hsing Yueh-wang chuan*, *chüan* 1, p. 32b.

16. Teng Kuang-ming, *Yueh Fei chuan* (Peking: San-lien shu-tien, 1955), pp. 1−5, esp. 5; Li Han-hun, *Yueh Wu-mu nien-p'u* (Taipei: Shang-wu yin-shu kuan, 1968), pp. 10−11.

17. Hsiung Ta-mu, *Yueh-wang chuan*, *chüan* 7, p. 35b.

18. Ibid., *chüan* 8, p. 7b.

19. *Sung-shih*, *chüan* 380, p. 11708.

20. *San-kuo yen-i*, 1:4; also C. H. Brewitt-Taylor, 1:5−6.

21. For the details of the death of Kuan Yü, see *San-kuo yen-i*, 2:629−35; for

the details of the death of Chang Fei, see *San-kuo yen-i*, 2:661−66; for the death of Liu Pei, see *San-kuo yen-i*, 2:675−97.

22. For official historical records of Sung Chiang and his band of outlaws, see *Sung-shih*, *chüan* 22, p. 407; also *chüan* 351, pp. 11113−14, esp. 11114; also *chüan* 353, pp. 11140−42, esp. 11141. For the earliest record of the *Shui-hu* stories, see *Hsuan-ho i-shih* in *Shui-hu* (120-chapter), pp. 1−8. For modern studies of the novel *Shui-hu chuan* see, among others, Hu Shih, "*Shui-hu chuan* k'ao-cheng," and "Pai-erh-shih-hui-pen *chung-i shui-hu chuan*," in *Hu Shih Wen-ts'un*, 1:500−547, 548−74; 3:404−40; Cheng chen-to, "*Shui-hu chuan* ti yen-hua," in *Chung-kuo wen-hsueh yen-chiu*, 1:101−57; Lu Hsun, *Chung-kuo hsiao-shuo shih-lueh*, pp. 107−16; Sun K'ai-ti, "*Shui-hu-chuan* chiu-pen k'ao," in *Ts'ang-chou chi*, 1:121−43; Chao Ching-shen, "*Shui-hu chuan* chien-lun," in *Shui-hu jen-wu yü Shui-hu chuan* (reprint, Taipei, 1971), pp. 121−54; Tso-chia ch'u-pan she ed., *Shui-hu yen-chiu lun-wen chi* (Peking, 1957); Yen Tun-i, *Shui-hu chuan ti yen-pien* (Peking: Tso-chia ch'u-pan she, 1957); Ho Hsin, *Shui-hu yen-chiu* (Shanghai: Shang-hai wen-i lien-ho ch'u-pan she, 1954); Sa Meng-wu, *Shui-hu chuan yü chung-kuo she-hui* (reprint, Macao: Wan-yu shu-tien, 1966). For English-language works on the novel, see, among others, James T. Y. Liu, *The Chinese Knight-Errant* (Chicago: University of Chicago Press, 1967), pp. 108−16; C. T. Hsia, "The Water Margin," in *The Classic Chinese Novel*, pp. 75−114; Ogawa Tamaki, "The Author of the *Shui-hu chuan*," *Monumenta Serica* 17 (1958): 312−330; Charles J. Alber, "A Survey of English Language Criticism of the *Shui-hu chuan*," *Ch'ing-hua hsueh-pao*, n.s. 7, no. 2 (August 1969): 102−19; Richard Irwin, *The Evolution of a Chinese Novel: Shui-hu-chuan*; Richard Irwin, "Water Margin Revised," *T'oung pao* 48, nos. 4−5 (1960): 393−415. For an English translation of the novel, see Pearl Buck, *All Men Are Brothers*; J. H. Jackson, *Water Margin*; and Sidney Shapiro, *Outlaws of the Marsh*. Also see Miyazaki Ichisada, *Suikoden* (Tokyo, 1972), esp. pp. 24−69, 192−215.

23. For a most detailed study of the numerous versions and editions of the novel *Shui-hu chuan*, see Yen Tun-i, *Shui-hu chuan ti yen-pien*, pp. 149−205; for a study of the *Shui-hu* in English, see Richard Irwin, *The Evolution of a Chinese Novel*, pp. 61−111.

24. See Li Chih's preface to the novel in *Shui-hu* (120-chapter), 1:1−4, esp. 1.

25. Yen Tun-i, *Shui-hu-chuan ti yen-pien*, pp. 31−32. For other discussions of *Shui-hu chuan* in connection with the Army of the Loyal and the Righteous, see chap. 1, n. 46. Also see Abe Kenya "Suikoden no bungakuseie no ikkōsatsu," *Nippon Chūgoku gakkai-hō* 24 (1972):167−87; Nakabachi Masakagu, "Suikoden no tai iminzoku ishiki ni tsuite," *Nippon Chūgoku gakkai-hō* 21 (1969):159−75.

26. A Japanese scholar also holds a similar opinion that there are no anti-alien feelings revealed in this novel. See Nakabachi Masakagu, "Suikoden no tai iminzoku ishiki ni tsuite," pp. 159−75.

27. *Shui-hu* (70-chapter), 2:496; *Shui-hu* (120-chapter), 1:688. The quoted passage is very similar in the above-mentioned two editions. For different punctuation, compare Cheng Chen-to, ed., *Shui-hu ch'üan-chuan* (reprint, Hong Kong, 1965), 2:679. For different English translations, see Buck, p. 745; Jackson, pp. 588–89; Shapiro, p. 673.

28. Cheng Chen-to, ed., *Shui-hu ch'üan-chuan*, 3:1012; also *Shui-hu* (120-chapter), 2:989.

29. Cheng Chen-to, ed., *Shui-hu ch'üan-chuan*, 3:1206–7; also *Shui-hu* (120-chapter), 2:1158–59.

30. Cheng Chen-to, ed., *Shui-hu ch'üan-chuan*, 3:1206; also *Shui-hu* (120-chapter), 2:1159. For the English translation, see C. T. Hsia, "The Water Margin," in *The Classic Chinese Novel*, p. 109.

31. *Shui-hu* (120-chapter), 2:1839–40; also C. T. Hsia, "The Water Margin," p. 114.

32. *Shui-hu* (120-chapter), 2:1839; also Cheng Chen-to, ed., *Shui-hu ch'üan-chuan*, 4:1811.

33. In his article "The Author of the *Shui-hu Chuan*," Ogawa Tamaki emphasizes that the idea of loyalty is given to Sung Chiang by the goddess Chiu-tien hsuan-nü. According to him, Sung Chiang was a rebel before he dreamed of the goddess. He cited Sung Chiang's poem boasting that he would out-do even the famous rebel Huang Ch'ao (d. 884) of the late T'ang times (from 875–884), as an example. But Sung Chiang was drunk when he wrote that poem. Later, when his friend asked him what he did write, Sung Chiang told him he did not remember. (See *Shui-hu* [70-chapter], 2:457). If Sung Chiang really meant what he wrote, he could not completely forget it. Besides, Sung Chiang signed his name to the poem. It seems unlikely that a rebel would openly declare his intention and invite his own arrest by the government troops.

34. For a different interpretation of Sung Chiang's motive, see C. T. Hsia, "The Water Margin" (p. 114), in which Professor Hsia suggests that it is out of his yearning for his dearest friend that Sung Chiang imposes a suicide pact upon Li K'uei. Here lies the difference between a literary critic and an intellectual historian. The literary approach stresses individual appreciation of the literary merit, while the historian generally must abide by the text.

35. For a detailed discussion on Chin Sheng-t'an's version of *Shui-hu*, see, among others, Sun K'ai-ti, "Pa Chin Sheng-t'an pen *Shui-hu chuan*," in *Ts'ang-chou chi*, 1:144–48; Chang Yu-luan, "Chin Sheng-t'an tsen-yang wu-mo Sung Chiang te," in *Shui-hu yen-chiu lun-wen chi* (Peking: Tso-chia ch'u-pan she, 1957), pp. 324–31; Sung Yun-pin, "T'an Chin Sheng-t'an," in *Shui-hu yen-chiu lun wen chi*, pp. 332–35; Ch'en Teng-yuan, *Chin Sheng-t'an chuan* (reprint, Hong Kong: T'ai-p'ing shu-chü, 1963); John Ching-yu Wang, *Chin Sheng-t'an* (New York: Twayne Publishers, 1972), pp. 53–81.

36. Both Pearl Buck's and J. H. Jackson's translations of the *Shui-hu* are based on the 70-chapter version. As to Sidney Shapiro's 100-chapter

translation, which is "based on a combination of the 70- and 100-chapter editions," the 70-chapter version is used "as the text of the first seventy chapters." With the final 30-chapter, "minor liberties" have been taken, according to Shapiro, to delete the poems that introduce each chapter as well as some of the redundancy and cumbersome detail. See Shapiro's "Translator's Note" in *Outlaws of the Marsh*.

37. For a brief, clear discussion of the 120-chapter *Shui-hu*, see Cheng Chen-to's preface to *Shui-hu ch'üan-chuan*, 1:1—7.

38. Mencius discusses benevolence and righteousness in the first chapter of the *Meng-tzu*, which together with *Lun-yü*, *Ta-hsueh*, and *Chung-yung* are included in the *Ssu-shu ta-ch'uan* (The Great Compendium of the Four Books), one of the official Confucian Classics published during the reign of the Yung-lo (1403—27). Students in every level at the state schools (the prefectural, subprefectural, and county levels) were required to study these texts. Even in the independent academies and other private schools these texts were an important subject of study.

39. *Pan-ku chih T'ang Yü chuan*, prefaced by Chung Hsing (microfilm copy, made in 1955, of the original Ming edition [Yü Chi-yueh ed.] in Naikaku Bunko, Japan), *chüan* 2, pp. 35a—42b; *Yu-Hsia chih-chuan*, prefaced by Chung Hsing (microfilm copy of the original Ming edition in Naikaku Bunko, Japan), *chüan* 1, pp. 58a—61b. For a historical version of the abdication stories of King Yao and King Shun, see *Shih-chi*, 1:21—48, 82—83. Parts of the stories can also be found in the *Book of History*, see *Shu-ching chi chuan*, pp. 3—5, 8, 12—14. For the dating of the legendary dynasties and sage-kings I have followed the traditional dates; for a different dating system, see Tung Tso-pin, *Chung-kuo nien-li tsung-p'u* (Hong Kong: University of Hong Kong Press, 1960), 1:255—58. In a recent study of the dynastic legend in early China, Sarah Allan has reached similar conclusions. The key theme of ancient Chinese dynastic legends, according to Allan, is the opposition between heredity and virtue—"the heir" versus "the sage." For details of her findings, see Sarah Allan, *The Heir and the Sage: Dynastic Legend in Early China* (San Francisco: Chinese Materials Center, 1981), pp. 141—46. For a brilliant discussion on the merit concept developed by various schools of thought in China, see Ping-ti Ho, *The Ladder of Success in Imperial China*, pp. 5—17.

40. For details of the story, see *P'an-ku*, *chüan* 2, pp. 35a—42b; also *Shih chi*, 1:21—48.

41. For details of the story, see *Yu Hsia*, *chüan* 1, pp. 58a—61b, also see *Shih-chi*, 1:82—83.

42. *Yu Hsia*, *chüan* 1, p. 61b.

43. Ibid., *chüan* 1, p. 61a.

44. Ibid., *chüan* 1, pp. 80a—81a.

45. *Han Fei-tzu*, annot. Wang Hsien-shen, *Han Fei-tzu chi-chieh* 4:52—63, esp. 53, 54. For English translation, see Burton Watson, trans., *Han Fei-tzu: Basic Writing* (New York: Columbia University Press, 1964), pp. 96—117, esp. 99.

46. *Yu-Hsia, chüan* 3, pp. 24a—36a.
47. Ibid., *chüan* 4, pp. 57b—76b.
48. *San-kuo yen-i,* 1:308—18; also Brewitt-Taylor, 1:386—402.
49. There are many references about Pai-li Hsi in classical and historical literature: for studies of Pai-li Hsi see, among others, Shang K'uei-chai, "Pai-li Hsi k'ao," in *Hsu, pai, wen-fa, ts'ung-k'ao, chuan-chi yen-chiu lun-wen chi* (Taipei: Ta-lu tsa-chih she, 1970), pp. 113—117; also Yü Cheng-hsieh (1775—1840), "Pai-li Hsi shih i tung-lun" in *K'uei-ssu lei-kao* (Taipei: Shih-chih shu-chü, 1960 reprint), pp. 397—400. In Official History, the story about Pai-li Hsi was recorded in the *Shih-Chi* (see 1:186). Earlier, in the *Tso-chuan,* a similar but much simpler story was recorded: However, here, the minister of Yü who was captured by the Chin was named Ching Po instead of Pai-li Hsi, as stated in the *Shih-chi.* Compare *Tso-chuan* (Taipei: Ch'i-ming shu-chü, 1952 ed.), p. 160. In a different section of *Shih-chi,* the "Ch'in Shih-chia," it says "Ching-po Pai-li Hsi" together; see *Shih-chi,* 5:1647.
50. For details of the story, see Yü Shao-yü, *Ch'un-ch'iu lieh-kuo chih-chuan* (microfilm copy made by Library of Congress of the original Ming Wan-li edition in the Rare Books Collection of National Peiping Library), *chüan* 4, pp. 18b—29a (hereafter abbreviated as *Lieh-kuo).* There is a brief statement at the beginning of the novel that the book is based on the historical text *Tso-chuan.*
51. *Lieh-kuo, chüan* 4, p. 21a.
52. Ibid., *chüan* 4, pp. 24a—25a.
53. Ibid., *chüan* 4, pp. 25a—26a.
54. Ibid., *chüan* 4, p. 23b.
55. Ssu-ma Ch'ien, *Shih-chi,* 1:186.
56. *Lieh-kuo, chüan* 4, p. 25a.
57. *Meng-tzu, Ssu-shu tu-pen* edition, 2:269—71.
58. For the details of the story, see *Shih-chi,* 7:2161—69; also Wu-men hsiao-k'o, *Sun P'ang tou-chih yen-i* (microfilm copy made in 1955 of the original 1636 edition in the Naikaku Bunko, Japan).
59. In the *Shih-chi,* Ssu-ma Ch'ien did not name Kuei Ku as Sun Pin's and Pang Chüan's teacher, but in different sections, "Su Ch'in lieh-chuan" and "Chang I lieh-chuan" (7:2241—2305), he named Kuei Ku as teacher of both Su Ch'in (fl. 349—326 B.C.) and Chang I (fl. 337—311 B.C.).

Chapter 5

1. *Meng-tzu, Ssu-shu tu-pen* edition, 1:88—89. English translation follows D. C. Lau, with minor revision; see Lau, *Mencius,* p. 82.
2. *Meng-tzu, Ssu-shu tu-pen* edition, 1:90. English translation follows D. C. Lau, with minor revision; see Lau, *Mencius,* pp. 82.
3. *Meng-tzu, Ssu-shu tu-pen* edition, 3:306—7. English translation follows D. C. Lau, see Lau, *Mencius,* p. 163.

4. *Ming-shih* (Taipei, 1962), 1:737, 808, 810; 2:934. For a discussion in English of far-reaching institutional changes of the Ming state, see Edward L. Farmer, *Early Ming Government: The Evolution of Dual Capitals* (Cambridge: East Asian Research Center, Harvard University, 1976), pp. 71−97. For a discussion in English on the growth of terror in the Ming government, see F. W. Mote, "The Growth of Chinese Despotism: A Critique of Wittfogel's Theory of Oriental Despotism as Applied to China," pp. 1−41, esp. 18−29.

5. For a detailed description of the eunuch-dominated secret service in the Ming government, see Ting I, *Ming-tai t'e-wu cheng-chih* (Peking: Chung-wai ch'u-pan she, 1950), pp. 1−44. For a discussion of the eunuch establishment and the degree of eunuch participation in the relations between sovereign and minister (either in the form of eunuch dictators ruling through delegated imperial authority, or of eunuch bureaucrats transmitting the imperial will and implementing imperial policies), see Edward L. Dreyer, *Early Ming China: A Political History 1355−1435* (Stanford, Calif.: Stanford University Press, 1982), pp. 244−48.

To learn the inside stories about the Ming eunuchs, a book entitled *Cho-chung chih* is most interesting since the author Liu Jo-yü was a eunuch who entered the palace service in 1601, at the age of seventeen. Liu's intimate knowledge of the imperial institutions in general, and of palace life in particular, sheds light on the various roles the eunuchs played in the imperial government. See Liu Jo-yü, *Cho-chung chih* (Shanghai: Shang-wu yin-shu kuan, 1935). For an English study on eunuch power in the Ming Dynasty, see Robert B. Crawford, "Eunuch Power in the Ming Dynasty," *T'ung Pao* 49:115−48.

6. *Shui-hu* (120-chapter), 1:14−23; also Pearl Buck, pp. 17−22; Sidney Shapiro, 1:15−24.

7. Jaroslav Průšek, contends that the author of *Shui-hu* "did not only want to describe the adventures of the band of robbers but he tried to show how a bad government made honest and brave people escape to the forest, in other words, describe how a popular uprising was created." See Jaroslav Průšek, *Chinese History and Literature* (Prague: Orient Institute, Academia, 1970), p. 32.

8. *Shui-hu* (120-chapter), 1:48−56; also Pearl Buck, pp. 53−60; Sidney Shapiro, 1:49−57.

9. *Shui-hu* (120-chapter), 1:316−34; also Pearl Buck, pp. 341−58; Sidney Shapiro, 1:318−33.

10. *Shui-hu* (120-chapter), 1:228−45.

11. *Shui-hu* (120-chapter), 1:610. For English translation, compare Pearl Buck's (p. 657) with Sidney Shapiro's (p. 597).

12. *Shui-hu* (120-chapter), 1:223; also Pearl Buck, p. 243; Sidney Shapiro, p. 229.

13. *Shui-hu* (120-chapter), 1:48−51. English translation follows, with minor changes, Pearl Buck, pp. 55−56; see also Sidney Shapiro, 1:49−51.

14. *Shui-hu* (120-chapter), 1:224. For English translation, compare Pearl Buck's (p. 243) with J. H. Jackson's (p. 179) and Sidney Shapiro's (p. 229).

15. Sa Meng-wu, *Shui-hu chuan yü chung-kuo she-hui*, pp. 154–55.

16. A Japanese scholar, Ogawa Tamaki, also has a theory about the existence of two sets of values in *Shui-hu*. According to Ogawa, the Liang-shan-p'o heroes represent "roughly two classes of society, one was concerned only with needs, the other with national needs. The one group lived for themselves, the other for their country. The one acted upon impulse, the other with restraint." See Ogawa Tamaki, "The Author of the *Shui-hu chuan*," pp. 312–30.

17. *Shui-hu* (120-chapter), 1:485–90; for an English translation of the actual massacre scene, see C. T. Hsia, "The Water Margin," in *The Classic Chinese Novel*, pp. 97–99.

18. For an account of Li K'uei's executing of Huang Wen-ping, see *Shui-hu* (120-chapter), 1:672; for an account of Yang Hsiung's lynching of his wife, see 1:767. See also Sidney Shapiro, 1:656, 747.

19. *Shui-hu* (120-chapter), 1:830–31; also Pearl Buck, pp. 899–900; Sidney Shapiro, 2:810.

20. In C. T. Hsia's study of the *Shui-hu*, he examines in depth these various aspects of violence in the novel. For his insight into these problems, see C. T. Hsia, *The Classic Chinese Novel*, pp. 97–104.

21. Feng Meng-lung, *Wang Yang-ming ch'u-shen chin-luan lu* (Taipei: Kwang-wen shu-chü, 1968), *chüan* 1, 16a–16b. For a historical account of Wang Shou-jen's career, see the official biography in *Ming-shih*, 17:5159–72; for an English account of Wang's political career, see Goodrich and Fang, eds., *Dictionary of Ming Biography*, pp. 1408–16.

22. Feng Meng-lung, *Wang Yang-ming*, *chüan* 2, pp. 24a–34a; *chüan* 3, pp. 1a–32a; *Ming-shih*, 17:5162–65. See also Cheng Chi-meng, *Wang Yang-ming chuan* (Taipei: Taipei shu-chü, 1957), pp. 57–106; Yu Chung-yao, *Yang-ming hsien-shen chuan chi* (Shanghai: Chung-hua shu-chü, 1923), *chüan* 3, pp. 1–14.

23. Feng Meng-lung, *Wang Yang-ming*, *chüan* 2, p. 27a; *chüan* 3, p. 30b; *Ming-shih*, 1:5169–70.

24. A recent study of Ming history gives a detailed description of some aspects of the daily life in the imperial palace and sheds light on the role the emperor played in Ming government. See Ray Huang, "The Wan-li Emperor" in *1587, A Year of No Significance* (New Haven, Conn.: Yale University Press, 1981), pp. 1–41.

25. Sun Kuo-liang, *Yü Ch'ien ch'üan chuan* (Hangchou: Che-chiang jen-min ch'u-pan she, 1981), pp. 95–112, 184–95. The novel *Yü Ch'ien ch'uan-chuan* (*Yü Ch'ien* hereafter) is a modern edition of the *Yü Shao-pao ts'ui chung ch'uan chuan* based on its Ming Wan-li edition; see "Ch'ien-yen" (Introduction) in *Yü Ch'ien*, pp. 1–4. For Yü Ch'ien's biography, see *Ming-shih*, 15:4543–51. Also see *Dictionary of Ming Biography*, pp. 1608–12.

26. The tendency or the certainty of corruption by authority discussed in this chapter is along the same vein as Lord Acton's maxim, "Power tends to corrupt and absolute power corrupts absolutely." See Acton's letter to Craighton dated April 5, 1887, in a collection entitled *Essays on Freedom and Power*, by Lord Acton (New York: Meridian Editions, 1955), p. 335. For a different approach that speaks of a specific "orient despotism" in terms of inevitable developments within the socioeconomic order, see Karl Wittfogel, *Oriental Despotism, A Comparative Study of Total Power*, pp. 101−8.

27. Mencius's comments about King Chou are a classical example of this theory. According to the book *Meng-tzu*, King Hsuan of Ch'i asked Mencius about King Chou's (the last king of the Shang dynasty) dethronement: "Is regicide permissible?" Mencius answered as follows:

    A man who mutilates benevolence is a mutilator, while one who cripples rightness is a crippler. He who is both a mutilator and a crippler is an "outcast." I have indeed heard of the punishment of the "outcast Chou," but I have not heard of any regicide.

    See *Meng-tzu*, *Ssu-shu tu-pen* edition, 1:52. For an English translation, see D. C. Lau, *Mencius*, p. 68.

28. *Ying-lieh chuan* (Shanghai: Shang-hai wen-hua ch'u-pan she, 1956), p. 49.

29. Ibid., p. 49.

30. Yen-shih shan-ch'iao, *Nan-Sung chih-chuan* in *Nan Pei Sung ch'üan-chuan* (6 vols. Chin-wen t'ang, 1866), vol. 6, *chüan* 10, pp. 28b−29a, esp. 29a; also in a different edition (8 vols. reprint. Shanghai: Chang-fu-chi shu-chü, 1913), vol. 8, *chüan* 4, pp. 15b−17a, esp. 17a.

31. *San-kuo yen-i*, 1:61−62; English translation follows Brewitt-Taylor with revision, 1:73.

32. *San-kuo yen-i*, 1:81−83; Brewitt-Taylor, 1:97−99.

33. *San-kuo yen-i*, 1:109−10; English translation follows Brewitt-Taylor, 1:131.

34. *Shih-chi*, 1:105.

35. Ibid., 1:108.

36. *Feng-shen yen-i* (Hong Kong: T'ai-p'ing shu-chü, 1970), 1:229−47, esp. 244.

37. *Feng-shen yen-i*, 1: chaps. 6−11, 17, 19. In *Feng-shen*, King Chou and Tan Chi dominated the first quarter of the novel; at least ten chapters deal with the cruelty and sadism exhibited by Tan Chi and King Chou in their harsh punishment of royal families and upright officials.

38. *Yu-Hsia chih-chuan*, *chüan* 4; also Feng Meng-lung, *Tung-Chou lieh-kuo chih*, pp. 1−13.

39. *Shui-hu* (120-chapter), 1:365−438.

40. There is a new theory suggesting that unfairness toward women in the *Shui-hu* does not represent a universal attitude, but reflects the mentality of a few desperate men who played a significant part in the creation and transmission of the *Shui-hu* stories before they were finally organized into a novel. See Phillip S. Y. Sun, "The Seditious Art of the *Water Margin*," *Chinese Scholars* 5 (July 1973): 75−101.

41. Ch'i-tung yeh-jen, *Sui Yang-ti yen-shih* (reprint, Taipei: T'ien-i ch'u-pan she, 1974), 1:2; reprint based on the Wan-li edition.
42. For a brilliant discussion on the stereotype of the bad last-rulers, see Arthur F. Wright, "Sui Yang-ti: Personality and Stereotype," in *The Confucian Persuasion*, ed. by Arthur Wright (Stanford, Calif.: Stanford University Press, 1960), pp. 47–76, esp. 61–76.
43. *Sui Yang-ti yen-shih*, 2:191–93, 197.
44. Hsi-wu lan-tao-jen, *Chiao Ch'uang t'ung-su hsiao-shuo* (microfilm copy made in 1955 of the original in Naikaku Bunko, Japan; hereafter referred to as *Chiao Ch'uang*), chap. 1, pp. 3b–4a.
45. *Chiao Ch'uang*, chap. 1, p. 5a.
46. For a fictional account of Li Yen, see *Chiao Ch'uang*, chap. 1, pp. 10a–11a. For a historical study of Li Yen and his role in Li Tzu-ch'eng's rebellion, see James B. Parsons, *The Peasant Rebellions of the Late Ming Dynasty* (Tucson: University of Arizona Press, 1970), pp. 90–93, 134, 136, 137, 163.
47. For a detailed discussion of the rebellion of Li Tzu-ch'eng, see James B. Parsons, *The Peasant Rebellions of the Late Ming Dynasty*, pp. 113–42, esp. 132–42. For source materials, see Cheng T'ien-t'ing et al., eds., *Ming-mo nung-min ch'i-i shih-liao* (Peking: Chung-hua shu-chü, 1954), pp. 421–56.
48. *Chiao-Ch'uang*, chap. 2, p. 8b.
49. Ibid., "Preface," pp. 1a–6b, esp. 1a.
50. Ibid., chap. 7, p. 3b.
51. In the Ming-Ch'ing transition period, the corrupting influence of the imperial favorites, especially the eunuchs, was regarded as one of the chief factors involved in the Ming downfall. In fiction and drama, the evils of the imperial favorites became a popular theme: Hung Sheng uses it in his most celebrated *Ch'ang-sheng tien* (The Palace of the Eternal Youth); and Li Yü elaborates on it in two of his plays, *Huang ch'iu feng* (The Female Phoenix Seeks the Male Phoenix) and *Yü sao-t'ou* (The Jade Pin), and also one of his short stories, "Tsui-ya lou" (The Tower That Collects All the Refinements), to name only a few examples.
52. Shelley Hsueh-lun Chang, "Li Yü hsi-chü hsiao-shuo chung so fan-ying te ssu-hsiang," p. 13.
53. *Meng-tzu, Ssu-shu tu-pen* edition, 1:20; D. C. Lau, *Mencius*, p. 54.

Chapter 6

1. For the history and development of the traditional religions, see, among others, J. J. M. de Groot, *The Religion of the Chinese* (New York: Macmillan, 1910), pp. 3–88; J. J. M. de Groot, *Sectarianism and Religious Persecution in China* (reprint, Taipei: Literature House, 1963), pp. 16–95; Laurence G. Thompson, *Chinese Religion: An Introduction* (Belmont,

Calif.: Dickenson Publishing Co., 1969), pp. 78—99; C. K. Yang, *Religion in Chinese Society* (Berkeley: University of California Press, 1967), pp. 104—24, 180—217; D. Howard Smith, *Chinese Religion* (New York: Holt, Rinehart and Winston, 1968), pp. 94—147; Kenneth Ch'en, *Buddhism in China: A Historical Survey* (Princeton: Princeton University Press, 1964), pp. 21—53; Arthur F. Wright, *Buddhism in Chinese History* (New York: Atheneum, 1965), pp. 42—85; Holmes Welch, *Taoism: The Parting of the Way* (Boston: Beacon Press, 1957), pp. 88—163; Fu Ch'in-chia, *Chung-kuo tao-chiao shih* (reprint, Taipei: Shang-wu yin-shu kuan, 1966), pp. 154—73.

2. For the Han theory of Yin-yang and the Five Elements, see, among others, Yang Hsiang-k'uei, *Chung-kuo ku-tai she-hui yü ku-tai ssu-hsiang yen-chiu* (Shanghai: Jen-min ch'u-pan she, 1962), 1:241—97; Li Han-san, *Hsien-Ch'in Liang-Han chih Yin-Yang Wu-Hsing hsueh-shuo* (Taipei: Wei-hsin shu-chü, 1968), pp. 103—90; Sun Kuang-te, *Hsien-Ch'in Liang-Han Yin-Yang Wu-hsing shuo ti cheng-chih ssu-hsiang* (Taipei: Chia-hsin shui-ni kung-ssu wen-hua chi-chin hui, 1969), pp. 1—54; Feng Yu-lan, *A History of Chinese Philosophy*, trans. Derk Bodde (Princeton: Princeton University Press, 1953), 2:7—10; C. K. Yang, *Religion in Chinese Society*, pp. 135—36.

3. Feng Yu-lan, *A History of Chinese Philosophy*, p. 57. For detailed discussion of Tung Chung-shu and his thought, see, among others, Chou Fu-ch'eng, *Lun Tung Chung-shu ssu-hsiang* (Shanghai: Jen-min ch'u-pan she, 1961), pp. 27—37; *Han-shu*, 8:2495—2528; Sun Kuang-te, *Hsien-Ch'in Liang-Han Yin-Yang Wu-Hsing shuo ti cheng-chih ssu-hsiang*, pp. 173—220; Wm. Theodore de Bary, et al., eds., *Sources of Chinese Tradition* (New York: Columbia University Press, 1960), pp. 171—72; Feng Yu-lan, *A History of Chinese Philosophy*, pp. 16—87; C. K. Yang, *Religion in Chinese Society*, pp. 139—43.

4. For selections from Tung Chung-shu, see *Chung-kuo che-hsueh shih chiao-hsueh tzu-liao hui-pien* [*Liang Han pu-fen*] (Peking: Chung-hua shu-chü, 1963), 1:127—74, esp. 134. English translation follows de Bary, with minor revision; see Wm. Theodore de Bary, *Sources of Chinese Tradition*, 1:171.

5. In the morality book *Tzu-chih lu* (The Record of Self-knowledge) written by Chu-hung (1535—1615), the leading Buddhist of the lay movement, the strong Confucian overtones are present. In the Category of Good Deeds of the book, for example, the first heading is "Loyal and Filial Deeds" while in the Category of Bad Deeds, "Disloyal and Unfilial Deeds" are also first singled out as bad deeds. For an English translation of the *Tzu-chih lu*, see Yü Chün-fang, *The Renewal of Buddhism in China: Chu-hung and the Late Ming Synthesis* (New York: Columbia University Press, 1981), pp. 233—59. For discussion of the *Tzu-chih lu*, see chapter 5 of Yü Chün-fang op. cit. For discussion of the lay Buddhism in the Late Ming, see Kristin Yü Greenblatt, "Chu-hung and Lay Buddhism in the Late Ming," in *The Unfolding of Neo-Confucianism*, ed. Wm. Theodore de Bary et al. (New York: Columbia University Press, 1975), pp. 93—140.

For discussion of the syncretism of Neo-Confucianism, Buddhism, and Taoism, see, among others, Judith A. Berling, *The Syncretic Religion of Lin Chao-en* (New York: Columbia University Press, 1980), pp. 1–13. Edward Ch'ien, "Chiao Hung and the Revolt against Ch'eng-Chu Orthodoxy," in *The Unfolding of Neo-Confucianism*, pp. 271–303; Araki Kengo, "Confucianism and Buddhism in the Late Ming," in *The Unfolding of Neo-Confucianism*, pp. 39–66.

6. Liu Ts'un-yan, "Taoist Self-Cultivation," in *Self and Society in Ming Thought*, ed. Wm. Theodore de Bary et al., pp. 291–330. Also Liu Ts'un-yan, "Taoism and Neo-Confucianists in Ming Time," *New Asia Journal* 8, no. 1 (February 1976): 259–96.

7. For the *Verifiable Records of the Ming*, I use the 1966 reprint published by the Academia Sinica at Taipei, Taiwan; See *Ming Shih lu* (Taipei: Chung-yang yen-chiu-yuan, 1966).

8. *Ming-shih*, 2:340; Fang Hsuan-ling et al, eds., *Chin-shu* (Peking: Chung-hua, 1974), 2:278–88, esp. 281. For discussion in English of the astronomical chapters in the Standard History, see Ho Peng Yoke, *The Astronomical Chapters of the Chin Shu* (Paris and the Hague: Morton and Co., 1966), pp. 13–41.

9. For understanding the historical development of the astronomical and cosmological thought, compare the chapters on astronomy and on Five-Phase cosmology in the *Ming-shih* with their counterparts in previous Standard Histories. See *Ming-shih*, 2:339–423, 425–512; Sung Lien et al., *Yuan-shih* (Taipei: Kuo-fang yen-chiu yuan, 1966), 1:386–408, 409–32; *Sung-shih*, 4:946–1316, 1317–1490; Hsueh Chü-cheng, *Chiu Wu-tai-shih* (reprint, Taipei: I-wen yin-shu kuan, 1955), 29:919–23, 932–36; Ou-Yang Hsiu, *Wu-tai shih-chi* (reprint, Taipei: I-wen yin-shu kuan, 1955), 28:813–42; Liu Hsu, *Chiu T'ang-shu* (reprint, Taipei: I-wen yin-shu kuan, 1955), 1:380–410, 411–12; *Chiu-shu*, 2:277–403; *Han-shu*, 5:1315–1522; *Shih-chi*, 4:1289–1353.

10. *Han-shu*, 4:1189–1222.

11. Historically, it was during the epoch of the Southern and Northern Dynasties (420–589) that people began to compare Buddhism and Taoism with Confucianism and created for them a new term, the *san-chiao* or Three Schools of Teaching. For example, according to Li Shih-ch'ien, of the early Sui dynasty (589–618), Buddhism can be compared to the Sun; Taoism, to the moon; and Confucianism, to the Five Planets. See Li Yen-shou's *Pei-shih* (reprint, Taipei: I-wen yin-shu kuan, 1955), p. 546. From then on scholars debated on the merits of these three doctrines. Records show that sometimes even the emperors took interest in these debates and had them held in the imperial court. See Ling-hu Te-fen's *Chou-shu* (reprint, Taipei: I-wen yin-shu kuan, 1955), pp. 39, 42, 224, 335. Influenced by the imperial government and its officials, the concept of Three Religions spread. The effect upon the populace was enormous. People actually began to worship them together, sometimes even in the same temple. In 1115, for example, the Taoist monk Tung Nan-yun

requested that the images of the three founders of Buddhism, Taoism, and Confucianism, which were sculptured together in a monastery named T'ien-ning (Heavenly Peace) at T'ai-chou (in modern Lin-hai-hsien, Chekiang), be destroyed. See Li Chih, *Huang-Sung shih-ch'ao kang-yao* (reprint, Taipei: Wen-hai ch'u-pan she, 1967), p. 404.

12. Chu Yuan-chang, "San-Chiao lun" (On the Three Teachings) in [*Ming T'ai-tsu*] *Yü-chih wen-chi* (reprint, Taipei: Hsueh-sheng shu-chü, 1965), *chüan* 11, pp. 8a—9b. Wu Han, *Chu Yuan-chang chuan* (Hong Kong: Chuan-chi wen-hsueh, 1976), pp. 218—25. Chu Yuan-chang's syncretic thought is also discussed in John D. Langlois, Jr., and Sun K'o-k'uan, "Three Teachings Syncretism and the Thought of Ming T'ai-tsu" *HJAS* 43, no. 1 (June 1983): 97—139.

13. Li Chih, *Fen-shu, Hsu fen-shu* (Peking: Chung-hua shu-chü, 1975), *Hsu fen-shu*, *chüan* 2, pp. 66—67. Ming Tai-tsu's view on the *Heart Sutra* is found in his "Hsin-ching hsü" (preface to the *Heart Sutra*); see Chu Yuan-chang, [*Kao Huang-ti*] *Yü-chih wen-chi* (photocopy of the original in Kyoto University, Kyoto, Japan), *chüan* 15, pp. 11a—12b. For Li Chih's own exposition of the Three Teachings, see *Hsü fen-shu*, *chüan* 2, pp. 75—76; for his exposition of the *Heart Sutra*, see *Fen-shu*, *chüan* 3, pp. 100—101. Yang Ch'i-yuan's precedent for using Buddhist ideas in the examination papers was pointed out by Ku Yen-wu; see Ku Yen-wu, *Jih-chih lu* (*Kuo-hsueh chi-pen ts'ung-shu* edition, Taipei: Shang-wu yin-shu kuan), 3:111—12.

14. Ku Yen-wu, *Jih-chih lu*, 3:113—14.

15. For Lin Chao-en's life and thought, see Liu Ts'un-yan, "Lin Chao-en, the Master of the Three Teachings," in *Selected Papers From the Hall of Harmonious Wind* (Leiden: E. J. Brill, 1976), pp. 149—74; Judith A. Berling, *The Syncretic Religions of Lin Chao-en*, pp. 62—89, 195—219, 235—38.

16. *Feng-shen yen-i*, 1:40—41. The novel is usually attributed to Hsu Chung-lin (d. ca. 1566). Supported only by a single, indirect bibliographical piece of evidence, the attribution has been rejected by Liu Ts'un-yan in favor of the Taoist priest Lu Hsi-hsing (1520—1601?). See Liu Ts'un-yan, *Buddhist and Taoist Influence on Chinese Novels*, vol. 1, *The Authorship of the Feng-sheng yen-i* (Wiesbaden: Kommissionsverlag Otto Harrassowitz, 1962).

17. Ibid., p. 138.

18. Ibid., p. 442, 447.

19. *Feng-shen yen-i*, 2:702, 755, 757. In these two chapters there are three occasions in which each of the three Taoist patriarchs (Yuan-shih, T'ung-t'ien, and Lao Tzu) reminisced about a conference among themselves some time ago, preparing for the forthcoming investiture of the gods. There the term *san-chiao* seems to refer to the three patriarchs themselves rather than three religions.

20. *Feng-shen yen-i*, 2:764, 822, 832.

21. Liu Ts'un-yan, *Buddhist and Taoist Influences on Chinese Novels*, 1:187−95. The orthodox conception that Confucianism, Buddhism, and Taoism were the Three Teachings under Heaven was so ingrained in people's minds that some fiction writers actually portray Confucius as a kind of religious patriarch. For example, in the introductory chapter of the novel *Hsi-yang t'ung-su yen-i* (The Western Voyages of the Grand Eunuch Cheng Ho), the novelist refers to Confucius, Buddha, and Lord Lao as patriarchs of the Three Teachings — Confucianism, Buddhism, and Taoism respectively. See Lo Mou-teng, [*San-pao t'ai-chien*] *Hsi-yang t'ung-su yen-i* (Shanghai: Kuang-i shu-chü, n.d.) pp. 1−3. The same approach toward the Three Teachings can be found in many short stories. For example, in the story "Chang Tao-ling ch'i-shih Chao Sheng" (Seven Times Chang Tao-ling Tested Chao Sheng), it is said that at the beginning of the world when the firmament was divided, there were Three Teachings: the T'ai-shang Lao-chun created Taoism, Sakyamuni created Buddhism, and Confucius created Confucianism. See Feng Meng-lung's *Yü-shih ming-yen* (Hong Kong: Chung-hua shu-chü, 1965), pp. 187−210, esp. 187. Again, in the same collection, in the prelude of the story "T'eng Ta-yin kuei-tuan chia-ssu" (Magistrate T'eng Settled a Property Dispute), the storyteller enumerates the canonical text of Confucianism, Buddhism, and Taoism. See *Yü-shih ming-yen*, pp. 145−164, esp. 145.

22. *Feng-shen yen-i*, 1:138. In the beginning of chapter 15, the novelist gives a brief introduction to the background of his story. In his description of the cosmic order, he mentions the existence of the Hao-tien shang-ti. But that is all he wants to say about this Sovereign on High in the Vast Heaven. He never mentions him again.

23. Following a long established tradition of capitalizing on magic warfare as a regular feature of historical tales, *Feng-shen* demonstrated the increasing prominence of magic cult in its grand scale of magic warfare. For an illuminating discussion on the element of magic warfare in historical novels, see C. T. Hsia, "The Military Romance," pp. 346−358.

24. Liu Ts'un-yan, *Buddhist and Taoist Influences on Chinese Novels*, 1:212, 240−42.

25. *Shui-hu* (70-chapter), 1:2. English translation follows, with revision, Pearl Buck, p. 2; also compare J. H. Jackson's translation, p. ii.

26. *Shui-hu* (70-chapter), 1:2. English translation follows, with revision, Pearl Buck, p. 3; also compare J. H. Jackson, p. ii.

27. *Shui-hu* (120-chapter), p. 14. English translation follows Sidney Shapiro, 1:13.

28. *Shui-hu* (100-chapter), 3:1227. English translation follows, with minor revision, Sidney Shapiro, 2:1421.

29. There are at least three novels that tell the legendary story about the Shang-Chou dynastic war. Besides *Feng-shen yen-i*, there are *Wu-wang fa-Chou p'ing hua* and *Lieh-kuo chih-chuan*. For the relation among these three novels, see Liu Ts'un-yan, "Yuan Chih-chih-pen *ch'üan hsiang*

Wu-wang fa-Chou p'ing-hua, Ming ken-pen *Lieh-kuo chih-chuan* chüan i yü *Feng-shen yen-i* chih kuan-hsi," *Hsin-ya hsueh-pao* 4, no. 1 (August 1959): 401—42.

30. Lo Fen, ed., *Yang-chia-chiang yen-i*, pp. 90—92, esp. 92. This novel is a revised edition of the original 1618 edition of *Pei-Sung chih-chuan* composed by Hsiung Ta-mu. For detailed information about the various editions of the novel, see Lo Fen's "Preface" in *Yang-chia-chiang yen-i*, pp. 1—4.

31. For Yang Yeh's official biography, see T'o T'o's *Sung-shih* (reprint, Taipei: I-wen yin-shu kuan, 1955), *chüan* 272, pp. 1a—19a. For a modern study of Yang Yeh and his family's legend, see, among others, Cheng Ch'ien, "Yang-chia-chiang ku-shih k'ao-shih cheng-su," in *Ching-wu ts'ung-pien* (Taipei: Chung-hua shu-chü, 1972), 2:1—84; Lo Fen's "Preface" to *Yang-chia-chiang yen-i*, pp. 1—4; Liu Chao-yu's "Hsu-lu" (Preface) to *Yang-chia-fu shih-tai chung-yung t'ung-su yen-i chih-chuan* (Taipei: Chung-yang t'u-shu-kuan, 1970), pp. 1—6.

32. *San-kuo yen-i*, 2:860, 861. English translation follows Brewitt-Taylor, 2:459—60.

33. *San-kuo yen-i*, 2:861. English translation follows, with revision, Brewitt-Taylor, 2:460.

34. *San-kuo yen-i*, 2:873. For English translation, see Brewitt-Taylor, 2:475.

35. For details of the story, see *Shui-hu* (70-chapter), 1:8; also Pearl Buck, p. 14; J. H. Jackson, pp. ix—x.

36. *Shui-hu* (70-chapter), 2:496—97, esp. 496. English translation follows, with minor changes, Pearl Buck, p. 745.

37. Lo Fen, ed., *Yang-chia-chiang yen-i*, pp. 172—74.

38. Professor C. T. Hsia regards Mu Kuei-ying as "an archetyped figure of consequence to subsequent military romances." See C. T. Hsia, "The Military Romance: A Genre of Chinese Fiction" in *Studies in Chinese Literary Genres*, pp. 371—78. The subsequent Ch'ing historical novels that contain the romantic element of lady-warriors and their love stories are, among others, *Shuo-T'ang, Lo T'ung sao-pei, Hsueh Jen-kuei cheng-tung, Hsueh T'ing-shan cheng-hsi*, and *Wu-hu p'ing-hsi*, to name the most popular ones.

39. *Shui-hu* (70-chapter), 2:598.

40. *Shui-hu* (70-chapter), 2:599. English translation follows Pearl Buck, p. 907.

41. *Shuo T'ang* (reprint, Hong Kong: Kwang-chih shu-chü, n.d.), pp. 268—74. This Hong Kong reprint is based on the 1961 edition of the novel edited by Ch'en Ju-heng (Shanghai: Chung-hua shu-chü, 1961). The "Editorial Explanation" (Chiao-ting shuo-ming) is a summary of Ch'en Ju-heng's original "Preface," only the name Ch'en Ju-heng is withheld.

42. Hsiung Ta-mu, *Ta-Sung chung-hsing yueh-wang chuan*, *chüan* 8, pp. 32a—47a.

43. Ibid., *chüan* 8, p. 37b.

44. *San-kuo-chih p'ing-hua*, pp. 1—6.

45. Feng Meng-lung, *Yü-shih ming-yen*, pp. 459—74.

46. *Feng-shen yen-i*, 2:755. English translation follows Liu Ts'un-yan, with minor revision; see Liu Ts'un-yan, *Buddhist and Taoist Influences on Chinese Novels*, 1:187.
47. *Feng-shen yen-i* 2:990. English translation follows Liu Ts'un-yan, pp. 154–55.
48. For a study of the Chinese cosmological thought, see John B. Henderson, *The Development and Decline of Chinese Cosmology* (New York: Columbia University Press, 1984), pp. 137–73. On the Ming attitude toward cosmological metaphysical speculation, see Wing-tsit Chan, "The Ch'eng-Chu School of Early Ming," in *Self and Society in Ming Thought*, pp. 29–52, esp. 33.

Chapter 7

1. For a different approach to the Ming novel, from the standpoint of literary criticism, see Andrew H. Plaks, *The Four Masterworks of the Ming Novel* (Princeton, N.J.: Princeton University Press, 1987), which was published after the completion of my research. For his discussions of the *Shui-hu* and the *San-kuo*, see chapters 3 and 4 of the book.
2. For a brilliant discussion on the rise of individualism and humanitarianism during the sixteenth and seventeenth centuries, see Wm. Theodore de Bary, et al., ed. *Self and Society in Ming Thought*, pp. 1–28, 145–247.
3. For studies of the novel *Chin P'ing Mei* in English language, see C. T. Hsia, "Chin P'ing Mei," in *The Classic Chinese Novel*, pp. 165–202; P. D. Hanan, "A Landmark of the Chinese Novel," in *The Far East: China and Japan*, ed D. Grant (Toronto: University of Toronto Press, 1961), pp. 325–35.
4. Both Li Chih and Ho Hsin-yin attached the greatest importance to relationships of friendship; see Li Chih, *Ch'u-t'an chi* (Peking: Chung-hua shu-chü, 1974), 2:311–33; Li Chih, *Fen-shu, Hsu Fen-shu*, pp. 88–90, 221–22; Ho Hsin-yin, *Ho Hsin-yin chi*, ed. Jung Chao-tsu (Peking: Chung-hua shu-chü, 1981), pp. 10–12, 28–29, 65–66.

   Ho Hsin-yin, who was always looking for the broader world so he could extend his love and respect equally to all men, believed that the narrow limits of self-family could best be overcome through the relationship among friends. For discussion of Ho Hsin-yin's thought in this regard, see Ronald G. Dimberg, *The Sage and Society: The Life and Thought of Ho Hsin-yin* (Honolulu: University Press of Hawaii, 1974), pp. 60–118.
5. Nicholas Berdyaev, *Slavery and Freedom*, trans. R. M. French (London: Geoffrey Bles, 1943), pp. 257–61; David Bonner Richardson, *Berdyaev's Philosophy of History* (The Hague: Martinus Nijhoff, 1968), pp. 39–40; Fuad Nucho, *Berdyaev's Philosophy: The Existential Paradox of Freedom and Necessity* (Garden City, N.Y.: Doubleday and Co., 1966), pp. 66–67.
6. For an interesting discussion of the national cult of Kuan Yü, see C. K. Yang, *Religion in Chinese Society*, pp. 159–61; for a discussion of Kuan

Yü as a composite hero in popular fiction, see Robert Ruhlmann, "Traditional Heroes in Chinese Popular Fiction," in *Confucianism and Chinese Civilization*, pp. 122—57, esp. 154—56. For a detailed account of the myths and legends about Kuan Yü and the evolution of the official worship of him, see E. T. C. Werner, *Myths and Legends of China* (reprint, London: George G. Harrap and Co., 1958), pp. 117—18.

7. *San-kuo yen-i*, 2:631—33.
8. *San-kuo yen-i*, 2:633; English translation follows C. H. Brewitt-Taylor, with minor revision; see C. H. Brewitt-Taylor, 2:182.
9. *San-kuo yen-i*, 2:632; English translation follows C. H. Brewitt-Taylor, with minor revision; see 2:180.
10. *Shui-hu* (120-chapter), 2:1842.
11. C. K. Yang, *Religion in Chinese Society*, pp. 158—165, esp. 159. For a handy dictionary of the heroes who were deified and became an essential part of Chinese popular religion and belief, see E. T. C. Werner, *A Dictionary of Chinese Mythology* (Shanghai, 1932).
12. For an excellent exposition of this issue in contemporary China, see Donald J. Munro, *The Concept of Man in Contemporary China* (Ann Arbor: University of Michigan Press, 1977), chap. 6.
13. *I Ching, Chou-i pen-i* (reprint, Taipei: Ch'i-ming shu-chü, 1952), *chüan* 1, p. 21. For a different English translation, compare James Legge, *The I Ching*, p. 230.
14. In the *Lun-yü* we have the famous quotation "the Master never talked of prodigies, feats of strength, disorder or spirits" as an example of Confucius's evasive attitude toward religion. As to Confucius's agnostic attitude, we have what the Master said, "Till you know about the living, how are you to know about the dead?" See *The Analects of Confucius*, trans. Arthur Waley, pp. 127, 155; also Yang Po-chün, *Lun-yü i-chu*, pp. 77, 120.
15. Note that in translating the Chinese character *shen*, the word "gods" is used here in its general and later context to replace "spirits" in its original classical context.
16. One example of such opinion was held by Hu Shih (1891—1962), leading member of the Peking University galaxy of intellectuals, who once made a statement that "China is a country without religion and the Chinese are a people who are not bound by religious superstitions" in an article entitled "Ming chiao," the religion of *Ming* (Names, etc.). See "Ming chiao" in *Hu Shih wen-ts'un*, 3:40—52, esp. 40.
17. For a modern illuminating analysis of the classic argument of the hero in history, see Sidney Hook, *The Hero in History* (Boston: Beacon Press, 1955). The most famous classic on the subject is, of course, Thomas Carlyle's *On Heroes, Hero-worship, and the Heroic in History* (London: Everyman's Library, 1940).

Glossary

an-chien yen-i (an-chien) 按鑑演義

chan-cheng chao-ch'in 戰陣招親
Chan-kuo ts'e 戰國策
ch'an-jang 禪讓
Chang Chung 張忠
Chang Fei 張飛
chang-i shu-ts'ai 仗義疏財
Chang Liang 張良
Chang T'ing-yü 張廷玉
Chang Yung 張永
Ch'ang-chou 長洲
Ch'ang-she Chen 長蛇陣
chao-hsien na-shih 招賢納士
Chao K'uang-yin (Sung T'ai-tsu)
　趙匡胤（宋太祖）
Chao Yun 趙雲
Ch'ao Kai 晁蓋
chen-jen 眞人
chen-sheng 眞聲
Ch'en Kung 陳恭
Ch'en She 陳涉
Ch'en Shou 陳壽
Cheng En 鄭恩
cheng-shih 正史
cheng-t'ung 正統
Ch'eng Yao-chin 程咬金
chi 紀
Chi-shih yü 及時雨
Chi Yuan-heng 冀元亨
Ch'i (King) 啟
ch'i-chü chu 起居注
chia t'ien-hsia 家天下

chiang-hsueh 講學
Chiang Shang 姜尚
chiang-shih 講史
chiang-shih hsiao-shuo 講史小說
Chiang Wei 姜維
chiao-chu 敎主
Chiao Ch'uang t'ung-su hsiao-shuo
　(*Chiao Ch'uang*) 勦闖通俗小說
chiao-t'u ssu, tsou-kou p'eng 狡兔死
　走狗烹
Chieh (King) 桀
Chieh-chiao 截敎
Chieh-ni 桀溺
Chien-yang 建陽
ch'ien-kuo 僭國
chih 志
chih 質
chih-chi 知己
chih-chuan 志傳
chih-kuai 志怪
chih-yin 知音
ch'ih 尺
Ch'ih-sung-tzu 赤松子
Chin (State of) 金
Chin-chi 晉紀
Chin-i-wei 錦衣衞
Chin P'ing Mei 金瓶梅
Chin Sheng-t'an 金聖嘆
chin-shih 進士
Chin-shu 晉書
Ch'in (State of) 秦
Ch'in Ch'iung 秦瓊
Ch'in Kuei 秦檜

243

Ching-chou 荊州

ching-chung pao-kuo 精忠報國

ch'ing-shih liu-ming 青史留名

Chiu-shih pien 舊事編

Chiu T'ang-shu 舊唐書

Chiu-t'ien Hsuan-nü 九天玄女

Chiu Wu-tai shih 舊五代史

ch'iu-hsien jo-k'o 求賢若渴

cho-hsing 卓行

Chou (King) 紂

Chou Ch'un-ch'iu 周春秋

Chou San-wei 周三畏

chu 主

Chu Ch'en-hao (Ning Wang)
  朱宸濠(寧王)

Chu Hsi 朱熹

Chu-hsien chen 朱仙鎮

Chu-ko Chün 諸葛均

Chu-ko Liang (K'ung-ming)
  諸葛亮(孔明)

Chu Kuei 朱貴

Chu Yuan-chang (Ming T'ai-tsu)
  朱元璋(明太祖)

Chü-i T'ing 聚義廳

chü-kung chin-ts'ui ssu erh hou i
  鞠躬盡瘁死而後已

Ch'u (State of) 楚

Ch'u-shih piao 出師表

chuan 傳

chüan 卷

ch'uan-ch'i 傳奇

Chuang Chou 莊周

Chuang-tzu 莊子

Ch'üan-Han chih-chuan (Ch'üan-Han) 全漢志傳

chui-chi 綴集

chün 君

Ch'un-ch'iu 春秋

ch'ün-hsiung ch'i-i 羣雄起義

chung 忠

Chung Hsing 鍾惺

Chung-i Shui-hu chuan 忠義水滸傳

Chung-i T'ang 忠義堂

chung-jen 眾人

Chung-k'ang (King) 仲康

chung-shu sheng 中書省

Ch'ung-chen (Emperor) 崇禎

Fan-ch'eng 樊城

Fang Hsuan-ling 房玄齡

Feng Meng-lung 馮夢龍

Feng-shen yen-i (Feng-shen)
  封神演義

Feng Sheng 馮勝

fu-mu kuan 父母官

Han Chen 韓貞

Han Fei 韓非

Han Fei Tzu 韓非子

Han Hsin 韓信

Han-shu 漢書

hao-han 好漢

Hao-t'ien Shang-ti 昊天上帝

Ho Hsin-yin 何心隱

Hou-Han shu 後漢書

Hou I 后羿

Hsi-ching tsa-chi 西京雜記

Hsi-Han yen-i (Hsi-Han) 西漢演義

Hsi-tsung (Emperor) 熹宗

Hsi-tsung (Emperor) 僖宗

Hsi-yu chi 西游記

Hsiang Yü 項羽

hsiao 孝

Hsiao-p'in chi 效顰集

hsiao-shuo 小說

hsiao-tao 小道

hsiao-yu 孝友

Hsien-chu chuan 先主傳

Hsien-ti (Emperor) 獻帝

Hsien-yang 咸陽

Hsin-ching 心經

Hsin lieh-kuo chih (Hsin lieh-kuo)
  新列國志

hsing-ling 性靈
Hsiu-jan-tzu (Chang Shang-te)
　修髯子(張尙德)
hsiu-te ch'in-cheng 修德勤政
Hsiung-nu 匈奴
Hsiung Ta-mu 熊大木
hsu 序
Hsu-chou 徐州
Hsu Shih-chi 徐世勣
Hsu Shu 徐庶
Hsu Ta 徐達
Hsu T'ai 許泰
Hsu tung-ch'uang shih-fan 續東窗事犯
Hsuan (King) 宣
Hsuan-ho i-shih 宣和遺事
Hsun Hsi 荀息
Hu San-niang 扈三娘
Hua-Hsia 華夏
Hua Jung 花榮
hua-pen 話本
Huang Ch'ao 黃巢
Huang-Ming k'ai-yun ying-lieh chuan
　(*Ying-lieh chuan*) 皇明開運英烈傳
Huang-shih-kung 黃石公
Huang Tsung-hsi 黃宗羲
Hui-chou 徽州
Hui-tsung (Emperor) 徽宗
hun-chün 昏君
Hun-t'ien 渾天
Hung 洪

I 夷
i 義
i 異
i-sh ì 藝術
I-tai chao 衣帶詔
I Yin 伊尹

jen 仁
Jen An 任安
Jen-huang shih 人皇氏
jen-tao 人道

Jen-tsung (Emperor) 仁宗
ju-lin 儒林

K'ai-p'i yen-i t'ung-su chih-chuan
　(*K'ai-p'i*) 開闢演義通俗志傳
Kan Pao 干寶
Kao Ch'iu 高俅
ko 戈
Ko Hung 葛洪
Ku-su chih 姑蘇志
Ku Yen-wu 顧炎武
Kuai (State of) 虢
Kuan Yü 關羽
Kuei-ku-tzu 鬼谷子
Kuo Tzu-hsing 郭子興
Kuo-yü 國語
Kung-sun Chih 公孫枝
Kung-sun Sheng 公孫勝

Lao Tzu 老子
li 禮
Li-chi 禮記
Li Chih 李贄
Li Chung 李忠
Li K'e-yung 李克用
Li K'uei 李逵
Li Ling 李陵
Li Mi 李密
li-ming 立名
Li Shan-ch'ang 李善長
Li Shih-min (T'ang T'ai-tsung)
　李世民(唐太宗)
li-shih yen-i 歷史演義
Li Ts'un-hsiao 李存孝
Li Ts'un-hsin 李存信
Li Tzu-ch'eng 李自成
Li Yen 李岩
Li Yü 李煜
Li Yü 李漁
Liang-shan po 梁山泊
Liao (State of) 遼

Lieh-kuo chih-chuan (*Lieh-kuo*) 列國志傳

lieh-nu 烈女

Lin-an 臨安

Lin Chao-en 林兆恩

Lin Ch'ung 林冲

Liu Ch'an 劉禪

Liu Chi 劉基

Liu Chin 劉瑾

Liu Hsien-t'ing 劉獻廷

Liu Huang-shu 劉皇叔

Liu Hui 劉翬

Liu I-ch'ing 劉義慶

liu-k'ou 流寇

Liu Pang (Han Kao-tsu) 劉邦(漢高祖)

Liu Pei 劉備

Liu Piao 劉表

Liu T'ang 劉唐

Liu-t'ao 六韜

Lo Ju-fang 羅汝芳

Lo Kuan-chung 羅貫中

Lu Chih-shen 魯智深

Lu Chün-i 盧俊義

Lu Su 魯肅

Lü Meng 呂蒙

Lü Shang (Chiang Shang) 呂尚(姜尚)

Lun-yü 論語

mao 矛

Mao Tsung-kang 毛崇崗

Meng-tzu 孟子

Mi-lou 迷樓

ming-ch'en 名臣

Ming-shih 明史

Ming Shih-lu 明實錄

Mo Hsi 妹喜

Mo-tzu 墨子

Mu Kuei-ying 穆桂英

Nai Te-weng 耐得翁

Nan pei shih yen-i 南北史演義

Nan-Sung chih-chuan (*Nan-Sung*) 南宋志傳

Nan-yang 南陽

nei-sheng wai-wang 內聖外王

Ning-wu 寧武

nü-chiang 女將

pa 跋

pai-kuan 稗官

pai-kuan hsiao-shuo 稗官小說

pai-kuan yeh-shih 稗官野史

Pai-li Hsi 百里奚

Pan Ku 班固

P'an Jen-mei 潘仁美

P'an-ku chih T'ang Yü chuan (*P'an-ku*) 盤古至唐虞傳

P'ang Chüan 龐涓

pao-chün 暴君

Pao Chen 包拯

pao-pien 包貶

Pao Ssu 褒姒

Pei-Sung chih-chuan (*Pei-Sung*) 北宋志傳

Pei-Sung Yang-chia-chiang (*Yang-chia-chiang*) 北宋楊家將

P'ei Sung-chih 裴松之

pen-chi 本紀

P'eng Yueh 彭越

pi-chi 筆記

Pi Kan 比干

Pien-liang 汴梁

p'ing-hua 平話，評話

p'ing-tien 評點

Po I 伯益

Po Yi 伯夷

Sa Meng-wu 薩孟武

san-chiao 三教

san-ch'ien kuan 三千貫

San-i chiao 三一教

san-kang 三綱

San-kuo chih 三國志

San-kuo-chih p'ing-hua 三國志平話

San-kuo chih t'ung-su yen-i (*San-kuo*) 三國志通俗演義

San-pao t'ai-chien hsi-yang t'ung-su yen-i (*San-pao*) 三寶太監西洋通俗演義

san pu-hsiu 三不朽

Shan-chiao 闡敎

Shan Hsiung-hsin 單雄信

shan-shu 善書

Shang Chou lieh-kuo ch'üan-chuan 商周列國全傳

Shang Chün 商均

Shang-ti 上帝

Shen Nung 神農

shen-tao she-chiao 神道設敎

Shen-tsung (Emperor) 神宗

Sheng-ch'ao 聖朝

Sheng-chih 聖旨

Sheng-chu 聖主

Sheng-chün 聖君

Sheng-en 聖恩

Sheng-shang 聖上

Sheng-ts'ai 聖裁

Sheng-yü 聖諭

sheng-yuan 生員

shih 史

Shih-chi 史記

Shih Chin 史進

Shih-ching 詩經

Shih Lao 釋老

Shih Nai-an 施耐庵

Shih-shuo hsin-yü 世說新語

Shou-yang 首陽

Shu Ch'i 叔齊

Shu-ching 書經

shu-ts'ai chang-i 疏財仗義

Shui-hu chuan (*Shui-hu*) 水滸傳

Shun (King) 舜

Shuo kung-an 說公案

Shuo T'ang 說唐

Soochow 蘇州

Sou-shen chi 搜神記

Ssu-ma Ch'ien 司馬遷

Ssu-ma I 司馬懿

Ssu-ma Kuang 司馬光

su 俗

Su Tung-p'o 蘇東坡

Sui-shih i-wen (*Sui-shih*) 隋史遺文

Sui-shu 隋書

Sui T'ang liang-ch'ao chih-chuan (*Sui-T'ang*) 隋唐兩朝志傳

Sui T'ang yen-i 隋唐演義

Sui Yang-ti yen-shih (*Sui Yang-ti*) 隋煬帝艷史

Sun Ch'üan 孫權

Sun P'ang tou-chih yen-i (*Sun P'ang*) 孫龐鬥志演義

Sun Pin 孫臏

Sun Wu 孫武

Sung Chiang 宋江

Sung-shih 宋史

Sung Wan 宋萬

ta-chang-fu 大丈夫

Ta-ssu-k'ung 大司空

Ta-Sung chung-hsing t'ung-su yen-i (*Ta Sung*) 大宋中興通俗演義

Ta-Sung chung-hsing Yüeh-wang chuan (*Ta Sung*) 大宋中興岳王傳

ta-tao 大道

Ta-tse 大澤

Ta-tu-t'u fu 大都督府

ta-t'ung 大同

Ta-Yüan lung-hsing chi 大元龍興記

Tai-tsung (Emperor) 代宗

T'ai-chia 太甲

T'ai-chou 泰州

T'ai-hang 太行

T'ai-k'ang (King) 太康

T'ai-shih 泰誓

Tan Chi 妲己

Tan Chu 丹朱

T'ang (King) 湯

T'ang Hsien-tsu 湯顯祖

T'ang-shu chih-chuan t'ung-su yen-i
  (*T'ang-shu*) 唐書志傳通俗演義
Tao 道
T'ao Ch'ien 陶謙
T'ao-yuan chieh-i 桃園結義
Ti 帝
Ti Ch'ing 狄青
Ti Jang 翟讓
t'i-t'ien hsing-tao 替天行道
T'ien Feng 田豐
t'ien-hsia wei-kung 天下爲公
t'ien-jen kan-ying 天人感應
T'ien-ming 天命
T'ien-tzu 天子
t'ing-chang 廷杖
t'ing-t'ien yu-ming 聽天由命
tsa-chi 雜技
Tsa-chuan pien 雜傳編
tsai 災
Ts'ai Ching 蔡京
Ts'an-T'ang Wu-tai-shih yen-i chuan
  (*Ts'an-T'ang*) 殘唐五代史演義傳
ts'an-ts'ai shih-chien 參采史鑑
Ts'ao Man chuan 曹瞞傳
Ts'ao P'i 曹丕
Ts'ao Pin 曹彬
Ts'ao Ts'ao 曹操
Tso-chuan 左傳
Tso Ju 左儒
Tu-ch'eng chi-sheng 都城紀勝
Tu Ch'ien 杜遷
Tu Fu 杜甫
Tu Pai 杜伯
Tung Cho 董卓
Tung-Chou lieh-kuo chih 東周列國志
Tung-ch'uang shih-fan 東窗事犯
Tung Chung-shu 董仲舒
Tung-Han yen-i (*Tung-Han*) 東漢演義
Tung Hsi Chin yen-i 東西晉演義
Tung Hsi Han t'ung-su yen-i
  東西漢通俗演義

Tung-hu shih 東戶氏
Tung-lin 東林
t'ung-hsin 童心
T'ung Kuan 童貫
t'ung-su yen-i 通俗演義
T'ung-t'ien chiao-chu 通天敎主
Tzu-chih t'ung-chien (*T'ung-chien*)
  資治通鑑
Tzu-chih t'ung-chien kang-mu
  (*Kang-mu*) 綱目
Tzu-lu 子路

Wa-kang chai 瓦岡寨
Wang Chen 王振
Wang Chin 王進
Wang Lun 王倫
Wang Ken 王艮
Wang Po-tang 王伯當
wang-tao 王道
Wang Yang-ming ch'u-shen
  ching-luan lu (*Wang Yang-ming*)
  王陽明出身靖亂錄
Wang Yen-chang 王彥章
Wei Chung-hsien 魏忠賢
Wei-chi 魏紀
wen 文
wen-hsueh 文學
Wen Shu 文殊
wen-yen 文言
Wu-chiang 烏江
wu-chiang 武將
Wu-chu chuan 吳主傳
Wu Kuang 吳廣
Wu San-kuei 吳三桂
Wu Sung 武松
Wu-tai shih-chi 五代史記
Wu-tai shih p'ing hua 五代史平話
Wu-t'ai 五台
wu-te chung-shih shuo 五德終始說
Wu-ti chi 武帝紀
Wu-tsung (Emperor) 武宗

wu-t'ung 梧桐
Wu-wang fa Chou p'ing-hua
武王伐紂平話
Wu-Yueh ch'un-ch'iu 吳越春秋
Wu Yung 吳用

ya 雅
Yang Ch'i-yuan 楊起元
*Yang-chia fu shih-tai chung-yung
yen-i* 楊家府世代忠勇演義
Yang-chia t'ung-su yen-i 楊家通俗演義
Yang-chou 揚州
Yang Hsiung 楊雄
Yang Huai-yü 楊懷玉
Yang Kung-cheng 楊公正
Yang Ting-chien 楊定見
Yang Tsung-pao 楊宗保
Yang Yeh 楊業
Yao (King) 堯
Yeh Chou 葉晝
yeh-shih 野史
Yen (King) 炎
Yen P'o-hsi 閻婆惜
yin-i 隱逸
yin-yang 陰陽
ying-hsiung ch'uan-chi 英雄傳奇
Ying Pu 英布
Ying-tsung (Emperor) 英宗
Yu (King) 幽
Yu-ch'iung (State of) 有窮

Yu Hsia chih-chuan (*Yu Hsia*)
有夏誌傳
Yu Shang chih-chuan (*Yu Shang*)
有商誌傳
Yü (King) 禹
Yü (State of) 虞
Yü Ch'ien 于謙
Yü-ch'ih Kung 尉遲恭
yü-fu yü-fu 愚夫愚婦
Yü Hsiang-tou 余象斗
Yü-huang ta-ti (Yü-ti) 玉皇大帝 (玉帝)
yü-i hsin-shih 羽翼信史
Yü sao-t'ou 玉搔頭
*Yü Shao-pao ts'ui-chung
ch'üan-chuan* (*Yü Shao-pao*)
于少保粹忠全傳
Yü Shao-yü 余邵魚
Yü-shih ming-yen 喻世名言
Yuan Chung-tao 袁中道
Yuan Hung-tao 袁宏道
Yuan Nien 袁年
Yuan Shao 袁紹
Yuan-shih t'ien-tsun 元始天尊
Yuan Tsung-tao 袁宗道
Yuan Yü-ling 袁于令
Yueh Fei 岳飛
Yueh Yun 岳雲
yung-shih shih 詠史詩
Yung-yü-tzu (Chiang Ta-ch'i)
庸愚子 (蔣大器)

Selected Bibliography

In a study of the scope and nature of this one, it would be unrealistic to attempt what may be called an exhaustive bibliography. Listed below are the principal Chinese, Japanese, and Western sources that I have consulted or cited.

Works in Chinese and Japanese

A Ying 阿英 [Ch'ien Hsing-ts'un 錢杏邨]. *Hsiao-shuo hsien-t'an* 小說閒談. Rev. ed. Shanghai: Ku-tien wen-hsueh, 1958.

Abe Kenya 阿部兼也. "Suikoden no bungakuseie no ikkōsatsu" 水滸傳の文學性への一考察, *Nippon Chūgoku gakkai-hō* 日本中國學會報 24 (1972): 167–87.

Chan-kuo ts'e 戰國策. Annotated by Kao Yu 高誘. 4 vols. Taipei: Shang-wu yin-shu kuan, 1956.

Chang Cheng-lang 張政烺. "Chiang-shih yü yung-shih shih" 講史與詠史詩, *Chung-yang yen-chiu yuan li-shih yü-yen yen-chiu so chi-k'an* 中央研究院歷史語言研究所集刊, no. 10 (1948): 601–45.

Chang Hsin-ch'eng 張心澂. *Wei-shu t'ung-k'ao* 偽書通考. 2 vols. Shanghai: Shang-wu yin-shu kuan, 1954.

Chang Hsueh-ch'eng 章學誠. *Ping-ch'en cha-chi* 丙辰劄記. In *Chu-hsueh-hsuan ts'ung-shu* 聚學軒叢書. Compiled by Liu Shih-heng 劉世珩. Vol. 16. Reprint. Taipei: I-wen yin-shu kuan, 1970.

Chang Kuo-kuang 張國光. "San-kuo chih t'ung-su yen-i ch'eng-shu yü Ming chung-yeh pien" 三國志通俗演義成書于明中葉辨. In *San-kuo yen-i yen-chiu chi* 三國演義研究集, pp. 266–79.

———. *Shui-hu yü Chin Sheng-t'an yen-chiu* 水滸與金聖嘆研究. Cheng-chou, Honan: Chung-chou shu-hua she, 1981.

Chang Kwang-chih 張光直. "Shang Chou shen-hua chih fen-lei" 商周神話之分類, *Min-tsu hsueh yen-chiu suo chi-k'an* 民族學研究所集刊, no. 14 (1962): 47–94.

Ch'ang-sun Wu-chi 長孫無忌 et al. *Sui-shu ching-chi chih* 隋書經籍志. Shanghai: Shang-wu yin-shu kuan, 1955.

Chang T'ing-yü 張廷玉 et al. *Ming-shih* 明史. 6 vols. Taipei: Kuo-fang yen-chiu yuan, 1962; 28 vols. Peking: Chung-hua shu-chü, 1974.

Chang Yu-luan 張友鸞. "Chin Sheng-t'an tsen-yang wu-mo Sung Chiang te" 金聖嘆怎樣誣蔑宋江的. In *Shui-hu yen-chiu lun-wen chi* 水滸研究論文集, pp. 324–31.

Chao Ching-shen 趙景深. *Shui-hu jen-wu yü Shui-hu chuan* 水滸人物與水滸傳. Reprint. Taipei, 1971.

Chao Ts'ung 趙聰. *Chung-kuo ssu ta hsiao-shuo chih yen-chiu* 中國四大小說之研究. Hong Kong: Yu-lien, 1964.

Chao Yeh 趙曄. *Wu-Yueh ch'un-ch'iu* 吳越春秋. Reprint. Taipei: Chung-hua shu-chü, 1970.

Chen Wei 甄偉. *Hsi-Han yen-i* 西漢演義. 2 vols. Reprint. Hong Kong: Hsiang-chi shu-chü, n.d.

Ch'en Chou-ch'ang 陳周昌. "San-kuo-chih t'ung-su yen-i hsing-ch'eng kuo-ch'eng lun-lueh" 三國志通俗演義形成過程論略. In *San-kuo yen-i yen-chiu chi*, 三國演義研究集, pp. 306–25.

Ch'en Ju-heng 陳汝衡. "P'ing-hua yen-chiu" 評話研究. *Shih-hsueh tsa-chih* 史學雜誌 2, no. 5 (April 1931): 1–16.

———. *Shuo-shu shih-hua* 說書史話. Peking: Tso-chia ch'u-pan she, 1958.

———, ed. *Shuo T'ang* 說唐. Shanghai: Chung-hua shu-chü, 1959. Reprint. Hong Kong: Kwang-chih shu-chü, n.d.

Ch'en Shou 陳壽. *San-kuo chih* 三國志. 5 vols. Shanghai: Ch'ung-hua shu-chü, 1964.

Ch'en Teng-yuan 陳登原. *Chin Sheng-t'an chuan* 金聖嘆傳. Reprint. Hong Kong: T'ai-p'ing shu-chü, 1963.

Cheng Chen-to 鄭振鐸. *Chung-kuo wen-hsueh lun chi* 中國文學論集. Shanghai: Kai-ming shu-tien, 1934.

———. [*Ch'a-t'u-pen*] Chung-kuo wen-hsueh shih [插圖本] 中國文學史. 4 vols. Hong Kong: Ku-wen shu-chü, n.d.

———. *Chung-kuo wen-hsueh yen-chiu* 中國文學研究. 3 vols. Reprint. Hong Kong: Ku-wen shu-chü, 1970.

———. "Yueh chuan te yen-hua" 岳傳的演化. In Cheng Chen-to, *Chung-kuo wen-hsueh yen-chiu*, pp. 300–312.

———, ed. *Shui-hu ch'üan-chuan* 水滸全傳. Reprint. Hong Kong, 1965.

Cheng Chi-meng 鄭繼孟. *Wang Yang-ming chuan* 王陽明傳. Taipei: Tai-pei shu-chü, 1957.

Cheng Ch'ien 鄭騫. "Yang-chia-chiang ku-shih k'ao-shih cheng-su" 楊家將故事考史証俗. In *Ching-wu ts'ung-pien* 景午叢編, vol. 2, pp. 1–84. 2 vols. Taipei: Chung-hua shu-chü, 1972.

Cheng Ho-sheng 鄭鶴聲. *Ssu-ma Ch'ien nien-p'u* 司馬遷年譜. Shanghai: Shang-wu yin-shu kuan, 1956.

Cheng T'ien-t'ing 鄭天挺 et al., eds. *Ming-mo nung-min ch'i-i shih-liao* 明末農民起義史料. Peking: Chung-hua shu-chü, 1954.

Chi Wen-fu 嵇文甫. *Wan Ming ssu-hsiang shih lun* 晚明思想史論. Ch'ung-ch'ing: Shang-wu yin-shu kuan, 1944.

Chi Yun 紀昀 et al. *Ssu-ku ch'üan-shu tsung-mu t'i-yao* 四庫全書總目提要. Shanghai, 1934. Reprint. Taipei, 1971.

Ch'i-tung yeh-jen 齊東野人 [pseud]. *Sui Yang-ti yen-shih* 隋煬帝艷史. Reprint. Taipei: T'ien-i ch'u-pan she, 1974.

Ch'ien Ching-fang 錢靜方. *Hsiao-shuo ts'ung-k'ao* 小說叢考. Shanghai: Ku-tien wen-hsueh ch'u-pan she, 1958.

Ch'in-huai Mo-k'o 秦淮墨客 [Chi Chen-lun 紀振倫]. *Yang-chia-fu shih-tai chung-yung yen-i chih-chuan* 楊家府世代忠勇演義志傳. 1606. Facsimile edition. 4 vols. Taipei: Chung-yang tu-shu-kuan, 1970.

Chou Fu-ch'eng 周輔成 . *Lun Tung Chung-shu ssu-hsiang* 論董仲舒思想 Shanghai: Jen-min ch'u-pan she, 1961.

Chou Li-po 周立波 . *"T'an San-kuo chih yen-i"* 談三國誌演義 . In *Chung-kuo ku-tien hsiao-shuo p'ing-lun chi* 中國古典小說評論集, pp. 51−64. Peking: Hsin-hua shu-tien, 1957; reprint, Hong Kong: Shang-hai shu-tien, 1960.

Chou Wei 周緯 . *Chung-kuo ping-ch'i shih-kao* 中國兵器史稿 . Peking: San-lien shu-tien, 1957.

Chu Hsi 朱熹 . *Ssu-shu chang-chü chi-chu* 四書章句集註. Peking: Chung-hua shu-chü, 1983.

———. *T'ung-chien Kang-mu* 通鑑綱目 . Chin Chieh Shu Yeh Teh Chi, Chia-ch'ing Chia-tzu (1804) edition.

Chu I-hsuan 朱一玄 and Liu Yü-ch'en 劉毓忱 . *San-kuo yen-i tzu-liao hui-pien* 三國演義資料滙編 . Tien-tsin: Pai-hua wen-i ch'u-pan she, 1983.

———. *Sui-hu chuan tzu-liao hui-pien* 水滸傳資料滙編 . Tien-tsin: Pai-hua wen-i ch'u-pan she, 1981.

Chu-ko Liang 諸葛亮 . *Chu-ko Liang chi* 諸葛亮集 . Peking: Chung-hua shu-chü, 1974.

Chu Yuan-chang 朱元璋 . *[Ming T'ai-tsu] Yü-chih wen-chi* [明太祖]御製文集 . Reprint. Taipei: Hsueh-sheng shu-chü, 1965.

———. *[Kao Huang-ti] Yü-chih wen-chi* [高皇帝]御製文集 . Photocopy of the original in Kyoto University, Kyoto, Japan.

Ch'ü Wan-li 屈萬里 . *"Shih-chi Yin-pen-chi chi ch'i-t'a chi-lu chung so-tsai Yin-Shang shih-tai ti shih-shih"* 史記殷本紀及其他紀錄中所載殷商時代的史事 . *Bulletin of the College of Arts, National Taiwan University* 14 (November 1965): 87−118.

Chuang-tzu 莊子 . *Chuang-tzu chi shih* 莊子集釋 . Annotated by Kuo Ch'ing-fan 郭慶藩 . 2 vols. Taipei: Shih-chih shu-chü, 1962.

Ch'un-ch'iu 春秋 . *Ch'un-chiu san-chuan* 春秋三傳 . Taipei: Ch'i-ming shu-chü, 1952.

Chung-kuo che-hsueh shih chiao-hsueh tzu-liao hui-pien [*Liang Han pu-fen*] 中國哲學史教學資料彙編：兩漢部分 . 2 vols. Peking: Chung-hua shu-chü, 1963.

Chung Ssu-ch'eng 鍾嗣成 et al. *Lu kuei pu (wai ssu-chung)* 錄鬼簿(外四種). Shanghai: Chung-hua shu-chü, 1959.

Fan Yen-ch'iao 范煙橋 . *Chung-kuo hsiao-shuo shih* 中國小說史. Suchou: Ch'iu-yeh she, 1927.

Fang Hsuan-ling 房玄齡 et al., eds. *Chin-shu* 晋書 . 10 vols. Peking: Chung-hua, 1974.

Feng Meng-lung 馮夢龍 . *Hsin lieh-kuo chih* 新列國志 . 2 vols. Facsimile ed. Taipei: Lien-ching ch'u-pan shih-yeh kung-ssu, 1981.

P'ing-yao chuan 平妖傳 . Peking, 1956.

———. *Tung Chou lieh-kuo chih* 東周列國志 . Peking: Tso-chia ch'u-pan she, 1955.

————. *Wang Yang-ming ch'u-shen chin-luan lu* 王陽明出身靖亂錄 . Taipei: Kwang-wen shu-chü, 1968.

————. *Yü-shih ming yen* 喻世明言 . Hong Kong: Chung-hua shu-chü, 1965.

Feng-shen yen-i 封神演義 . 2 vols. Hong Kong: T'ai-p'ing shu-chü, 1970; Peking: Tso-chia ch'u-pan she, 1955.

Fu Chen-lun 傅振倫 *Chung-kuo fang-chih hsueh t'ung-lun* 中國方志學通論 . Reprint, Taipei, 1968.

Fu Ch'in-chia 傅勤家 . *Chung-kuo tao-chiao shih* 中國道教史 . Reprint. Taipei: Shang-wu yin-shu kuan, 1966.

Fu I-ling 傅衣凌 . *Ming-tai chiang-nan shih-min ching-chi shih-t'an* 明代江南市民經濟試探 . Shanghai: Jen-min ch'u-pan she, 1963.

Fu Ssu-nien 傅斯年 . "Chou tung-feng yü Yin i-min" 周東封與殷遺民 . In *Fu Meng-chen hsien-sheng chi* 傅孟眞先生集 . (Taipei: Tai-wan ta-hsueh, 1952), 4: 28.

Han Fei-tzu 韓非子 . *Han Fei-tzu chi chieh* 韓非子集解 . Annotated by Wang Hsien-shen 王先愼 . 4 vols. Taipei: Shang-wu yin-shu kuan, 1956.

Ho Hsin 何心 [Lu Tan-an 陸澹安]. *Shui-hu yen-chiu* 水滸研究 . Shanghai: Shang-hai wen-i lien-ho ch'u-pan she, 1954.

Ho Hsin-yin 何心隱 . *Ho Hsin-yin chi* 何心隱集 . Edited by Jung Chao-tsu 容肇祖 . Peking: Chung-hua shu-chü, 1981.

Hou Wai-lu 侯外廬 . "Shih-ch'i shih-chi te Chung-kuo she-hui ho ch'i-meng ssu-ch'ao te t'e-tien" 十七世紀的中國社會和啟蒙思潮的特點 . In *Chung-kuo tzu-pen chu-i meng-ya wen-t'i t'ao-lun chi*, pp. 91–125. Peking: San-lien ch'u- pan she, 1957.

Hsi-wu lan-tao-jen 西吳懶道人 [pseud]. *Chiao Ch'uang t'ung-su hsiao-shuo* 勦闖通俗小說 · . Microfilm copy of the original in Naikaku Bunko, Japan.

Hsieh Wu-liang 謝無量 . *Lo Kuan-chung yü Ma Chih-yuan* 羅貫中與馬致遠 . Shanghai: Shang-wu yin-shu kuan, 1935.

Hsia Chih-ch'ing 夏志清 . "*Sui-shih i-wen* ch'ung-k'an hsu" 隋史遺文重刊序 . In *Sui-shih i-wen*, pp. 1–20. Reprint. Taipei: Yu-shih yueh-k'an she, 1975.

Hsiung Ta-mu 熊大木 . *Nan Pei Sung ch'üan-chuan* 南北宋全傳 . *Pei-Sung chih-chuan t'ung-su yen-i t'i-p'ing* 北宋志傳通俗演義題評 , 10 *chüan*; bound with *Nan-Sung chih-chuan t'ung-su yen-i t'i-p'ing* 南宋志傳通俗演義題評 , 10 *chüan*. Microfilm copy made in 1955 of the original Shih-te t'ang 世德堂 edition in Naikaku Bunko, Japan.

————. *T'ang-chuan yen-i* 唐傳演義 . Microfilm copy of the original 1619 edition in Naikaku Bunko, Japan.

————. *T'ang-shu chih-chuan t'ung-su yen-i* 唐書志傳通俗演義 . Microfilm copy of the original 1553 edition in Naikaku Bunko, Japan.

————. *Ta-Sung chung-hsing t'ung-su yen-i* 大宋中興通俗演義 . 8 *chüan*. Ming Wan-li edition.

————. *Ta-Sung chung-hsing Yueh-wang chuan* 大宋中興岳王傳 . 8 *chüan*. Microfilm copy of San-t'ai-kuan edition in Naikaku Bunko in Japan.

Hsu Hao 徐浩 . *Nien-wu shih lun-kang* 廿五史論綱 . Reprint. Hong Kong: Nan-hsing shu-chü, 1964.

Hsu Shih-nien 徐士年 . *Ku-tien hsiao-shu lun-chi* 古典小說論集 . Shanghai: Shanghai Ch'u pan kung-ssu, 1955.

Hsueh Chü-cheng 薛居正 . *Chiu Wu-tai shih* 舊五代史 . Reprint. Taipei: I-wen yin-shu kuan, 1955.

Hu Shih 胡適 . *Hu Shih wen-ts'un* 胡適文存 . 4 vols. Reprint. Taipei: Yuan-tung tu-shu kung-ssu, 1971.

Hu Wan-ch'uan 胡萬川 . "Feng Meng-lung yü Fu-she jen-wu" 馮夢龍與復社人物 . In *Chung-kuo ku-tien hsiao-shuo yen-chiu chuan-chi* 中國古典小說研究專集 , pp. 123–36. Taipei: Lien-ching ch'u-pan she, 1979.

―――. *P'ing-yao chuan yen-chiu* 平妖傳研究 . Taipei: Hua-cheng shu-chü, 1984.

―――. "Ts'ung *Chih-nang, Chih-nang pu* k'an Feng Meng-lung" 從智囊、智囊補看馮夢龍 . In *Chung-kuo ku-tien hsiao-shuo yen-chiu chuan-chi*, pp. 137–50.

Hu Yin-ling 胡應麟 . *Shao-shih shan-fang pi-ts'ung* 少室山房筆叢 . 2 vols. Shanghai: Chung-hua shu-chü, 1964.

Huang Lin 黃霖 and Han T'ung-wen 韓同文 . *Chung-kuo li-tai hsiao-shuo lun-chu hsuan* 中國歷代小說論著選 . Nan-ch'ang: Chiang-hsi jen-min ch'u-pan she, 1982.

Huang Tsung-hsi 黃宗羲 . *Ming-ju hsueh-an* 明儒學案 . 12 vols. Taipei: Shang-wu yin-shu kuan, 1965.

Hung Shih-ti 洪世滌 . *Ch'en Sheng, Wu Kuang* 陳勝、吳廣 . Shanghai: Jen-min ch'u-pan-she, 1972.

I Ching 易經 . *Chou I pen-i* 周易本義 . Wu-ching tu-pen edition. Taipei: Ch'i-ming shu-chü, 1952.

I Su- 一粟 [Chou Shao-liang 周紹良]. "T'an T'ang-tai te San-kuo ku-shih" 談唐代的三國故事 . In *Wen-hsueh i-ch'an tseng-k'an* 文學遺產增刊 10(1962): 117–26. Peking: Chung-hua shu-chü, 1962. Reprinted in Chou Shao-liang, *Shao-liang ts'ung-kao* 紹良叢稿 , pp. 223–33. Chi-nan: Ch'i-lu shu-she, 1984.

Jao Tsung-i 饒宗頤 . *Chung-kuo shih-hsueh shang chih cheng-t'ung lun* 中國史學上之正統論 . Hong Kong: Lung-mang shu-tien, 1979.

Jung Chao-tsu 容肇祖 . *Ming-tai ssu-hsiang shih* 明代思想史 . Reprint. Taipei: K'ai-ming shu-tien, 1973.

Kan Pao 干寶 . *Sou-shen chi* 搜神記 . In *Shuo-k'u* 說庫 . Reprint. Taipei: Hsin-hsing shu-chü, 1973.

Ko Hung 葛洪 . *Hsi-ching tsa-chi* 西京雜記 . In *Pi-chi hsiao-shuo ta-kuan hsu-pien* 筆記小說大觀續編 . Reprint. Taipei: Hsin-hsing shu-chü, 1962.

Ku Yen-wu 顧炎武 . *Jih-chih lu* 日知錄 . Kuo-hsueh chi-pen ts'ung-shu edition. Taipei: Shang-wu yin-shu kuan.

―――. *T'ien-hsia chün-kuo li-ping shu* 天下郡國利病書 . Ssu-pu ts'ung-k'an edition, 1936.

K'ung Ling-ching 孔另境 . *Chung-kuo hsiao-shuo shih-liao* 中國小說史料 . Shanghai: Ku-tien wen-hsueh ch'u-pan she, 1957.

Kuo Ch'ang-ho 郭昌鶴 . "Chia-jen ts'ai-tzu hsiao-shuo yen-chiu" 佳人才子小說研究 . *Wen-hsueh chi'k'an* 文學季刊 1, no. 1 (1 January 1934): 194–215; no. 2 (April 1934): 302–23.

Kuo Shao-yü 郭紹虞. *Chung-kuo wen-hsueh p'i-p'ing shih* 中國文學批評史. 3 vols. Reprint. Taipei: Shang-wu yin-shu kuan, 1970.

Kuo-yü 國語. Annotated by Wei Chao 韋昭. Taipei: Shang-wu yin-shu kuan, 1956.

Lao tzu 老子. *Lao-tzu pen-i* 老子本義. Annotated by Wei Yuan 魏源. Hong Kong, 1964.

Li Ch'ang-chih 李長之. *Ssu-ma Ch'ien chih jen-ko yü feng-ko* 司馬遷之人格與風格. Reprint. Hong Kong, 1963.

Li-chi 禮記. *Li-chi chi-shuo* 禮記集說. 2 vols. Taipei: Ch'i-ming shu-chü, 1952.

————. *Li-chi chin-chu chin-i* 禮記今註今譯. Annotated by Wang Meng-ou 王夢鷗. 2 vols. Taipei: Shang-wu yin-shu kuan, 1969.

Li Chih 李壐. *Huang-Sung shih-ch'ao kang-yao* 皇宋十朝綱要. Reprint. Taipei: Wen-hai ch'u-pan she, 1967.

Li Chih 李贄. *Ch'u-t'an chi* 初潭集. 2 vols. Peking: Chung-hua shu-chü, 1974.

————. *Fen-shu* 焚書. Peking: Chung-hua shu-chü, 1961.

————. *Fen-shu, Hsu fen-shu* 焚書，續焚書. Peking: Chung-hua shu-chü, 1975.

————. *Ts'ang-shu* 藏書. Taipei: Hsueh-sheng shu-chü, 1974.

Li Chih-chung 李致忠. "Ming-tai k'o-shu shu-lueh" 明代刻書述略. *Wen-shih* 文史, 23:127−58. Peking: Chung-hua shu-chü, 1984.

Li Han-hun 李漢魂. *Yueh Wu-mu nien-p'u* 岳武穆年譜. Taipei: Shang-wu yin-shu kuan, 1968.

Li Han-san 李漢三. *Hsien-ch'in liang-Han chih yin-yang wu-hsing hsueh-shuo* 先秦兩漢之陰陽五行學說. Taipei: Wei-hsin shu-chü, 1968.

Li Hsiao-ts'ang 李嘯倉. *Sung Yuan chi-i tsa-k'ao* 宋元伎藝雜考. Shanghai: Shang-tsa ch'u-pan-she, 1953.

Li Hui-ying 李輝英. *Chung-kuo hsiao-shuo shih* 中國小說史. Hong Kong: Tung-ya shu-chü, 1970.

Li Kuang-pi 李光璧. *Ming-chao shih-lueh* 明朝史略. Wu-han: Hu-pei jen-ming ch'u-pan she, 1957.

Li T'ai-fen 李泰芬. *Fang-chih hsueh* 方志學. 1935. Reprint. Taipei: Shang-wu yin-shu kuan, 1968.

Li Tou 李斗. *Yang-chou hua-fang lu* 揚州畫舫錄. Peking: Chung-hua shu-chü, 1960.

Li Yen-shou 李延壽. *Pei-shih* 北史. Reprint. Taipei: I-Wen yin-shu kuan, 1955.

Liang Ch'i-ch'ao 梁啓超. *Ku-shu chen-wei chi ch'i nien-tai* 古書眞僞及其年代. Peking: Chung-hua shu-chü, 1962.

————. "Yin-yang wu-hsing shuo chih lai-li" 陰陽五行說之來歷. In *Ku-shih pien* 古史辨, edited by Ku Chieh-kang 顧頡剛, 5(1935):343−62. Reprint. Taipei: Ming-lun ch'u-pan she, 1970.

Ling-hu Te-fen 令狐德芬. *Chou-shu* 周書. Reprint. Taipei: I-wen yin-shu kuan, 1955.

Liu Chao-yu 劉兆祐. "Hsu-lu" 叙錄. In Ch'in-huai Mo-k'o, *Yang-chia-fu shih-tai chung-yung yen-i chih-chuan*, vol. 1, pp. 1−6.

Liu Hsien-t'ing 劉獻廷. *Kuang-yang tsa-chi* 廣陽雜記. Peking: Chung-hua shu-chü, 1957.

Liu Hsiu-yeh 劉修業. *Ku-tien hsiao-shuo hsi-ch'u ts'ung-k'ao* 古典小說戲劇叢考. Peking: Tso-chia ch'u-pan she, 1958.

Liu Hsu 劉昫 et al., comps. *Chiu T'ang-shu* 舊唐書. Reprint. Taipei: I-wen yin-shu kuan, 1955.

————. *T'ang-shu ching-chi i-wen he-chich* 唐書經籍藝文合志. Shanghai: Shang-wu yin-shu kuan, 1956.

Liu I-ch'ing 劉義慶. *Shih-shuo hsin-yü* 世說新語. Hong Kong: Hsueh-lin shu-tien, n.d.

Liu Jo-yü 劉若愚. *Cho-chung chih* 酌中志. 2 vols. Shanghai: Shang-wu yin-shu kuan, 1935.

Liu Shih-te 劉世德. "*Feng-shen yen-i* te ssu-hsiang nei-jung ho i-shu miao-hsieh" 封神演義的思想內容和藝術描寫. In *Ming Ch'ing hsiao-shuo yen-chiu lun-wen chi* 明清小說研究論文集, pp. 244-55. Peking: Jen-min wen-hsueh, 1959.

————. "T'an *San-kuo chih yen-i* chung te cheng-t'ung kuan-nien wen-t'i" 談三國志演義中的正統觀念問題. *Wen-hsueh yen-chiu chi-ken* 文學研究集刊 3 (September 1956): 174-94.

Liu Ta-chieh 劉大杰. *Chung-kuo wen-hsueh fa-ta shih* 中國文學發達史. Reprint. Taipei: Chung-hua shu-chü, 1966.

Liu Ts'un-yan 柳存仁. "Yuan Chih-chih-pen *ch'üan hsiang Wu-wang fa-Chou p'ing-hua*, Ming ken-pen *Lieh-kuo chih-chuan* chüan i yü *Feng-shen yen-i* chih kuan-hsi" 元至治本全相武王伐紂平話明刊本列國志傳卷一與封神演義之關係, *Hsin-ya hsueh-pao* 新亞學報 4, no. 1 (August 1959): 401-42.

Lo Chin-t'ang 羅錦堂. "Chung-kuo hsiao-shuo kuan-nien te chuan-pien" 中國小說觀念的轉變. In *Ta-lu tsa-chih yü-wen ts'ung-shu* 大陸雜誌語文叢書 2, no. 6 (1970): 333-37.

Lo Fen 羅奮, ed. *Yang-chia-chiang yen-i* 楊家將演義. Shanghai: Shang-hai wen-hua ch'u-pan she, 1956.

Lo Mou-teng 羅懋登. [*San-pao t'ai-chien*] *Hsi yang t'ung-su yen-i* 〔三寶太監〕西洋通俗演義. 2 vols. Shanghai: Ku-chi ch'u-pan she, 1985.

Lo Yeh 羅燁. *Tsui-weng t'an-lu* 醉翁談錄. Shanghai: Ku-tien wen-hsueh ch'u-pan she, 1957.

Loh Hsueh-lun 駱雪倫 [Shelley H. L. Chang]. "Li Yü hsi-chü hsiao-shuo chung so fan-ying te ssu-hsiang" 李漁戲曲小說中所反映的思想, *Ta-lu tsa-chih* 大陸雜誌, 50, no. 2 (February 1975): 4-35.

Lu Hsun 魯迅. *Chung-kuo hsiao-shuo shih-lueh* 中國小說史略. 1930. Reprint. Hong Kong: Chin-tai t'u-shu kung-ssu, 1965.

————. *Chung-kuo hsiao-shuo te li-shih pien-ch'ien* 中國小說的歷史變遷. Hong Kong: Chung liu ch'u-pan she, 1957.

————. *Hsiao-shuo chiu-wen ch'ao* 小說舊聞鈔. Shanghai: Lu Hsun Ch'uan-chi ch'u-pan she, 1947; Taipei: Wan-nien-ch'ing shu-lang, n.d.

Lun-yü 論語. *Lun-yü cheng-i* 論語正義. Liu Pao-nan 劉寶楠 commentary edition. Hong Kong: Chung-hua shu-chü, 1963.

————. *Lun-yü i-chu* 論語譯註. Edited and annotated by Yang Po-chün 楊伯峻. Shanghai: Chung-hua shu-chü, 1965.

Lung Wen-pin 龍文彬. *Ming Hui-yao* 明會要. 2 vols. Taipei: Shih-chieh shu-chü, 1963.

Ma Yu-yuan 馬幼垣 . *Chung-kuo hsiao-shuo shih chi kao* 中國小說史集稿 . Taipei: Shih-pao ch'u-pan kung-ssu, 1980.

Meng Sen 孟森 . *Ming-tai shih* 明代史 . Taipei: Chung-hua ts'ung-shu wei-yuan hui, 1957.

Meng-tzu 孟子 Annotated by Chiang Po-ch'ien 蔣伯潛 . In *Ssu-shu tu-pen* 四書讀本 , edited by Shen Chih-fang, 沈知方 . Taipei: Ch'i-ming shu-chü, 1952.

Meng Yao 孟瑤 . *Chung-kuo hsiao-shuo shih* 中國小說史 . 4 vols. Taipei: Chuan-chi wen-hsueh she, 1969.

Meng Yuan-lao 孟元老 et al. *Tung-ching meng-hua lu (wai ssu-chung)* 東京夢華錄 (外四種) . Shanghai: Chung-hua shu-chü, 1962.

Ming Shih lu 明實錄 . 133 vols. Taipei: Chung-yang yen-chiu-yuan, 1962–66.

Miyazaki Ichisada 宮崎市定 . *Suikoden* 水滸傳 . Tokyo, 1972.

Mo-tzu 墨子 . *Mo-tzu hsien-ku* 墨子閒詁 . Annotated by Sun I-jang 孫詒讓 . 4 vols. Reprint. Taipei 1965.

Nai Te-Weng 耐得翁 . *Tu-ch'eng chi-sheng* 都城紀勝 . In *Tung-ching meng-hua lu (wai ssu-chung)* 東京夢華錄(外四種) , by Meng Yuan-lao 孟元老 et al. Shanghai: Chung-hua shu-chü, 1962.

Nakabachi Masakagu 中鉢雅量 . "Suikoden no tai iminzoku ishiki ni tsuite" 水滸傳の對異民族意識について. *Nippon chūgoku gakkai hō* 日本中國學會報 21 (1969): 159–75.

Nan Pei Sung ch'üan-chuan 南北宋全傳 . Revised by Yen-shih shan-ch'iao 研石山樵 . Collated by Chih-li ch'i-jen 織里畸人 . 6 vols. Chin-wen t'ang, 1866. 8 vols. Shanghai: Chang-fu-chi shu-chü, 1913.

Osaka Shiutsu Daiaku Chūgoku Bungaku Kenkyūshi 大阪市立大學中國文學研究室 . *Chūgoku no hachi dai shosetsu* 中國の八大小說 . Tokyo, 1965.

Ou-yang Chien 歐陽健 . "Shih lun *San-kuo chih t'ung-su yen-i* ti ch'eng-shu nien-tai" 試論三國志通俗演義的成書年代. In *San kuo yen-i yen-chiu chi* 三國演義研究集 pp. 280–95.

Ou-Yang Hsiu 歐陽修 . *Wu-tai shih-chi* 五代史記 . Reprint. Taipei: I-wen yin-shu kuan, 1955.

Ou-yang Hsiu and Sung Ch'i 宋祁 . *T'ang-shu* 唐書 . 3 vols. Reprint. Taipei: I-wen yin-shu kuan, 1955, 1965 ed.

Pan Ku 班固 . *Han-shu* 漢書 . 12 vols. Peking: Chung-hua shu-chü, 1964.

P'an-ku chih T'ang Yü chuan 盤古至唐虞傳 . Microfilm copy, made in 1955, of the original Ming edition (Yü Chi-yueh edition) in Naikaku Bunko, Japan.

Pei-ching ta-hsueh chung-wen hsi i-chiu-wu-wu chi 北京大學中文系一九五五級 . *Chung-kuo hsiao-shuo shih kao* 中國小說史稿 . Peking: Jen-min wen-hsueh, 1960.

Sa Meng-wu 薩孟武 . *Shui-hu chuan yü chung-kuo she-hui* 水滸傳與中國社會 . Reprint. Macao: Wan-yu shu-tien, 1966.

Sakai Tadao 酒井忠夫 . *Chūgoku zensho no kenkyū* 中國善書の研究 . Tokyo, 1960.

San-kuo chih p'ing-hua 三國志平話 . Peking: Chung-hua shu-chü, 1958.

San-kuo-chih t'ung-su yen-i 三國志通俗演義 . Facsimile reprint. 8 vols. Peking: Jen-min wen-hsueh, 1975. Microfilm copy of the original in Naikaku Bunko, Japan. Prefaces dated 1494 and 1522.

———. Chin-ling, 1591. Chou Yueh-chiao 周日校 edition. Microfilm in Peking Library rare book series, no. p—110, and in Michigan series, no. G50, 51.

San-kuo yen-i 三國演義. 2 vols. Peking: Tso-chia ch'u-pan she, 1953.

[Ch'uan-t'u hsiu-hsiang] [全圖綉像]. *San-kuo yen-i* 三國演義. Mao Tsung-kang 毛宗岡 commentary edition. 3 vols. Huhohet: Nei-Meng-ku jen-min ch'u-pan she, 1981.

San-kuo yen-i yen-chiu chi 三國演義研究集. Cheng-tu: Ssu-ch'uan She-hui k'o-hsueh yuan, 1983.

San-kuo yen-i yen-chiu lun-wen chi 三國演義研究論文集. Peking: Tso-chia ch'u-pan she, 1957.

San Sui p'ing-yao chuan 三遂平妖傳. 20 chapter version. Peking: Peking University Press, 1983.

Shang K'uei-chai 尚遂齋. "Pai-li Hsi k'ao" 百里奚考. In *Hsu, pai, wen-fa, ts'ung-k'ao, chuan-chi yen-chiu lun-wen chi* 序跋文法叢考傳記研究論文集, pp. 113—17. Taipei: Ta-lu tsa-chih she, 1970.

Shih-ching 詩經. *Mao Shih cheng-i* 毛詩正義. Annotated by K'ung Ying-ta 孔穎達. 6 vols. Hong Kong: Chung-hua shu-chü, 1964.

Shimzu Taiji 清水泰次. "Min dai no ryūmin to ryūzka" 明代の流民と流賊, *Shigaku Zasshi* 史學雜誌 46, no. 2 (March 1935): 192—230; 46, no. 3 (March 1935): 348—84.

Shu-ching 書經. *Shu-ching chi-chuan* 書經集傳. *Wu-ching tu-pen* edition. Taipei: Ch'i-ming shu-chü, 1952.

Shui-hu chuan 水滸傳. *Shui-hu* (*Shui-hu* [70-chapter]), 2 vols. Hong Kong: Chung-hua shu-chü, 1970.

———. *Shui-hu chuan hui-p'ing pen* 水滸傳會評本 (*Shui-hu* [70-chapter variorum ed.], 2 vols. Peking: Pei-ching ta-hsueh, 1981.

———. *Shui-hu chuan* (*Shui-hu* [100—chapter]), 3 vols. Peking: Jen-min wen-hsueh ch'u-pan she, 1975.

———. *I-pai erh-shih hui ti Shui-hu* 一百二十回的水滸 (*Shui-hu* [120-chapter]), 2 vols. Hong Kong: Shang-wu yin-shu kuan, 1969.

Shui-hu yen-chiu lun-wen chi 水滸研究論文集. Peking: Tso-chia ch'u-pan she, 1957.

Ssu-ma Ch'ien 司馬遷. *Shih-chi* 史記. 10 vols. Shanghai: Chung-hua shu-chü, 1959.

Ssu-ma Kuang 司馬光. *Tzu-chih t'ung-chien* 資治通鑑. Peking: Ku-chi ch'u-pan she, 1957.

Su Tung-p'o 蘇東坡. *Chih lin* 志林. In *Pi-chi hsiao-shuo ta-kuan* 筆記小說大觀, 2:799—829. Reprint. Taipei: Hsin-hsing shu-chü, 1973.

Sun K'ai-ti 孫楷第. *Chung-kuo t'ung-su hsiao-shuo shu-mu* 中國通俗小說書目. Reprint. Hong Kong: Shih-yung shu-chü, 1967. Rev. ed. Peking: Jen-min wen-hsueh ch'u-pan she, 1982.

———. *Jih-pen Tung-ching so-chien Chung-kuo hsiao-shuo shu-mu* 日本東京所見中國小說書目. Peking: Jen-min wen-hsueh, 1958. Reprint. Peking: Jen-min wen-hsueh ch'u-pan she, 1981.

———. *Su-chiang shuo-hua yü po-hua hsiao-shuo* 俗講說話與白話小說. Peking: Tso-chia ch'u-pan she, 1956.

————. *Ts'ang-chou chi* 滄州集 . 2 vols. Peking: Chung-hua shu-chü, 1965.

Sun K'o-k'uan 孫克寬 . *Sung Yuan Tao-chiao chih fa-chan* 宋元道敎之發展 . Taichung: Tung-hai ta-hsueh, 1965.

Sun Kuang-te 孫廣德 . *Hsien-Ch'in Liang-Han Yin-Yang Wu-hsing shuo ti cheng-chih ssu-hsiang* 先秦兩漢陰陽五行說的政治思想 . Taipei: Chia-hsin shui-ni kung-ssu wen-hua chi-chin hui, 1969.

Sun Kuo-liang 孫高亮 . *Yü Ch'ien ch'üan chuan* 于謙全傳 . Hangchou: Che-chiang jen-min ch'u-pan she, 1981.

Sun Shu-yü 孫述宇 . [Phillip Sun]. *Shui-hu chuan te lai-li, hsin-tai yü i-shu* 水滸傳的來歷、心態與藝術 . Taipei: Shih-pao wen-hua ch'u-pan shih-yeh, 1981.

Sung Lien 宋濂 et al. *Yuan-shih* 元史 . Taipei: Kuo-fang yen-chiu yuan, 1966.

Sung Yun-pin 宋雲彬 . "T'an Chin Sheng-t'an" 談金聖嘆 . In *Shui-hu yen-chiu lun-wen chi* 水滸研究論文集, pp. 332−35.

Ta-Sung Hsuan-ho i-shih 大宋宣和遺事 . Taipei: Tai-wan shang-wu yin-shu kuan, 1966.

T'an Cheng-pi 譚正璧 . *Hua-pen yü ku-chü* 話本與古劇 . Shanghai: Ku-tien wen-hsueh ch'u-pan she, 1957.

T'ao Tsung-i 陶宗義 . *Cho-keng lu* 輟耕錄 . Taipei: Shih-chieh shu-chü, 1963.

Teng Kuang-ming 鄧廣銘 . *Yueh Fei chuan* 岳飛傳 . Peking: San-lien shu-tien, 1955. Rev. and enl. ed. Peking: Jen-min ch'u-pan she, 1983.

Ting I 丁易 [Yeh Ting-i 葉丁易]. *Ming-tai t'e-wu cheng-chih* 明代特務政治 . Peking: Chung-wai ch'u-pan she, 1950.

T'o T'o 脫脫 et al. *Sung-shih* 宋史. 7 vols. Reprint. Taipei: I-Wen yin-shu kuan, 1955. 40 vols. Peking: Chung-hua shu-chü, 1977.

————. *Sung-shih i-wen chih, pu, fu-pien* 宋史藝文志 ,補 ,附編 . Shanghai: Shang-wu yin-shu kuan, 1957.

Ts'an-T'ang Wu-tai-shih yen-i chuan 殘唐五代史演義傳 . 8 *chüan* in 6 vols. Microfilm copy made by the Library of Congress of the original Ming edition in the Rare Books Collection of the National Peiping Library. Modern ed. Peking: Pao-wen t'ang shu-tien, 1983.

Ts'eng Tsu-yin 曾祖蔭 et al. *Chung-kuo li-tai hsiao-shuo hsu pa hsuan-chu* 中國歷代小說序跋選注. Hsien-nien: Ch'ang-chiang wen-i ch'u-pan she, 1982.

Tso-chuan 左傳 . *Ch'un-ch'iu Tso-chuan tu-pen* 春秋左傳讀本 . Annotated by Wang Po-hsing. Hong Kong: Chung-hua shu-chü, 1965.

————. *Tso-chuan hui-chien* 左傳會箋 . Annotated by Takezoe Kōkō 竹添光鴻 . 2 vols. Reprint. Taipei, 1970.

————. *Wu-ching tu-pen* edition. Reprint. Taipei: Ch'i-ming shu-chü, 1952.

Tu Ying-t'ao 杜穎陶 . *Yueh Fei ku-shih hsi-ch'ü shuo-ch'ang chi* 岳飛故事戲曲說唱集 . Shanghai: Ku-tien wen-hsueh, 1957.

Tung Hsi Chin yen-i 東西晉演義 . 1606. 6 vols. Facsimile ed. Taipei: Chung-yang t'u-shu kuan, 1970.

Tung Hsi Han t'ung-su yen-i 東西漢通俗演義 . Microfilm copy of the original (1612) Ch'ien-hsiao-ko p'i-p'ing 劍嘯閣批評 edition in Naikaku Bunko, Japan. *Hsi-Han yen-i chuan* 西漢演義傳 by Chen Wei 甄偉 . *Tung-Han yen-i chuan* 東漢演義傳 by Hsieh Chao 謝詔 .

Tung Tso-pin 董作賓. *Chung-kuo nien-li tsung-p'u* 中國年曆總譜. 2 vols. Hong Kong: University of Hong Kong Press, 1960.

Uchida Michio 內田道夫, ed. *Chūgoku shōsetsu no sekai* 中國小說の世界. Tokyo, 1970.

Wang Ao 王鏊. *Ku-Su chih* 姑蘇志. 2 vols. Reprint. Taipei: Hsueh-shen shu-chü, 1965.

Wang Hsin-i 王馨一. *Liu Po-wen nien-p'u* 劉伯溫年譜. Shanghai: Shang-wu yin-shu kuan, 1936.

Wang Ku-lu 王古魯. "Nan-Sung shuo-hua jen ssu-chia ti fen-fa" 南宋說話人四家之分法. In *Erh-k'o p'o-an ching-ch'i* 二刻拍案驚奇, 2: 805−12. 2 vols. Shanghai: Ku-tien wen-hsueh ch'u-pan she, 1957.

Wang Li-ch'i 王利器. "Lo Kuan-chung yü *San-kuo chih t'ung-su yen-i*" 羅貫中與三國志通俗演義. In *San-kuo yen-i yen-chiu chi*, pp. 240−65.

———. "*Shui-hu chuan* shih tsen-yang tsuan-hsiu ti" 水滸傳是怎樣纂修的. In *Wen-hsueh p'ing-lun* 文學評論, no. 3 (1982): 86−101.

———. "*Shui-hu* chung so ts'ai-yung ti hua-pen tzu-liao" 水滸中所採用的話本資料. In *Shui-hu yen-chiu lun-wen chi*, pp. 312−13.

———. "*Shui-hu* ti chen-jen chen-shih" 水滸的眞人眞事. In *Shui-hu cheng-ming* 水滸爭鳴 1(1982): 1−18, and 2(1983): 13−39.

Wei Chü-hsien 衞聚賢. *Feng-shen-pang ku-shih t'an-yuan* 封神榜故事探源. 2 vols. Kowloon: Wei-hsing yin-wu so, 1960.

Wei Cheng 魏徵 et al. *Sui-shu* 隋書. Reprint. Taipei: I-wen yin-shu kuan, 1955.

Wei Yin-ju 魏隱儒. *Chung-kuo ku-chi yin-shua shih* 中國古籍印刷史. Peking: Yin-shua kung-yeh ch'u-pan she, 1984.

Wen Chi 文輯. "T'an *San-kuo yen-i*" 談三國演義. In *Chung-kuo ku-tien hsiao-shuo chiang-hua* 中國古典小說講話, pp. 67−120. Reprint. Hong Kong: Shang-hai shu-tien, 1960.

Wen-hsueh i-ch'an pien-chi pu 文學遺產編輯部, ed. *Wen-hsueh i-ch'an tseng-k'an* 文學遺產增刊. 13 vols. Peking: Tso-chia ch'u-pan she (later, Chung-hua shu-chü), 1955−63.

Wu Ch'eng-en 吳承恩. *Hsi-yu chi* 西游記. 3 vols. Hong Kong: Shang-wu yin-shu kuan, 1963. Rev. ed. Peking: Jen-min wen-hsueh, 1980.

Wu Han 吳晗. *Chu Yuan-chang chuan* 朱元璋傳. Hong Kong: Chuan-chi wen-hsueh, 1976.

———. "Li-shih chung ti hsiao-shuo" 歷史中的小說. In *Chung-kuo wen-hsueh yen-chiu* 中國文學研究, pp. 1201−17. Hong Kong: Lung men shu-tien, 1964.

Wu Hsiao-ju 吳小如. *Chung-kuo hsiao-shuo chiang-hua chi ch'i-t'a* 中國小說講話及其他. Shanghai: Ku-tien wen-hsueh ch'u-pan she, 1956.

Wu-men hsiao-k'o 吳門嘯客 [pseud.]. *Sun P'ang tou-chih yen-i* 孫龐鬥志演義. Microfilm copy of the original 1636 edition in Naikaku Bunko, Japan.

Wu-tai shih p'ing-hua 五代史平話. Hong Kong: Kuang-chih shu-chu, n.d.

Wu-wang fa Chou p'ing-hua 武王伐紂平話. Peking: Chung-hua shu-chu, 1958.

Yang Hsiang-k'uei 楊向奎. *Chung-kuo ku-tai she-hui yü ku-tai ssu-hsiang yen-chiu* 中國古代社會與古代思想研究. 2 vols. Shanghai: Jen-min ch'u-pan she, 1962.

Yeh Lang 葉朗 . *Chung-kuo hsiao-shuo mei-hsueh* 中國小說美學 . Peking: Pei-ching ta-hsueh ch'u-pan she, 1982.

Yeh Te-chün 葉德均 . *Sung Yuan Ming chiang-ch'ang wen-hsueh* 宋元明講唱文學. Shanghai: Chung-hua shu-chü, 1959.

Yen Tun-i 嚴敦易 . *Shui-hu chuan ti yen-pien* 水滸傳的演變 . Peking: Tso-chia ch'u-pan she, 1957.

Ying-lieh chuan 英烈傳 . Edited and annotated by Chao Ching-shen 趙景深 and Tu Hao-ming 杜浩銘 . Shanghai: Shang-hai wen-hua ch'u-pan she, 1956.

————. [Hsin-k'e huang-Ming k'ai-yün chi-lueh wu-kung ming shih] *Ying-lieh chuan* [新刻皇明開運輯略武功名世] 英烈傳 . Microfilm copy of the original San-t'ai kuan 三台館 edition in Naikaku Bunko, Japan.

Yu-Hsia chih-chuan 有夏誌傳 . Microfilm copy of the original Ming edition in Naikaku Bunko, Japan.

Yü Cheng-hsieh 俞正燮. "Pal-li Hsi shih i tung lun" 百里奚事異同論 . In *Kuei-ssu lei-kao* 癸巳類稿 , pp. 397−400. Taipei: Shih-chieh shu-chü, 1960.

Yü Chung-yao 余重耀 . *Yang-ming hsien-shen chuan tsuan* 陽明先生傳纂 . Shanghai: Chung-hua shu-chü, 1923.

Yü Shao-yü 余邵魚 . *Ch'un-ch'iu lieh-kuo chih-chuan* 春秋列國志傳 . Microfilm copy of the original Ming Wan-li edition in the Rare Books Collection of National Peiping Library.

Yuan Hung-tao 袁宏道 . *Yuan Chung-lang ch'üan-chi* 袁中郎全集 . Hong Kong: Kuang-chih shu-chü, n.d.

Yuan K'o 袁珂 . *Chung-kuo ku-tai shen-hua* 中國古代神話 . Taipei: Shang-wu yin-shu kuan, 1955.

Yuan Yü-ling 袁于令 . *Sui-shih i-wen* 隋史遺文 . Reprint. With a long Preface by Hsia Chih-ch'ing 夏志清 . Taipei: Yu-shih yueh-k'an she, 1975.

Works in Western Languages

Acton, John E. E. D. *Essays on Freedom and Power*. New York: Meridian Editions, 1955.

Alber, Charles J. "A Survey of English Language Criticism of the *Shui-hu chuan*." *Ch'ing-hua hsueh-pao*, n.s. 7, no. 2 (August 1969): 102−19.

Allan, Sarah. *The Heir and the Sage: Dynastic Legend in Early China*. San Francisco: Chinese Materials Center, 1981.

Allan, Sarah, and Cohen, Alvin P., eds. *Legend, Lore, and Religion in China*. San Francisco: Chinese Materials Center, 1979.

Bauer, Wolfgang. *China and the Search for Happiness*. Translated by Michael Shaw. New York: Seaburg Press, 1976.

Berdyaev, Nicholas. *Slavery and Freedom*. Translated by R. M. French. London: Geoffrey Bles, 1943.

Berling, Judith A. *The Syncretic Religion of Lin Chao-en*. New York: Columbia University Press, 1980.

Birch, Cyril, ed. *Studies in Chinese Literary Genres*. Berkeley: University of California Press, 1974.

Bishop, John L. *The Colloquial Short Story in China.* Cambridge: Harvard University Press, 1965.

Blake, William. "On Homer's Poetry." In *Poetry and Prose of William Blake*, edited by Geoffrey Keynes, pp. 582−83. London: Nonesuch Library, 1956.

Blofeld, John, trans. *The Book of Changes.* London: Allen and Unwin, 1965.

Bodde, Derk. "Comments on the Paper of Arthur F. Wright." In *Generalization in the Writing of History*, edited by Louis Gottschalk, pp. 59−65. Chicago: University of Chicago Press, 1963.

Brewitt-Taylor, C. H., trans. *Romance of the Three Kingdoms.* 2 vols. Shanghai, 1925. Reprint, Taipei: Ch'eng-wen Publishing Co., 1969.

Brinton, Crane. *Ideas and Men: The Story of Western Thought.* 2d. ed. Englewood Cliffs, N.J.: Prentice-Hall, 1963.

Buck, Pearl, trans. *All Men Are Brothers.* New York: Grosset and Dunlap, 1937.

───. *The Chinese Novel.* New York: John Day, 1939.

Burke, Peter. *Popular Culture in Early Modern Europe.* New York: Harper Torchbooks, 1978.

Cam, Helen. *Historical Novel.* London: Historical Association, 1961.

Carlyle, Thomas. *On Heroes, Hero-Worship, and the Heroic in History.* London: Everyman's Library, 1940.

Chadwick, H. M., and Chadwick, N. K. *The Growth of Literature.* 3 vols. Cambridge: Cambridge University Press, 1932−40.

Chai, Ch'u, and Chai, Winberg, trans. and eds. *A Treasury of Chinese Literature.* New York: Appleton-Century, 1965.

Chan, Albert. *The Glory and Fall of the Ming Dynasty.* Norman: University of Oklahoma Press, 1982.

Chan, Hok-lam. "Liu Chi: Dual Image of a Chinese Imperial Adviser." Ph.D. diss., Princeton University, 1967. Microfilm.

───. "Liu Chi (1311−75) in the *Ying-lieh chuan*: The Fictionalization of a Scholar-Hero." *Journal of the Oriental Society of Australia* 5, no. 12 (December 1967): 25−42.

Chan, Wing-tsit. "The Ch'eng-Chu School of Early Ming." In *Self and Society in Ming Thought*, edited by Wm. Theodore de Bary, pp. 29−52. New York: Columbia University Press, 1970.

Chang, Chun-shu, and Chang, Hsueh-lun (Shelley). "K'ung Shang-jen and his *Tao-hua shan*: A Dramatist's Reflections on the Ming-Ch'ing Dynastic Transition." *Journal of the Institute of Chinese Studies of the Chinese University of Hong Kong* 9 (1978): 307−37.

───. "P'u Sung-ling and His *Liao-chai chih-i*: Literary Imagination and Intellectual Consciousness in Early Ch'ing China." *Renditions* 13 (Spring 1980): 60−81.

───. "The World of P'u Sung-ling's *Liao-chai chih-i*: Literature and the Intelligentsia during the Ming-Ch'ing Dynastic Transition." *Journal of the Institute of Chinese Studies of the Chinese University of Hong Kong* 6, no. 2 (1973): 401−23.

————. *State, Society, and Literature in Seventeenth Century China: The Life, Times, and Ideas of Li Yü (1611–1680)*. Forthcoming.

Chang, H. C., trans. *Chinese Literature: Popular Fiction and Drama*. Edinburgh: Edinburgh University Press, 1973.

Chang, Kwang-chih. *Art, Myth, and Ritual: The Path to Political Authority in Ancient China*. Cambridge: Harvard University Press, 1983.

Chang, Shelley Hsueh-lun. "Intellectual and Social Themes in Ming Fiction and Drama," *Chine ancienne*, in *Actes du XXIXe Congress international des orientalistes*, pp. 31–36. Paris: L'Asiatheque, 1977.

Ch'en, Kenneth. *Buddhism in China: A Historical Survey*. Princeton, N.J.: Princeton University Press, 1964.

Ch'en, Shou-yi. *Chinese Literature*. New York: Ronald Press, 1961.

Ch'ien, Edward. "Chiao Hung and the Revolt against Ch'eng-Chu Orthodoxy." In *The Unfolding of Neo-Confucianism*, edited by Wm. Theodore de Bary et al., pp. 271–303. New York: Columbia University Press, 1975.

Ching, Julia. *To Acquire Wisdom: The Way of Wang Yang-ming*. New York: Columbia University Press, 1976.

Cohen, Paul A. *Discovering History in China*. New York: Columbia University Press, 1984.

Crawford, Robert B. "Eunuch Power in the Ming Dynasty." *T'ung Pao* 49:115–48.

Creel, H. G. *The Origins of Statecraft in China*. Chicago: University of Chicago Press, 1970.

Crump, J. I., Jr. "*P'ing-hua* and the Early History of the *San-kuo chih*." *Journal of the American Oriental Society* 71, no. 4. (1951): 249–56.

de Bary, Wm. Theodore et al., eds., *Self and Society in Ming Thought*. New York: Columbia University Press, 1970.

————. *Sources of Chinese Tradition*. 2 vols. New York: Columbia University Press, 1960.

————. *The Unfolding of Neo-Confucianism*. New York: Columbia University Press, 1975.

de Groot, J. J. M. *The Religion of the Chinese*. New York: Macmillan, 1910.

————. *Sectarianism and Religious Persecution in China*. Reprint. Taipei: Literature House, 1963.

DeWoskin, Kenneth J. "The Six Dynasties *Chih-kuai* and the Birth of Fiction." In *Chinese Narrative: Critical and Theoretical Essays*, edited by Andrew H. Plaks, pp. 21–52. Princeton, N.J.: Princeton University Press, 1977.

Dimberg, Ronald G. *The Sage and Society: The Life and Thought of Ho Hsin-yin*. Honolulu: University of Hawaii Press, 1974.

Dreyer, Edward L. *Early Ming China: A Political History 1355–1435*. Stanford, Calif.: Stanford University Press, 1982.

Dubs, Homer H., trans. *The History of the Former Han Dynasty*, by Pan Ku. 3 vols. Baltimore, Md.: Waverly Press, 1938–55.

Eisenstadt, S. N., and Graubard, S. R., eds. *Intellectuals and Tradition*. New York: Humanities Press, 1973.

Elman, Benjamin A. *From Philosophy to Philology: Intellectual and Social Aspects of Change in Late Imperial China*. Cambridge: Council on East Asian Studies, Harvard University, 1984.

Elvin, Mark. *The Pattern of the Chinese Past*. Stanford, Calif.: Stanford University Press, 1973.

Fang, Achilles. *The Chronicle of The Three Kingdoms (220–265)*. Cambridge: Harvard University Press, 1965.

Farmer, Edward L. *Early Ming Government: The Evolution of Dual Capitals*. Cambridge: East Asian Research Center, Harvard University, 1976.

Feng, Yu-lan. *A History of Chinese Philosophy*. Translated by Derk Bodde. 2 vols. Princeton, N.J.: Princeton University Press, 1953.

Feuchtwanger, Lion. *The House of Desdemona or the Laurels and Limitations of Historical Fiction*. Translated by Harold A. Basilius. Detroit, Mich.: Wayne State University Press, 1963.

Foster, George F. "What Is Folk Culture?" *American Anthropologist* 55, no. 21 (1953): 159–73.

Gardner, Charles. *Chinese Traditional Historiography*. Cambridge: Harvard University Press, 1961.

Geertz, Clifford. *The Interpretation of Cultures*. New York: Basic Books, 1974.

Giles, Herbert. *A Chinese Biographical Dictionary*. 1898. Reprint. Taipei: Literature House, 1964.

Goodrich, L. Carrington, and Fang, Chao-ying. *Dictionary of Ming Biography*. New York: Columbia University Press, 1976.

Greenblatt, Kristin Yü. "Chu-hung and Lay Buddhism in the Late Ming." In *The Unfolding of Neo-Confucianism*, edited by Wm. Theodore de Bary et al., pp. 93–140.

Hanan, P. D. "The Authorship of Some *Ku-chin hsiao-shuo* Stories." *HJAS* 29 (1969): 190–200.

———. *The Chinese Short Stories: Studies in Dating, Authorship, and Composition*. Cambridge: Harvard University Press, 1973.

———. *The Chinese Vernacular Story*. Cambridge: Harvard University Press, 1981.

———. "The Composition of the *P'ing-yao chuan*." *HJAS* 31 (1971): 201–19.

———. "The Development of Fiction and Drama." In *The Legacy of China*. London: Oxford University Press, 1964.

———. "The Early Chinese Short Story, a Critical Theory in Outline." *HJAS* 27 (1967): 168–207.

———. "A Landmark of Chinese Novel." In *The Far East: China and Japan*, edited by D. Grant, pp. 325–35. Toronto: University of Toronto Press, 1961.

———. "Sung and Yuan Vernacular Fiction: A Critique of Modern Methods of Dating." *HJAS* 30 (1970): 159–84.

Hegel, Robert E. *The Novel in Seventeenth-Century China*. New York: Columbia University Press, 1981.

———. "*Sui T'ang yen-i*: The Sources and Narrative Techniques of a Traditional

Chinese Novel." Ph.D. diss., Columbia University, 1973. Microfilm.

Henderson, John B. *The Development and Decline of Chinese Cosmology.* New York: Columbia University Press, 1984.

Hennessey, William D., trans. *Proclaiming Harmony.* Ann Arbor, Mich.: Center for Chinese Studies, University of Michigan, 1981.

HJAS (Harvard Journal of Asiatic Studies), various issues.

Ho, Peng Yoke. *The Astronomical Chapters of the Chin Shu.* Paris and the Hague: Morton and Co., 1966.

Ho, Ping-ti. *The Cradle of the East.* Chicago: University of Chicago Press, 1975; Hong Kong: Chinese University of Hong Kong, 1975.

————. *The Ladder of Success in Imperial China: Aspects of Social Mobility, 1368–1911.* New York: Columbia University Press, 1962. Reprint. New York: John Wiley and Sons, Inc., 1964.

————. *Studies on the Population of China, 1368–1953.* Cambridge: Harvard University Press, 1959.

Hook, Sidney. *The Hero in History.* Boston: Beacon Press, 1955.

Hsia, C. T. *The Classic Chinese Novel.* New York: Columbia University Press, 1968.

————. "The Military Romance: A Genre of Chinese Fiction." In *Studies in Chinese Literary Genres*, edited by Cyril Birch, pp. 339–90. Berkeley: University of California Press, 1974.

————. "Time and the Human Condition in the Plays of T'ang Hsien-tsu." In *Self and Society in Ming Thought*, edited by Wm. Theodore de Bary et al., pp. 249–90.

Hsia, C. T., and Hsia, T. A. "New Perspectives on Two Ming Novels: *Hsi-yu chi* and *Hsi-yu pu.*" In *Wen-lin: Studies in the Chinese Humanities*, edited by Chow Tse-tsung, pp. 229–45. Madison: University of Wisconsin Press, 1968.

Huang, Ray. *1587, A Year of No Significance.* New Haven, Conn.: Yale University Press, 1981.

Hucker, Charles. *The Ming Dynasty: Its Origins and Evolving Institutions.* Ann Arbor, Mich.: Center for Chinese Studies, University of Michigan, 1978.

Hughes, E. R., and Hughes, K. *Religions in China.* London: Hutchinson's University Library, 1950.

Hughes, H. Stuart. *Consciousness and Society.* New York: Vintage Books, 1961.

Idema, W. L. *Chinese Vernacular Fiction: The Formative Period.* Leiden: E. J. Brill, 1974.

————. "Novels about the Founding of the Sung Dynasty." *Sung Studies Newsletter*, no. 9 (June 1974): 2–9.

————. "Some Remarks and Speculations Concerning *p'ing-hua.*" *T'oung pao* 60 (1974): 121–72.

————. "Storytelling and the Short Story in China." *T'oung Pao* 59 (1973): 1–67.

Irwin, Richard G. *The Evolution of a Chinese Novel.* Cambridge: Harvard University Press, 1966.

———. "Water Margin Revised." *T'oung Pao* 48, nos. 4–5 (1960): 393–415.

Jackson, J. H., trans. *Water Margin*. Shang-wu Yin-shu kuan 1937. Reprint. Cambridge, Mass.: C and T Co., 1976.

James, Henry. *The Future of the Novel*. New York: Vintage Books, 1956.

Johnson, David. "Communication, Class, and Consciousness in Late Imperial China." In *Popular Culture in Late Imperial China*, edited by David Johnson, Andrew J. Nathan, and Evelyn S. Rawski, pp. 34–72. Berkeley: University of California Press, 1985.

Karlgren, Bernard, trans. *The Book of Documents*. Stockholm: Museum of Far Eastern Antiquities, 1950.

Kengo, Araki. "Confucianism and Buddhism in the Late Ming." In *The Unfolding of Neo-Confucianism*, edited by Wm. Theodore de Bary et al., pp. 39–66.

Langlois, John D., Jr., and Sun, K'o-k'uan. "Three Teachings Syncretism and the Thought of Ming T'ai-tsu." *HJAS* 43, no. 1 (June 1983): 97–139.

Lau, D. C., trans. *Tao Te Ching*. Harmondsworth, England: Penguin Books, 1963.

———. *Mencius*. Harmondsworth, England: Penguin Books, 1970.

———. *The Analects (Lun Yü)*. Harmondsworth, England: Penguin Books, 1979.

Legge, James, trans. *The Chinese Classics*. Vol. 1, *The Confucian Analects, the Great Learning, and the Doctrine of the Mean*; Vol. 2, *The Works of Mencius*; Vol. 3, *The Shu King, or the Book of Historical Documents*; Vol. 4, *The She King, or the Book of Poetry*; Vol. 5, *The Ch'un Ts'ew, with the Tso Chuen*. Reprint. Hong Kong: Hong Kong University Press, 1960.

———. *The I-Ching*. Reprint. New York: Dover Publications, 1963.

———. *Sacred Books of China*. Reprint. Delhi: Matilal Banarsidass, 1966.

———. *The Works of Mencius*. Reprint. Tokyo, 1936.

Li, Chi. *The Beginnings of Chinese Civilizations*. Seattle: University of Washington Press, 1957.

Li, Chi. "The Changing Concept of the Recluse in Chinese Literature." *HJAS* 24 (1962–63): 234–47

Li, Tien-yi. *Chinese Fiction: A Bibliography of Books and Articles in Chinese and English*. New Haven: Far Eastern Publications, Yale University, 1968.

Liu, James T. C. "Yueh Fei (1103–41) and China's Heritage of Loyalty." *The Journal of Asian Studies* 31, no. 2 (February 1972): 291–97.

———. "Yueh Fei—An Analysis in Historiography and Intellectual History," *Chinese Scholar*, no. 2 (September 1971): 43–58.

Liu, James T. Y. *The Chinese Knight-Errant*. Chicago: University of Chicago Press, 1967.

Liu, Ts'un-yan. *Buddhist and Taoist Influences on Chinese Novels*. Vol. 1, *The Authorship of the Feng-shen yen-i*. Wiesbaden: Kommissionsverlag Otto Harrassowitz, 1962.

———. *Chinese Popular Fiction in Two London Libraries*. Hong Kong: Lung men Bookstore, 1967.

———. "Lo Kuan-chung and His Historical Romances." In *Critical Essays on Chinese Fiction*, edited by Winston Yang and Curtis Adkins, pp. 85–114.

————. *Selected Papers from the Hall of Harmonious Wind.* Leiden: E. J. Brill, 1976.

————. "Taoist Self-Cultivation." In *Self and Society in Ming Thought,* edited by Wm. Theodore de Bary et al., pp. 291–330. New York: Columbia University Press, 1970.

————. "Taoism and Neo-Confucianists in Ming Time." *The New Asia Journal* 8, no. 1 (February 1967): 259–96.

Liu, Wu-chi. *An Introduction to Chinese Literature.* Bloomington: Indiana University Press, 1966.

Lowenthal, Leo. *Literature and the Image of Man: Sociological Studies of the European Drama and Novel, 1600–1900.* Boston: Beacon Press, 1957.

Lukacs, Georg. *The Historical Novel,* translated by Hannah and Stanley Mitchell. London: Merlin Press, 1962.

Ma, Y. W. "The Beginnings of Professional Storytelling in China: A Critique of Current Theories and Evidence." In *Etudes d'historie et de litérature chinoises offertes au Professeur Jaroslav Průšek,* pp. 227–45. Paris, 1976.

————. "The Chinese Historical Novel: An Outline of Themes and Contexts." *Journal of Asian Studies* 34, no. 2 (February 1975): 277–94.

Matthews, Brander. *The Historical Novel and Other Essays.* New York: Charles Scribner's Sons, 1901.

Meskill, John, ed. "Academies and Politics in the Ming Dynasty." In *Chinese Government in Ming Times: Seven Studies,* edited by Charles O. Hucker, pp. 149–74. New York: Columbia University Press, 1969.

————. *The Pattern of Chinese History: Cycles, Development, or Stagnation?* Boston: D. C. Heath and Co., 1965.

Metzger, Thomas A. *Escape from Predicament.* New York: Columbia University Press, 1977.

Miller, Andrew. "Introduction." In *Romance of the Three Kingdoms,* translated by C. H. Brewitt-Taylor, 1:v–xii.

Mote, F. W. "The Growth of Chinese Despotism: A Critique of Wittfogel's Theory of Oriental Despotism as Applied to China." *Oriens Extremus* 8, no. 1 (August 1961): 1–41.

Munro, Donald J. *The Concept of Man in Contemporary China.* Ann Arbor: University of Michigan Press, 1977.

Nucho, Fuad. *Berdyaev's Philosophy: The Existential Paradox of Freedom and Necessity.* Garden City, N.Y.: Doubleday and Co., 1966.

Parsons, James B. *The Peasant Rebellions of the Late Ming Dynasty.* Tucson: University of Arizona Press, 1970.

Plaks, Andrew H., ed. *Chinese Narrative: Critical and Theoretical Essays.* Princeton, N.J.: Princeton University Press, 1977.

————. *The Four Masterworks of the Ming Novel.* Princeton, N.J.: Princeton University Press, 1987.

Průšek, Jaroslav. "The Beginnings of Popular Chinese Literature; Urban Centres—The Cradle of Popular Fiction." *Archiv Orientalni* 36 (1968): 67–115.

————. *Chinese History and Literature.* Prague: Orient Institute, Academia, 1970.

————. *The Origin and the Authors of the Hua-pen.* Prague: Orient Institute, Academia, 1967.

————. "Researches into the Beginning of the Chinese Popular Novel." *Archiv Orientalni* 11 (1938–39): 91–132; 23 (1955): 620–22.

Raleigh, John H. *Time, Place, and Idea: Essays on the Novel.* Carbondale: Southern Illinois University Press, 1968.

Rawski, Evelyn S. "Economic and Social Foundations of Late Imperial Culture." In *Popular Culture in Late Imperial China*, edited by David Johnson, Andrew J. Nathan, and Evelyn S. Rawski, pp. 3–33.

Redfield, Robert. "The Folk Society." In *Readings in Anthropology*, edited by Morton H. Fried, pp. 497–517. New York: Thomas Y. Crowell Company, 1968.

————. *The Little Community and Peasant Society and Culture.* Chicago: University of Chicago Press, 1960.

Richardson, David Bonner. *Berdyaev's Philosophy of History.* The Hague: Martinus Nijhoff, 1968.

Riftin, Boris L. "Summary." In *Ot mifa k romanu*, pp. 352–58. Moscow: Nanka 1979.

Roberts, Moss, trans. and ed. *Three Kingdoms: China's Epic Drama.* New York: Pantheon Books, 1976.

Ropp, Paul S. "The Seeds of Change: Reflections on the Condition of Women in the Early and Mid Ch'ing." *Signs: Journal of Women in Culture and Society* 2, no. 1 (Autumn 1976): 5–23.

Ruhlmann, Robert. "Traditional Heroes in Chinese Popular Fiction." In *Confucianism and Chinese Civilization*, edited by Arthur F. Wright, pp. 122–57. New York: Atheneum, 1964.

Sakai, Tadao. "Confucianism and Popular Educational Works." In *Self and Society in Ming Thought*, edited by Wm. Theodore de Bary et al., pp. 331–66.

Shapiro, Sidney, trans. and ed. *Outlaws of the Marsh.* 3 vols. Peking: Foreign Language Press, 1980. 2 vols. Bloomington: Indiana University Press, 1981.

Shih, Vincent Y. C. *The Taiping Ideology: Its Sources, Interpretations, and Influences.* Seattle: University of Washington Press, 1967.

Shils, Edward A. "Intellectuals, Tradition, and the Traditions of Intellectuals: Some Preliminary Consideration." In *Intellectuals and Tradition*, edited by S. N. Eisenstadt and S. R. Graubard, pp. 21–34.

Smith, D. Howard. *Chinese Religion.* New York: Holt, Rinehart and Winston, 1968.

Sun, Phillip S. Y. [Sun Shu-yü] "The Seditious Art of the *Water Margin.*" *Chinese Scholars* 5 (July 1973): 75–101.

Tamaki, Ogawa. "The Author of the *Shui-hu chuan.*" *Monumenta Serica* 17 (1958): 312–30.

Tebbel, John. *Fact and Fiction: Problems of the Historical Novelist.* Lansing: Historical Society of Michigan, 1962.

Thompson, Laurence G. *Chinese Religion: An Introduction.* Belmont, Calif.: Dickenson Publishing Co., 1969

Tu, Wei-ming. *Neo-Confucian Thought in Action: Wang Yang-ming's Youth*

(1472—1509). Berkeley: University of California Press, 1976.

Voelker, John. *About the Historical Novel*. Lansing: Historical Society of Michigan, 1970.

Wakeman, Frederic, Jr. "The Price of Autonomy: Intellectuals in Ming and Ch'ing Politics." *Daedalus* 101 (Spring 1972): 35—70.

Waley, Arthur, trans. *The Analects of Confucius*. New York: Vintage Books, 1938.

Wang, John Ching-yü. *Chin Sheng-t'an*. New York: Twayne Publishers Inc., 1972.

Watson, Burton. *Early Chinese Literature*. New York: Columbia University Press, 1962.

———. *Ssu-ma Ch'ien, Grand Historian of China*. New York: Columbia University Press, 1958.

———, trans. *The Complete Works of Chuang-tzu*. New York: Columbia University Press, 1968.

———, trans. *Han Fei-tzu: Basic Writing*. New York: Columbia University Press, 1964.

———, trans. *Records of the Grand Historian of China*. 2 vols. New York: Columbia University Press, 1961.

Watt, Ian. "Fielding and the Epic Theory of the Novel." In *The Rise of the Novel: Studies in Defoe, Richardson and Fielding*, pp. 239—59. Berkeley: University of California Press, 1964.

Watt, John R. *The District Magistrate in Late Imperial China*. New York: Columbia University Press, 1972.

Welch, Holmes. *Taoism: The Parting of the Way*. Boston: Beacon Press, 1957.

Werner, E. T. C. *A Dictionary of Chinese Mythology*. Shanghai, 1932.

———. *Myths and Legends of China*. Reprint. London: George G. Harrap and Co. 1958.

Wilhelm, Hellmut. "From Myth to Myth: The Case of Yueh Fei's Biography." In *Confucian Personalities*, edited by Arthur Wright and Dennis Twitchett, pp. 146—61. Stanford: Stanford University Press, 1962.

Wittfogel, Karl. *Oriental Despotism, A Comparative Study of Total Power*. New Haven: Yale University Press, 1957.

Wolf, Arthur P. "Gods, Ghosts, and Ancestors." In *Studies in Chinese Society*, edited by Arthur P. Wolf, pp. 131—82. Stanford: Stanford University Press, 1978.

Wright, Arthur F. *Buddhism in Chinese History*. New York: Atheneum, 1965.

———. "On the Use of Generalization in the Study of Chinese History." In *Generalization in the Writing of History*, edited by Louis Gottschalk, pp. 36—58. Chicago: University of Chicago Press, 1963.

———. "Sui Yang-ti: Personality and Stereotype." In *The Confucian Persuasion*, pp. 47—76.

———. "Values, Roles and Personalities." In *Confucian Personalities*, edited by Arthur Wright and Dennis Twitchett, pp. 3—23.

———, ed. *The Confucian Persuasion*. Stanford: Stanford University Press, 1960.

Wright, Arthur, and Twitchett, Dennis, eds. *Confucian Personalities*. Stanford: Stanford University Press, 1962.

Yang, C. K. *Religion in Chinese Society*. Berkeley: University of California Press, 1967.

Yang, Hsien-i, and Yang, Gladys, trans. *A Brief History of Chinese Fiction*, by Lu Hsun. Peking: Foreign Language Press, 1959.

Yang, Winston. "The Literary Transformation of Historical Figures in the *San-kuo chih yen-i*." In *Critical Essays on Chinese Fiction*, edited by Winston Yang and Curtis P. Adkins. Hong Kong: Chinese University Press, 1980.

————. "The Use of the *San-kuo chih* as a source of the *San-kuo-chih yen-i*." Ph.D. diss., Stanford University, 1971. Microfilm.

Yang, Winston, and Adkins, Curtis, eds. *Critical Essays on Chinese Fiction*. Hong Kong: Chinese University Press, 1980.

Yü, Chün-fang. *The Renewal of Buddhism in China: Chu-hung and the Late Ming Synthesis*. New York: Columbia University Press, 1981.

Index

Abdication stories: of King Yao,
113–14, 126; of King Shun, 114, 126
Abe Kenya, 228n25
An-chien yen-i, 3, 199n6, 200n7
Analects. See *Lun-yü*
Ancestor worship, 153, 158, 163
Apotheosis of departed heroes, 191, 192,
193, 194
Araki Kengo, 237n5
Astrology: masters of, 77, 162, 172

Berdyaev, Nicholas, 190
Berling, Judith, 237n5, 238n15
Book of Changes. See I-ching
Book of History. See Shu-ching
Book of Poetry. See Shih-ching
Book of Rites. See Li-chi
Buddhism, 92, 101, 157, 158, 161, 162,
164, 165, 175, 176, 185, 187, 188. *See
also* Three Teachings syncretism
Burke, Peter, x, 207n49

Chan-cheng chao-ch'in, 174, 175
Chan-kuo ts'e, 5
Chang Fei, 44, 45, 80, 83, 87, 107
Chang Hsueh-ch'eng, 201n9
Chang-i shu-ts'ai, 137, 138, 139
Chang Kwang-chih, 213n7
Chang Liang, 61, 69, 74, 75, 76, 77, 78
Chang T'ing-yü, 41
Ch'ang-she Chen, 45
Chao-hsien na-shih, 71
Chao K'uang-yin (Sung T'ai Tsu), 42,
48, 61, 62
Chao Yun, 45, 66, 80, 82, 83
Ch'ao Kai, 137, 139
Chen Wei, 11, 40, 99

Ch'en Kung, 147
Ch'en She, historical revolt of, 50, 51,
52, 62
Ch'en Shou, 4, 36, 50
Ch'eng-Chu Neo-Confucianism, 30, 85,
97, 101, 132, 146, 186, 187, 188, 189
Ch'eng Yao-chin, 45, 80
Chi Yun, 204n23
Ch'i (king), 115, 116, 117
Chiang Shang, 45, 75, 76, 77, 78, 79, 178
Chiang-shih (historical narration or
historical narratives): as a school of
storytellers, 13, 14, 15, 16; as a genre
of literature, ix, 198n3. *See also* Ming
historical novels
Chiang Ta-ch'i. *See* Yung-yü-tzu
*Chiao Ch'uang t'ung su hsiao-shuo
(Chiao Ch'uang)*, 21, 151, 152, 153,
154
Chieh (king), 35, 74, 118, 148, 149, 150,
151
Chieh-chiao, 165. *See also* Taoist
religion
Chieh-ni, 91, 92
Chih-kuai, 9
Ch'ih-sung-tzu, 77
Chin-chi, 8
Chin-i-wei, 133
Chin P'ing Mei, 182
Chin Sheng-t'an, 29, 108, 111, 112, 140
Chin-shu, 5
Ch'in Ch'iung (Ch'in Shu-pao), 45, 61,
80, 88
Ch'in Kuei, 105, 141
Ching-chung pao-kuo, 103, 104, 106
Ch'ing-shih liu-ming, 58, 59
Chiu-shih pien, 8

273